HERR HEMPEL

AT THE

GERMAN LEGATION
IN DUBLIN

1937–1945

JOHN P. DUGGAN

IRISH ACADEMIC PRESS

DUBLIN • PORTLAND, OR

First published 2003 by
IRISH ACADEMIC PRESS
44 Northumberland Road, Dublin 4, Ireland

and in the United States of America by
IRISH ACADEMIC PRESS
c/o ISBS, 920 NE 58th Avenue, Suite 300, Portland
Oregon 97213-3786

Website: www.iap.ie

British Library Cataloguing in Publication Data

Duggan, John P., 1918–
    Herr Hempel at the German legation in Dublin, 1937–1945
    1. Hempel, Edward 2. Neutrality – Ireland 3. Ireland – Foreign relations –
    Germany – 4. Ireland – Foreign relations – Great Britain 5. Germany – Foreign
    relations – Ireland 6. Great Britain – Foreign relations – Ireland
    I. Title.
    941. 7'0822

ISBN 0-7165-2746-4 (cloth)
0-7165-2757-X (paper)

Library of Congress Cataloging-in-Publication Data

Duggan, John P.
    Herr Hempel at the German legation in Dublin, 1937–1945/John P. Duggan.
        p. cm.
    Includes bibliographical references and index.
    ISBN 0-7165-2746-4 – ISBN 0-7165-2757-X (pbk.)
        1. Ireland – Foreign relations – Germany. 2. Germans – Ireland – History – 20th
    century. 3. Germany – Foreign relations – Ireland. 4. Ireland – Foreign relations –
    1922. 5. Germany – Foreign relations – 1933–1945. 6. World War, 1939–1945 –
    Ireland. 7. Hempel, Eduard. I. Title.

DA964.G3 D84 2002
940.53'25417–dc21   2002032724

Typeset in 11 pt on 13 pt Baskerville by
FiSH Books, London WC1
Printed by MPG Books Ltd, Bodmin, Cornwall

In memory of Eva Hempel

CONTENTS

ILLUSTRATIONS

ABBREVIATIONS

F & CO   Foreign and Commonwealth Office, London.

PRO   Public Record Office, Kew.

PAAA   Politisches Archiv des Auswärtigen Amtes, Bonn.

BA   Bundesarchiv, Koblenz.

MILA   Militärchiv, Freiburg.

Otherwise conventional abbreviations are observed.

ACKNOWLEDGEMENTS

A query from the *Auswärtigen Amt*, Bonn, for specific information on Eduard Hempel, the Reich's last envoy to Ireland, in the context of preparing a handbook on the German diplomatic staff, (1871–1945), prompted a revisit to my TCD thesis on him (1979). I would like to renew my thanks already expressed to Trinity and to all who made that possible.

The intention to refurbish a thesis after a quarter of a century, rapidly became a fresh requirement to rebuild thematically and compartmentalise chronologically.

When I came across Hempel's telegrams in the British Foreign Office over thirty years ago, I recommended that copies be sent to Dublin. My thanks to Mr Noel Kissane of the National Library who, in the course of this revision, eventually located them there under *Manuscript Sources for the History of Irish Civilisation* (1965).

I am particularly grateful to the Hempel family for their kind co-operation in the process, to the very many who lent support en route, and to Tom Dunne for his co-operation with translating the Appendices.

PREFACE

Dr Herr Eduard Hempel was a conservative career diplomat. That is not to say that he was immune from the 'Führer fever' that gripped Germany in the 1930s. Very few Germans were.

Many of his acquaintances in Ireland absolved him: 'he was not a Nazi, you know'. Who was a Nazi and who was not a Nazi in Hitler's Germany, judging from the hysteria reflected in the newsreels of the day, is debatable. The post-war de-Nazifying sorting process became blurred in the following 'Cold War' climate. It is not easy therefore to pigeon-hole Hempel. Even Enno Stephan's outstanding original research *Spies in Ireland* fails to fully focus on him, his mission and his Legation. This is an attempt to present, from his reportage, a fuller portrait of the Reich's representative in wartime neutral Ireland, to try to trace a pattern in Hitler's foreign policy, with regard to Ireland, and to examine it through German diplomacy, in the period preceding and during World War II. It is set against the background of Hitler's general strategic and political plan, as far as that can be pinned down. The main source has been Hempel's own chameleon telegrams.

However, all German documents relating to Ireland seem to terminate in late 1944, even though it seems (according to Frau Hempel) that Herr Hempel telegraphed (through Switzerland) his reportage right up to the end of the war. These were the days in Berlin of Hitler's Bunker and of saturation bombing – aerial initially, and finally with Russian artillery – superimposed indiscriminately. In the end there was street fighting in the 'Wilhelmstrasse'. The 'Auswärtiges Amt' was burnt down. On 10 April 1945, an order was issued to destroy secret files. (Only a fragment of Ribbentrop's files (Büro RAM) have been recovered.) Hempel complied diligently with this order.

Apart from Bewley's special pleading in his *Memoirs of a Wild Goose*, there is no formal documentation in the tidy accepted sense for covert operations of the type involving Veesenmayer, Kerney, Clissmann and, less directly, Bewley. The main problems for a conventional diplomat lay in dealing with these covert elements in his mission. To resolve and reconcile this dilemma, he tried to achieve an impossible objectivity in his reporting, to try to see all sides of the question. Nazi officials tended to report what they reckoned their masters wanted to hear, and Hempel's 'on the one hand, and on the other' style of reporting exasperated, and to some extent, frustrated officials in Berlin, particularly Ribbentrop, Veesenmayer and Haller. Haller described him as an 'unenterprising, dry-as-dust, dyed-in-the-wool civil servant: 'ein trockener Beamter' (Frank Aiken called him 'a cold fish'). However, his pedantry, penchant for protocol, conventional correctness, and 'keeping himself covered' were crucial factors in enabling de Valera to successfully steer his policy of Neutrality 'with a certain consideration' for a disbelieving, disgruntled and at times, desperate Britain. As Frau Hempel saw it, her husband saw his mission as trying to keep Ireland out of the war, a task for which his character was suited and he was grateful to be involved, in times of hate and aggression. Whatever about irritating Ribbentrop, Veesenmayer and Haller, she pointed out that, more importantly, her husband did not frustrate the correct Weizacker and Woermann.

In wartime Dublin, he was the principal means of intergovernmental communication at a time when other means of communication were restricted and a need for communication was pressing. He had to establish personal credibility with both governments, keeping 'official channels' open. He had the difficult task of recognising and circumventing, as far as possible, misunderstandings – all within the constraints of established diplomatic conventions. Being seen to be correct was a task for which Hempel's temperament and training were suited. De Valera pronounced him to have been 'invariably correct'.

He was eminently suitable for the portion of that work that required him to be a legitimate source of intelligence for his own government in this part of the world. He could establish 'official' sources and process and transmit information via normal diplomatic channels. Newspapers, in spite of censorship, were mines of information. Hempel was a good report writer. It was part of the job he had been trained for.

But, because non-governmental groups were important in Ireland and because these subversive groups had links with some of the meddling maverick proliferating agencies in Germany, Hempel was sometimes pushed, sometimes pulled, sometimes inclined to go, into the grey area of spying and subversion. He was not 'at home' in this world, which was at odds with the externals of diplomatic conventions and his background. He had a natural inclination for the trappings of protocol.

The dramatic interest lies in the tension which this particular diplomat experienced because of the conflict between the overt and covert requirements inherent in being a representative of a Nazi government at war with neutral Éire's nearest neighbour and 'ancient enemy'. The changing fortunes of the war indexed, perceptibly and imperceptibly, the changing attitudes of the Irish government to the German minister and their varying interpretations of 'a certain consideration for Britain', in implementing their policy of pragmatic neutrality.

De Valera insisted, in the national interest, on 'a certain consideration for Britain'. When the danger of invasion was imminent, the Taoiseach delegated total responsibility for national security to Ulsterman, Lt. Gen. Dan McKenna. The combat-ready army which he forged constituted a crucial constraint, not only on Britain, but in Hempel's reckonings. That 'consideration' did not remove the British threat. The dangers to national security from Allied miscalculation were ever present but German-cum-IRA irresponsibility was a constant concern. Throughout, the situations arising were of a non-transparent, hair-trigger nature.

PART I

1937–39, THE CONCEPTION OF NEUTRALITY

CHAPTER 1

Ireland and Germany in 1937

Background: Ireland and Germany

The personality and concepts of American-born Éamon de Valera strongly influenced the pattern of events in Ireland from 1916 to 1937, the year of the arrival in Dublin of Herr Eduard Hempel as the diplomatic representative of Adolf Hitler's Third Reich.

After the failure of the Easter Rising (which the Germans had half-heartedly attempted to aid by sending arms in the ill-fated *Aud* and, in a U-Boat, the equally ill-fated Sir Roger Casement of the amateur-ish German 'Irish Brigade') the British commuted the sentence of death passed on de Valera. They were influenced by the consideration that executing an American citizen would alienate opinion in the United States at a critical stage of American deliberations on entering World War I.

His opponents in the Civil War (1922–23) which followed the establishment of the Irish Free State in 1922 also forbore to shoot him.[1] This was not because of any love for him or appreciation of his past achievements in the War of Independence (1919–21) which were not substantial anyway – he was in America for most of it. Civil War bitterness ran too deep for such sentimentalities. It was a pragmatic recognition of his mystique and the influence he was able to exert over his more extreme followers. For many of them, deifying de Valera's identification with a cause was enough to salve their republican consciences. When it came to a choice, political polemics or doctrinaire ambivalences did not deflect their support for the 'Chief,' as de Valera was called. Therefore, the pragmatists too could negotiate with him when it came to the point, assured that he could speak for the majority of his followers.

Later (12/8/1927), de Valera's deductions allowed him – and the party he had founded – Fianna Fáil (the Republican Party) – to take their seats in Leinster House. Although this involved a break between him and the Sinn Féin Party of Miss Mary MacSwiney, it did not entail a complete severance with the IRA,[2] who shared objectives, idealism, sympathies and a common social-political background with Fianna Fáil. Fianna Fáil was 'republicanism by parliamentary means' according to Seán Lemass, de Valera's second-in-command. He defined Fianna Fáil as 'a slightly constitutional party'.[3] Nevertheless, their entry into Leinster House was regarded as a great turning point in the history of parliamentary government in Ireland. It consolidated Irish political democracy:[4] although, indicating the still uncertain times, the revolvers bulging in their pockets were obvious and ominous.

By 1932 however the Cumann na nGaedhael government had become stubbornly, and almost obsessively, a 'law and order' government. There was therefore substantial IRA backing for de Valera to 'put Cosgrave out'. Soon afterwards Fianna Fáil reached a position of strength from which they were no longer dependent to the same extent on IRA support. The focus of their attack on the Cumann na nGaedhael government, under its party leader W.T. Cosgrave, had been the question of the Oath of Allegiance – an oath which Dáil Deputies were then required to take to the King of England. In office the Fianna Fáil government abrogated that parliamentary oath; in addition the right of appeal to the judicial committee of the privy council was abolished and Irish citizens ceased to be regarded in Irish law as British subjects (Irish Nationality and Citizenship Act 1935). Advantage was taken of the Abdication crisis in Britain (1936) to substitute external association for full membership of the Commonwealth (1936). An economic war was fought and the opportunity used to pursue a policy of economic self-sufficiency.[5] By 1937 a draft Constitution had been prepared, which deleted reference to the Crown in internal Irish politics and laid *de jure* claim to the territory of the 32 Counties. (Articles 2 and 3 of the Constitution, for the sake of peace in Northern Ireland, relinquishing that claim, were repealed on 22 May 1998). The Neutrality stage was being prepared.

In Germany in the corresponding period up to 1937 another charismatic leader, Adolf Hitler, was exerting his influence and leaving his mark on events which were, of course, on a much larger scale than the happenings in Ireland. Another major difference between the situations in the two countries was that while Hitler operated from a contrived basis of dictatorship, de Valera's activities and ambitions were tempered by the democratic processes of government. A series of circumstances had combined in Germany to create a climate for Hitler's party of National Socialism to become a strong party, filling the vacuum left by the ostensible failure of democracy in the Weimar Republic. The irks and restrictions of the 'Versailles Humiliation' jarred national pride. The economic chaos, following inflationary pressures of the international depression years and an inner disposition of the German people to respond to catch-cries and propaganda for a strong national State, helped Hitler's bid for power. He articulated the distress felt by all classes of society. The pull of the party was felt by workers, middle-class and members of the nobility alike. He prescribed remedies that satisfied yearnings for order. Anti-Semitism and other oversimplifications were accepted as part of the panacea prescription: under the swastika a career was promised for everyone; for all 'Germans', that is. Dr Hans Frank told a convention of lawyers (1936): 'There is in Germany today only one authority, and that is the authority of the Führer. Hitler, by 1937, had used that authority to eliminate opposition, to regiment the State and to repress individual freedom. He cloaked this by abolishing unemployment and by getting the wheels of industry and commerce turning again. There was, however, no great meeting of minds between Ireland and Germany: both still trying to rehabilitate after ruinous wars, albeit of a vastly different scale, with Britain. This, in theory, gave them a common enemy and they both had a burning desire to assert sovereignty. However, it did not make bedfellows of them.

Establishment of Irish–German Relations

From practically the foundation of the Free State up to 1937 Irish trade links with Germany had proved to be positively difficult. This was to be seen well before Hitler came to power. Some of the difficulties may have had their roots in the well-known deference of German Foreign Ministry officials to their British counterparts in the Foreign Office, a deference traceable back to the days of Victoria and Albert and the then emerging German Foreign Service, which looked to the British for example. It was a deference that paradoxically persisted even in wartime and, subsequently,

British hauteur to the fledgling Free State parvenu may have influenced ingrained German subservient attitudes. Replies to Irish queries from official German sources tended to be condescending, curt and unhelpful: talking down, British style.

Von Dehn, the German representative in Liverpool, initially also dealt with matters affecting the Free State. From the beginning he snobbishly counselled caution in dealing with the new State: he felt that they might be getting 'too big for their boots'. A request through him from the Irish Minister for Defence in 1928 for a prototype German helmet for the Irish Army was curtly turned down by him, citing a regulation that this was impossible. The order was subsequently placed in Vickers for 5,000 of them. So another symptomatic anomaly was added to Anglo-Irish Relations. The Irish Army was issued with German-style helmets, made in Britain.[6]

The German history of the bullying iron fist with small nations and minorities, coupled with this fawning obsequiousness to Britain, is convoluted. In the past, they arrogantly disregarded the national movement of Lithuanians, Letts and Estonians.[7] In the case of Ireland they took the time from the British.

Until 1929 the Irish Free State, as a member of the British Commonwealth of Nations, was represented in Berlin by the British Ambassador. In a draft of a Commercial Convention between the Irish Free State and Germany (1926) the preamble named as their respective plenipotentiaries:

> His Majesty, the King of the United Kingdom of Great Britain and Ireland and of the British Dominions beyond the Seas, Emperor of India
>
> AND
>
> The President of the German Reich.[8]

The correspondence of the time conveys the tone and tenor of negotiations culminating in the appointment in 1929 of Professor D.A. Binchy as Irish Minister to Germany in Berlin. The Minister for External Affairs 'had the honour to be, Sir, your most obedient, humble Servant, P. McGilligan, Minister for External Affairs' to the Secretary of State for Dominion Affairs. Making due allowance for diplomatic 'speak', the language used confirmed official status and obsequious relationships.

This pro-British deference came naturally to the so-called 'Clongowes Mafia', who ruled the External Affairs' roost. Walsh, the Secretary, taught Binchy French at Clongowes. The Minister, McGilligan, was also a Clongowes man, as was Kevin O'Higgins (Justice), Burke (Lands) and Hogan (Agriculture). When Fianna Fáil eventually replaced Cumann na nGaedheal in government, Seán Lemass remarked that it was mostly a matter of Christian Brother boys taking over from the Clongowes fellows. However, not all the Clongowes fellows were West Britishers. Jim O'Donovan, who taught Chemistry there, later became the chief *Abwehr* (German Intelligence) agent in Ireland during the war. And beneath the 'West British' class veneer they were ardently patriotic and competent, albeit in some cases reluctant, public servants. Binchy had to be persuaded to become Minister to Germany.

The main motivation behind the persuasion of the reluctant Binchy to take the Berlin posting was the compulsion to shut out Germanophile Charles Bewley who hungered for the appointment. Seán T. O'Kelly of the Fianna Fáil opposition also opposed him, but for different reasons: he wanted to get even with him for mercilessly prosecuting Civil War prisoners in Castlebar. Bewley later managed to add Hempel to the long list of those who regarded him as a dangerous pest.

When Binchy finally gave as a reason for his reluctance to go to Berlin that he did not like the Germans, he was told that was exactly the reason he should go. He went, still reluctantly, as he was then at the height of his academic powers and revelling in it.

He was born on 2 June 1899 in Charleville, Co. Cork and educated at Clongowes Wood College and University College, Dublin. He studied law and history in the Universities of Munich and Paris, and special legal studies in the Hague and Geneva. He was Professor of Jurisprudence and International Law at UCD since 1924. His *magnum opus, Corpus Iuris Hibernicis (The Body of Irish Law)*, was published by the Dublin Institute for Advanced Studies. He was an example of the new Irish talent coming to the fore after the British had left.

The British however, never missing an opportunity to keep the new State in its place, insisted that Binchy be designated as 'Minister for the Irish Free State' and not as 'Irish Minister'. (It was from this climate that von Dehn took his cues). That nit-picking did not bother Binchy, who resigned in 1932 after two and a half years of office, preferring to return to the academic world. He (according to Bewley, which Binchy contemptuously dismissed) 'moved by an equal dislike of Hitler and de Valera, had sent in his resignation after the accession to power of the National Socialists and the Hosts of Destiny'. (He and de Valera both grew up in Charleville, Co. Cork). It did not stop Binchy making his mark.

He wrote an article on Hitler (*Studies* March 1933) that put him permanently in the 'black books' with the Nazis. It was a prophetic analysis of the phenomenon of Hitler and demonstrated that the Irish government had a well-informed and perceptive minister in Berlin between 1929 and 1932. It illustrated that, unlike his controversial successor Bewley, one senior Irish minister at least had few illusions about Hitler. Another penetrating study by him on Hindenburg *Studies June 1937*, analyses the pathos of the 'now very old and very tired' 'venerable Field Marshal', playing into Hitler's hands. Hitler accepted all the conditions and broke them all in turn. The President had not read *Mein Kampf* was Binchy's caustic conclusion. However, Binchy's academic eminence did not modify von Dehn's superiority pro-British leanings complex nor his over protested reverence for 'Der Führer'. Relations between the two countries were uneasy.

Difficulties Posed by Germany in Commercial Matters

Hard attitudes continued to be struck by Germany in exploring the possibilities of establishing an export trade with Ireland in live cattle and sheep, pigs, bacon and eggs even though the disparity of trade was very much in their favour. Their version was, that as far as they were concerned, the Irish Free State had only Dominion status and should therefore only get the same treatment as New Zealand: Danish opinion had also to be taken into account. Dieckhoff was specific (13/8/1932): *nothing was to be done with regard to the Irish Free State that might be prejudicial to the interests of German relations with England.*[9] Mr Leo T. McCauley, the acting representative for a year and a half after Binchy's resignation (Bewley was not appointed as successor to Binchy until 1933) experienced the effects of the application of this policy. In the matters of meeting sudden orders regarding butter storage affecting Irish quotas and leakages of information (to everyone but him), he wrote to Baron von Plessen of the Foreign Office:[10]

> When, after hearing the bad news from you, I rang him up on Saturday morning in Hamburg to where he had proceeded in the meantime, he referred at once to this information and pointed out how much better informed the other Legation had been than this one. He will of course bring the news back to Ireland; and my only defence will be that I kept closely in touch with the *Auswärtiges Amt*, and had every reason to believe that timely information would be given to the Legation before the order came into force.

The previous September, as another instance of this peremptory attitude towards the Irish Free State, an order of the Senate of Hamburg, dated 7 January 1927, was quoted forbidding the importation of live ruminants. This abrupt and arbitrary method of doing business with the Irish persisted and the following December (30/12/32) a Mr David O'Connor – the Chief Translator of English in the Foreign Office in Berlin – wrote to the *Irish Independent*:

> Last September the German government allowed the Saorstát to export to their country 5,000 tons of butter on a quota basis. Before anything like 5,000 tons had gone, the Germans took a new and far-reaching decision under which the Saorstát quota was reduced to 600 lb per annum. It is incomprehensible and all points to the existence of an organised conspiracy in Dublin to misrepresent Ireland abroad.[11]

German-Irish trade relations continued to be influenced by relations with England and the gold standard devaluation of the pound.[12] By 1935, on the other hand, Anglo-Irish trade relations were experiencing a thaw in the Economic War: the quota of cattle was increased by $33\frac{1}{3}$ per cent in return for increased purchases by the Irish; Great Britain had a virtual monopoly in the supply of coal.[13] A German overseas organisation – the dubious *Auslandsorganisation* – overtly concerned itself with promoting trade in Ireland to Germany's advantage. It had, like all the Nazi organisations, a double life. Quota quarrelling and quibbling went on. It was founded in 1931 and after 1933 acted as if it were a foreign office on its own. In addition to fostering trade it exercised surveillance over German nationals abroad to ensure that they

remained loyal to the Nazi Party. It sent agents abroad to propagate
Nazi doctrines and to extend party discipline. It also maintained
contact with subversive organizations – in Ireland, the IRA. From
1937 on, no Third Reich diplomat or consul could be appointed
unless his National Socialist credentials were cleared by the
Auslandsorganisation. In spite of all the protestations that he was not
a Nazi, Hempel seems to have got through that test. The notorious
Adolf Mahr, head of the *Auslandsorganisation,* a mole in the National
Museum, made the organisation's presence felt with Hempel. Mahr
had been appointed Senior Keeper of Irish Antiquities there in
1927 and by 1934 had worked his way, with de Valera's acquiescence,
to the top museum post. There he was well placed to promote Nazi
propaganda. The Germans, however, still arrogantly rode rough-
shod over Irish economic sensibilities but were blind to the effects
of their boorish behaviour. They blamed everyone but themselves
when things went wrong.

On 28 February 1936 the German Economic Office in Dublin (W.
Hahn of 69 Fitzwilliam Square) attributed the failure in economic
negotiations to a recently concluded British–Irish trade treaty.[14] De
Valera had earlier declared that this policy, directed towards freeing
Ireland from economic domination by Britain, did not mean a
complete severance in relations between the two states.[15] Ireland
remained dependent on Britain and exports to Germany continued
to be difficult. By May 1937 the Irish Cabinet were still giving
consideration to the problems of exporting cattle to Germany and
agreeing that in the event of the Minister for Agriculture being
unable to secure better terms he might accept prices which might
not, as far as could be foreseen, cover the costs of the shipments
which would be required, under the contract, to export to
Germany.[16] Germany's efforts in the first years of Nazism to achieve
'a good understanding with England'[17] were not matched by
corresponding efforts to accommodate Ireland. Wished-for line-ups
in the looming war sidelined it. Contingency IRA links were in the
shadows at this stage.

German Foreign Policy: Impact on Ireland

The Führer's 'Grand Design' may have been a partial explanation
for this dismissive German policy towards Ireland. Hitler had been

able to get Germany's industry moving again because he had it geared towards the erection of a mighty military machine, which would be used as an instrument to enable him to achieve his goals of foreign policy. The Clausewitz theory of war as an extension of diplomacy by other means was being followed.

Evolving German foreign policy, relating traditional territorial demands to the new expansionist strategy of the Third Reich, was now rooted in Hitler's *Stufenplan*.[18] This plan aimed firstly to restore to her pre-war eminence Germany's status as a Great Power; then to achieve pre-eminence in Europe, prior to subjugating the Soviet Union in order to secure continental hegemony and 'Lebensraum' in the East. Finally Hitler would lead this 'Greater German Reich of the German Nation' to overseas global expansion.[19] The essence of Hitler's conceptions was to be seen in *Mein Kampf* and the *Second Book* (1928).[20]

There is no specific reference to Ireland in *Mein Kampf* though Hitler had a knowledge of relations between Great Britain and Ireland.[21] Hitler had pinned his hopes on an alliance with Britain for his projects, and particularly so on Neville Chamberlain, who by May 1937 had succeeded Stanley Baldwin as Prime Minister. Chamberlain's obsessive preoccupation was for the preservation of the British Empire: the interest of peoples in Central Europe took second place. In this period of wooing England, the Irish rocking the boat in the Economic War was looked on with askance from Berlin.[22] What the Germans did not know apparently was that, by May 1936, the British, inspired by the new Dominion's Secretary, Malcolm MacDonald, had renewed attempts to reach an understanding with the Irish in security, defence, trade and industry.[23] Survival in the looming war was the spur.

Irish Foreign Policy: Impact on Germany

On the other hand, the 'coin of political controversy' in the Ireland of the period, in contradistinction with early Nazi aspirations and attempts to seek an alliance and an accommodation with the British Empire, produced a foreign policy that, on the face of it, involved confrontation with Britain. In 1932 de Valera orated:

> What now of the treaty imposed under threat 'of immediate and terrible

war?' What about the Governor-General residing in the old vice-regal lodge and symbolising the presence of the Crown in the Constitution? What about Irish neutrality with the treaty ports in British hands? What about the right of secession itself.[24]

The right of secession and neutrality had been a preoccupation of de Valera for a long time. In an interview given to the *Westminster Gazette* in February 1920 he suggested the example of the 1910 Treaty between the United States and Cuba to Britain as a means of safeguarding herself against foreign attack. He suggested that a British declaration of the Monroe Doctrine for the two neighbouring islands would produce wholehearted co-operation by the Irish side: they would co-operate 'with their whole soul'. On the question of neutrality, as far back as November 1927 de Valera had stated his view that in the event of war the right of maintaining Irish neutrality should be insisted on.[25] Neutrality was, even then, obviously a question occupying politicians' minds. The previous April (28/2/27), the German representative for Ireland, the ever-egregious von Dehn-Schmidt, reported[26] that, in view of her geographical situation, he doubted Ireland's ability to remain neutral in the event of Britain becoming involved in a war. He also referred to the Dáil debates of 16 February 1927 where the question of co-operation between the British and Irish Forces in the event of an attack by a third party was considered. He quoted the then Minister for Defence – Desmond Fitzgerald – as saying that the two armies must co-operate: that it was out of the question that the Irish Army would become involved in combat with Great Britain.

The advent of de Valera to power ended cosy assumptions from such assurances in British official circles, and a great deal of disquiet ensued. In 1932 J.H. Thomas, Secretary of State for Dominion Affairs, stated in Ottawa that their hopes lay in the newly formed opposition – the Army Comrades' Association – triumphing in a Civil War in Ireland and that then they would be dealing with a different government.[27] On Monday 6 June 1932, when Thomas arrived in Dublin, he was rather ominously accompanied by Lord Hailsham, who held the Portfolio of War.[28] The subjects under dispute were the Oath of Allegiance, Land Annuity payments, Partition, British occupation of the ports and finance in general. The British at that point considered the riposte of financial reprisals.[29] Relations deteriorated and led to the Economic War. The passage of routine secret information between the Foreign Office and Dublin was restricted and certain categories of information were withheld.[30] However 'Irish' solutions were gestating. Anglo-Irish relations were not only a puzzle to foreigners but sometimes to the parties themselves.

By 1936 the paradox was that the clumsy German efforts to seek a British accommodation, as spearheaded by Ribbentrop – the German Ambassador to London (1936–38) – tended to reveal gaps that were to prove to be unbridgeable. On the other hand, the pressures of the international situation, geographical contiguity and historical links, moved Anglo-Irish relations, under the guiding hands of de Valera and Malcolm McDonald,[31] towards a mutual recognition of the need for a rapprochement and the working out of a *modus vivendi*. These drifts inevitably coloured mutual survival policies, which were in the process of uneven evolution. A note by the British Secretary of State (24/3/36) on a conversation with de Valera remarked: 'Naturally he has keen sympathy with Germany in her struggle to establish equality with other nations'.[32] McDonald felt that de Valera had been greatly comforted by the British failure to react to Hitler's reoccupation of the Rhineland and that it could have given him encouragement to think that he too could face the British with a *fait accompli* on the ports and partition.[33]

That reaction, as outlined by McDonald, did not purport to imply that there was universal Irish approbation for German foreign policy; neither does it refute it. The internal policy of the Nazis towards the Jews – denying them office and even citizenship – does not appear to have provoked significant noticeable Irish public reaction. Ireland after all, in spite of de Valera's care to foster relations with the non-Catholic section of the population,[34] did herself have one or two anti-Semitic outbursts. These were not typical however. The case of Limerick has been blown out of all proportion: the peddled version is inaccurate and mischievous.

Local businessmen, jealous of travelling Jewish entrepreneurs introducing hire purchase, influenced a fundamentalist Redemptorist, Father Creagh, to fulminate predictably from the pulpit against this. He was not representative. Jews in the Christian Brothers' school in Limerick were treated the same as the rest. There was no general awareness in Ireland of the Nazi abomination against Jews. The extent of the horror and heinousness of such a crime was inconceivable. The historical ethnic cleansing by the likes of Cromwell could give no notion of such horrors. The Irish people simply did not know – and had no way of knowing – of the Holocaust crime against humanity.

Germany's anti-Catholicism however was another matter. That was publicised at the time – not that much was – or could be – done about it. There was no comparison with the Holocaust. All in all, while the youth may have envied Germany's physical fitness, emphasis and sexual freedom, the general Irish attitude to Germany was one of reservation. There were many reasons for this.

It had been reported (14/1/1934) that the Gospel of St John had been revised in Germany to make it more acceptable to the National Socialists. It was anti-Jewish and contained no Hebrew words. The author (Bishop Weidemann of Bremen) sought to modify Christian teaching to bring it into harmony with the Nazi world outlook based on 'blood and soil'. Care was taken to distinguish between the Jews and Jesus.[35]

'Mit brennender sorge' (with burning sorrow) Pope Pius XI opened his encyclical of 14 March 1937 on the condition of the Catholic Church in Germany. It condemned the persecution of the Church, the new neo-paganism and the campaign against denominational schools which had been guaranteed by the Concordat (1933). The failure of the Concordat was attributed to 'machinations that, from the beginning, had no other aim than a war of extermination'. Tension between Germany and the Holy See had been heightened. The Archbishop of Chicago, Cardinal Mundelein, spoke out in support of the Vatican:

> Perhaps you will ask how it is that a nation of sixty million intelligent people will submit in fear and servitude to an alien, an Austrian paper hanger, and a poor one at that and a few associates like Goebbels and Göring who dictate every move of the peoples' lives . . . American Catholics must fight back.[36]

Irish-Americans of course constituted an influential section of the American Catholic population. The reactions of Irish public opinion were also reflected. The *Irish Independent* (1/7/1937) reported the strong protests by the Catholic Bishop of Berlin on behalf of the German Episcopacy against 'the flood of filth' which had filled the German Press in connection with the trials of priests on charges of immorality.

The *Irish Press* (12/7/1937) reported Cardinal Pacelli's (later Pope Pius XII) comparison between Pope Pius XI's stricture on Nazi Germany and the manner in which St Ambrose imposed penance on the Emperor Theodosius: 'neither revolutionary violence and the sacrilege of masses blinded by false prophets nor the sophisms of those who are trying to deChristianise public life have been able to conquer the resistance or check the words of censure of this intrepid patriarch'.[37] Resistance was becoming more outspoken. *The Irish Times* (16/7/1937) commented: 'No folly seems to be too extreme for the leaders of the Nazi Party'. The reference was to the arrest of Dr Martin Niemöller, pastor of the famous Protestant Church in Dahlen, one of Germany's popular U-Boat war heroes and an outspoken opponent of the Nazi campaign against the Christian Church. 'He was lodged in Moabit prison, an institution that will be remembered by many Irish prisoners of war'.[38] Some 'righteous gentiles' in Germany also took a stand against Nazism but they were few.

This attitude to the Christian Churches constituted a fundamental divergence in the policies between the two countries. The draft Constitution in preparation in Ireland was acknowledged to be based on the Papal Encyclicals and had indeed gone so far as to accord a special place to the Catholic Church.[39] That is not to imply that there was no disagreement in Irish Affairs: but, under the force of de Valera's personality control, dichotomy on expressed policy was not discernible to any great extent among members of the government. The German Legation sent a cutting from *The Irish Times* (31/7/36) quoting 'The Three Voices', 'Britain in Time of War', giving the opinions of Mr De Valera, Seán T. O'Kelly and General O'Duffy. They were all seeking the ending of partition in varying tones of militancy. Koester, who signed the report,[40] doubted the efficacy of these protestations. His opinion was that the 'birds in the hand' were what counted: the retention of the ports and Northern Ireland would serve, initially at any rate, – he thought – to secure Ireland for Britain in the event of war. He did not discern any significant reaction from the British to the argument that, in war, Ireland would place facilities willingly at Britain's disposal, on condition that her national aspirations were first fulfilled. His finger was not on the pulse of the rapprochement between Britain and Ireland that was bringing the Economic War to a close and a Ports deal closer. Mutual self-interest was gradually impelling the British and Irish towards reconciling their differences. The British problem was how to deal with an Irish Republic outside the Commonwealth, assuming, that 'the 26 Counties'was what was meant by an Irish Republic. The special act passed in December 1936 after the abdication of the Germanophile Edward VIII changed fundamentally the relations of the Free State with the Commonwealth. As a result of the new act the King no longer figured in the Free State Constitution. The British chose to look on the brighter side of this and observe that for the first time in Irish history an English king had been recognised spontaneously by the people of 'Southern' Ireland. Mr de Valera by his own free will had chosen to keep the Free State in the Commonwealth for external purposes. The King would still have to accredit and receive diplomatic representatives to and from Ireland. That, of course, included representatives from Adolf Hitler's Germany, namely Herr Hempel, when he came. This could be tricky, the way things were developing.

German reports from the Dublin Legation however indicated growing cleavages in Anglo-Irish relations. Their reports were based on Ireland's intention to remain neutral in the event of a European conflict (30/1/1936);[41] Irish refusal to attend the Coronation celebrations (1/8/1936),[42] Ireland and the Oath of Allegiance (25/2/1937),[43] de Valera's broadcast to Australia on Anglo-Irish relations, the wrong of partition (17/3/1937);[44] and on de Valera's declaration regarding Ireland's non-participation in the Imperial Conference.[45]

It was against such a background that the Cabinet approved on 21 May 1937 the proposed appointment by the German government of Herr Eduard Hempel as Envoy Extraordinary and Minister Plenipotentiary of the German Government at Dublin and the Minister for External Affairs (Éamon de Valera) was authorised to advise the King accordingly.[46] Herr Hempel was to take over from the unattached Legation Counsellor, Herr Schroetter, who had been acting temporarily in office as a 'Chargé d'Affaires' since the death of the previous representative, Herr Kuhlmann in 1936.[47]

CHAPTER 2

Hempel, his Legation and his Irish Counterparts

Hempel's Appointment

In Berlin on 22 June 1937 Herr Hempel's letter of credence was signed by the Reich's Chancellor, Adolf Hitler, and the Foreign Minister, Freiherr von Neurath. It was addressed from Hitler to 'His Majesty, King of Great Britain, Ireland and the British Dominions beyond the Seas, Defender of the Faith, Emperor of India'. Hempel, as Envoy Extraordinary and Minister Plenipotentiary of the German government, was recommended on account of his proven personal qualities as a worthy successor to the late von Kuhlmann. The hope was expressed that Hempel would earn the good will of 'His Majesty' and so strengthen and deepen the bonds between the two peoples (British and German). Hitler requested that the Envoy be given a good reception and that full credence be accorded to any undertakings he carried out in the name of the German government. The opportunity was availed of to conventionally assure 'His Majesty' of Hitler's 'absolute esteem' and 'sincere friendship' and to express his best wishes for the well-being of 'His Majesty' and the development and prosperity of the Irish Free State. A translated copy of this letter of credence was later presented to the President of the Executive Council of the Irish Free State.[1]

Hempel's Background[2]

Eduard Hempel was born on 6 June 6 1887 in Pirna, Saxony, where his father was a judge. His mother, Olga Elwine Ponfick, came from a German family – 'totally German' Frau Hempel hastened to stress – who had lived for some generations in St Petersburg and in Moscow. The Hempel family had estates near Bautzen, where Herr Hempel's father ended his career as District President, when in 1898 he had to retire to Davos in Switzerland with lung trouble.

Here 'in the great nature of the Alps' the three Hempel children (two boys and a girl) grew up. The family bought the house of the widow of a John Adington Symonds and friendly relations between the two families prevailed over and outlasted the two wars. After his *Abitur* (Leaving Certificate) examination in 1906, Eduard studied law in Munich, Heidelberg, Berlin and finally in Leipzig where he completed his studies. There is no indication that he ever sowed any student 'wild oats' during that period.

His father died in 1911. In 1913 his mother took him with his brother and sister for an extended tour of India, China and Japan. The younger son made his way home in June 1914 and wondered why so many Russian troops were travelling westwards. As it turned out, there was no time left for Eduard to go back to his job at the District President's Office in Saxony from where he had taken leave for the journey.

When war broke out (August 1914) he joined his regiment, the one with which he had done his military service in 1910–11. As a lieutenant of the reserve he served with his regiment – the Saxon Mounted Guard Regiment – in Poland, where he was wounded. In 1915 he was posted to the Military Headquarters in Charleville and in 1917 he was transferred to the German Board of Management in Rumania. After the war he passed his second examination and for two years worked again in Saxony. In 1921 he was sent to the Saxon Legation in Berlin (such a Legation existed there until 1933). He was incorporated into the Foreign Ministry in 1926. On 24 May 1928 he married Eva Ahlemann.[3] After his marriage he went to Oslo as First Secretary for four years. In 1932 he returned with his wife and son, Andreas,[4] to Berlin to a job he found not entirely congenial. From November 1932 to July 1937 until he was sent to Dublin by Hitler, on the advice of Foreign Minister von Neurath, he was concerned with the administration abroad of the property of the Foreign Ministry. His wife thought that, although he did not like that job very much, it was nevertheless not uninteresting because it involved a lot of travel. Conveniently for the Dublin requirement, it provided a neutral background.

Hitler saw Hempel before he left for Dublin and the Führer impressed him with the extent of his knowledge of Ireland. The German leader was well versed on the difficulties in Anglo-Irish relations and also was well aware that the religious factor posed a potential problem for harmonious German–Irish relations. Frau Hempel held that there were no special instructions to the Envoy from Hitler. The meeting was not photographed: it was private. Herr Hempel's rank for his new appointment was Minister Class I.

On 2 July 1937 Reuter's News Agency reported: 'The new German Ambassador to the Irish Free State, Dr Eduard Hempel, left last night to take up his post. Dr Hempel is an old member of the German Foreign Office and has seen much of his foreign diplomatic service in different capitals. He was received yesterday by Hitler'. He did not in fact have Ambassador status: he was an 'Envoy Extraordinary and Minister Plenipotentiary'.

The *Irish Press*[5] noted, without comment, the Envoy's arrival with his family at Dún Laoire. The *Irish Independent*[6] had a picture of his wife, a radiant Frau Eva Hempel, holding a bunch of pink carnations, which had been presented to her by Dr Koester, Chancellor of the German Legation. Beside her stood her middle-aged husband looking well pleased with himself. The *Irish Times*[7] gave the most coverage and comment to his arrival in HMS *Cambria* at Dún Laoire. It expanded effusively on the magnificence of Germany's motorways (the autobahn) which provided 'a paradise for tourists', without commenting on their military significance. The new Minister and his wife were officially received at the boat pier by representatives of the Free State Ministry of External Affairs and the German Legation.[8]

> The new Minister who succeeds the late Herr von Kuhlmann is a tall well set-up man who does not look within ten years of his age although he was born fifty years ago. He is a native of Saxony and was educated there and in Switzerland. He is a Doctor of Law. He comes to Ireland for the first time from the Foreign Office in Berlin and has seen much service as a diplomat in many European capitals and in the Far East and India.
>
> Frau Hempel is tall and fair. She is the daughter of a General of the old German Army and is the mother of three children, two boys and a girl from two to six years.

It did not remark that much about Hempel's service in foreign capitals (1932–37) was in an administrative capacity – looking after the property of the Foreign Ministry. In fact, Frau Hempel's father retired with the rank of Lt. Colonel at the end of the First World War. Her grandfather was a General.

The Hempels were accompanied by their three children: Andreas (aged 6 years, born in Oslo); Constantine aged 4 and Lief aged 2, both born in Berlin.[9]

By 16 July 1937, Kitty Clive, a gossip columnist in *The Irish Times*, writing that the members of 'our diplomatic Corps' added considerably to the social life of Dublin, referred specifically to Frau Hempel as 'an interesting and elegant arrival to Dublin's hostesses'. This columnist also reported that the German Legation was seeking a residence for the new Minister and that it was not an easy task to find just the necessary accommodation in a house close enough to the city and large enough for receptions and other social functions.[10] The Italian Minister and Signora Lodi Fe who resided in Foxrock were also reported to be trying to get nearer town. Even then apparently the Italians were trying to 'keep up with the German Joneses'.

At the beginning of August the new German Minister and his wife were the cynosure of all eyes in their box at the Dublin Horse Show.[11] They were a good advertisement for Hitler's Germany: they looked well and behaved well. The fate of Herr Hempel's predecessors in office did not seem to perturb them or anyone else in the Ireland of the day. It had its own troubles, internally and, as ever, with the 'ancient enemy'. The Civil War was only fourteen years past and the War of Independence a mere sixteen.

His Predecessors

Hempel had been preceded by Dr Georg von Dehn (1930–34 – he was Consul-General from 1923 to 1930); Wilhelm von Kuhlmann (1934–37) and Dr Erich Schroetter, who was temporarily representing the Legation during von Kuhlmann's long illness 1936–37.[12] If Hempel had been superstitious, the bad luck that had dogged his predecessors could have been a cause for concern.

The sudden unexpected death in Munich of von Dehn after a slight operation might have afforded an illustration of one of the hazards of representing the German government in Dublin. As Consul General, Chargé d'Affaires and finally Minister (1923–30) von Dehn had become very popular with a certain section in Ireland. When the Nazis came to power he supported them staunchly, though it may, at times, have 'gone against the grain'.[13]

Before leaving Dublin in 1934 he made the usual round of farewell visits to his diplomatic colleagues. When saying goodbye to his friend, the Papal Nuncio, he followed the usual practice of kissing Dr Robinson's ring as he came away from the nunciature in the Phoenix Park. The photograph of the incident, snapped by a Press photographer, was duly forwarded to Germany by the foxy Adolf Mahr, the omniscient guru of the *Auslandsorganisation*. It found its way into the hands of the notorious Julius Streicher[14] (of Jew baiting infamy) and was reproduced with an offensive caption in the Nuremberger *Stürmer*. By the time it appeared Dr Von Dehn had settled into his new post as German Minister in Bucharest where he was said to have established himself as one of the outstanding members of the diplomatic corps and to have won the respect and personal friendship of King Carol.

As soon however as the photograph in the *Stürmer* was brought to Hitler's notice, von Dehn was peremptorily summoned to Berlin and in spite of all the efforts of Baron von Neurath, the Foreign Secretary – the man who had later selected and recommended Hempel for the Dublin post[15] – to save him, the Führer insisted on his instant dismissal on the grounds that by kissing the Nuncio's ring he had acted in a manner unworthy of a German representative abroad. The fact that he had turned down an invitation to attend a Nazi Party Rally in Nuremberg in 1934 was probably also 'on the record'.[16] He was given his full pension and allowed to retain his title as Minister of the Third Reich but it was made clear to him that he could hope for no further appointment under the Nazi government. Adolf Mahr duly responded by vilifying Schmidt in Dublin, constantly referring to him as a 'swine'. When *The Irish Times* editor Smyllie, who was a friend of his, later visited him,[17] he found him 'a broken man who has to weigh every word and watch every step'.

He had however been apparently in excellent health but he underwent a slight operation at the end of June 1937. By 14 July, a week after Hempel's arrival in Ireland, he was dead. Smyllie thought that he died of a broken heart and he does not hint at foul play in the hospital; though this was 'weeding-out' time with a vengeance by the Master Race in Nazi Germany.[18] Opposition to Hitler's dictatorship was being ruthlessly eradicated on fabricated pretexts. The lesson was there to be learned by succeeding representatives that, as von Dehn's experience illustrated, it did not enhance career prospects or increase life expectancy to be out of step with their Nazi masters. Diplomats, like everyone else, were now having to conform to Nazi doctrine. The early Nazi expedient of initially leaving 'foreign affairs in the hands of the experts' had passed. It is only fair to say however, that Frau Hempel was indignant when I appraised her of such implications. 'He died a normal death' she insisted, 'otherwise I would have heard of it'. She did not comment when I mentioned that Professor Binchy class-consciously told me that shallow Schmidt has abrogated the 'von Dehn' from a neighbour who had adopted him. Actually his father was a vet. The pre-Nazi snobs never let him forget his origins and never, ever, referred to him as 'von Dehn', only contemptuously as 'Der Schmidt'. Ironically, he was now also out of court with the egalitarian Nazis. For different reasons he had not endeared himself to the Fianna Fáil government either. He had been thought well of by the pro-British Cosgrave administration and he had been snobbishly outspoken in his criticism of the change of government. Fianna Fáil apparently matched the upstart image he had of the foundation of the Irish State. Fact and discretion were not von Dehn's strong points and most people saw through him. At a luncheon he was regaling Mons. Boylan, the noted Celtic Studies scholar, about his visit to the Bishop in Köln. The conversation was in German and the Monsignor remarked that the way he was going he would become a 'Roman' and judging a pause for von Dehn – Schmidt to inflate himself at his success as a raconteur, – added, 'in the interests of the Reich of course'. He was also, according to Dr Michael Rynne symptomatically unhelpful towards a request (infrequent) to assist with the proposed emigration of a Jew from Germany to Ireland.

Von Dehn's successor, Herr Wilhelm Erich Edmund von Kuhlmann, appointed Minister in October 1934 was also dogged by bad luck. In this instance however there is no evidence of party machinations; he was apparently seriously ill when he arrived in Dublin; he was reported as having a 'grave disease'. To add to his trouble his mother died in a fire at his home in Brennanstown House, Cabinteely.

He returned to Germany for medical treatment and when news of his death in Wiesbaden in January 1937, after a long illness, reached

Dublin, the French Minister, M. Pierre Guerlet said: 'I am very sorry to learn of Herr von Kuhlmann's death; although I knew he had been ill, I did not realise he was so bad'.[19] Though the French Minister's tone cannot be recaptured, it is not possible to read anything sinister into that observation. Frau Hempel certainly did not see anything sinister but she only saw the good side of Nazism at the time. So did millions of her contemporaries, in spite of the evidence of things happening to those who said something their Nazi masters did not want to hear.

Shortly after his arrival von Kuhlmann had occasion to report 'Down with Hitler' slogans in Dublin and protesting women carrying 'Free Thälmann' placards.[20] The Irish government expressed regret for these incidents. Not everyone however was meek and mute. During von Kuhlmann's watch, the Nazi regime was virulently criticised in Ireland by the left-wing Press. *The Worker*[21] reported that Rudolf Claus, the working class leader and Communist Deputy, was 'beheaded by the Nazi butchers'. It also carried a 'News from the Front' feature on the Spanish Civil War by Frank Ryan, who was fighting on the republican side against the Hitler-backed Franco. The *Irish Workers' Voice*,[22] another left-wing paper, also attacked the Nazi regime:

> The Nazis are keeping up their propaganda in Dublin. Hardly a week goes by now without some speech-making or social function to attract the serried ranks of 'seonínism': They took over the Metropole last week for another dance graced by von Kuhlmann, Seán McEntee and Alfie.[22] And the Tricolour and the Swastika of the fascist murder gang were draped in unholy matrimony in the ballroom. But where, oh where, were the 'young men' of the CYMS, that they made no protest here against the dictatorship, that had outlawed all religious association and is arresting clergymen of every denomination.[23]

In the same issue, Seán Nolan accused the German colony in Dublin of being the mouthpiece of propaganda for Hitler's Fascism and castigated the *Independent* for vilifying the 'worker's Russia', 'the country of real freedom', while remaining silent on Hitler's jailing of priests and boosting 'Mussolini's war of plunder in Abyssinia'. There was no cheer for the Nazis from the *vox populi* in Dublin. They tended to shoot the messenger.

Hempel's immediate predecessor, Herr Schroetter, had been sent on temporary attachment to represent von Kuhlmann for the duration of the latter's illness. He thought of himself as a Chargé d'Affaires and newspaper reports referred to him as such. The German records however do not accord him this title: 'unattached Legation Counsellor charged with temporary representation of the Legation' keeps that record straight.[24]

The *Auslandsorganisation* was instrumental in his downfall. It was getting more brazen about manifesting its Nazi Party concerns with the loyalties, real or imagined, of German nationals living abroad: (that of course would also, when the time came, include Hempel). It was established in 1931 and after 1933 became a 'Foreign Office' of its own. Woe betide anyone who crossed it. It sent agents abroad to propagate Nazi doctrines and to extend party discipline over German nationals. It was also given the task of maintaining contacts with subversive organisations.[25] It favoured thought-control and toeing the party line in word and deed. The conduct and administration of all matters affecting German citizens living abroad, falling within the competence of the Foreign Office, was entrusted to this 'Organisation'.[26] No German diplomat or consul from the beginning of 1937 could be employed who had not 'given proof of his National Socialist attitude in closest co-operation with the *Auslandsorganisation*.[27] It did not pay to be the bearer of uncomplimentary tidings. Hempel, obviously, gave satisfactory proof of his attitudes; otherwise he would hardly have been appointed. Schroetter apparently did not: he was removed. Schroetter's removal was an index of the power of the *Auslandsorganisation*, as masterminded by its chief, Bohle, who 'prowled around the corridors of Wilhelmstrasse'.[28] Making their own policy was now a *fait accompli*.

Herr Adolf Mahr, Curator of the National Museum, head of the *Auslandsorganisation* in Dublin swaggered accordingly. He shafted Schroetter. The museum provided perfect cover. He felt free to strut German pretensions in an Ireland where, with good reason, the only real 'baddies' were the Black-and-Tans. At the age of forty, Austrian archaeologist Mahr had come to Dublin in 1927 with his wife, Maria (27), son and baby daughter, from Vienna's Natural History Museum to take up the Dublin post. He was soon ruling the Germany colony roost. There were no specific accusations against Schroetter but he did have a Greek wife and this was enough to offend the Nazi racial purists of the time. Shafting him gave Mahr a chance to curry favour with these master racists in Berlin. Schroetter put himself further offside by reporting in a hand-washing manner the Irish government's misgivings about suspected espionage activities of a German national residing in Ireland who was head of the German Academic Exchange Service,[29] Helmut Clissmann. That again was not what they wanted to hear and again they identified the messenger with it. The head of the *Auslandsorganisation* in London frostily thanked Schroetter for this report but included an admonishment to be more benevolently disposed towards the alleged spy, pointing out his adroitness and reliability in carrying out his mission.[30] The DA (*'Gesellschaft der Berliner Freunde der Deutschen Akademie'*) chimed in with a mention of the necessity to protect 'the spy' from intrigues.[31] The finger now pointed at the outsider diplomat rather than at the insider 'spy'. He was coolly received.

An intriguing exercise in duplicity followed. Having sown the seeds for Schroetter's downfall, Mahr then proceeded to compliment him personally, saying that it was a shame that he had to go. In this double-dealing Mahr received a peremptory rebuke on behalf of an aggrieved Gauleiter Bohle from Berlin: it was, after all, Mahr who had prompted Bohle to remove Schroetter. Now a letter (6/7/937) turned up which shed light on his double-dealing.[32] Coincidentally, Hempel was just about to leave to take up his appointment in Dublin. Mahr was curtly ordered to have no further correspondence whatsoever with the Legation. But there were wheels within wheels and the restriction did not unduly curb Mahr.

There is no available evidence of what impact these incidents had on Hempel's assessment of his new position but it is plausible to suggest that they must have had, had he known of them, some influence on his appreciations of situations. He would have to take the abiding *Auslandsorganisation* into account. The rebuke from Bohle to the overreaching Mahr could have the effect of protecting the non-Nazi image of Hempel in Dublin, though such subtlety and sensitivity was not a Nazi characteristic. In more ways than one Hempel would have to watch his back as well as his step. Betrayal was the life-blood of Nazism. Least of all could he trust his colleagues.

Colleagues

The story persisted that the Irish government had informed German sources that they would not favour the appointment of a National Socialist as German Minister in Ireland.[33] That was a double-edged condition. When Hempel arrived in Dublin, he discovered that he was the only non-party man in the German Legation – the members of which met him on his arrival at Dún Laoire. The spin maintained that, although a patriotic German, Hempel was never a Nazi and that his diplomatic training before the advent of Hitler's national socialism ensured that he would follow normal diplomatic procedures in loyally serving his government but would do so 'free from Nazism'. The report did not say how this exercise in ambivalence in loyally serving a Nazi government on the one hand, and not being a Nazi on the other, could be carried out. Nor does it indicate how the Envoy could have satisfied the *Auslandsorganisation* with proof of his National Socialist attitudes before being appointed.[34]

Frau Hempel summarily dismissed all this. Her husband, she explained had intended to quit the service, but von Neurath and Weizacker prevailed on him to stay on. There was no hidden Nazi agenda, she held. She admitted that her brother was 'high-up' in the Nazi organisation, holding the *Blut-Orden*,[35] a decoration for being wounded in the cause of the Nazi struggle for power. She conceded that this connection may have worked in her husband's favour in securing the appointment, which puts a different complexion on that situation and the status of Thompsen.

Herr Hennig Thomsen,[36] who was transferred to Dublin on 25 October 1938 and appointed First Secretary 20 November 1938, explained the initial softly-softly Nazi party connection with the diplomats.[37] Hitler, he said, unexpectedly, but very cleverly, deliberately did not touch the Foreign Service initially. Later however, German diplomats abroad were given the option of joining the Nazi Party or leaving the service. Refusal to join would have barred the person concerned from any post in the public service and very likely qualified them for 're-education'. It was an offer they could not refuse so both Hempel and Thomsen joined.[38] Hempel may not have been happy with being coupled with him.

Thomsen did acknowledge that he himself had for some time

previously belonged to the Mounted SS[39] and had no hesitation about publicly displaying Nazi emblems. He explained that there were two versions of the party badge: he sported one, the size of a five shilling piece in black and white on red colour with a big swastika in the centre; and the other – the so-called *Hoheitsabzeichen* in silver, about half the size as that worn on every military cap. Members of the Legation (according to Thomsen), including Dr Hempel, preferred the less eye-catching silver *Hoheitsabzeichen*.[40] Wearing the less ostentatious badge in Dublin, however, may have been due more to diplomatic expediency, bearing in mind Hitler's expression to Hempel prior to his departure, of a feeling in Ireland against the Nazi treatment of religion. Hitler's main concern, to achieve an accommodation with England, persisted.

By the end of 1937 however, German foreign policy, Hitler's Anglophile ambivalence notwithstanding, was increasingly acquiring an anti-British flavour.[41] In contradistinction, Irish anti-British foreign policy, emanating from de Valera (Taoiseach and Minister for External Affairs), conscious of the threat of war, was progressively coming around to the realisation of the need for a mutual understanding with Britain: the British were in reciprocal mood.[42] The turn-about in trends of earlier respective policies received impetus under the good rapport established between Malcolm McDonald and de Valera, truly a turning point in Anglo-Irish relations. Mutual survival was the compulsion: word games, played for domestic galleries, were part of it. The people had to be brought along: de Valera was brilliant at this.

The small scale of the British-focussed policies of the Irish government made possible the concentration of foreign policy in the hands of de Valera. On the other hand the large-scale multi-sided German aspirations inevitably made for fragmentation. In Germany, in addition, a proliferation of poaching agencies tended to usurp the functions of the Foreign Ministry.[43] The influence of the Foreign Minister was noticed to have markedly weakened from the moment (1933) the weak and indolent von Neurath, for personal reasons, had identified with Hitler.[44] By 1934 Hitler was forging his own unique brand of policy which flouted the normal conventions of professional diplomacy. Ostensibly, for the sake of unity of the conduct of foreign policy, the European and British Departments were merged in a Bismarck-style reorganisation in

1936.[45] It did little to remedy this wayward state of affairs. Nor did the appointment of Ribbentrop as Foreign Minister (4/2/38) to replace von Neurath: his contention was that the Nazi Party had a more realistic view of the international situation than the Foreign Office. His *Dienststelle* (*Büro*) *Ribbentrop* had been founded by Hitler as a 'paradiplomatic' agency in 1933.[46] Then there was Rosenberg's 'Foreign Policy Office', which held that foreign policy was the business of the entire nation, and not the prerogative of a small few. Other competing organisations in the field of foreign policy were Himmler's notorious *Volksdeutsche Mittelstelle* and his *Reichsicherheitshauptamt*, foreign intelligence units with Goebel's Propaganda Ministry[47] and the *Fichtebund*.[48]

Another factor, which influenced Herr Hempel as a 'practitioner' of German diplomacy, was that, in common with all German Civil Servants, he now (1937) had to put the Nazi Party first and the State second. Officials were required to swear an Oath that they would be 'true and obedient to the Führer of the German Reich and people, Adolf Hitler'.[49] The sinister *Auslandsorganisation*[50] increasingly exercised jurisdiction over diplomatic representatives abroad, to ensure that they kept their Oath and remained loyal to Nazi doctrine. This surveillance activity, delegated to them by Hitler (30/1/37), was a serious blow to the independence of the Foreign Office, which the *Auslandorganisation* blackened as inept and incompetent. Fortunately for Ireland, Dr Hempel generally tended to operate within the canons of conventional diplomacy, though like most Germans of the day, after the Fall of France (1940) he got 'carried away' and de Valera found him 'insufferable' at that time.

The Irish Team

By comparison with the confusion and overlapping inevitably arising from this labyrinthine proliferation of Nazi organisations, the Irish Department of External Affairs was more tangible and more coherent. It was smaller and more competent: the Head of the Government was also the Minister for External Affairs. Depending on the weight of the matter of the moment, Hempel dealt mainly with either the Minister (de Valera), the Secretary (Joe Walsh) or the Assistant Secretary, the comparatively youthful 31-year-old F.H. Boland,[51] a product of Clongowes Wood College and Trinity

College. (Another Clongowes man, D.A. Binchy had been on the board which had selected Boland for External Affairs). Excellence was a pursuit of the Irish team, though in exceptional cases, e.g. Bewley, brilliance did not always denote dependability. Hempel quickly established a rapport with F.H. Boland with whom he had a good deal of contact – they used to go for walks together in the Dublin mountains. He was never a Nazi, according to Boland.[52] Boland's feeling was that Frau Hempel was more pro-Nazi than Hempel was. Both Hempel and Boland shared a dislike for parading academic distinctions. Hempel disliked being called 'Doctor' because, he believed that every second person in Germany was a doctor of one kind or another. And Boland was reported to have turned down at one stage the offer of an Honorary Doctorate. Other players on the Irish side were John Dulanty, the Irish High Commissioner in London; Robert Brennan the Minister to the United States, who had been Oxford educated and Charles Bewley, a Catholic convert from the Quaker religion and an ex-Free State Army Officer, Irish Minister in Berlin. Bewley undiplomatically, and unwisely, as it turned out, expressed a strong antipathy to what seemed, to his extremist view, to be de Valera's dilution of republican ideals for political expediency.[53] His recall (8/3/39) was the culmination of differences of opinion between himself and de Valera/Walshe regarding the interpretation and implementation of foreign policy. He continued to supply the German Foreign Office with quirky information[54] on matters pertaining to Irish Foreign Policy. Bewley had aspirations to high political office in Ireland in the event of a Nazi victory in the looming war. De Valera however kept a firm grip on the details of evolving foreign policy and a tight rein, eventually, and finally, a lasso, on maverick Bewley.

In contrast to W.T. Cosgrave's reluctance to become involved in the formulation of foreign policy[55] feeling perhaps, that significant developments in this sphere were more properly left to the British – de Valera was the conceiver and the implementer of his own brand of foreign policy.[56] This policy was obsessed with readjustments with Britain, particularly with regard to partition, and contrasted with the previous preoccupation with establishing legations to encourage trade. Walshe had experience of both of those worlds.[57]

Born in Limerick in 1889, he initially intended a career in the Church but had to leave the Jesuits, ostensibly for health reasons.

He never actually filled a diplomatic post abroad and augmented his knowledge of International Affairs from his experience as a member of the League of Nations' delegation. There are many stories to indicate that, from the outset, his relations with his staff were uneasy and prickly, and worsened as time went on:[58] though he did, it seems, develop a rapport with Miss Sheila Murphy, a Third Secretary, whom, according to contemporaries, 'he should have married'.[59] He developed a reputation in some quarters for 'blowing hot and blowing cold'.[60]

He was also accused of running his department with unbelievable incompetence. No minister was adequately briefed on foreign policy, the accusation ran. Walshe did not read the reports of his colleagues from other capitals; requests for instructions in particular cases were either not answered or regarded as an intrusion into the private affairs of the Secretary. De Valera, appeared to condone Walshe's parsimony and negativity: the distribution of instructions and the circulation of reports etc. would not be possible without engaging two more typists. They were not engaged. De Valera, like his predecessor, Cosgrave was sensitive to any small expenditure that smacked of extravagance. Walshe made it his business to get on well with him.

Walshe also got a name of being subserviently associated with Britain at all levels, keeping up a constant correspondence with minor officials in the Dominion and Foreign Office, who treated him with condescending friendship, which seemed to impress him. He was also enthusiastic at this stage for the Jewish cause and had travelled to Palestine at Jewish expense. The story concluded that he was hostile to Irish Independence and claimed to have weaned de Valera away from the notion of a Republic.

It was during the early days of Hempel's representation (17/11/1937) that the Envoy made the following remark in the context of reporting a conversation with Walshe: 'it is customary here to say agreeable things without meaning everything that is said'.[61] He was to learn that hard things could also be said and meant. When the tide of war ebbed for Germany he was to feel the sharp edge of Walsh's tongue. However, a lot of water had to flow under the bridge before that turn of events. Policy had to be made 'on the hoof'.

CHAPTER 3

The Diplomat as Official Observer, 1937–September 1939

In the period of 1937–39, Hempel's reportage from Dublin etched the emerging policy of 'unlikely' neutrality which was uncertainly evolving. Mr de Valera perceived the likelihood of a European war and determined to resolve outstanding Anglo-Irish problems prior to that event. The issues were partition, defence, agriculture and finance. Partition and defence were diplomatically linked in de Valera's mind. For this he was suspected in some quarters – notably by the IRA and by Bewley – as being too pro-British.[1] The Irish representative in Berlin (Bewley) compared de Valera adversely with John Redmond who he said: 'had the courage to declare himself openly before the public whereas de Valera was keeping his policy dark even from his own followers'. Neutrality was hardly yet in 1937 a firm policy, much less a quasi-doctrine. Northern Ireland and Anglo-Irish relations were two of the main factors circumscribing the neutrality concept and Hempel's reports dealt largely with matters relative to these areas. In that context the IRA inevitably obtruded and received his assessment. He also appreciated them (the IRA and 'radical nationalists' opinion') as potential allies and acknowledged the US influence on Irish affairs. These areas were broadly to represent his reporter's canvas for this period (1937–39).

Hempel was reporting back to a government now firmly embarked on a *Lebensraum* policy, which was to be achieved through 'military might and determination' – a policy which recognised that 'Great Britain might well have to be regarded as an enemy'.[2] This was a change, attitudes towards Ireland, to whom England was 'the ancient enemy' inevitably modified, imperceptibly at first: Hitler never lost his sneaking regard for Britain.

Mussolini's visit to Berlin in September 1937 had cemented the Axis. Lord Halifax's visit to Germany in November 1937 was a major step in the Anglo-French policy of appeasement. These objectives and the 'strong arm' methods of Nazi diplomacy came increasingly to dominate German Foreign Policy.[3] Before leaving for London for consultations, the British Ambassador to Germany (Henderson) received from the German Foreign Minister, Neurath, a memorandum outlining the German position on colonies, limitation of bombing, the League of Nations, Austria and Czechoslovakia. Neurath insisted they would not make concessions on other questions in order to obtain colonies. It is thought provoking that nearly two years before the outbreak of war 'the question of bombing could possibly be discussed independently some time but in any case not in connection with colonial questions'.

The Anglo-French charade of appeasement however did not allay the general underlying current of apprehension that war was inevitable though 'von Ribbentrop and Hitler were agreed that Great Britain would never take on a risk of a large scale war on account of a crisis in Central Europe'.[4] In that situation the importance of Ireland to Germany lay in the context of her relations with Great Britain. British influence on Ireland was deemed to be 'pervasive',[5] and 'penetrating'.[6] Walshe told Hempel that he hoped that an easing of German–British tension would favourably affect the settlement of Anglo-Irish relations 'which could be expected sooner or later'.[7] In Walshe's opinion Britain was in a difficult situation and he believed that the anti-Comintern pact was aimed at her. An understanding with Germany was essential for Britain, Walshe told Hempel, and in his opinion, there were prospects that Germany's demand for a return of her colonies would be successful: 'sooner or later the Sudeten German question must move towards a fundamental solution'. These Irish views, as articulated by Walshe and reported by Hempel, made reassuring reading in Berlin. It was at this point that Hempel sounded his '*cum grano salis*' note of caution about the Irish: they did not always mean everything they said, he warned. The only disquieting observations of Walshe that were reported were the references to the Catholic Lord Halifax being thought highly of in Ireland.

On the 'home front' Hempel's first six months in Ireland introduced him to some of the essential elements in an evaluation of the possibility of a policy of neutrality. Ostensibly his mission during this period (1937–39) was keeping Ireland neutral, i.e.

discouraging a closer alignment with Britain and France to counteract the possible effect of a blockade by them in wartime.

Hempel's routine reporting[8] of the general election and the plebiscite on the new Constitution that had just taken place gave him insights into the local political scene. He reported that Fianna Fáil (de Valera's party) had got 69 seats out of a total number of 138. Fine Gael (Mr Cosgrave's Treaty (1922) party which had a reputation for being pro-British) got 48; Labour 11 and Independents 8. De Valera would become a minority government, leaving a delicate political situation. The new Cabinet was: Mr de Valera, President of the Executive Council (and Minister for External Affairs, though this was overlooked in the photograph); Mr Seán T. O'Kelly, Vice-President and Minister for Local Government and Health; Mr P.J. Ruttledge, Justice; Mr Seán Lemass, Industry and Commerce; Dr J. Ryan Agriculture; Mr Frank Aiken, Defence; Mr G. Boland, Lands and Fisheries; Mr Oscar Traynor, Posts and Telegraphs.

Hempel felt that government Ministers Seán Lemass and Oscar Traynor were bluffing[9] when they threatened that Fianna Fáil would go to the country again to get an absolute majority. Labour Party votes were essential to keep the minority government in office. Labour's funds had been significantly reduced after the previous election. Hempel thought that the threats of Lemass and Traynor were made to keep them in check and to secure their support.

An unflattering picture of an impoverished country with depleted coffers and an unfavourable trade balance was painted by him, with Fine Gael attacking the government for their lack of planning in industrialisation and for their failure to come to an agreement with England.[10] When the country did go to the polls the following June (1938), the German representative wryly refrained from forecasting a result, observing only 'that in Ireland the unexpected always happens' ('*In Irland gesthieht immer das Unerwartete*').[11] Fianna Fáil had converted its minority position into one of an overall majority of five. This gave de Valera a freer hand to formulate foreign policy.

Northern Ireland was a fundamental factor in any consideration of the formulation of a policy of neutrality so Hempel took pains to regularly report the situation there. Constitutionally Northern Ireland was part of the United Kingdom; the Dublin government aspired to have it part of a United Ireland, 'reunited' with the rest of the island. This left Hempel with two shrines to tend: the king to whom he was accredited; and Mr de Valera to whom he was Envoy and Minister Plenipotentiary.

The carnival aspect of the 'Twelfth of July' celebrations in 1937 was the first thing to strike him. He tried to explain[12] that it was the 247th anniversary of the decisive victory at the Battle of the Boyne (1690) by William of Orange, catapulted onto the English throne by warring factions, over King James (commanding the so-called Irish Forces, his allies). Before he completed his report however he had made clear the strength of the British connection with Northern Ireland in reporting Lord Craigavon's (the Northern Premier) 'hands off Ulster' warning to the South. He did not translate the 'hands off Ulster' phrase nor the phrase used by Dr Little in his contemptuous retort to de Valera's expressed wish that his new Constitution[13] be seen to embrace Northern Ireland. In the plebiscite held on the same day as the general election a majority in the Irish Free State had voted for Mr de Valera's new Constitution: for 686,042; against 528,362. The majority was 157,686. It was a narrow enough majority, particularly when 104,805 spoiled votes were taken into account. Ulster, Little declared, would never swerve its loyalty from the British Royal Family to a president 'of a visionary halfpenny, make-believe Republic'.

Hempel enclosed with his report the comprehensive cover given by *The Irish Times* ('the Anglo-Irish paper') and a leading article from the *Irish Press* indicating the strong opposition that existed among Ulster people to the Northern Ireland government. In a later report[14] (3/8/1937) on IRA[15] acts of sabotage against the visit of the king and queen to Belfast, reminiscent of the methods used in the Civil War (1922), Hempel concluded that the British and the Irish sides wished to 'play down' these incidents. He recalled de Valera's own links with the IRA during the War of Independence but observed that that organisation was now officially prohibited. He indicated the unpredictability of the Irish temperament and inconclusively examined the different shades of republicanism, stemming from the Sinn Féin split in the Civil War: a reuniting of Fianna Fáil and Fine Gael was, for the time being anyway, ruled out as a solution to their differences. The bitterness from the Civil War was still too near the surface. However IRA assassination attempts during Armistice Day Celebrations in 1937 were coldly reported on by him[16] – although it was realised that the Free State government did not celebrate that occasion and that police protection was needed for those who did dare to celebrate it.

Before the end of 1937 an incident occurred to remind us that Herr Hempel also had a wife and family and ordinary domestic problems. The German Minister, perhaps petulantly, felt that this incident illustrated the weakness of Fianna Fáil's still minority government. A dock strike in Dublin had held up the delivery of his furniture, which had been shipped from Germany by Bugsier. Hempel grew quite hysterical and rounded on the government: it was their responsibility to see that he got his furniture and, if necessary, they should call in the army to see to it. Walshe soothed him and said that if they did that they would have to give the Envoy permanent military and police protection. Hempel put all this down to government weakness, remarking that they were dependent on the Labour Party to remain in office. Walshe offered to have the furniture taken out by soldiers but Hempel was sensitive about this. He felt that calling in the army to protect 'the diplomatic representative of a so-called fascist State' as he put it, could cause complications, acidly adding that, 'in keeping with a facility acquired over the centuries, the people in this country would not think twice before shooting'. He lashed out at the dockers for their lack of consideration and wildness and that, he said, went for the rest of the country as well.[17] His exasperation caused his diplomatic veneer to slip. The previous summer a building strike had lasted for seven months.[18] He repeated that it was the government's responsibility and that there would have to be a question of compensation.

The ending of the strike came suddenly on a Sunday evening and the Envoy's subsequent report (13/12/1937)[19] took on a softer tone. It stated that government intervention was not now needed and added that the idea of military intervention had originated with the government and not with Hempel. It seemed to Hempel now that the dockers were not such bad fellows after all. The Strike Committee had in fact looked after his furniture and protected it from the rain. He had obviously cooled down and went on to compliment the government: the decisiveness, he said, with which they handled the case, deserved recognition. Diplomatic 'speak' had obviously returned; the domestic crisis was over and he could get back to his job of observing, reporting and communicating the intentions of each government to the other. The media of transmitting these communications presented no problem at this stage.

Back at work Hempel (20/12/1937)[20] analysed at length (over 4,000 words) the significance of the new Constitution due to come into force at the end of the year (1937), from the point of view of Ireland's position within the Commonwealth and with regard to Anglo-Irish relations generally. This study brought him to the heart of the matter of his theme during the period leading up to the 'Last Days of Peace': how would Ireland stand in relation to Britain in the circumstances of a future European conflict. It provided him with insights into de Valera's thinking. Deviousness is not necessarily a pejorative term in a politician charged with the awesome task of charting his country through a perilous world crisis: it is a prerequisite and one politician's deviousness is another politician's adroitness.

Hempel did not feel that so far (20/12/1937) the new Constitution was working out as hoped, for political success for de Valera. It gave shape to the constitutional developments in Ireland since the Anglo-Irish Treaty of 6 December 1921. This development towards independent Dominion status in accordance with the Statute of Westminster, negotiated by McGilligan in the previous government, favoured de Valera in his aspiration for complete emancipation from British tutelage but, so far however, this break with Britain and the Commonwealth had eluded him. As Hempel saw it, Britain's power base in Ireland remained undisturbed: she still held on to Northern Ireland and had other occupation rights guaranteed by the Treaty. He did not hold out much hope that de Valera would achieve his long-sought goal of a United Ireland and felt that the practicalities of a solution to the present Anglo-Irish confrontation would centre around British possession of the ports, the adjustment of financial problems (namely, the land annuities) and the ending of the Economic War. In a wide-ranging dissertation Hempel linked the left wing of the Fianna Fáil Party with the IRA in their dissatisfaction with de Valera's progress towards 'breaking the connection with England'. On the other hand, he summed up England's interest in Ireland in a nutshell with the phrase that the island, in a strategic and supply sense, was 'the key to the Atlantic

Ocean'. He identified Fine Gael with the Anglo-Irish element of the population as wishing to remain 'under the Crown'. He analysed the complexities of Ireland's continuing membership of the Commonwealth in the light of the External Relations' Act of 12 December 1936, reviewing the period when Britain impeded Ireland's progress towards full Dominion status. He also reported de Valera's efforts to reply to his own party critics (including Mrs Tom Clarke, widow of the executed 1916 leader). Ireland was a mother country, Dev told the Fianna Fáil Ard-Fheis, and the King of England was a foreign king.

This populist rhetoric did not alter the facts: the king may have been removed from the 1922 Constitution by de Valera's constitutional revision in the 1936 External Relations Act but he was still the representative of the country in external relations: 'the link' remained. De Valera, according to Hempel was prepared, with United States support, to do a deal with England for the sake of the appearance of unity. However, Hempel saw the Protestants of Ulster as an intractable factor preventing any solution of this kind. He outlined Northern ethnic history and indicated that Ulster Protestants wanted to take up arms rather than come in with the South – even if, for the sake of expediency in life or death defence matters, such a course proved to be acceptable to Britain. He did not see much prospect of such an acceptance as the British Labour Party Conference had already rejected that concept of a United Ireland by a large majority – even though the percentage of unemployed people in Ulster was twice what it was in the Free State.

Against that he instanced petrol storage facilities in Dublin Harbour and the presence of an airbase near Limerick as factors awakening suspicion in anti-British circles that, in the event of war, de Valera would reach a settlement with Britain. De Valera, maintained Hempel, had repeatedly asserted that Ireland wished to remain neutral in a future war and that, in particular, the island would not be permitted to be used as a base for an attack against Britain. Neutrality however, de Valera qualified, was going to be very difficult to implement and a defence treaty with Britain had to be taken into consideration. Hempel recognised these as bargaining postures and reckoned that, in the uncertain political climate in Europe, it behoved both countries, whose destinies were so intertwined, to come to an understanding. He displayed a comprehensive political grasp of the essentials of the Anglo-Irish situation – and his reporting at that point has an objective detached quality about it. This may have been influenced by Hitler's previous policy of seeking an accommodation with Britain. There is no evidence of lip-service to the party line. Objectivity seems to have been the keynote. That was in tune with the Irish government's indication that an obvious strident Nazi party member would not be welcome as minister. That did not change the cross-channel climate.

On the same day Hempel was writing that report (20/12/1937), a practical manifestation of the restrictions of the External Relations Act cropped up when the king declined to put his signature to the Accreditation of a Representative to a proposed Irish Legation in Rome on the grounds that the King of Italy was not recognised by the British as Emperor of Abyssinia. Hempel observed that Ireland at this point felt less bound by the League of Nations than formerly and that, in any case, Britain, by acknowledging a Consul-General for Abyssinia, had already given *de facto* recognition to Italian sovereignty.[21] He later reported (29/12/1937) Walshe's trip to London to resolve the matter and the rumour in political circles that, in the event of the king's signature not being forthcoming, Ireland would settle for a Trade Representative.[22] In spite of de Valera's dismissiveness of the Article in the Constitution, retaining for whatever purposes, the link with the Crown 'as an external organ or instrument', it did have significance: it could be effective. Hempel gave chapter and verse for the Article (Artikel 29, Ziff. 4) in his report and translated it. De Valera's biographers, Longford and O'Neill, explained:

> The whole question of the continued existence of diplomatic representatives in Ireland was involved, and de Valera was particularly concerned regarding those of the Vatican and of the United States of America. Thus the retention of the king in foreign affairs was considered prudent. A further factor too was de Valera's view that the keeping of this shadowy link with Britain might help towards the ultimate reunification of Ireland.[23]

In the later case of Kieran,[24] (attempting to take up his appointment to replace Bewley as Irish representative in Berlin) – recognising the king as a symbol for accreditation purposes was a matter de Valera was not disposed to make an issue of. He, after all, in the External Relations Act of 1936, was the chief architect of that device and was aware of its purpose and limitations.

In the circumstances it is hardly surprising that Hempel reported a muted coming into force of the new Constitution on 29/12/1937.[25] Simple religious ceremonies in the Catholic Pro-Cathedral, the Protestant St Patrick's Cathedral and in the Jewish Synagogue marked the occasion.[26] At the Pro-Cathedral service, where the greater portion of the government and TD's participated, the Chief Justice was sworn in with the first sitting of the Commission which would function in the absence or default of the first president (yet to be elected).[27] In addition to these constitutional aspects Hempel also depicted the externals: flags were flown from public buildings but only in a few cases from private buildings; Sinn Féin ('who today represented radical republicans') flew a black flag and condemned the Constitution as a betrayal of republican ideals; and the diplomatic and consular corps apparently received no invitations to the celebrations.

Hempel condescendingly attributed this omission to Irish lack of experience in protocol procedure, something, he remarked sharply, that he had observed since his arrival. This attitude lived up to his reputation for being very correct and punctilious.[28] He refuted however the derogatory story told gleefully by the *Daily Mail* that the diplomatic corps had turned down the invitations. Hempel also included in his report a summary of de Valera's speech (directed principally to the Irish people in America), which explained the significance of the Constitution in terms of unity of national territory, a freedom of the Irish people to decide their foreign relationships and of Christian democracy. Predictably, said Hempel, the *Irish Press* praised the speech, the *Independent* criticised it and *The Irish Times* gave it a cool reception. Hempel was a great 'What the papers say' reporter. All the papers, he said, had given wide coverage to the remarks of the *Berliner Tageblatt* which dealt with the merits of de Valera and the reasonable attitude of Italian, English Dominion and English reactions, Hempel drew attention to the friendly comments in the *Manchester Guardian* and the *Daily Express.*

The German Minister however did not attempt to translate what he called the most important thing of the day – the communiqué from Downing Street. It was Britain's riposte: nothing had changed as far as they were concerned; they could call themselves anything they wanted to. It made no difference to them: if the 26 Counties wanted to call themselves 'Éire', they had no objections.[29] The name 'Éire' began to be used, often in a pejorative sense, by the British as a term in English for the 26 Counties. When war broke out (1939) the British tabloids used manglings of the word to rubbish neutrality. Irish people never took to the word: the British used it to dominate and dismiss.

Hempel did not send separate congratulations to de Valera on the coming into force of the Constitution: he coupled them with his Christmas and New Year Greetings. Perhaps he too, was affected by a general absence of any manifestation of great enthusiasm for the new Constitution (widely held to be the brainchild of de Valera) though he did say that in the West of Ireland its enactment got a better reception. Hempel could not have been expected to have known at this stage all de Valera's machiavellian insights into the significance of the Constitution. Longford and O'Neill summed it up: 'And Britain had acquiesced'. The British government declaration of 29 December 1937, stated that the Constitution did not affect membership of the Commonwealth. By the time the two governments reached the negotiation table early in 1938, it will be seen that the constitutional question in regard to the 26 Counties did not need to figure, and did not figure in fact. It can be argued that if constitutional difficulties had not been previously ironed out it would not have been possible for de Valera's government and the British government to come to the table to discuss matters of mutual concern, centring on defence:

> We now know that the British decision to give up the ports removed one of the most serious obstacles to effective Irish neutrality in time of war. In effect the Irish State became freer than ever before to pursue an independent foreign policy. But it won this freedom of action at a dangerous time. The League of Nations was dying and with it the concept of collective security. The place of the small independent neutral state had again become an extremely uncertain one. The evacuation of the Irish ports by the British, therefore, gave two related problems, neutrality and defence, an urgency and an importance they had not previously known in Irish politics.[30]

Hempel observed and reported meticulously on those two related problems and in the word picture he diligently narrated to Berlin one factor emerged as an unchanging constant, i.e. the implacable hostility and contempt of Northern Ireland Unionist opinion to what they conceived to be de Valera's machinations. The German Minister used their own word – 'affront'[31] to convey loyalist reactions – North and South – to the effect of the new Constitution on the king's position. At the beginning of 1938 Woermann from the London Embassy quoted the *Belfast Telegraph*'s snide remark that the changing of the name 'Irish Free State' to 'Éire' had the same significance as the changing of 'Kingstown' to 'Dún Laoghaire' or 'Queenstown' to 'Cobh'.[32]

The signing of the Anglo-Irish Agreement did not alter those attitudes. Lord Craigavon's analysis in Stormont[33] of the extent of British subsidies to Northern Ireland put the matter beyond question. Economically, Northern Ireland was irrevocably and inextricably linked to Britain, and would remain so whatever. Hempel had a good grasp of the situation. He had been perceptive in his Northern Ireland judgements and the election results there had borne him out.[34]

Unionists	39	(previously 36)
Independent Unionists	1	(previously 3)
Nationalists	8	(previously 1)
Labour	1	(previously 2)
Independents	1	(previously 1)
Independent Labour	1	(previously 1)

However, pinning down neutrality and linking neutrality with defence proved to be a more elusive exercise for him. To anchor his assumptions (15/1/1938) he included (in English) extracts from the Treaty of 6/12/1921 relative to the ports.[35] He also referred to de Valera's Document No. 2 (de Valera's alternative to the 1922 Treaty) and thought it worthwhile embodying the following extract (Article V) from it:

Ireland accepts and the British Commonwealth guarantee the perpetual neutrality of Ireland and the integrity and inviolability of Irish territory; and both in its own interest and in friendly regard to the strategic interests of the British Commonwealth binds itself to enter into no compact, and to take no action, nor permit any action to be taken, inconsistent with the obligation of preserving its own neutrality and inviolability and to repel with force any attempt to violate its territory or to use its territorial waters for warlike purposes.

He obviously saw this as a clear relevant formulation of de Valera's on-going intentions.

In the same report he expressed doubts about neutrality being a practical proposition. An accompanying *Sunday Times* cutting (16/1/1938) headlined 'De Valera and Defence: Éire's big part in a future blocade'.[36] This naval correspondent speculated that a comprehensive understanding between the two countries on defence might lead to a resumption of the pre-war tradition of manning certain warships with Irish names exclusively with Irish personnel. Before the war HMS *Erin* and HMS *Emerald* were so manned and now there was a new HMS *Emerald*. In Berlin it was conceivable that the Irish side might be prepared, for certain concessions, 'to bury the hatchet' with England. Working obviously on Hempel's report they estimated that the British occupation of the ports constituted a threat to the prospects of Irish neutrality.[37] The Agreement in April removed that particular threat to neutrality but not all the misgivings that a neutrality policy might prove impossible to implement in the event. Both de Valera and Hempel shared these doubts. Intertwined in the Anglo-Irish coming together was the factor of the influence of the Irish in the US. Hempel found it 'interesting', that the Parliamentary Secretary to the Minister for Lands indicated that a special British interest in reaching a settlement was motivated by the hope that Irish-American influence would then work for them in promoting a closer identity with the US.[38]

Hempel closely monitored – as far as was possible for him – the remainder of the negotiations, together with discussions in the Senate on Defence questions.[39] Significantly, as his report indicates, the Senate debate on the Agreement centred on neutrality and defence. De Valera saw parallels between British and Irish interests and remarked that the Agreement was more worthwhile for Britain than for Ireland. On the question of defence, de Valera was quoted in the report as not wanting to have Ireland placed in an unsatisfactory position in the event of war, such as had been the case while the British occupied the ports.[40] The Envoy again expressed doubts about the practical possibilities of implementing a policy of neutrality,[41] and noted further the importance of the Irish overseas in these matters, when he reported de Valera's broadcast to them on St Patrick's Day (1938).[42] He saw the Irish overseas, notably in America, as an ever-present factor in Anglo-Irish negotiations affecting reunification. He reported the Agreement (25/3/1938) briefly and factually under three headings: the handing back of the ports; the settlement of the Land Annuities and the signing of a three-year trade agreement.[43] He urged an extension of the existing German-Irish Trade Agreement.

When he had time to reflect, Hempel submitted a more comprehensive report.[44] It was astonishing, he commented, how swiftly those two sister islands, who had been traditional enemies for centuries, reached accord; especially when de Valera's inflexible, doctrinaire-aggravated obstinacy in the pursuit of his goals against Britain, was taken into account.[45] But he observed the fact had become obscured that de Valera had long wished for friendly co-operation and association with Britain in return for reunification. More than any of his countrymen de Valera was champion of the ideals of western democracy, believing that democracy was the most difficult form of government but the best. Hempel's opinion of de Valera's purpose was that Ireland, in return for reunification, would join a British–US Commonwealth camp. He retraced what he portrayed as de Valera's machiavellian steps from the time the Taoiseach had seen his way free to introduce the External Relations Act. De Valera foresaw, Hempel said, the coming European war and with it the compromised position in which Ireland was placed as a result of the occupation by a Britain involved in such a war: this situation would render Irish aspirations towards neutrality illusory. But he believed de Valera was concerned to protect Britain's interests. He did not share the IRA aspiration that 'England's difficulty was Ireland's opportunity'. He took the poor state of the country's economic and financial conditions into account. The report mentioned de Valera's old thesis that Britain and Ireland were both mother countries, that Ireland, as much as England, could be proud of its Commonwealth achievements and that both lands should rebuild a friendly partnership. In a long report Hempel relayed Chamberlain's and de Valera's denial that there was any secret understanding on matters of defence and touched on Ireland's position of being, next to the US and Canada, one of Britain's biggest suppliers. De Valera's queries on the possibility of being able to implement a policy of neutrality in the event of a large-scale war were again recorded.[46] Hempel granted de Valera popular acclaim for completing the Agreement but sounded a warning about IRA disenchantment with him. Some of the latter, he asserted, were idealists and adventurers, but others were worthwhile types who would show a clear understanding towards a new Germany and her aims; but that remained to be seen. Hempel was more speculative than usual in this report.

He soon returned 'to brass tacks' and reported progress on the German-Irish Trade Agreement.[47] It was de Valera's wish, he said, to expand trade with Germany, something that had been retarded during recent Anglo-Irish negotiations and which he now wished to redress. Hempel undertook to look into the matter during his coming holidays when he planned to visit Berlin.

During his absence, his representative, Marchtaler, submitted the clearest report to date on the evolution of a neutrality policy, which was to prove to be definitive in linking neutrality and defence.[48] Its clarity was due not merely to an improvement on Hempel's circuitous style of reporting: it was more perhaps because de Valera was now clear in his own mind as to the projected patterns of Irish foreign policy. The report outlined Mr de Valera's replies to the Opposition questions on foreign policy: he refuted vehemently that Ireland's League of Nations policy was dictated by the British. In reply to General Mulcahy (Fine Gael), who asked, if in a coming war, as a result of the Agreement, Ireland would ally with Britain or remain neutral, it was stated comprehensively that Irish policy in a future war was in no way firmly laid down; they were fully free to act in 'the best interests of the country'; Ireland's first interest was to remain neutral, though the difficulties of carrying out this policy in a future war were recognised. It was not enough merely to wish for neutrality: the other sides were required to recognise and respect that wish; if they did not, Ireland would defend itself by every means in its power. The report further gives de Valera's version of the circumstances of relations to Britain; the circumstances in which Ireland would seek British aid on the one hand and, on the other, the circumstances in which Britain was the aggressor. It was hoped that the latter situation would never arise but if it did Ireland would make such aggression as costly as possible to Britain. The fact was, however, that Britain provided a bulwark for Ireland against an attack from the Continent and therefore it was in Ireland's interest that Britain remained in a position to execute this defensive function. A free and united Ireland would be better able to co-operate, militarily, politically and psychologically with Great Britain to achieve this end. Therefore the removal of Partition, for which the Irish government would continue to strive, was in Britain's interest. The report concluded with de Valera's assertion that if they could remain neutral they would still endeavour to continue trade with all countries – and that included regularly sending supplies to England.

In October 1938 Hempel interpreted Ireland's reaction to the European crisis of the previous September.[49] There was widespread apprehension and a general desire to stay out of any coming conflict between Britain and Germany, though the Anglo-Irish openly rallied to the British colours. Less ostentatiously, for whatever reasons, economic or otherwise, so did a significant proportion of the population.

On the other hand, an appreciation was shown for the Sudetenland coup, analogies being drawn between that situation and the Six Counties' position; the transfer of populations seemed to find acceptance as a solution. The conflict with the Catholic Church and in particular the plight of Cardinal Innitzer in Austria was looked on with disfavour. Hempel further reported rumours of a split in the Cabinet with Seán T. O'Kelly taking a negative attitude towards Britain compared with de Valera, who was alleged to be more and more pro-British, while at the same time wishing to spare his country from the horrors of war. The burning question, the report stated, was whether the supply of essential commodities to England, i.e. food and petrol, would constitute a breach of neutrality and if that, in turn, would bring countermeasures such as an attack on Irish territory. Seán T. O'Kelly had blurted out to Hempel that he did not see how a policy of neutrality could be implemented: there were rumours, the report said, of Seán T., as he was popularly known, being shifted as Ambassador to Paris on the one hand and, on the other, taking over External Affairs: this latter move by Anglophobe O'Kelly would, Hempel thought, hardly please the British. But in Anglo-Irish relations nothing was ever black and white.

Hempel's long report[50] on de Valera's interview in the *Evening Standard,* which labelled the Partition of Ireland as a 'dangerous anachronism', and suggesting a devolved solution, construed this ploy as further evidence of de Valera's longstanding wish for an association with Britain: 'to keep afloat with Britain'. Lord Craigavon predictably retorted 'No Surrender'. However, Hempel was not finding it all that easy to make his reports labelling de Valera as absolutely 'pro-British' stick. The following month he was reporting de Valera's speech to the Fianna Fáil Ard Fheis in which he declaimed that as far as Ireland was concerned England was a foreign country ('England sei für Irland Ausland'): the association with England was not a statutory necessity; it was merely a gesture to a part of Irish people.[51] De Valera also addressed a note (31/11/1938) to Hempel, giving him his full title, accepting the German proposal to extend the Irish-German Trade Agreement for a further period of one year as from the 1 January 1939 and concluding 'Accept, Excellency, the renewed assurance of my highest consideration'.[52] This could be construed as another move on de Valera's part to keep his options open. He was nothing if not flexible: devious where necessary, in the national interest. His moves however, while maybe politically adroit, did not signify a groundswell of approval for Germany.

Towards the end of 1938 the Jewish question was making an impact outside Germany and Hempel reported an unfavourable Irish reaction to the treatment of Jews there following the assassination of diplomat, von Rath.[53] He had already circulated to German Jews living in Dublin the Nazi edict that German male Jews must have 'Israel' inserted in their passports as part of their first names: for females the insertion was 'Sarah'. At least one Jewish refugee family in Dublin at the time refused to comply, though summoned to the Legation in this connection. He was Professor Ernest Lewy (formerly b a o für Allgemeine Sprachwissenschaft), who had been summarily dismissed from his post at Berlin University, and later (1937) at his wife's instigation, had sought refuge in Ireland – they did not return from holidays. According to Professor Binchy, who knew him, he was a very likeable good-natured character, who gave lie to the stereotype of the money-grabbing Jew. For the sake of appearances and on account of his proven eminence in scholarship, the Nazis offered him back-pay compensation to return to his post. This would have represented a substantial amount of money for the professor and his family, but in principle, as a protest against the Nazi regime, he declined the offer and chose to eke out in relative poverty in Ireland (£400 p.a.).[54] However the story that Hempel was rude to Lewy and snubbed him is not substantiated by the professor's son. On the contrary his recollection was that Hempel was liked by the Dublin Jewish Community and was far from being anti-Semitic. That recollection however included an impression that 'Hennig Thomsen was the Gestapo man sent to keep an eye on Hempel'.[55]

The German Jews in Dublin were never invited to any function in the Legation. Lines were being firmly drawn: in January 1939 Ribbentrop forbade all social relations between his subordinates and the American Embassy in Berlin.[56]

Frau Hempel was impatient with negative interpretations of these events, even naïve. 'How could one ask the Jewish families to Legation functions', she expostulated. 'It was a matter of tact. We did not even ask Germans of whom we knew their feeling.' Herr Thomsen, she explained, was young and ambitious and her husband was careful with him. She did not believe that he was a Gestapo agent. Many people did.

The real question for Hempel was to discern where Irish sympathies lay. He reported that de Valera was the only one in the League of Nations' Assembly who had welcomed Chamberlain's decision to go to Berchtesgaden. De Valera also told him – asking him to treat it in confidence – that he had been considering appealing directly to the Führer, the Chancellor and Mussolini in a solo effort to preserve peace – not in his capacity as President of the League of Nations' Assembly (Hempel had previously attributed de Valera's appointment to this post as having been due to British support) but as Prime Minister of Éire. 'His Excellency the German Minister' seemed to have been singled out for special confidences by the Taoiseach, who had previously requested that, no matter what happened, Irish-German relations should not be broken. The Envoy promptly telegraphed the contents of de Valera's confidences to Berlin,[57] and no doubt this is what de Valera intended.

From then until the outbreak of war the following September, Hempel continued to monitor the refinements and nuances of de

Valera's utterances on his neutrality policy: doubts still existed as to the possibility of implementing it. The question of Northern Ireland and the attitudes of the Irish in America remained recurring factors affecting the resolution of this problem. This situation was aggravated by the introduction of a more sinister factor which called into question the capability of the democratically elected government to govern. Its fundamental right of being the body in whom alone was vested the right to declare and wage war was being challenged by the IRA ultimatum (12/1/1939) which formally opened their ill-conceived counter-productive bombing campaign in England.[58] Hempel reported his meeting with de Valera and the implications were that a 'mailed fist in a velvet glove' type conversation took place.[59] The Taoiseach left the German Minister in no doubt as to his disapproval of alleged German links with the IRA, making the point that they, as the legally elected representatives, would under no circumstances use illegal methods to resolve the Northern Ireland problem. He warned Hempel that it would be a mistake to overrate the IRA and he (de Valera) was convinced that intra-Irish strife, particularly in the context of a future European war, would have no decisive role against England. Ireland could only be interested in a strong Britain, that would be prepared to defend the island if attacked. Hempel scotched the rumours of German involvement in the IRA bombing in Britain and blamed the British Press for circulating this smear.

He then (16/2/1939) reported in detail[60] the Dáil debate on the army vote for 1938/39. In spite of Frank Aiken's buoyant projections (including a statement that the preparations for the erection of an ammunition factory were completed) Hempel remained unconvinced. The provision of £3,200,600 as against the previous year's £2,000,000 would in his opinion, only afford marginal strengthening of installations and personnel. He also enclosed an *Irish Times* analysis of budget increases for equipment and stores (£5,000,000) and for the building and equipping of installations, airfields and possibly a munitions factory an expenditure of £4,200,000 was forecast. He reported strengths and the government's plan for recruiting for the army and ARP. As regards policy, he reported the Minister for Defence's statement that the general staff had drawn up plans based on the following guidelines:

1.   That the sovereignty of Ireland as presently constituted by the 26 Counties is respected and internationally recognised.
2.   That the Dáil as the assembly of the elected representatives of the people was the only body empowered to declare war.
3.   That the government had no policy of aggression towards any nation and that Ireland had no obligation to take part or become involved in a war.
4.   That it was the policy of the government to resist any attack which might be made on Irish soil.

Hempel reported this as ruling out the possibility of a war with Great Britain unless, of course, Britain was the aggressor. Therefore, the conclusion was that the only conditions to be taken into account were the maintenance of neutrality and an attack by a power with whom Great Britain was at war. It was unlikely that a power not at war with Great Britain would attack Ireland and in all probability, his surmise ran, such an attack would come from a power wanting to make Ireland a theatre of operations or a base for attack against Great Britain.

However, as his report of the following day (17/2/1939)[61] indicated, tidy interpretations of the implications of following a policy of neutrality were thrown into confusion by de Valera's contribution to the debate. The Taoiseach had just retorted to a query from the leader of the Opposition if they would co-operate with Britain for the defence of Ireland if Ireland was attacked. He brought bluntly into the open the consideration that the maintenance of neutrality in wartime would be a precarious business, scarcely possible to carry through. He seemed to be saying that Ireland would almost inevitably be drawn into any war in which Britain was involved. Hempel reflected the confusion – even in government circles, his report said – caused by this intervention but he preferred to await the official version of the speech before finally committing himself. At this stage however, the Envoy maintained that there was no essential difference from his previous interpretations of this situation except that no illusions were left by de Valera about the danger of depending on Great Britain in wartime and this, Hempel held, was what had implications for Germany. However, he chose to append the following in English, a practice he followed when he found de

Valera's verbal subtleties too convoluted to translate into German black and white:

> The desire of the Irish people, and the desire of the Irish government is to keep the nation out of war. The aim of the government policy is to maintain and preserve our neutrality in the event of war. The best way, and the only way to secure our aim is to put ourselves in the best position possible to defend ourselves, so that no one can hope to attack us, or violate our territory with impunity. We know, of course, that should an attack come from a power other than Great Britain, Great Britain in her own interests must help us to repel it.
>
> Mr de Valera also said that the Irish government had not entered into any commitments with Great Britain. His government was free to follow any course that Irish interests might dictate.

Reporting on the Defence Debate was continued by his No. 2, Henning Thomsen, while Hempel went on leave towards the end of February. He was back at his desk in time to try to unravel the effects of a diplomatic gaffe arising out of Hitler's celebrated reply to Roosevelt's appeal (15/4/1939) that Germany would not attack or invade the territory of a listed thirty-one nations.[62] Germany had queried all of them except Poland, Russia, Britain and France. Roosevelt apparently had linked Britain and Ireland and the Germans seemed to follow suit in coupling Ireland with Britain when they queried the other countries as to whether they felt threatened by Germany or if they had authorised Roosevelt to make his proposals. Negative replies were received. Hitler, although referring to Ireland in his reply, had obviously omitted to separately consult the Dublin government.

> I must draw Mr Roosevelt's attention to one or two historical errors. He mentioned Ireland for instance and asks for a statement that Germany will not attack Ireland. Now I have just read a speech by de Valera, the Irish Taoiseach, in which, strangely enough and contrary to Mr Roosevelt's opinion, he does not charge Germany with oppressing Ireland but he reproaches England with subjecting Ireland to continuous aggression.

And referring to the incorporation into the Reich of Bohemia and Moravia, Hitler also said: 'Just as English measures in, say, Northern

Ireland, whether they be right or wrong, are not subject to German supervision, this is also the case with these German constituencies'. Hempel was agitated at omissions by Hitler to consult: he felt they would offend Irish sensitivities. He reported that General Mulcahy had raised the matter in the Dáil asking what were the 'implications'. De Valera replied that it was not possible for anyone to discover 'implications'.[63] Tempers were getting frayed: liberties were being taken by the Germans in relation to Ireland.

Hempel referred again to de Valera's Anglophile tendencies. He further implied that public opinion was flushing de Valera out from his pro-British posture, which his pious aspirations about neutrality had served to cloak.[64] The Taoiseach, he maintained, was now showing more decisiveness than formerly in reiterating the 'wish' (the inverted commas are Hempel's) of his government to remain neutral. His own opinion however, following a conversation with Walshe, was that de Valera, while painstakingly avoiding identification in foreign affairs with British policy, would not allow British vital interests to be compromised, even if that 'considera-tion' jeopardised the neutrality position. He mentioned the resurgence of national feeling and the re-emergence of the IRA who in a coming war (expected, he believed, the coming September), would operate not only against Northern Ireland but also perhaps against de Valera's government. He added that, not only in his own interests, but also out of consideration for Britain, de Valera had introduced the Offences against the State Bill and the Treason Bill, but that these had met with opposition even within the government party. In spite of de Valera's repeated denials of the existence of any secret deals with England, Hempel recorded the opinion that there was more in the Anglo-Irish Agreement than was publicly revealed: de Valera had cleverly exploited that Agreement to spring and win a general election, something, Hempel thought, he would not have been able to accomplish a year later. The German Minister's opinion was that it was fear of an adverse reception from Irish nationalists that prompted de Valera to call off his proposed US trip. Seán T. O'Kelly went instead to represent the Taoiseach for the opening of the Irish Pavilion at the New York World Fair. As Hempel read the position, Seán T. was sent because his reputation for keeping alive the fighting spirit of Irish nationalism made him more acceptable than de Valera to Irish-American audiences. Hempel did not report the greater possibility that the trip may have been called off at America's insistence, under British pressure, to deny de Valera a transatlantic anti-partition platform.

The nationalists however suspected that de Valera's method of solving the Partition problem was to obtain a US guarantee of the neutrality of a free Irish State which would serve to protect vital British interests and secure her west flanks. Walshe told Hempel that there was no truth in these rumours: de Valera would pay no price for the return of Northern Ireland which he regarded as an integral part of his country. On the other hand (and it was this 'on the other hand' style of reportage that was said to be the despair of officials like Veesenmayer in Berlin trying to draw conclusions from his reports),[65] Hempel (in a long sentence of 174 words) illustrated a widening gulf between the British and Irish governments, instancing the removal of the king's name from Irish passports, the treatment of IRA prisoners in English Courts and the anti-conscription campaign, to support this view. There again, Hempel concluded, de Valera did nothing to conceal his sympathy for the democracies: the Anglo-Irish remained implacably opposed and the Catholic Church feared that a German victory would increase the danger of the suppression of Christianity and the abolition of the traditional freedoms of Western Europe.

Hempel had already reported on Seán T. O'Kelly's anti-British nationalism and now (27/5/1939) he reported[66] on diverse tongues[67] within the Irish Cabinet. Northern Ireland-born Seán McEntee sounded pro-British and saw defence policy as not merely protecting Irish freedom but also as having a function in repelling possible attacks on British interests. Hempel then cited Seán Lemass as saying (in a by-election speech) that the only people we had a quarrel with was Great Britain; that we had no obligation to get involved and were only interested in remaining neutral. He did not refer to another Minister, Frank Aiken, who was alleged to be sympathetic to the Central European power,[68] but rounded off his report by observing that Sinn Féin wanted not merely neutrality in the event of war – but had demanded a campaign against Britain.

He then reported verbatim[69] an extract from de Valera's by-election speech. The sentiments expressed by de Valera on this occasion did not accord with the pro-British picture of him which Hempel's previous reports portrayed. It was a recruiting speech for the Volunteers: 'I appeal to the young people to get into the ranks and defend what has been won, and, if necessary, BE PREPARED TO SECURE WHAT HAS NOT YET BEEN WON'.[70]

This could be interpreted in Berlin as an indication of a narrowing of whatever gap existed between de Valera and the IRA as to the aims and methods of securing freedom. He later reported Dr O'Higgin's (Fine Gael) criticism that the army did not know whom they were supposed to fight against. De Valera retorted that they would fight not alone against the Axis Forces but against anyone else who might attack them: Government policy was to keep Ireland out of the war, though he acknowledged that this was going to be difficult if normal trading with Britain was pursued as intended.[71] Hempel expressed doubts that de Valera's intentions to continue normal trading could be compatible with neutrality.

On 7 August 1939 Hempel telegraphed a warning that *The Sunday Times* was trying to involve Ireland in the war by goading Germany to take precipitate action.[72] *The Times* was quoting German papers who were saying that Ireland would be dragged into the war on the side of Germany's enemies. He warned them to be careful as British propaganda was extremely active.

German foreign policy at this stage was to isolate Poland by diplomatic means: the largely predictable factors of logistics and weather would determine the date for the commencement of the military campaign.[73] Towards the end of August, Walshe in a meeting with Hempel stressed that Ireland would remain neutral unless attacked and suggested that Germany declare that she had no aggressive aims on Ireland but, on the contrary, had sympathy for Irish aims and aspirations, with particular reference to Northern Ireland.[74] Referring to the possible dropping of bombs on Irish towns, Walshe said that he could not believe the Germans would ever do such a thing: for one thing they could not be indifferent to Irish sympathy especially in view of American-Irish influence which could be exercised against the formation of a British-American alliance and also deter the British from violating Irish neutrality. Ribbentrop instructed Hempel as to how to reply in friendly terms:

In accordance with the friendly relations between ourselves and Ireland we are determined to refrain from any hostile action against Irish territory and to respect her integrity *provided* that Ireland for her part

maintains unimpeachable neutrality towards us in any conflict. Only if
the condition should no longer obtain as a result of a decision of the
government themselves or by pressures exerted on Ireland from other
quarters, should we be compelled as a matter of course as far as Ireland
was concerned too to safeguard our interests in the sphere of warfare in
such a way as the situation then arising might demand of us.[75] (My italics).

There was no direct mention of Northern Ireland but there was a
reference to the wide sympathy felt in Germany for the national
aspirations of the Irish people. Irish nationals were to be permitted
to remain in Germany and Ireland was expected to reciprocate: an
awareness of the problems involved in the difficulties of the
geographical position of Ireland was expressed. The message may
have been delivered in a friendly fashion but the authoritative tone
was evident. De Valera took up the challenge on ground of his own
choosing. Professor Desmond Williams has written: 'Few politicians
have paid more attention to the significance of detail in the use of
words'.[76] Hempel was not alone in being wary but he also found out
that de Valera could be steely unambiguous when circumstances
demanded it.

The Taoiseach sent for Hempel and received him in the presence
of Walshe. He told the Minister Plenipotentiary in no uncertain
terms that he could not accept the expression 'unimpeachable'[77]
(translated as 'non-objectionable'). Ireland's dependence on
Britain for trade vital to Ireland and the possibility of British
intervention rendered it inevitable for the Irish government to show
'a certain consideration for Britain', which in similar circumstances
would be shown to Germany. De Valera warned Hempel of danger
points: any violation by Britain or Germany of Irish territorial
waters; exploitation of the anti-British radical nationalist movement;
or any hostile action against the population on the other side of the
border who wanted to return to the Irish state. 'My general
impression' concluded Hempel in his report (Telegraph No. 52
31/8/1939) 'was one of sincere effort to keep Ireland out of the
conflict, but of great fear which de Valera discussed in his usual
doctrinaire[78] fashion, which betrays his real weakness.'

Next day, 1 September 1939, Germany invaded Poland. On 3
September Britain declared war on Germany. A long threatening
had come at last. In de Valera's words there had been 'one crisis too

many'. On 2 September he introduced a bill to amend Article 28 of the Constitution in order to pass emergency legislation.[79] 'The Emergency', as the period of World War II was known in Ireland, had begun.

Hempel had been at his post representing the Third Reich in Dublin for just over two years. During that time he had observed the political scene with perception and, *inter alia*, monitored de Valera's unfolding blueprint for a solution to the foreseen related problems of neutrality and defence. He reported de Valera's utterances of the difficulties to be encountered in implementing policies to deal with those two problems, which were complicated by the history of Anglo-Irish relations (including the unresolved problem of Partition, which involved the IRA in an apparent identity of aim with the government). De Valera had told the Dáil[80] that it was very difficult to remain neutral. Hempel had reported him as saying that it was 'hardly possible' to uphold Irish neutrality in time of war.[81] But it was Hempel's report and not de Valera's statement which implied that neutrality was probably impossible ('von vornherein zu sagen, dass Neutralität unmöglich sei').[82] De Valera's advance planning for neutrality now fell into shape and place and the day before war broke out Hempel's telegram to Berlin recorded that Ireland, fearful, but firm and sincere and piloted by the 'doctrinaire' de Valera was determined to stay out of the coming conflict.[83]

The time had come for all sides to put the intelligence gathered in peacetime to military use. Irish intelligence reassessed German peacetime information gathering. They had not been biking, hiking, photographing, camping all around Ireland just for the good of their health.

Information gathered in enterprises like the Shannon Scheme was drawn on. Social comment, however was of the British-prompted nineteenth-century 'Punch variety'. (A British encyclopedia entry referred to the Irish as 'aborigines'.) Hempel's part in this aspect was not overt: it could not be.

CHAPTER 4

The Diplomat as Intelligence Agent?
1937–September 1939

Diplomacy and Intelligence

It may sound too melodramatic to refer to a career diplomat in peacetime as an Intelligence Agent: to put that association into context a number of factors must be taken into consideration. Firstly, Dr Hempel represented a regime which, under Hitler defied the cautious canons of professional diplomacy in implementing foreign policy. Secondly, the relationship between information-gathering and the intelligence process must be comprehended before a circumstantial link with the German Minister can be postulated. Thirdly, the connection between military intelligence and spy-networks is clear only to the extent that military objectives are clear and in Germany, this extraordinary proliferation of agencies, meddling in policy-making, produced friction and fragmentation and a blurring of objectives. Fourthly, to an extent, all embassies and legations are information-gatherers for their countries: there is a notoriously grey area between information gathering and spying in those circumstances. Hempel only moved to make direct contact with IRA extremists through Herr Clissmann just before the outbreak of war.[1] He probably reckoned that such surveillance was the function of other organisations like the *Auslandsorganisation* or Clissmann's own Academic Exchange organisation.[2] His detachment may have had a 'need to know' basis, which, on security grounds, is established intelligence practice. Finally, the type of information gathering overtly indulged in by Hempel at that time was well established practice in the German Legation and elsewhere.

Historically speaking, when at the beginning of this century Graf Metternich was appointed Ambassador to London, he addressed his staff thus: 'Gentlemen, I'll make the politics: your job is to keep me informed who breakfasts with whom and who sleeps with whom'.[3] By the time Hempel took up his Dublin post, however, the age of the 'great ambassadors' who were policy-makers in their own right was well over. An ambassador was half-jokingly referred to as 'an honest man sent to lie abroad for the good of his country'.[4] German diplomats of the old school – Hempel was one – generally sought to exploit their position to promote Germany's post-Versailles revisionist aims, without jeopardising the national existence. Their loyalty to the State was exploited by Hitler for his own ends: though not policy-makers, the diplomats were the implementers of policy abroad, the emissaries in keeping up appearances and the purveyors ('spinners') of essential information. Nevertheless, as other parties could now also claim to be well informed about conditions in other countries, the diplomat was no longer regarded as the sole source of information.[5] He was however – and this was the case with Hempel – the principal means of intergovernmental communication: that meant at surface level establishing 'official' sources and transmitting information via normal diplomatic channels. This information would then presumably be fed into the intelligence process. Hempel's contribution in this respect was copious and apparently directed towards his country's aims, to the extent, that is, that the career diplomat, whom some would describe as a 'front man', was fully appraised of those aims.

A stereotyped approach to the processing referred to would require that the following stages be more or less followed: stating what the problem is; making an intelligence estimate related to the solving of that problem: collection of information and then the three stages of intelligence handling: collation, interpretation and dissemination. Hitler's ambivalent attitude towards the British during this period did not lend itself to a clear-cut determination in Berlin of the problem as far as Ireland was concerned. To add to the fog, Halifax, in his visit to the Führer in November 1937, had intriguingly classified Germany as the bulwark of the West against Russia.[6] He also expressed the hope that what in effect was an appeased Germany would rejoin the League of Nations.[7]

It was essentially a psychological warfare period, so the requirements from Hempel would have been somewhat different from those concerned simply with conventional military intelligence. Information for psychological operations should comprise political, psychological, religious, social and economic aspects. This, Hempel – if somewhat subjunctively – did diligently. He reported fully on Dáil debates and transparently from the newspapers through normal diplomatic channels: it is a cliché in intelligence work that much of the required information for processing is freely available and that selectively 'milked' newspapers are rich sources of such information. The Dublin Legation had an important role to play, officially collecting information to be processed into intelligence. Therefore Hempel was legitimately in this period (1937–39) a source of intelligence for his own country in this part of the world: that was part of his job as a diplomat. And if the military objective of the *Wehrmacht* was to keep Ireland neutral initially, then Hempel's reportage was an important contribution to making an intelligence estimate of that situation. With regard to neutrality he strove to establish the courses open to the British and soberly listed the indications pointing to the course they were likely to adopt.

But, of course, colloquially – and in practice – the word intelligence had a more pejorative implication – a 'cloak and dagger' connotation, with sinister subversive undertones. Two factors lent significance to this aspect. First of all, non-governmental groups in Ireland, who did not recognise the authority of the democratically elected government of the 26 Counties, were significant in themselves. Secondly, the proliferation of agencies in Nazi Germany already referred to – each striving 'to have its finger in the policy-making pie'– recurringly made for a lack of cohesion and control in intelligence work. Maintenance of the aim is a principle of war; but in the case of German intelligence operations in Ireland that aim does not seem to have been either accurately determined or clearly defined. Confusion was bound to ensue: co-ordination was haphazard and whimsical. This turned out to be the greatest hazard towards maintaining the policy of neutrality, which was gestating during this period (1937–39) and which Hempel, to the best of his ability was carefully monitoring.

Intelligence Prior to 1937

In 1937 Admiral Canaris (Head of German Intelligence) was finally given a free hand with regard to intelligence operations in England.[8] The previous general prohibition for England was relaxed somewhat in 1936 but was bungled: the German agent, Herman Goertz, who later featured prominently in Irish wartime espionage was sentenced in March 1936 to four years penal servitude for spying in England. As always, he was accompanied by a young nubile German maiden and this encumbrance may have been a factor in his apprehension. The alleged 'strict injunction' not to trouble the Irish was not formally revoked at that point.

The assumption however, that because of that, no prior German 'intelligence' work took place in Ireland was not fully accurate, but could perhaps be explained by recognising that such operations have lives of their own and burrow away, sometimes out of co-ordination, even after an army has been defeated in the field. Espionage has been called the second oldest profession in the world. It goes on all the time but is rarely fully documented. It has a life of its own.

In the far background of World War I this report (10/1/1914) emanated from the German Embassy in Washington to the Foreign Minister in Berlin: 'An Irish priest named Michael Collins and Sir Roger Casement are going to Germany in order to visit prisoners'.[9] Things are rarely what they seem in intelligence work. No ruse is too old-fashioned or too new and the obvious and open can sometimes be the best cover. Hempel had a lot to learn to cope with the situation in which he found himself.

In 1937 his predecessor set the precedent of reporting on the strength of the Irish Army and Reserve and speculating about the ability of Ireland being able to remain neutral in the event of Britain being involved in a war; (he doubted it).[10] He also reported Dáil debates on defence, quoting a past minister, Desmond Fitzgerald, on the necessity for co-operation between the British and Irish Forces, in the event of an attack by a third party: an attack on these islands, for Fitzgerald, automatically involved both Great Britain and Ireland. Full reports were also made on army organisations,[11] with the details of establishment tables, the names of officers going on courses abroad,[12] lists of training manuals, dress regulations, appointments and promotions, pay and pensions, included in these reports.

A recurring preoccupation was the role of the Irish Army and this question of military relations with Great Britain. On the other hand, as an index to the existence of another military level in Ireland, the

Consulate in Dublin reported General Murphy of the Garda Siochána as alleging (1928) that he had evidence of links between a Johann Otto Egestorff[13] and an illegal organisation and that he had letters in code, which even Scotland Yard failed to decipher. (The IRA was represented at the World Congress of the Anti-Imperialist League by Seán MacBride and Donald O'Donoghue in Frankfurt-am-Main in 1929).[14] Prior to this period (15/3/1927), the German Sea Union (foreign) (*Hauptverband Deutscher Seevereine im Ausland*) looked for the names of agents that they could trust in Ireland. They got them.

Anything related to defence was deemed by the German Representation to be worthy of note. One explanation for this could be deduced from a report of (21/2/1935) an article carried by the Paris weekly magazine *Gringoire* to the effect that the English government was aware that the continuing wide field of negotiations between Ireland and Germany was a prelude to a military treaty in the event of war.[15] The gist of the reported article was that Ireland had no army to speak of but that the country could be an important base and strong point for Germany's aircraft and U-Boats in the event of war with Great Britain.

In the general historical precedents for Hempel's information-gathering activity, one consideration took on a grand strategy, *Weltanschauung*, dimension when Freiherr Geyr von Schweppen-burg,[16] the German Military Attache in London (1933–37) was concerned enough during his tour of duty to visit Foynes and the Mouth of the Shannon to make an appreciation of the strategic significance of Ireland's geographical location, with particular reference to the Foynes-Newfoundland air route. He had made an accurate forecast of the World War II Order of Battle aligning Italy and Japan with Germany, thereby allowing the Luftwaffe freedom to poise itself lethally at the heart of the 'British Motherland', as he put it. His visualisation took the following shape: at the other end of the gigantic defence front that stretched from Port Darwin in Australia stood the might of the Japanese fleet. German-Spanish politics sought for naval and air bases which posed a threat through the Mediterranean to the Cape; the Mediterranean route itself would be rendered insecure for Britain by the position of Italy in a future war. The position of Ireland remained a conundrum in this strategic jigsaw. The route to the USA had the disadvantage of being flanked by Ireland and von Schweppenburg's theory was that in the coming war the USA, while remaining nominally neutral, would give *de facto* support to England and that this gave unusual importance to Foynes in the context of transatlantic traffic development. He saw British politics as being previously militarily motivated, using British diplomacy to clarify relationships with a view to securing this vulnerable Irish flank. In January 1938 one of the questions put to the British Chief of Staff's Sub-Committee included a question as to whether the importance of the Irish ports was so great as to warrant military operations to regain possession and use of them.[17] The reply indicated that this would require a campaign of Gallipoli proportions if it were carried out in the face of opposition: denying their use to the enemy was what was paramount; to this end a friendly Ireland was essential; in addition German intelligence work would thrive better in an environment unfriendly to Britain.

Contacts with the IRA

There were forces in Ireland actively 'unfriendly to Britain'. On 31 October 1936 Sean Russell, Quartermaster General of the IRA, then Special Envoy to the US, wrote to the German Ambassador in the USA, regretting the reported refusal by the Irish 'Free State' government of landing rights to Germany for an international air service, 'a right apparently conceded without question to England, the traditional enemy of the Irish race'. The puppet 'Free State' government, the letter conveyed, was doing its British masters bidding but the IRA was disposed to 'make return to her friends in Germany for valued assistance in the early days of our present phase of the fight'.

Notwithstanding these protestations of being comrades in arms however, no overt empathy seemed to emanate in the IRA's direction from the Third Reich: the early years of Nazism had a slogan for 'a good understanding with England'. The Nazi paper *Völkischer Beobachter* in June 1936 praised de Valera for disciplining the IRA.[18] When Koester of the German Legation was reporting the suppression of the IRA, he associated this with the murder near Cork of Vice-Admiral Sommerville, who was supposed to be a recruiting agent for the British Navy.[19] This report did not indicate any sympathy for the IRA: 'they had it coming' was the message.

By January 1939 however, when the IRA bombing campaign in Britain began[20] the prospect of a German understanding with England had greatly receded: the Sudeten crisis had soured relations already disturbed by the occupation of the Rhineland and the annexation of Austria. The *Frankfurter Zeitung* now (24/1/1939) editorialised favourably about the IRA bombing. The *Völkischer Beobachter* also changed its tune from a few years previously. 'Sooner or later there would be a war with Great Britain and allies would then be needed.'[21] The interest of the *Abwehr* (Intelligence Organisation) was awakened. Or was it 'reawakened'? The files were called for and Oscar C. Pfaus was dispatched on his mission as contact man to the IRA.[22] Kurt Haller, former Section Leader in *Abwehr II*'s Office I in West Berlin, confirmed the assertion of Pfaus that the *Abwehr* were in the dark about Ireland and the IRA up to this: he said that neither *Abwehr* Division I, the Espionage Division, nor Division II, the Sabotage Division,[23] had previously troubled themselves over Ireland. *Abwehr II* at that time was apparently only represented by one man, Major Voss (cover name, Director Magnus), a specialist for all discontented minority groups ranging from the Flemish and Bretons to the people of South Tyrol and the Irish.

The *Deutsche Fichtebund*, of which Pfaus was a member, was founded in 1914 by Heinrich Kessemeyer for the global dissemination of pro-German propaganda. At the time of Pfaus' recruitment to the *Abwehr* that organisation was in the process of a rapid pre-war expansion. The division concerned with Ireland (Division II) was under Lt. Col. Lahausen. The tasks of this division which dealt with discontented minority groups were sabotage and special operations.

The Pfaus encounters in Ireland moved with the pace of a Chicago gangland 'movie'. He made contact with the IRA through the offices of Blueshirt Leader, Gen. Eoin O'Duffy and his adjutant Captain Liam Walsh.[24] (O'Duffy incidentally is stated to have been a frequent visitor to Hempels). Pretty, young, Joy Paine – referred to pejoratively by Colonel Dan Bryan, Director of Intelligence as 'a flapper, not a student' and by Stephan (P. 29) as 'a patriot and a reader of *Fichtebund* material' – helped to make the contact. She fell madly in love with Pfaus, who invited Seán Russell, the then (February 1939) IRA Chief of Staff, to send an agent to Germany where he would be instructed in the procurement of small arms and hand grenades. Jim O'Donovan was the nomination who emerged and he became the Chief *Abwehr* agent in Ireland, known as 'V. Held'. O'Donovan, an M.Sc., an ex-Clongowes Wood College teacher, was an employee of the Electricity Supply Board. He had been a leading member of the IRA in the early twenties and returned at Russell's request to train young men in explosive and sabotage materials for the bombing campaign in England. He was the instigator of the 'S' Plan – the Sabotage Plan.[25] A torn pound note, one half to the *Abwehr* and the other to be produced by the IRA emissary to Germany was to provide the means of identification and recognition. O'Donovan visited Germany in February, April and finally on 23 August 1939. In May he checked the route to France of the Breton courier, Paul Moyse. The third trip to Germany just before war broke out nearly shattered the liaison, when an over-officious German cutoms officer had Mrs Monty O'Donovan, who was accompanying her husband on the trip, strip-searched as a result of discovering an underdeclared packet of cigarettes. O'Donovan consequently, for a time, became very critical of things German. However, there had been confirmation of the IRA decision to collaborate with Germany; plans, in the event of a war between Germany and England, were considered, links between agents were discussed and possibilities were weighed up about sending the IRA weapons for the fight against the Six Counties.[26] But the three meetings omitted to arrange a secret code for the future wireless traffic. Kurt Haller thought out three English words containing as many letters as possible but incorporating a minor error for security purposes namely, House of Parliaments. It was however 1 September – the twelfth hour. Paul Moyse was hurriedly dispatched on the courier route to London and there delivered to the IRA contact the code, instructions for transmissions, co-operation etc. and a large sum of money.[27] During this time Jim O'Donovan had no contact with Hempel. Later on he did visit the German Minister's house but beat a hasty retreat when the policeman on duty there – 'G-men' as O'Donovan himself termed them – asked him his business.[28]

Intelligence Sources

Legitimate sources of information, relevant to the intelligence process, were availed of by the German representation in Dublin since the foundation of the Irish State (1922): pre-1937, less overt sources also existed. In addition, up to 1939, military geographical data on Ireland was being collected for the Department of War Maps and Survey in Berlin. This was a widespread activity carried out by the Department of Military Geography and not confined to Ireland alone. However, it required more information collection than would have been available through relatively normal channels to produce volumes with situation descriptions, historical background, areas, frontiers, administrative structures, surface forms, types of ground and vegetation, climate, weather and waters of Ireland and which also discussed population, health, industry, transport, communications and traffic, to conclude with a general military estimate. Routine production, German style, it may well have been, but routine production too must have a purpose.

Intelligence appreciations are always considered from the enemy's point of view in order to put the intelligence staff more clearly in the mind of the enemy. An Irish Army Intelligence Officer writing in *The Defence Journal* (*An Cosantoir*)[29] on these documents on Irish life produced by the Germans, asks who supplied all of the pictures and clippings from magazines, the beach data etc. for such a work. He acknowledges the existence of 'friendly' sources but comments on the following comparison of the 1936 Census with the 1946 Census of those born outside Ireland:

	1936	1946	Decrease
Germany	529	460	−69
Italy	325	298	−27
Czechoslovakia	134	85	−49

While many of these figures are irrelevant the German figure may be of interest. It is fair to assume that a percentage of the persons shown would, in the normal way, supply some of the mass of data accumulated. Indeed, there were more than a few 'refugees' from the Continent in Ireland during the 1930s. If they had one thing in common it was a passion for photography and the open air. Many of these were to be seen in coastal areas where, presumably, they could have made the necessary close examination of beaches called for in this study. The firms involved in the building of the Shannon Power Station would have had access to the plans of that installation and would also be aware of the capacity of Irish waterways if this were not already available elsewhere. There were those nationals from the Continent in Ireland involved in research and study in such fields as archaeology, which would give them access to a fund of knowledge and a wide range of maps and charts that could be translated into intelligence. Indeed there is evidence for the presence of army reservists from the Continent here at the time who were subsequently called up for service in their home countries...Thus we see the compilation of this work as something going on over a long period involving a hard core of professionals doing a routine job assisted by an 'army' of amateurs.

The article further comments that the biggest exodus, forty-two, of the German population ('before, during and immediately after the war') was from the Munster area, noting that Munster was shown by the German study to be the most likely point of entry for an invasion force.

The IRA of course was another intelligence source. Before Pfaus was recruited, the *Abwehr*, because either of confusion or incompetence, or for some other reason, had rejected a ready-made source of information available in this area namely, Helmut Clissmann.[30] Clissmann's association with Ireland went back to 1930, when – then a member of the left-wing Young Prussian League – he made a trip to Dublin as a student. In 1933 he returned as an exchange student and later returned to do a doctorate thesis on 'The Wild Geese in Germany' at Frankfort University. Before he came back to Dublin (*Irish Press* 28/1/1936) he attended a lecture there entitled 'Celtic Leaders from Vercingetorix (55 B.C.) to de Valera'.

In spite of all this 'Green' and Celtic complexion however, official attitudes towards him remained cool. Official apprehension had been conveyed to the German Legation that Clissmann's activities in the German Academic Exchange Service (he established branches in Dublin, Cork and Galway) were regarded as a front for a form of espionage activities.[31] Schroetter got very little thanks for passing on this information to Berlin. There had been tension between Clissmann and the *Auslandsorganisation* probably on account of his membership of a left-wing organisation; but on the occasion of his being accused of being a spy, there had been a closing of ranks and they rallied to his support. It was Schroetter who was 'left out on a limb'. The Nazis in Berlin had judged where loyalties lay. On the other hand, Clissmann's application for permission to get married ended with the customary 'Heil Hitler'.

Loyalties were shifting: expediency dictated power-following allegiances.

In the summer of 1938, Clissmann got a tip-off from his prominent IRA friends of developments in the IRA.[32] Confirming earlier official misgivings about his espionage activities, he promptly made his way to Germany to inform the *Abwehr*. Incredibly, believable only at a certain level of German bureaucracy, Captain Marwede alias Dr Pfalzgraf of *Abwehr II*, turned him away on the grounds that it was forbidden to become involved in Irish questions.[33] This alleged attitude of Pfalzgraf does not easily fit in with the allegation that the *Abwehr* made its first contact with the IRA in 1937 through a Breton, Mill Arden, who was married to an Irishwoman, or that another contact with the IRA had been established through Eivars and McCutcheon, two ex-Trinity College students, who were supposed to be sympathetic to Nazi activities and who went to Germany to study.[34] There is no indication that Clissmann's membership of a left-wing organisation had anything to do with the cold-shouldering in Berlin. When the IRA bombing began the following January it does not seem to have occurred to *Abwehr II* that Clissmann was the man on the spot to establish contact with the IRA. Nor – before they turned to Pfaus – do they seem to have considered recruiting a contact man from the ranks of *Auslandsorganisation*. The Nazi chain of command spawned proliferating mavericks.

Nevertheless Hempel remains the principal means of inter-governmental communication. He was not however the sole means of official communication at that level: the *Auslandsorganisation* also had quasi-official status. It was drawn in the main from members of the German colony in Ireland which facilitated the discreet maintenance of contact with subversive organisations. The fate of Schroetter had revealed the extent of party discipline over these German nationals but it also, to some extent, exposed the limits of its power. Still, they did have power and they were extremely well insinuated into the Irish commercial scene.[35] For example, Wolfgang Hahn (economic advisor to the Dublin Group of A.O.) was a Consulting Engineer at 69 Fitzwilliam Square; Karl Krause (on the staff of the commander of the local A.O.) was a representative of the A.E.G. in Dublin; Frederick Winkelmann (reputed to be Gauleiter designate for Ireland)[36] was Director of the Irish Glass

Bottle Manufacturers Ltd; Oswald Müller-Dubrow (Deputy Leader of the local A.O. Group and Chairman of Siemens-Schuckert Ltd, Ireland; the other Director was also an A.O. member Henri Broekhoven – a Dutchman); and the thrusting leader of the organisation was Dr Adolf Mahr, Curator of the National Museum. Another leading member was Colonel Fritz Brase, Director of the Irish Army School of Music who had been made a professor by Hitler. The Irish Army authorities gave him a choice: leave the army or leave the *Auslandsorganisation*. He formally chose the latter.[37]

Perhaps Hempel was aware of the extent of this penetration by the *Auslandsorganisation* or perhaps, in deference to its mission to maintain contact with subversive organisations, he had not, it seems, cultivated relations with extreme nationalist opinion. The war organisation (*Kriegsorganisation*; *K.O.*) assumptions were that if an intelligence service was to function in wartime it should be acquired in peacetime and camouflaged as a commercial undertaking or found some suitable niche in existing German official overseas missions.[38] It was true that Hempel moved in 'radical nationalist' circles but these, whether they liked it or not, were now incorporated in the establishment. Hempel referred to them as representing 'responsible radical opinion', so he kept in touch with them respectively. His interest in art for instance brought him into close contact with Dr L.S. Gogan, a '1916 man' and, inexplicably, Adolf Mahr's subordinate in the National Museum. Hempel was prompted to feel something more was required: 'extreme nationalist opinion' was perhaps coming close to the IRA. He sent for Herr Clissmann and gave him the task of bridging the gap.[39] He obviously knew about Clissmann, whom Peadar O'Donnell in the left-wing paper *The Worker* had pilloried as a spy.[40] In his Trinity days, his contemporaries were amused but convinced that he (with his companion Jupp Hoven) was a spy.[41] Clissmann not alone had contacts with prominent IRA men, particularly Frank Ryan, but also had contacts with the A.O. in London.[42] (Dr Thierfelder, Prof. Sieverts, Dr Steuber, Prof. Riddell and Herr Bene. Herr Bene, 'State Group Leader for Great Britain and Ireland', had come under scathing criticism from another left-wing paper, *The Irish Workers' Voice*, for his propaganda stunts in Ireland.)[43] If left-wing criticism was anything to go by, Clissmann should have by now purged his 'Young Prussian League' associations in Nazi eyes. Time was short but Clissmann introduced Hempel to Seán MacBride 'and a few others' (Clissmann's phrase). Hempel thereafter regularly consulted with Seán MacBride and he and Frau Hempel regularly visited the MacBrides in Roebuck. MacBride had the formidable task of constantly counselling Hempel: his golden rule for him was not to appear to be on the wrong side of the law at any time.[44]

But Clissmann went back to Germany when war broke out and, in spite of Hempel's assurance that he would be back, he did not return until after the war. Clissmann maintains that he was called up because of official bungling. Another story[45] is: when his name did not appear on the list of Germans to be sent home from Ireland after 1 September 1939, the British, aware of the extreme company he kept, asked the Irish government to add his name to the list and he was asked to leave. Nowadays when there is some idea of the extent of the British infiltration and permeation of the German Intelligence Service – even Canaris[46] himself is suspect – it is not fantastic to conceive a link between the two incidents. Clissmann was accompanied by forty-two key members of the colony – scientists, academics and administrators. This move was later regretted as it was felt that they could have done more to help the German cause if they had remained in Ireland.[47] What that could have been can only be surmised with concern.

The Effects in Berlin

Bewley, the Irish representative in Berlin up to August 1939, was convinced 'that National Socialism, whatever might be the defects, should be upheld by the Western Powers as the strongest, perhaps the only, force which could prevent the spread of the Communist Empire over half Europe'.[48] That, he said, did not imply an unquestioning acceptance of all the practices of Hitler's regime. Among the diplomats of the old school in Germany he found no sympathy for Ireland: they regarded it as the same disturbing element in the British Empire as Alsace-Lorraine had been in the German Reich.[49]

So what? In spite of the circuitous nature of much of Hempel's reporting, he influenced the political Department in Berlin. They saw the difference between the Irish government and the IRA as lying mainly in methods. In February 1940 they sent this message to Hempel in response to his telegrams:

> The government hopes to attain its objective by legal political means while the IRA tries to achieve success by terrorist means. Most of the members of the present Irish Government formerly belonged to the IRA. By reason of its militant attitude towards England the IRA is a natural ally of Germany. *Abwehr already has strictly secret connections with the IRA*, a part of which utilised a channel which is *now* closed as the result of the war. The interest of the Intelligence Department is confined to promoting acts of sabotage.[50]

Perhaps a looseness in some of Hempel's reportage (it would be possible in some of his reports to mistakingly interpret references to 'radical nationalist opinion' as a euphemism for the IRA) contributed to this type of thinking but it had probably gone further than he had intended. Later the German Minister would express firmer opinions about the IRA capabilities and the *modus operandi* of intelligence operations in a neutrality situation. On the other hand, information supplied by the Envoy, verbatim, untranslated and without qualification on de Valera's statements of appealing to the young people to 'be prepared to secure what has not yet been won',[51] contributed to this colouring of intelligence processing especially when it was leavened by supplementary contributions from the Chief *Abwehr* agent, Jim O'Donovan.[52]

Hempel's reporting was certainly a key factor in the intelligence process of the period 1937–39. It had a crucial effect in Berlin on the intelligence appreciation of the neutrality situation in Ireland. Those benevolent references of the Envoy to 'radical nationalist opinion', when coupled with the denigration of de Valera's alleged pro-Britishness and implied praise for Seán T. O'Kelly's fighting spirit of nationalism, served to substantiate subversive fantasies that they, with the IRA, represented the 'soul' of Ireland and were the true patriots. To that extent Hempel – sometimes unwittingly perhaps – contributed to the creation of a climate that made possible the interjection later on from underground sources of a bizarre assortment of 'agents'. These interpositions were to present problems for the very conventional career diplomat representing, in a small neutral country, which was strategically located, his Nazi government, which was at war with that neutral country's historically and geographically intertwined neighbour and 'ancient enemy'. That situation, which implicated a diplomat like Hempel in peacetime in the related activities of an intelligence agent, is by its nature convoluted. Intelligence operations are rarely simplistic, though these operations may require the performance of simple overt tasks of the kind Hempel was seen to perform punctiliously. The 'need to know' canon often implied that, by design, the left hand did not know what the right hand was doing. In effect, albeit unintentionally ambidextrous reportage fed with both hands: the one promoting; the other, cloying. This added to the ongoing tensions, endemic in representing a disordered Nazi government at war with his mission's neighbour. These tensions undulated with the ebb and flow of war, presenting a seamless series of dilemmas for the diplomat throughout his tenure.

Hempel's activities were not a major concern to the beset Irish Government at this time. He was not engaged in any discernible 'cloak and dagger' activity. The tiny Irish Army intelligence service was aware of IRA-Abwehr links but its focus at that time was on the IRA threat rather than a German one. There was nothing 'phoney' about the IRA menace in the overtaking 'Phoney War' period. They had already usurped the functions of the democratically elected government by declaring war on England, thereby provoking the possibility of a precipitate counter-attack — the major danger to neutrality in an anti-Irish climate. The British media scurrilously attacked Éire's neutrality. The 'certain considerations for Britain' were peremptorily dismissed. Demarcations were blurred accordingly. The 'Phoney War' in Ireland was opaque in more ways than one and Hempel was part of that opacity: an essential part, as it turned out.

PART II

1939–41, THE DIPLOMAT'S DILEMMA

CHAPTER 5

The Phoney War, September 1939–May 1940

The Situation, Irish Responses and Phoney Diplomacy

If the Clausewitz concept that war is an extension of diplomacy by other means is accepted, then phoney war is, by definition, an extension of phoney diplomacy. Hempel was affected by this phoney diplomacy at different levels. At a fundamental level, without specifying Hempel, opinions were expressed that the constitutional device for the accreditation of foreign diplomats to Éire was in itself phoney. Bewley, the former Irish representative in Berlin, was particularly caustic about the 'way out' he alleged de Valera had found 'which would convince Ireland of his independence and England of his loyalty' as 'he (de Valera) could not afford to defy his British patrons or jeopardise his standing at Geneva':

> Such was the constitutional position: the Irish government could neither sign a treaty nor appoint an ambassador except through the medium of the king, and King George VI for foreign states was still Head of the State. But it was still possible for the Irish government to treat these reserved powers as a mere formality, to regard His Majesty in the words of a former Irish minister as a 'rubber stamp' useful for registering the decision of a native government.[1]

De Valera had regarded the Constitution as a republican one which nevertheless retained a link with the Commonwealth. Bewley referred to this as an attempt 'to square the circle' but in de Valera's mind he was aiming at the form of external association which he had first suggested in 1921.[2] That aim however, demanded an element of phoney posturing to deal with the question of Éire's membership or non-membership of the British Commonwealth. But international diplomacy generally also had a phoney façade. There is evidence of this in the pre-war peace 'feelers', which can be put into perspective by recalling that Hitler, as far back as 3 April 1939, had fixed 1 September 1939 as the date for launching an attack on Poland.[3]

Conceptually, and in terms of relative combat power, the Polish campaign was a case of 'horses versus tanks'. In addition there was, from a military point of view, the inexplicable inertia of Britain and France in failing to engage Germany, while the principal German armies were allowed a free hand in Poland. 'The Phoney War was the time when those who had declared war on Hitler did not fight'.[4] As British General J.F.C. Fuller has observed, the French Army, then reckoned to be the strongest in the world, with no more than twenty-six German divisions facing them, sat still and sheltered behind steel and concrete while a quixotish valiant Polish army was being exterminated. British bombers dropped leaflets, not bombs, over Germany while Poland was being ruthlessly overrun. On the other hand, if they *had* dropped bombs, they were ill-prepared to counter any retaliation: the 1,000 bomber raids of Air Marshal Albert ('Bomber') Harris on Köln, Hamburg and finally Dresden were not possible at that time. The supporting British psychological warfare campaign consisted of empty 'pop-song' threats to 'Hang out the Washing on the Siegfried Line', accompanied by a sneer campaign at the Nazi leaders. Low, the famous British newspaper cartoonist had already dubbed Ribbentrop (now Hempel's Foreign Affairs' Minister), 'Herr von Brickendrop'.[5] The former champagne salesman's period as German Ambassador in London had been marked by a series of gaffes, like giving the Nazi salute when being presented to the king.

In neutral Éire on the day Poland was invaded (1/9/1939) a solitary senry with a fixed bayonet was posted symbolically at the Northern-line Amiens Street Station: 'as a purely precautionary measure', a formal army statement was issued to reassure the Irish public.[6]

Britain declared war on Germany on 3 September 1939 and the following day, de Valera called a press conference at which he spoke of the German Envoy's visit to him a week before on 31 August. Hempel had conveyed to the Taoiseach that Germany would, under certain conditions, respect Ireland's neutrality. De Valera had stressed that the aim of the Irish government *was* to preserve Irish neutrality.[7] To accomplish this aim a National Emergency was declared.[8] The Offences against the State Act was applied.[9] The Special Criminal Court was set up.[10] Powers of requisition were extended to authorised officers.[11]

Shortly after the outbreak of war, Hempel, for the first time, found himself with a British counterpart in Dublin. Heretofore, disagreement about title had proven to be a barrier to British diplomatic representation in Éire. 'High Commissioners' had too many imperial connotations to be acceptable in Ireland while the British baulked at the appointment of an ambassador or minister as they felt that such action would be tantamount to recognising Irish independence. De Valera's dexterity in placing prepositions – substituting 'to' for 'in' – made possible the acceptance of a title for the proposed post: 'United Kingdom Representative *to* 'Éire'. Sir John Maffey's appointment to the post was approved on 22 September 1939.[12] Chamberlain thanked de Valera for solving the title problem: de Valera sympathised with Chamberlain in his anxieties. This newly created diplomatic climate however did not deter the Irish government from an emphatic assertion of neutrality in the form of an *aide-mémoire* which was handed by Dulanty to a perturbed Anthony Eden on 12 September 1939 and read out by Dr Michael Rynne to Lafocarde, the French representative and to Herr Hempel. Hempel's response was 'classical'.

The German Minister referred the *aide-mémoire* to Berlin, which stated, through Hempel, that they would accept the neutrality declaration providing it was 'non-objectionable' – 'einwandfrei'. The other belligerent ignored the communication and asked the Irish not to publish it. Walshe was not consulted about the composition of this *aide-mémoire*: the task was given directly by de Valera himself to Rynne. (Rynne composed it overnight and when de Valera read it the following morning he congratulated Rynne, saying he could have done better himself). Walshe felt somewhat aggrieved and was less than enthusiastic about the presentation, which announced the prohibition of the use of Irish territorial waters and air space to belligerents. The point Walshe – the reputed 'éminence grise' of the implementation of the neutrality concept – made, was the less put on paper about it the better.

The job of Hempel's British counterpart, Maffey, was to make these restrictions 'less embarrassing' for Britain.[13] Hempel's job, at this stage, was to see that the Irish government complied with the conditions required to ensure that Germany would respect chameleon Irish neutrality:

The little phrase 'a certain consideration' for Britain' turned out to be the key to Irish neutrality, and Hempel could scarcely have guessed at the extent to which ostensible neutrality would be bent in favour of Britain as the war progressed.[14]

German Attitudes towards Irish Neutrality

The Phoney War provided a suitable setting for the phoney protocol inherent in Anglo-Irish relations, arising out of the difficulties of reconciling a policy of qualified neutrality with the actual external relations aspects of the Constitution. A case in point was the attempt to appoint Dr Kiernan as the new Irish Minister to Germany to succeed Bewley, who had finally severed his relations with the Irish government just before the war. (Bewley had retired voluntarily under pressure from de Valera and not having completed fifteen years service was, in his own words 'unemployed without even the consolation of a pension').[15] The First Secretary, Mr William Warnock, had been promoted Chargé d'Affaires to act as representative until a new appointment was made. (As events turned out he carried on alone, until relieved by Cornelius Cremin in 1944). When Kiernan was nominated, Hempel 'cleared' him to Berlin. He was, he wrote, 'kind, careful, reticent, a good worker, an MA; had served in the Income Tax Department and had been Director of Radio Éireann; he was versed in economic questions and had an interest in Celtic Studies'. Kiernan's wife, the ballad singer Delia Murphy, did not impress Hempel to the same extent. His condescending report snobbishly presumed her to be of humble origins from the West of Ireland.[16]

Kiernan's departure was delayed and Warnock pointed out to the German Foreign Ministry (25/2/1939) the difficulties in sending Kiernan abroad in a wartime situation with a wife and five children. Hempel perceived that there was a constitutional snag and on 16 October 1939 he expressed his doubts that the king would sign Kiernan's accreditation.[17] However, he continued to request Berlin for material to give to the Irish government for the briefing of Kiernan in the event of the latter receiving accreditation. In considering the alternative of either de Valera or President Hyde signing the accreditation, the Envoy concluded that protocol insisted that it would require Hyde's signature before the Führer could receive Kiernan: de Valera's signature could only confer minister status on the Irish representative. Nevertheless, the Envoy doubted that, in the eventuality, either de Valera or Hyde could or would sign, as this would disturb the Commonwealth link. In this analysis he was correct because it was obvious that, although the Irish government kept up a pretence of wanting full accreditation for Kiernan, de Valera had no intention of disturbing the Commonwealth link of which he was the architect. The case was still not resolved by the following March (1940) and Hempel reported that the constitutional impediment to accreditation was now compounded by political considerations, as a consequence of the conviction and hanging of IRA prisoners in Birmingham. Anthony Eden had had a word with de Valera over the difficulties arising from asking the king to sign credentials addressed to Herr Hitler and the Taoiseach did not push to resolve the anomaly: 'he felt it unwise to pursue the matter'. That position – not surprisingly – was not conveyed to Hempel. Nevertheless the Envoy in Éire 'got the message'. His report however had reservations about the disparity in representation: a minister as against 'a young secretary acting as Irish Representative'. Still he implied that it was just as well to let the matter drop as Warnock seemed to be doing a good job and anyway he now, in a volte-face, remarked that Kiernan did not seem to have anything special to recommend him.[18]

Hempel's pre-war reports consistently reflected de Valera's developed conceptions of neutrality and his delineations of the difficulties of maintaining a neutral posture. The German Minister had featured the Taoiseach's Dáil speech (23/2/1939) declaring that neutrality was not only the most difficult but also the most costly of all the courses to implement, because whoever adopted a neutral stand had to be prepared to defend himself against the possibility of an attack from either side.[19] Such doubts about the capability of remaining neutral in the circumstances of contiguity to and trade with Britain could account for the steely edge of German attitudes towards Ireland in wartime. Their conditions and expectations were somewhat stiffly presented to de Valera by Ribbentrop through his minister Hempel. If Ireland strayed from the path of neutrality 'as a result of a decision by the government themselves or by pressure exerted on Ireland from other quarters' the Germans would safeguard their interests in the sphere of warfare in accordance with the demands of the situation.[20] Hempel took great care with the wording of a simultaneous press release by the two governments indicating where they stood in this matter (1/9/1939).[21]

When Warnock was later (27/9/1939) observing strict protocol in giving official notification of Irish neutrality in Berlin, he politely enquired how Hempel had been communicated with, so that the Envoy could inform the Irish government of German willingness to respect neutrality.[22] The existence of a secret German transmitter in Hempel's Legation in Dublin – a hazard to neutrality by the German side – was not known to the Irish authorities at this stage, or if it was they did not let on. All irons had to be kept in the fire.

Woermann lamely replied that he did not know how the communications had been effected and mentioned the possibility of an American route. At the beginning of the war when the US was nominally neutral, that route was effective and the transmitter was used only sparingly. Even in the field of communications a 'phoney' situation prevailed that protocol could not fully cover up. Diplomatic speak developed to accommodate the mutuality of the day.

All the protocol however, together with the flying of an Irish flag, did not prevent the *Inver Liffey* being sunk in September 1939 by a German U-Boat.[23] The 'phoney' side of the war was shown to be not all a matter of mere play-acting. The killing game was barely below the surface, biding its time. This action seemed to upset Hempel to the extent that he queried Berlin about such behaviour. He need not have been over-concerned. De Valera played down the incident: the ship, Taoiseach exonerated, was carrying contraband to a country at war and so ran the risk of being sunk. As he saw it, the U-Boat Commander had done nothing out of the way; other combatants would do the same. De Valera was bending over backwards, so as not to provoke the feared Germans. Hempel however, warned the Foreign Ministry against making too much capital out of this in the German Press and Radio and went on to give details of the sailing of American steamers *St John* and *Arcadia* and in the same report to request details of the wiring and operating of a condenser for his secret transmitter. The German Minister felt that Irish neutrality should work as a favourable factor in the U-Boat campaign[24] but on the other hand, he did not feel that the sinking of the passenger ship *Athenia* was a matter of pride.[25] The irony was that the probability existed that Hempel himself was the source of information that led to the sinking of another ship the

Iroquois and Walshe conveyed the Irish government's embarrassment to the German Minister at an American report that neutral Ireland had been quoted as a source of the information that led to the sinking.[26] Hempel over protested about Petersen's innocence in this affair, mentioning in passing his own 'careful telegram'. Woermann eventually had to more or less tell the Envoy to keep quiet and let the matter rest, especially as Hempel had now – in what seemed to be a frantic effort to divert suspicion away from himself – also pointed the finger at a possible IRA involvement.[27] That could open up the covert side of German underhand liaisons with the subversive illegal organisation. That was not the image they wished to project at this point.

The ship sinkings notwithstanding, it would appear that Germany wished to be seen to be respecting Irish neutrality, but intending in addition to be vigilant in seeing that no unfair advantage from that position accrued to Britain. Hempel busied himself in reporting on possibilities of the re-export of goods from Ireland to Britain when neutral ships had been allowed through with certain goods for Ireland. This, he pointed out, could have a big significance in the event of the USA abandoning its neutrality laws and not recognising Western Irish ports as a war zone.[28] In this comprehensive economic report the German Minister stressed that a long war would be detrimental to Irish economic life and that the British were using the opportunity of Irish economic difficulties to apply pressure on Ireland and to make political use of economic dependence. He indicated that a continuing Irish interest in imports from Germany would be welcome but that payment would present problems, as would the danger of British connections and the mechanics of exports. An Italian connection might be a solution and the Envoy 'left it to themselves' to examine whether Irish cattle and trade could be procured in such a way. He had got an undertaking, he reported, regarding the re-export of goods, from Boland and had extracted from Woermann in Berlin a message that German naval forces had been instructed to strictly observe Irish neutrality.[29] These were significant contributions from the German representative working towards preserving the externals in the fabric of neutrality. Words were important but deeds more so.

He had already rebuked German Radio for their English language broadcast that the Dublin 'blackout' was favouring the

British.[30] In that report of an angry Dáil reaction to the broadcast, Hempel used an interesting word – 'bagatellisierend' – to describe de Valera's answer playing down the affair. Walshe had told Hempel 'confidentially' that the blackout was implemented solely at the hands of the Irish Minister for Defence and that it was also directed against possible eventual British flying intentions: the effect on other neutrals of lifting the blackout was also pointed out by Walshe. Hempel warned the Foreign Ministry that, in view of the strenuous efforts of the Irish government to maintain neutrality, such defamatory remarks as had been broadcast must cease. The Envoy seemed to be adopting opinions of his own and taking a stronger line with his Berlin base. He was after all 'the man on the spot'. However, the main factor influencing his responses was the firm but flexible leadership adroitly exercised by the Irish side.

In any case, the German Minister in Éire had been able to confirm in early October (1939) that Irish neutrality was being strictly observed, had wide popular support and should also be supported by Germany.[31] The warning notes he sounded indexed German predilections which he was seeking to counter or modify. Caution, he advised, should be exercised in submarine warfare; special treatment was required in the application of the blockade to Ireland; interference in Irish internal conflicts should be avoided. He made the point that leading British statesmen and officials – including probably Eden – were said not to have any significant objections to Irish neutrality; but that other influential groups did object and that resulted in a fear on the part of the Irish of British demands for harbours and airports if the war situation worsened. Irish neutrality, he continued, was being very closely watched in the USA and any abandonment of US neutrality would constitute a threat to Irish neutrality. Coupled with his recommendation that Germany should continue to support Irish neutrality it was also recommended that they should also support Irish independence 'on a broad national basis'. He felt that the Irish question in press and radio should be handled on a 'facts only' basis and that any attempts to directly exploit stories for propaganda against England should be avoided. These he obviously found to be counter-productive, marred possibly by an inappropriate phrasing. He pointed out that Ireland rejected belonging to the British Empire and recognised only a loose connection with that body for foreign policy purposes. He also noted that in Ireland if a foreigner said a word against England the Irish reacted negatively. It was alright for them to do it, but dare an outsider open his mouth against the British.

Again, to counter an inclination to persist with certain attitudes, he repeated his advice against any interpositioning in Irish affairs and particularly opposed giving German aid to the IRA.[32]

The Envoy's report was pragmatic and no point of 'principle' relating to neutrality was invoked. It was simply to state unambiguously that interference now could 'rob the IRA of all chances of future success' by giving England a pretext to intervene – 'and Irish neutrality as well as the possibility of a future use of the Irish cause for German interests would be prematurely destroyed'. This situation, he continued, would probably change if Irish neutrality were to be violated or if England were weakened sufficiently to make the prospects of regaining Northern Ireland more favourable. In that case then there would be a prospect of a broad national rising supported by the Irish overseas and this would force the Germans to make a decision to promise Ireland support and the return of Northern Ireland at the conclusion of peace. Hempel passed on the rumour that hope for such an outcome had been expressed by Dáil deputies (but not by de Valera, he stressed). With 'Wild Goose' opponents like Veesenmayer the Envoy felt that he could not be pragmatic enough in clarifying Germany's best interests. The Envoy's expressed firm opinion was that the time for such involvement was not yet ripe: 'the proper moment has not yet arrived'. He had already pointed out that the IRA was not strong enough for significant action against England and was also 'probably lacking in a leader of any stature'. This, however, did not deter him from rather coyly mentioning in a later report (30/11/1939) that the IRA had informed him that in the event of British action against his Legation, they (the IRA) would be prepared to defend them and take them to safety.[33] He added, as an afterthought apparently, that the government would also, probably, be willing to do the same.

German propaganda reflected German attitudes and Hempel monitored it. The German broadcasts in English were listened to everywhere, he mentioned, and were the best of propaganda, though he had reservations about the efficacy of the sharp personal attacks on Churchill, which he felt achieved the opposite of the intended effect, especially in England.[34] On the other hand, as far as Ireland was concerned, he reported that the Irish-speaking broadcasts worked brilliantly and both the government and Irish speakers were well pleased with this 'first international recognition of the Irish language'.[35] This was the line to go on, he urged: tone down on the propaganda, stick to culture and the importance of German 'know-how' and skills to revive old Irish cultural traditions; stress German-Irish relations. He paid tribute to the Irish used in the broadcast but counselled avoiding using the word 'Gaelic'. He advised using the word 'Irish' instead. The German Minister had also advised against sending certain types of material through the post.[36] as this would militate against his increasingly successful measures against British propaganda.[37] His representations in that respect had led to the banning of the more violently anti-German British tabloids.

But there was also at this time, at a level other than the one in which Hempel's official representation operated, a more sinister development in German attitudes. This was the direction by the Foreign Ministry[38] to formally appoint Veesenmayer, the *coup d'état* specialist, to foment an Irish rebellion.[39] At that stage, and on that point (early 1940), the *Abwehr* were responding to instigations from the Foreign Ministry.[40] Mystify and mislead was the name of the game. Nothing was what it seemed to be on the surface. The biggest danger arose from the proliferating German agencies misleading each other. There was no unity of command in the *Abwehr*.

Hempel and Peace Feelers

The peace initiatives put about underlined this and epitomised the phoney aspects of the 'Phoney War' and its phoney diplomacy. Hempel's name was also associated with the 'Peace Feelers'. His initial assessment of Maffey noted him as a possible player in Italian-prompted peace overtures, initiated following the overrunning of Poland.[41] The reason Hempel gave for this was that the new British Representative in Ireland – who, he said, had been partly educated in Germany and was former Under-Secretary of State for the Colonies and Governor General of the Sudan – had been the author of reports on the Ethiopian conflict which were favourable to Italy.

However – as per usual – the Envoy immediately hedged his speculations on Maffey's usefulness. He telegraphed thus:

> The first impression is good; thus there is hope of useful mediation, *but on the other hand* (my italics) there is concern on the part of nationalist circles. The government is hoping that he will be appointed Minister which would signify the recognition sought by Ireland of her special position with reference to the Commonwealth.[42]

Hempel had already reported (3/10/1939) that Chamberlain and an influential section of the Cabinet would welcome peace, if British prestige could be preserved in the process.[43] In spite of his persistent obsession with the dangers of British provocation, he himself had connections with British bishops in this matter of peace initiatives.[44] The difficulty was that the only peace terms acknowledged by the Germans were those announced in Hitler's Reichstag speech of 6 October 1939,[45] and Woermann had lugubriously commented on Chamberlain's decision for war after 'the Führer's hand of peace had been brutally rejected'.[46] Hempel took pains to point out to Berlin that he was following the party line in any movement towards 'peace feelers'. Referring to de Valera's probing to try to help Chamberlain's efforts in this regard 'against Churchill and the other war supporters in the British Cabinet', he wrote: 'In that instance too I strictly adhered to the directives of your telegraphic instruction No. 185 of October 24 1939'.[47]

But the Peace Initiative that literally hit the front page and embarrassed Hempel was the bizarre business of Lord Tavistock. The 51-year-old Lord, a former active Communist, and a self-professed expert on Social Credit, later gravitated towards nazism, fascism and the Anglican Pacifist Fellowship. In an article in the British Union of Fascists' journal (January 1940), he accused the British government of being responsible for the war. In one of his reports Hempel referred to him as 'a crank'.[48]

In March 1940 Tavistock published a leaflet setting out alleged German peace terms which he said he had obtained from the German Legation in Dublin through an 'Irish friend'. The 'friend' turned out to be a Craig (or Gregg) of Belfast who had a German wife.[49] Tavistock (later the Duke of Bedford) held that he was led to believe by the Dublin Legation that the German government was prepared to allow Czechoslovakia full independence provided she remained neutral; similarly in the case of Poland, provided an outlet to the sea with necessary rail communications and the use of the Vistula was granted to Germany. The Germans, according to him, were interested in an international disarmament pact and were ready to join a reformed League of Nations; they were prepared to hold a plebiscite in Austria and undertook to co-operate with an international body to find a national home for the Jews; but they wanted the return of their former colonies.[50]

In spite of Hempel's vehement denials that any such information was given, the impression remained that there was 'no smoke without fire'. One way or another, his circumspection in refusing to see Tavistock himself but in passing him on to Thomsen was justified.[51] Had the German Minister given Tavistock an interview he could have been compromised. Tavistock had passed information on to Lord Halifax who, while showing little interest and describing Tavistock's action as irregular, did little to deter the unorthodox Lord and in the end gave him permission to visit Dublin to check if the terms were authentic. The Bedford version then was that about that time, the Germans, having been snubbed in their peace overtures just after the outbreak of the war, were becoming evasive and were not prepared to give official sanction to these new approaches.

If that version were correct it illustrated one more aspect of the 'phoney war', because the Germans, while they were posturing as the injured peacemakers, were at the same time reliably reported behind the scenes to be increasing military activity all along the Reich frontiers with Belgium, Luxembourg and the Netherlands. They were in fact 'forming up' for the coming Blitzkrieg (May 1940). And, as the Political Department admitted the previous February, the *Abwehr* had secret connections with the IRA to forge an alliance against England.[52] Also Hitler, in outlining a five-point programme in an interview to the American government representative Summer Welles, stated that they were ready for a long war.[53]

The five points were:

1. German retention of Bohemia – Moravia and Poland (the retention of Austria was taken for granted).
2. Renunciation by Britain of her demands to intrigue in or

exercise her influence in Scandinavia.
3.   Disappearance of Britain's bases at Malta, Gibraltar and Singapore.
4.   A 'Monroe Doctrine' for Germany in Central Europe.
5.   Return of Germany's former colonies.

Tavistock felt that he was not getting an adequate response to his 'peace feelers' and John McGovern MP, who had been associated with him in this enterprise, suggested telling the whole story to the press. The resultant political storm was an embarrassment to Halifax, as a member of the government who could not disclaim knowledge of the affair, and to Hempel, whose cautious approach in the first instance now served to extricate him. He was pleased with the way the *Irish Press* handled his rebuttal of the business.

As well as McGovern, George Landsbury, Labour MP for Bow and Bromley, and the Most Revd William Temple, Archbishop of York, had been involved in peace overtures and Martin traces the Hempel connection.[54] The links were thought to be with an English Peace Party, to which the Archbishop of York belonged and which included Lords Buccleuch, Buxton, Darnley, Farringdon and Holden and the spokesman, Labour MP Stokes. There remains much more to be disclosed in this area.[55] Chamberlain, Halifax, Simon, Hoare, Londonderry and Astor are mentioned; even the Duke of Windsor seems to have played a part as a Germanophile appeaser. Hempel quoted reports from the Irish High Commissioner in London around Christmas (1939) indicating increasing optimism for peace tendencies among the British Cabinet but '*on the other hand*', oppositely, this had stimulated an inclination to carry on the war against Germany.[56] It was hard to pin Hempel down to unequivocal assertions.

Hempel's Reports

Nevertheless, no matter how circuitously couched, Hempel's reports at this time were designed to help Ireland to remain on the path of neutrality. He did advocate support for neutrality; caution in the application of the blockade to Ireland and in submarine warfare and a warning about getting mixed up with the IRA. He accurately read British policy towards Ireland and in this area reported soberly and with balance. His handling of the field of communications did not make a similar contribution to the preservation of neutrality. From the beginning of the war, the only qualms he had about using the secret transmitter were, not unnaturally, to avoid detection if possible. He was preoccupied with securing proper condensers and concerned himself with appropriate frequencies to ensure sending and receiving messages on the clandestine set.[57] He was not alone in this practice. The British too had their own clandestine transmitter in Romania.

His reports in this period indicate that he was a veritable sleuth-hound, snooping after firms like McGee and Beck and Scott to uncover breaches of neutrality. He had heard that timber was being re-exported to Harland and Wolfe and the Ulster Timbucktoo Company, who were acting for a Swedish pulp company in Maidenhead, London.[58] A lot of this information was fed gratuitously, for whatever reason, through his letter-box. He pressed the Irish government for clarification of regulations and for explanations and occasionally embarrassed them.[59] Boland kept him reassured on those points and Hempel in turn put in a word looking after Irish interests. He requested that in the event of a tightening of the blockade that a protected route should be found for the relatively small imports of goods from countries other than Britain: Anglo-Irish trade, he cautioned to Berlin, had but a minimum effect in jeopardising neutrality.[60] His motive was to avoid driving Ireland into English hands.[61]

The German Minister's report on the IRA's successful raid on the Irish Army armoury in the Magazine Fort at Christmas 1939 developed into an analysis of de Valera's strengths and weaknesses.[62] He stated that De Valera was being criticised for his pacifist attitude towards Northern Ireland and he interpreted de Valera's statement that Northern Ireland would not be a bargaining counter for a cattle deal as applying also to a deal relating to the ports. De Valera had conveyed to the German representative – 'perhaps not unintentionally' – that his intention was to let the Northern Ireland question lie for the time being, but Hempel wondered whether the 'national movement' (euphemism for the IRA) would permit such a course of action/inaction. He did not see the opposition, whom he classified as more pro-British and anti-IRA than Fianna Fáil, as an alternative government. He predicted an increase in tension between the government and the 'Nationalists'. There seemed to be an increasing blurring of Nationalist and IRA in that report which could possibly be attributable to the initial impact of the raid. It seemed to have been successful; they seemed to have got away with it; Hempel had hinted at Irish Army collaboration. It would appear, as a result of the raid, as if they (the IRA) were a force to be reckoned with Hempel vacillated.

He had difficulty making up his mind about the role of the Irish Army. In October 1939 he wrote: 'The Irish Army is supposedly ready to defend neutrality in all directions in spite of the presence of pro-British elements'.[63]

The following May – Hempel was assuming that the Irish government would only make concessions concerning harbours if the British resorted to force. In those circumstances, he felt, the government might put up armed resistance but on the other hand, in view of the small size of the armed forces, they might not. He added a different slant to the one he had given the previous October:

> In the Irish Army which is quite likely permeated with elements in close contact with the IRA – as is said to be the case especially among the volunteers – feelings are clearly divided.[64]

Hempel never did quite get the pulse of the Irish Army, partly for the reason that after the Magazine Fort raid, the reformed army totally reasserted itself. De Valera emerged from the raided fort with his brow as black as thunder. The Civil War was only seventeen years past and thoughts of treachery inevitably came to mind. There was undoubtedly IRA infiltration but they were rounded up and weeded out. Heads rolled and what might be called a reign of punctilious terror for orderly duty officers ensued. Then de Valera made an inspired choice. He selected Major-General Dan McKenna to replace General Michael Hogan as Chief of Staff of the Defence Forces. In the space of a couple of years he transformed, through sweat and tears, a gathering of Volunteer and Emergency men into a combat-ready force ready to fight and die for their country. 'If we have to die for it, we will die for it.' It was a governing factor in deterring hasty aggression. The IRA in particular remained a dangerous Trojan horse as far as the security of Éire was concerned.

A 'snakin' regard for the IRA by some sections of the public confused Hempel at times but he did immediately grasp essentials: the IRA was an illegal subversive organisation. But there again he was representing a Nazi government which itself had scant respect for the rule of law. Anyway he had a wide range of subjects to cover during the 'Phoney War' period. In addition to policy matters and the IRA, there were also his own man-management problems. He reported on difficulties with Petersen, the DNB reporter, whom he had taken on his staff at the outbreak of the war and to whom he paid 500 marks per month. This newspaperman had a flair for getting himself into scrapes. Boland thought he was an ass[65] – so did Francis Stuart.[66] But Petersen's wife's opinion was that he (Petersen) was 'the only one of them' at the Legation who was not a Nazi.[67] Hempel damned him with faint praise and put his shortcomings down to youth and political inexperience abroad, but he said he was doing a good job as a press liaison officer. Anyway he saw no way of getting rid of him by repatriation and asked what form of rebuke he should administer.[68] Contradicting his earlier commendation he now asserted that Petersen also had practical work-related problems. It was time for a face-to-face meeting.

Hempel's efforts to return to Berlin for a conference with Woermann at the beginning of the 'Phoney War' were based initially on unrealistic assumptions. Such assumptions however were symptomatic of the climate prevailing during that 'Phoney War' time. The prospect of enlisting Irish co-operation in the matter of securing safe conduct through England was sounded out and the precedent of the facilitation of German diplomats stranded in Europe at the outbreak of the war to return to their posts in South America was cited. No such facilitation however was forthcoming from the circumspect Irish side. Warnock pointed out the problems incidental to Hempel's intimation that he intended to travel to Germany in wartime with his wife and now five children. That ignores the 'phoney' back-drop which influenced his thought-process.

The 'phoney' side of the general situation is however more comprehensible when it is recalled that the United States and Italy were still neutral at the time and so lines of communications were open to both of those countries. In that context perhaps the aspiration of Hempel and Woermann to have a conference in Berlin which involved Hempel travelling through enemy territory does not sound so phoney and unreal, especially if it is considered in conjunction with an *aide-mémoire* (27/12/1939) issued concerning reciprocal arrangements for diplomats and their families:

> The American Chargé d'Affaires in Berlin has been authorised by the British government to maintain its present practice respecting the treatment of German diplomats and consular officers as defined in the aide-mémoire of 25 December 1939 so long as the German authorities act in the same manner towards similar categories of British subjects.[69]

The old phoney 'Sitzkrieg' in the West was quite a gentlemanly affair in the beginning. The officers did not have their swords sharpened – which was the first thing they did in August 1914 – and it would seem that time-honoured procedures on laws and usages of war might be followed. Hempel was a very strict follower of protocol and procedure. The Irish side however did not mediate to get the German Minister an English guarantee of a safe passage: they had to take their position on neutrality into consideration. It is interesting to speculate how the War Office (at that point, in some opinions, hide-bound prisoners of practice and procedure) would have reacted to such a formal request from, in their eyes, an errant Éire. In any event Hempel did not go, though he cherished the illusion up to May (1940), contemplating routes through Switzerland on a *noblesse oblige* axis. That day was gone, but it took starchy Hempel some time to realise it.

However, the sinkings of cargo ships was a sharp reminder that the war might not continue to be waged in this droll, gentlemanly fashion.[70] There were also disquieting reports, which Hempel purported to have got from a reliable Irish 'Nationalist', that a British offensive was planned in Belgium and the Caucasus[71] and later in Norway.[72] Britain obviously did not have such capabilities and the reports may have been 'spun' on the net for their own purposes by some shadowy *Abwehr* level.

Two channels of communication from Ireland were in operation: Hempel to the Foreign Office and the IRA to the *Abwehr*. Image was most important. A series of *Daily Telegraph* articles reprinted in the *Irish Press* prompted Walshe to suggest to Hempel that the Germans supply a series of articles favourable to Germany which could also be published in *The Irish Times*.[73] The Irish attitude towards Germany at

this stage was to appear to show their understanding that there was
a war on. That could and did change. Hempel had reported in
October 1939 that the attitude of the Irish government towards him
at that point was definitely friendly.[74] Misgivings over the conquest of
Poland remained, but the Envoy in December 1939 was able to
report that many Christmas gifts had been sent from Ireland to
German POWs in England.[75] There was residual goodwill from 1916
for 'our gallant allies in Europe' the Germans. Simplistically, in
some minds (not de Valera's) Britain was still regarded as an enemy:
Black-and-Tan memories were still fresh.

De Valera Condemns Invasion

In 1940 a dramatic change in attitudes came about. De Valera had
held his tongue on the occupation of Denmark and Norway:[76] 'An
té ná fuil laidir, ni foláir dó bheith glic' (an Irish proverb: 'he who
is not strong must be clever'.) Anyway those countries were
comparatively far away and England was in between to act as a
protective buffer. The invasion of the Low Countries was much
closer to home. De Valera felt that he could no longer remain silent:

> Today two small nations are fighting for their lives and I think I would
> be unworthy of this small nation, if on an occasion like this, I did not
> utter our protest against a cruel wrong which has been done them.[77]

The 'Phoney War' was over. Hempel's mission was due for a change,
now that German armies had overrun France, which had previously
been judged the strongest military power on the continent.[78] Only a
reeling Britain stood between Hitler's Reich and unfettered Central
and Western European hegemony, with its further promise of
Lebensraum in either the colonies or elsewhere. Ideally, at this stage,
Hitler's concept envisaged a partnership with Britain on the basis of
'partitioning the world', with Britain as the strongest sea power and
Germany the supreme land power. However, as there was no reliable
sign of British willingness to yield, the Führer was constrained to
discuss the problem of a landing in Britain with Admiral Raeder
(21/5/1940).[79]

History and Geography demanded that the 'Ireland Factor' be
taken into account in considering a landing in Britain. Partly for

reasons of Hitler's ambivalence about contact with Britain and his fixation about *Lebensraum* in Russia, this estimate was not based on a continuous logical military thought-process. It was of an *ad hoc* piecemeal nature, tackled 'by jolt', as it were. It was not an estimate characterised by the traditional professionalism of German High Command Staff work. The proliferation of agencies already referred to also bedeviled the cohesion and coherence of these flawed estimates. Hempel was to be embarrassed as a consequence of such faulty decision-making processes, which lacked an overall co-ordination, as far as Ireland and its German representative were concerned:

> It is necessary, therefore, to bear in mind that, at least until Hitler had spoken, and not always even then, it was not safe to assume that any line of policy or expression represented settled German policy.[80]

The 'Emergency' now justified its name. It was a crucial test for Hempel: the Irish nation showed its teeth to Germany, instead of accommodating 'understanding'. This time they *did* mean what they said. They armed accordingly. Hempel reacted predictably.

CHAPTER 6

The Invasion Crisis: summer 1940

'When the tide of war flowed in Germany's favour in the early war years he (Hempel) could be inflexible'.[1] In June 1940 the German people were in a state of euphoria. It would be unnatural for Hempel, whose profession demanded concern for Germany's interest, not to be similarly infected. Canaris was an exception in divining that the phenomenal military success, which brought German armies to the French Coast on the Atlantic to directly menace 'the British Isles', concealed a fundamental ignorance of strategy.[2]

The Third Reich was at the height of its power. 'To many Germany appeared invincible' and de Valera was no exception.[3] It took courage therefore on his part to condemn the German invasion of Belgium and Holland. There were, however, limits to which a small nation like Éire, with a low grade military capability, could push such a protest. The Germans were very angry with de Valera over this speech and Hempel was instructed to convey a sharp rebuke in protest against the remarks made.[4] The Envoy was able to report that he had anticipated his government's instructions and had already protested on his own initiative. As befitted their relative combat power the Irish government made muted responses to the protests and these were taken by the German side as apologies for de Valera's 'unfriendly speech'.[5]

A previous report of Hempel's (10/5/1940) had included a significant point made by the Minister for Defence in the Dáil in reply to a question asking if there was an agreement with England in the event of Ireland being attacked. The reply then was to the effect that in such circumstances the Danish example would *not* be followed.[6] (The Danes had not opposed in arms the German invasion of their country). However, in the wake of the overwhelming 'blitzkrieg', the Irish tone now was conciliatory: Boland mollified Hempel to an extent tantamount to apologising.[7] Hempel's recall was that Boland explained that the people over here did not really know what the

Germans had to put up with from those Dutch agents and from other Allied machinations.[8] 'De Valera did not see him (Hempel). F.H. Boland received him on de Valera's behalf. He poured oil on troubled waters and apparently instructed Warnock in Berlin to do the same. According to German records – but not to the Irish – both expressed themselves in an 'appropriate manner'.

Warnock's mien, according to a memorandum by the Director of the Political Department in Berlin (21/5/1940), was correspondingly meek and fulsomely apologetic. 'Mr Warnock had already been informed by his government and expressed himself in a similarly apologetic manner as the deputy of the Irish minister had done to our minister[9].'

Warnock's task was difficult, especially as his predecessor, Bewley, now in the guise of an ultra-patriot, was still in the wings (based in Italy), prompting the German government in Irish affairs. Nevertheless, considering the Irish government's avowed policy of neutrality, some of Warnock's alleged remarks read rather oddly. Having made the point that Ireland wished to remain neutral towards all powers, the Irish representative in Berlin added an anti-British implication of his own. Speaking 'personally', he explained that Ireland in the last war against England had struck too early but this time, he implied, that mistake would not be repeated.[10]

Warnock was a Protestant from the Ringsend area of Dublin – a graduate of Trinity College who was an enthusiast for the Irish language. He had been a teacher before joining the diplomatic service. Nevertheless, any expression of such extreme Wolfe-Tone type views, at variance with his government's declared policy, would have been out of character in a career diplomat. As against that, it is unlikely that he had been misunderstood; Warnock spoke fluent German. But there was no misunderstanding the note of menace in the German retort as expressed by Woermann (Director of the Political Department) to Hempel: 'In view of the German successes the question however was whether Ireland would not come too late'.[11]

Warnock did not deny that, in the circumstances, he may have made some such remarks as were attributed to him by Woermann.[12] (Woermann later remarked (19/7/1940) that Warnock was definitely anti-British: '*der Geschäftsträger, dessen anti-englische Einstellung ausser Frage steht*'). The Irish diplomat recalled that he may have made the '1916' remarks 'off the cuff', 'as he was getting his coat' or 'they may have been prompted'. It was fashionable at home and expedient in his position to be anti-British. The point he has since asserted was that he was not specifically instructed to make remarks of that kind though he had been instructed by Boland to more or less 'pour oil on troubled waters'.[13] This apparently was his way of doing so; it reflected perhaps the prevailing 'healthy respect' for the intimidating German military might of the time.

But, as Hempel quietly reported (23/5/1940), another attitude was also current: feeling in Ireland for Germany – except for outspoken Irish nationalists elements – had materially deteriorated since the invasion of Belgium and the Netherlands, especially in Church circles, influenced as they were by the Pope's attitude.[14] The Envoy's opinion was that any German intervention in Ireland before a British attack would be counter-productive and he saw no imminence of such an attack. The British, in his opinion, would attack only in an emergency if they suspected that this move were necessary in order to avoid being forestalled by Germany. Hempel however acknowledged that any German assistance, especially if accompanied by a proclamation of a German aim to liberate Northern Ireland, would probably give a powerful boost to 'the anti-English nationalist movement'. On the other hand he doubted that a move by them on Northern Ireland would best serve German interests. (Frau Hempel asked impatiently: 'Was he not right to show what German interests would be?')

Hempel further 'war-gamed' with perception the consequences of invasion. A German intervention, he judged, would meet with strong resistance; the army would obey orders although it contained IRA elements, particularly among the Volunteer Forces, who, in possible collaboration with 'the nationalist population', might have been happier waging a form of guerilla warfare against an English attack. In the face of such a threat, i.e. a German invasion, de Valera, supported automatically by the British, would he thought, proceed ruthlessly against the IRA, exploit the situation, involve the USA and press for a return of Northern Ireland. He speculated how this danger of possible Irish involvement might pressurise Britain to take a decisive step to settle the Northern Ireland question. He thought it conceivable – without elucidating – that the French government could be interested in such a move.

As he saw it, de Valera was the only leader of any stature who could keep 'the nationalists' under control, while at the same time – compelled by geographic factors and economic dependence as well as being impelled by his democratic principles – maintain a friendly understanding with England, even if that meant risking the threat of becoming involved in the war. On balance however, he did not see any voluntary political concessions being made which would violate neutrality and he felt that de Valera would maintain this line of approach even if England were defeated. He suggested that such an outcome would not prevent the Irish leader from continuing to exploit Britain's weakness and, by working as de Valera had done for a long time in the USA, so secure the return of Northern Ireland. As a result he foresaw a strengthening of the Taoiseach's position, possibly redounding to Britain's advantage in the USA, 'which perhaps has a hand in the game'.

Up to now (25/5/1940), Hempel's continuous estimate on the various aspects and outcomes attendant on an invasion of Ireland had the comparatively calm detached air of a scenario for a staff college exercise; a certain remoteness was discernible. Suddenly (24/5/1940) his reports became more agitated and shrill. It was as if he was abruptly forced to realise that the invasion he had theorised about could become a reality. The subject was no longer an academic exercise for a detached dissertation but a live possibility involving incredibly bizarre methods – methods involving sabotage, espionage and questionable covert operations. Whether willing or unwilling, whatever the nature of these links, the events arising from them inevitably threatened to compromise him. This greatly disturbed the correct diplomat who set such store on appearances and being seen to do the right thing at all times.

The Envoy's report to the Foreign Ministry giving details of the arrest of an Irishman named Held because of his contacts with a German called Brandy indicated that the Irish government too were showing signs of panic.[15] The report outlined that Brandy was a lodger in Held's house and that in his room plans of Irish ports and defence lay-outs; transmitters; $20,000; a secret code; a parachute; insignia of the German Luftwaffe; German World War I decorations; a military cap and a black tie of German origin had been discovered. Hempel was very perturbed and reminded the Foreign Ministry that he had already warned them about Held on account of his association with Hamilton, an English provocateur, whose aim, he held, was the destruction of Irish neutrality and, incidentally, the German Legation.[16] Held was the son of an unmarried couple (father German, mother Irish). He was separated from his US wife and lived in Templeogue, Dublin with his mistress, the wife of a serving RAF man. Hamilton got a reputation for being 'a chancer' who could not be trusted.[17]

Hempel appeared to have been convinced that this whole business was a 'frame-up', an act of vengeance against himself and Held and that the supposed Brandy was in fact a British agent. He expressed himself strongly on this subject saying he would speak to Boland about the renewed provocation by the British and 'shall express the firm expectation of a satisfactory attitude on the part of the Irish government'. His attitude in this case poses queries as to either his lack of information or to his histrionic capacity: the likelihood however is that he was unaware of the details behind the Held affair. It was Nazi policy not to tell diplomats more than they needed to know.[18] At the funeral of a Herr Wengel somebody whispered to the Envoy the news of the arrival of the German (Goertz). He expressed complete surprise: whether feigned or not, it is impossible to state categorically.

Hempel's 'spiel' was that credulous pro-German Held was 'taken in' by a 'planted' British agent called Brandy, who disappeared after leaving the incriminating material in Held's house. However, a further remark in the same report saying that 'the English also knew about W.D.' would seem to indicate that the German representative was not entirely the 'innocent abroad' that he purported to be. The initials (W.D.) would appear to refer to a case involving a certain Weber-Drohl, concerning which the minister had been negotiating.[19] Weber-Drohl was an *Abwehr* agent whose mission had been the strengthening of German intelligence relations with the IRA. He had been apprehended by the Irish authorities. He was a strong man whose physique seemed to excite some harbouring Irish ladies, though by all accounts, his later sexual performances did not always live up to promise. It did last long enough for him to father a child, which the girl's mother claimed as her own for children's allowance purposes. That was how the affair came to light. The point is, that in the climate of that particular time, there was a haven in Ireland for German undercover agents. Hempel nevertheless, persisted in his efforts to absolve the Germans and point the finger at the British.

But then with the arrest of Mrs Iseult Stuart[20] – on suspicion of harbouring Brandy – the pretexts of English intrigues were upset and the finger pointed unmistakably at the Germans, thereby seriously threatening to compromise Hempel's personal position, since he had open friendly relations with the Stuarts. Mrs Stuart lived in Laragh in Wicklow, a place frequented by the Hempels for weekends.[21] The Hempels were very fond of Iseult Stuart. They did not know her husband, Francis Stuart, all that well. They knew of him of course: Hempel had helped him to return to Germany. He introduced him to no less a person than Ernest von Weizacker, Foreign Ministry State Secretary. How much did Hempel know? Did he know that one of Stuart's missions was to procure a transmitter? Did he know that Stuart was having marital problems and, both as a husband and a writer, had got itchy feet etc.? He was not his later uxorious self with Iseult and he felt cramped by Irish society. He suited IRA purposes and Hempel, wittingly or unwittingly, aided and abetted.

The Irish government took a very serious view of what they saw as a German move at a high level to support subversive activity against it as a possible prelude to invasion. It was a delicate situation and Hempel complained to Berlin that an article by a Herr Pockhammer in an Essen newspaper did not help relations. The article, he said, was indiscreet and disturbing. He mentioned that all political parties supported the government and he referred to the 'influential' Bishop of Galway as being 'anti-German'.[22] He worried about the consequences for himself and remarked on the 'unsparing' publication of the details of the case. He feared that the inevitable exploitation of the affair in England and America would critically undermine his position.[23] He was particularly worried about the possible discovery of indiscreet statements in Stuart's letters from Germany and the dangers from people like the bishop to his mission, as he saw it, in Germany's best interests, to keep Ireland neutral, out of the war, of no benefit to Britain.

Hempel's wild accusations in attempting to dissociate himself from the Held business did hot help his credibility. His gratuitous raking up of the attempted suicide of Edith Brandy, because she had been spurned by her English lover, had no relevance to the situation. There *was* in fact an arms dealer in Dublin named Brandy and he *did* have a daughter named Edith. It is not clear why agent Goertz plucked that name as a *nom de guerre*. Once more, as previously in the case of the sinking of the *Iroquois*, it was time for Berlin to put right their Dublin Minister, who again seemed to be protesting too much.

Woermann told him straight that Brandy was in fact a German agent, entrusted with special missions directed exclusively against England via Ireland and for this purpose he was to make use of personal connections with the Irish.[24] Woermann explained that Goertz (Brandy's real name) was expressly forbidden to take any activity against the Irish government, though he acknowledged that subversive plans against the Irish government had frequently been submitted by certain Irish personalities – he did not name them – but had been rejected. Woermann does not seem to have fully grasped that using Ireland to attack England *was* action against Ireland and that de Valera was fully determined that Ireland was not to be used *in any circumstances* as a base for operations against Britain. The blame for the existence of this 'blind spot' on the part of the German Political Department can not be entirely apportioned to Herr Hempel. Other sources (e.g. Clissmann, Stuart, perhaps Bewley or erratic IRA feed-back) are more likely to have been responsible for this myopic frame of mind. The IRA lived in a fantasy world ridiculously claiming a 'mandate from history', whatever that was, to subvert the democratically expressed will of the people. Bewley's unreal, opinionated green opiate was equally fantastic.

Hempel's assessments of government attitudes were more realistic. He had pointed out that de Valera would never allow Ireland to be used as a base for an attack of any kind against England; and for all his hedging embroideries and euphemisms about 'radical nationalists' the Envoy had stated, unequivocally enough, that the IRA lacked leadership and military capability; that they were not ready; that the time was not yet ripe to use them.[25] It was a question of timing in his general acquiescence to their later use. It would appear that his timing advice had not been carefully listened to by all the agencies in Berlin.

The Irish government was thoroughly alarmed: 'panic' was the recurring word used to describe the prevailing situation. However, de Valera managed to keep a clear head in the long-term national interest. In the midst of the invasion crises in 1940 he found time to introduce the Dublin Institute for Advanced Studies, Act (signed 19/6/1940). It met with opposition from philistines all round, in the academic world, the Dáil, the Civil Service, and even within his own party. But he persisted and was more than justified. Its international prestige, wrought by dedication, now ranks the Dublin Institute with its famous US sister research institute, Princeton, a ranking generously acknowledged by its American counterpart. His focus was pure research for its own sake undistracted by commercial considerations. However, de Valera's social and cultural foresight did not dilute his concern or slacken his focus on the German threat.

One of Hempel's main tasks at this time was to dispel Irish fears of a German invasion of Ireland. These were not groundless fears: ever-present Irish distrust of 'perfidious Albion' was now matched with a growing distrust of Germany. 'Brandy' Goertz had a general sabotage mission which required Irish connections to implement. This course of action would inevitably have led to a head-on confrontation with the Irish government determined at all costs to maintain its policy of neutrality. Contrastingly, the German High Command had agreed that no instructions of any kind for sabotage in or from America would be given, although for 'compelling military reasons' the procurement of intelligence from that country could not be dispensed with.[26]

The Irish government were not then aware that Plan 'Kathleen' (Artus) discovered in Held's house, proposing a German landing in Northern Ireland in the vicinity of Derry, assisted by the IRA from a concentration area in County Leitrim, was an IRA, and not a German concept. They were not aware either that the Germans regarded it, for what it was, as a piece of logistical nonsense, the work of an ignoramus in military matters.[27] Still, the Germans played along with these fanciful notions in order to keep the IRA in tow for possible future developments. This touched directly on one of de Valera's main fears: if Germany overestimated the strength of the IRA they might be tempted to use them against Britain; if Britain were determined to occupy Irish bases these IRA links with Germany presented them with a ready-made plausible pretext for intervention. There was plenty of cause for concern and now the Held case produced the hard evidence to prove that the British fears were by no means fantastic or groundless. It could happen, and it looked as if the Germans were scheming to make it happen.

Speaking in Cork (25/5/1940) de Valera said that the IRA were providing incidents which could have been readily availed of as an excuse for invasion by some who found neutrality inconvenient and were restive of it.

In the climate of the time it was not unexpected therefore that Britain would renew proposals (through Malcolm McDonald) for 'Éire to enter the war on the side of the United Kingdom and her allies forthwith'. De Valera refused to bargain about partition, as he regarded the offer in that regard as illusory and the spectre of John Redmond's fate was ever-present.[28] Overtly then, the proposals brought by McDonald met with little success. Meaningful contacts at official levels had however been made and maintained. A British Army Officer, Lt.-Col. Dudley, had been given the mission of persuading the Irish government to allow General Huddleston, GOC Northern Ireland, to send a mobile column across the border to help the Irish to oppose any German attack that might occur.[29] This deadly serious business involving Clarke, Joe Walshe and Colonel Liam Archer of Irish Army Intelligence was conducted with the props for farce – whisking from the Phoenix Park to the hills overlooking Baldonnel military airfield, through the bowels of Government Buildings to the Shelbourne Hotel.

Farce and deadly serious business walked hand-in-hand in a Gilbertian situation. Varied, sometimes fanciful, opinions were publicly expressed which provide an index to British pressures. Sir Charles Legart had reported to the British Cabinet that Éire was crawling with German agents and that 2,000 German troops could capture the whole country.[30] Chamberlain, in a change before death from dove to hawk, embarrassing even Churchill in the process, told the British Cabinet that the IRA was strong enough to overrun the Éire Defence Forces.[31] Lord Haw-Haw (William Joyce) broadcast that the 'Irish Army could not beat the tinkers out of Galway'. Joyce (ironically, an ex-Auxiliary Black-and-Tan) executed for treason after the war, had a wide, vicarious audience and a host of mimics. 'Germany calling, Germany calling', his call sign was imitated in every pub in the country. He did influence. He was rumoured (incorrectly) to have said; 'we will bomb Amiens Street station because so many Irishmen use it to go North to join the British Army'. And 'we must bomb the South Circular Road because so many Jews live there'. Bombs did fall there and in the Curragh subsequently but Hempel chose to see them as British bombs dropped to justify the rumours and to bring the Irish Army in on the side of the British. The bombs were German, but facts did not halt either side's rumour machines. Gauche British interventions by well-known personalities were particularly unhelpful. There was no shortage of cranks and, in the climate of fear prevailing, they all got a hearing.

The Marchioness of Londonderry pressed for an adequate defence for the whole of Ireland and the application of some form of conscription.[32] The Duke of Abercorn felt invasion 'almost certain' and suggested that neutrality at sea be ignored and the coast of Ireland mined. Allegedly pro-German Cardinal McRory thought that, even if de Valera declared for 'them', the people might not follow him.[33] In a letter to Churchill, Lord Rotherham said that the German 5th Column in Ireland – 'starting with the German Minister' – was enormous and that the Germans had promised the Irish a United Ireland.[34] A landing in the West or South of Ireland would meet with little resistance, he believed, and the Germans already knew every nook and cranny through the Shannon Scheme Project: a footing in Ireland would put key factories in the West of England within range. Lord Londonderry, writing from Park Lane, saw nothing to stop a German landing in the South of Ireland, and attacked Chamberlain's concessions, but Ernest Bevin's solution was to recommend a United Ireland and a Joint Defence Council.[35] It all created a climate which egged Churchill 'to come to close quarters with Éire'.

The advent of Churchill to replace Chamberlain (10/5/1940) renewed Irish apprehensions about Britain's intentions. Hempel duly forwarded the official text of some of Churchill's bulldog bellicose sentiments.[36] The notion that these strong comments by Churchill were made to bolster de Valera's domestic position *vis-à-vis* the IRA[37] is not matched by the understandably desperate mood of the time in Britain or with the revised estimates of the outgoing Chief of the Imperial Staff-Ironside.[38] In a previous report (13/2/1940), Hempel had listed Churchill, Hanley and Anderson as being foremost amongst the warmonger clique in the British Cabinet, adding that Anderson was an ex 'Black-and-Tan'.[39] The German Minister had branded Maffey as a mouthpiece of British propaganda and reported the complaint of the Department of

External Affairs to the British representative about British propaganda, which was geared, Hempel stated, to provoking Germany into striking the first blow and, according to his Irish-American sources, Britain had already given commitments to Ireland based on such an eventuality.[40] He urged counter-propaganda, especially against stories originating in Zurich that Germany was intent on fabricating a pretext to invade Ireland. He regretted that the German Radio had not featured de Valera's assertion of Ireland's determination to remain neutral.[41] Hempel was remarkably well-informed, particularly on Anglo-Irish unity moves and the part played in these moves by the new American minister to Ireland, David Gray.[42]

He could not, of course, fully appreciate the covert rapport generated by the intelligence links then established between the British and Irish Secret Services.[43] Very few did. Unrealistic neutralists who thought that maintaining neutrality was simply a matter of making pious protestations from high moral ground would have been appalled. These links endured throughout the war, political exploitation, Churchill's fulminations and de Valera's polemics notwithstanding. The Irish side nevertheless was always wary that 'perfidious Albion' would use the information which they (the Irish Intelligence) had promptly and diligently furnished, to prove a British point that neutrality was not being maintained. They had to ensure they never dropped their guard. De Valera made no bones about the fact that, in the national interest, neutrality as practised by Ireland, was pragmatic, not doctrinaire. National survival was what counted, not unrealistic doctrine. Belgium was a sad example of reliance on words alone. In wartime power flowed out of the barrel of a gun.

The Irish government had good reason to remain apprehensive and suspicious of both the British and the Germans. Hempel's task of reassuring them for the German side was not made easier by the fact that he apparently had not been fully informed about the Goertz sabotage mission. His righteous denials dented his credibility. Another impediment to their reassurance was the recurring evidence of the mentality of the Political Department in Berlin. As revealed repeatedly to Hempel, it was, blindly, erroneously considered there that it would be acceptable to the Irish government if Goertz did not direct his activities specifically against them, but used his Irish connections to operate only against Britain. This concern confounded Hempel's confusion. The bewildered German Minister rattled off a flurry of telegrams, between 4 and 8 June 1940, seeking guidance on the Held-Stuart case.[44] On 15 June Woermann instructed him to get in touch with the Irish government 'in a confidential way', and to point out that since Britain was the major common foe of both countries, Germany counted on the greatest possible understanding from Ireland despite her neutrality.[45] Again, a note of menace can be detected in this message but an incentive was also to be conveyed by Hempel: the outcome of the war would be of decisive importance for the Irish nation and the final realisation of its national demands. But the German Minister was also detailed to warn the government and the press to handle the Held affair with care and to go easy with the publicity side of it.

The stance taken generally by the Irish government up to now seemed (as befitted a small weak nation dealing with a rampant military superpower) to be deliberately unprovocative.[46] De Valera broke that mould courageously with his protest over the Low Countries' invasion, but Walshe, who appeared 'to have become convinced that Germany would soon win the war', tried to accommodate Hempel by saying agreeable things to him where at all possible.[47] In a blatant effort to placate, Walshe hinted that he had not ruled out the involvement of an English agent in the Held case. Hempel, aware now of his gaffe over Brandy, should have winced somewhat at this hypocritical attempt by Walshe to exonerate the Germans. It would be extraordinary if Walshe really believed what Hempel reported that he said in this connection. But a certain 'starchiness' seemingly blunted Hempel's perception too, especially in those heady days of victory, and he was disarmed when Walshe counselled caution all round in handling the matter. That was the message which the Envoy had come to formally convey: Walshe had said it for him! Hempel reported that the conversation in which Walshe expressed great admiration for the German achievements, went off in a very friendly way.

The German Minister Plenipotentiary continued his somewhat priggish superior report with the remark: 'I presented our view of what now as before appeared to be advisable'. The Envoy brushed aside in his representations the possibility of a German landing being linked specifically to the Held affair but declined Walshe's

request to guarantee that the Germans would *not* make a landing in
Ireland. Hempel took the stand that such a declaration was
impossible in the present military situation and he added that 'in
the case of any collision between Irish interests and German
measures, complete and realistically wise understanding on the part
of Ireland was to be expected'. For some reason, not readily
apparent, this seemed to relax Walshe who responded in a *c'est la
guerre* philosophical fashion, that they understood the German
position: war was war, and in the vigorous prosecution of the war
against Britain in a blockade situation, difficulties were to be
expected. Walshe then remarked (and it is difficult to assess
whether this was just 'talk' as reported by Hempel or whether it had
a basis in realities) that the Irish government was more worried
about a possible British attack than by a German invasion. While the
outstanding Irish Chief of Staff, Ulsterman Lt. Gen. Dan McKenna,
in the interests of procuring the only accessible armament for his ill-
equipped army, had established a soldierly rapport with his British
counterparts in the North, there was no telling what impulsive
Churchill might spark off or implacable selfish, unpredictable
Ulster Unionists would get up to. Walshe followed his remark, with
a switch of emphasis. He probably now judged that the time had
come to indicate once more to Hempel some mail in the velvet
glove, by 'slipping in' the point that, as a result of the latest
measures to increase the army and its equipment, de Valera had 90
per cent of the people behind him.

In a change of tone, Walshe quizzically questioned Hempel about
the Führer's forlorn hopes of seeking a separate peace with Britain:
he hoped that Hitler's declaration that he had no intention of
destroying the British Empire did not imply the abandonment of
Ireland.[48] It was hard to know what he was getting at. He was living up
to Colonel Dan Bryan's assessment of him of 'blowing hot and cold'.

It was Hempel's turn to demur and to reassure: the outcome of
the war, he insisted, *was* important for the final realisation of Irish
national demands. This especially interested Walshe and ensured
for the Envoy a summons to meet de Valera. From the way Walshe
and Warnock were conducting themselves, it was possible on
occasions to take the impression that the best Irish hopes for the
realisation of national demands lay in a German victory. The
Taoiseach took a longer view.

De Valera, as expected, requested Hempel to call on him (16/6/1940). In the presence of Walshe, a lengthy conversation was held in 'a forthright and pleasant manner'.[49] Hempel distanced himself from the Held case but made his point about German concern for careful handling of publicity associated with that matter. Walshe supported him. De Valera listened with interest but laid stress on his continued policy of observing strict neutrality. Then he deviated somewhat from the point about England which Walshe had previously made. At the beginning of the year fear of English intervention had been their biggest worry, but so far at any rate – though this could change – the British had respected Irish neutrality. Their main anxiety now was concerning possible German intentions to use Ireland as a base for attacks on England by exploiting the 'weak minority which has been working against the government policy'.[50] The gloves were coming off. This seemed to be different to what Walshe had told Hempel about the government being more worried about a possible British invasion than a German one. Hempel obviously thought it worthwhile to quote de Valera verbatim on this matter and thought that this anxiety on the part of the government had been aggravated by alarmist reports from the Irish in America.

The German Minister also thought that the recent efforts of pro-British groups in Northern Ireland, who in his opinion were seeking co-ordination in defence measures in order to insidiously under-mine Irish neutrality, had no prospect of success. He did not comment that de Valera's reaction to the proposals in question was negative,[51] nor did he specify who these 'groups' in Northern Ireland were. Craigavon had rejected all advances for a rapproche-ment with the Irish State, an indication, Hempel felt, of the waning of the Roosevelt influence, assumed to have been moderately exercised to catch the Irish-American vote in the forthcoming November election. He now surmised that, from their position of strength, possible German action for the return of Northern Ireland would find 'ready acceptance in non-radical nationalist circles, among others, allegedly, the influential far-seeing Cardinal McRory' (Primate of all Ireland).

As usual, having uttered an opinion in this area, Hempel immediately qualified it: on the other hand, the defence forces of Northern Ireland had been substantially strengthened 'among other things by recruitment to the UDF'. He commented on recruiting in the Irish Army, which had received about 50,000 applications, many from 'old freedom fighters'. Hempel's impression was, in spite of reports of growing pro-German feeling in the army, that the Held case had turned the Irish people against the Germans: the primary fear was now of a German invasion and radical nationalism seemed to be losing public opinion. He had attributed machiavellian motives to de Valera for manipulating the Held case so as to be better armed against the British and to gain political advantage at home 'against the largely anti-German Cosgrave opposition'. But he was in no doubt that de Valera would not allow Ireland to become a point of departure for an attack against England: 'it was only by giving such an undertaking that de Valera succeeded in obtaining the return of the ports'. The minimum loose external connection with the British Empire, provided for in the Constitution, was merely intended to facilitate the future return of Northern Ireland to the Irish State, and except for the strong economic dependence on England, Ireland made no other distinction between Britain and Germany. If it came to an invasion, Ireland would become a battlefield, with either English assistance to fight the Germans or German assistance to fight the English, depending on who was the first to attack.[52] It was a question of 'first come, first served' in designating the invader, though in Hempel's view there was a growing realisation of the obvious weakness of the democracies.

The main fear at government level at this point remained one of a German invasion. There were other threats however which had also to be dealt with. Boland told Hempel that the English pressure already referred to for the abandonment of Irish neutrality, accompanied apparently by the bait of the future concessions in respect of Northern Ireland, had been 'vehemently rejected' by de Valera.[53] Hempel thought that de Valera had also exploited this situation to further augment the strength of the army troops. The new 2nd Spearhead Division, under Major-General McNeill, was alleged to be confronting a massed British force – estimated by Hempel as between 100,000 and 300,000 – along the Border.[54]

On 26 June, Weizacker (Secretary of State) instructed Hempel[55] that in order to avoid misunderstandings he could intimate, without stressing the point, that the measures against England mentioned in

Instruction No. 190 were not intended to include the landing of German troops in Ireland.[56] Hempel now hoped that his conversations with de Valera and Walshe had had a calming effect after the panic caused by the Held incident: he expected 'a continuance of their understanding neutral attitude'.

He was soon to find out the limits of this understanding and incidentally, the independence of the Irish judiciary. On 27 June, Held was sentenced to five years imprisonment for giving aid and support to persons unknown, in receiving instructions for the collection of information, particularly such as would affect the security of the State and for possession of a radio transmitter.[57] The 'understanding' shown to Mrs Stuart, wife of Hempel's friend in the university in Berlin, had probably more to do with her mother, Madame Gonne MacBride (widow of a patriot executed after the 1916 Rising) and IRA aspects of internal politics, or perhaps her possible future use as a 'bait' to track Goertz, than with any representations made by the German Minister. On 2 July following a two-day trial, she was acquitted.[58] That pleased her friends, the Hempels.

Hempel's self-assurance was waning. The Held knuckle-rapping had left its mark.[59] He complained that, although he had done everything, within the limitations imposed on him to minimise suspicion of an impending German attack, the Irish government, still apprehensive from the Held affair and the Stuart connection, refused to be reassured. He thought that a factor in this was pressure on de Valera by the British and Americans who, in his opinion, were playing a dangerous game on the question of Northern Ireland. De Valera, he added, did not intend to yield to this pressure.[60] The Envoy cited his Italian colleague to support this contention. There was no indication at this point of the tensions which existed between the German and Italian representatives[61] and the Italian Berardis was instrumental in relaying de Valera's wish to elicit a reassurance from the Axis powers that there was no intention of an attack on Ireland. It was an unhappy conduit: the uneven behaviour of Berardis disconcerted Hempel but, apart from that, the discovery of a spy with German connections in the Italian Legation (19 May 1940) raised tensions. The spy was a certain Captain Liam Walsh who was associated with the German *Fichtebund* propaganda organisation.

Hempel felt that de Valera's request involving references to strategic dispositions, was unrealistic. He agreed however that something should be done to restore de Valera's confidence and to strengthen his position against British pressure, in order to bolster Irish determination to maintain neutrality. The strong influence Walshe and Boland were exercising on de Valera had convinced him of this determination. This report seemed to give the credit for this determination more to Walshe and Boland than to de Valera. Therefore, the German Minister recommended that a German statement or declaration be made, indicating continuing respect for Irish neutrality and the absence of any intention to sponsor fifth-column activities in preparation for the future use of Ireland as a military base against England. His opinion that the mid-June (1940) declaration fell short of reassuring the Irish government had the effect of eliciting a frank response from Woermann that German policy was primarily concerned with the prevention of any rapprochement between Ireland and Britain.[62] He suggested however that Hempel, 'off his own bat', could renew previous assurances of German intent to continually respect Irish neutrality: the Envoy could repeat the contents of Telegram No. 72 of 31 August 1939, but it was not to be given out as a fresh declaration. Woermann, in addition, told Warnock that they all knew how Germany felt about Ireland and that in any case assurances had already been given – in August 1939 and in mid-June (1940).[63] Wary, however, of de Valera's ability to manipulate words to suit his purposes, the German representative said that there should be no ambiguity and that de Valera should be given a statement in a strictly guarded form to avoid possible misuse. He referred, without specifying, to 'the rapid course of developments'. This obviously was a reference to dramatic British efforts to dangle the prospect of Irish unity in front of de Valera as an inducement to de Valera to abandon neutrality. There was great pressure from the British and US Press for the use of the ports and for Ireland to side with Britain. Joe Carroll called it, 'Britain Plays the Unity Card'.[64] Hempel asked as to how matters previously discussed relating to Northern Ireland could also be taken into account.[65]

The memorandum he got back from the Director of the Political Department (Woermann) was so couched that it would confirm any misgivings Hempel may have held about that department's lack of political acumen as far as Ireland was concerned.[66] It seemed to ascribe the fears of the Irish government to a misconception that the German plans were for a landing in the Irish Free State, whereas in the *Artus* plan, they had specified Northern Ireland. This, in Berlin's mind, was supposed to clear the matter up. It is symptomatic of a lack of full comprehension that this same memorandum felt it necessary to warn against reprisals for the sentencing of Held, on the grounds that he was an Irish citizen and that German interest in the case should not be demonstrated.

Ribbentrop intervened again (11/7/1940) to give Hempel guidance: the minister was to emphasise in all conversations Germany's primary interest in the preservation of Irish neutrality: *as long as Ireland remained neutral Germany would respect her neutrality.*[67] The Foreign Minister's telegram was terse and curt: he declared that suspicions that Germany intended to use Ireland as a base against England, through a 'so-called fifth column', were utterly unreasonable: they were in the realm of fancy and had no basis in fact. Such a fifth column, he held, did not exist:

> If the British government in dealing with the Irish government makes use of the idea of a union of Northern Ireland with Southern Ireland it is evident that this is only a sham, which is only engaged in for the purpose of manoeuvring Ireland out of her neutrality and drawing her into the war. The question of how Germany would act in case of the establishment of the unity of Ireland is therefore wrongly posed and purposeless.

These statements did not carry conviction, when viewed against the background of the insertion of German agents by sea and air. Hempel's reports however did nothing to erode that Ribbentrop hubris. He relayed the impression, said to exist in the Irish Ministry for External Affairs, that peace on reasonably tolerable terms would be welcomed by Chamberlain, Halifax, Simon and Hoare and in conservative circles represented by the Astors, Londonderry, high officialdom (Wilson), the 'City' and *The Times*. The middle-class and the lower classes were depressed and longed for a speedy peace he believed but – the ruling class was preponderantly in favour of going on with the war. The British, he maintained, had written off their lost position in Europe.[68] His attitude to Roosevelt was inconsistent.

He concluded that, if Roosevelt were to declare for peace, he could influence US public opinion in a favourable direction: such an eventuality was rendered unlikely by Roosevelt's anti-Axis speech (19/7/1940) which had encouraged resistance to the totalitarian powers.[69] Hempel referred to this speech but he did not seem to have fully evaluated it when he considered Roosevelt to be a possible appeaser or peacemaker.

By the end of July, he felt that Roosevelt was not in favour with the Irish government and that his possible re-election would increase the danger for Ireland.[70] In Hempel's view the re-election of Roosevelt would lessen British and US inhibitions about coercing Ireland, as considerations for the Irish-American vote could, in those circumstances, be set aside, for the time being, as a deterring factor. Though Roosevelt had declined Churchill's request to send a US squadron to Irish ports, he had nevertheless been prepared to use any means possible – even the Pope – to pressurise the Irish into relinquishing neutrality. American opinion was worried that there would not be effective resistance in Ireland to a German invasion but, on the other hand, if the British had to seize the ports for their survival it might alienate Irish-American opinion. In any event, as Roosevelt told Gray, the American Minister, though Irish independence was very close to the American heart, there could be 'no question as between invasion by Germany and protection by England'.[71]

There were compelling reasons therefore for Hempel to analyse the American scene and the effect of political development there on future German policy towards Ireland.[72] He was sure that regard for American public opinion had so far deterred the British from attacking. Walshe in another of his mood swings intimated to the German Minister that discreet closer co-operation between Irish, German and Italian elements in the States could exert a powerful influence, without compromising the Dublin government. Walshe and Boland, Hempel reported, were putting their hopes in a German interest in a fully independent Ireland: they were suspicious of English retaliation even if the British were defeated. He recommended that an undertaking be given – in a manner to avoid the Irish being compromised by Britain and subject to reservations based on the example of Czechoslovakia in World War I – that Germany would not abandon Ireland.[73] For Walshe and many others the war was as good as won by Germany.

But the greatest danger of Ireland being compromised came from proposals arising from Admiral Ritter's closely knit estimate as to whether Ireland should be excluded or included in a blockade of England.[74] In the end the Führer wished to make an exception in some form for Ireland, as otherwise, he said, instead of being separated from England, Ireland would be forced into her arms. A special secret arrangement with the Irish government was proposed.[75] Ribbentrop's telegram – to be deciphered personally by Hempel – outlined that the German Forces would not attack ships under the Irish flag *provided* these ships were especially marked and reported by the Irish government, *if* these ships and their cargoes were promptly reported by telegraph, *if* they obeyed the instructions of the German forces and *if* they had on board only goods which the Irish government guaranteed would remain in Ireland. In the straitened circumstances of the time, the German reckoning was that this was an offer the Irish could not refuse.

Walshe in reply, again pointed out the problems of entering into an agreement with Germany and played for time, without rejecting outright the German offer.[76] He explained to Hempel the complication of Irish overseas trade, which was mainly with England and in British ships. The government was also concerned to avoid giving the British grounds for a charge of unneutral behaviour. A decision was deferred by diplomatically suggesting that the proposal be discussed through the Irish Chargé d'Affaires in Berlin.

William Warnock's apologetic *aide-mémoire* to the German Foreign Ministry provided tangible reasons for not 'rejecting the German offer out of hand':

The Irish Legation has the honour to state that its government has been informed that the following five steamships, the entire cargoes of which comprised grain for exclusive consumption in Éire were sunk by unidentified submarines at times and in positions indicated hereunder.

1. *Violando N.T. Mulvanis* Greek at 10.15 a.m. on 10 June
2. *Adamandious Georgandis* Greek at 17.15 GMT on 19 June
3. *Petsamo Finnien* at 11.45 a.m. on 10 July
4. *Kzetis A* Greek at 3.20 p.m. on 14 July
5. *Nafitkus* Greek at 9.30 p.m. on 15 July[77]

The Irish Legation has been instructed by its government to bring the foregoing to the attention of the German Foreign Office. The Legation would be grateful if the Foreign Office would be good enough to have enquiries made and to furnish the Legation with any information at the disposal of the German government as to the circumstances of the sinking of these vessels.

The time was not propitious for thumping the table.

Once more, Hempel's renewed counsel that consideration be given to Irish shipping when it was not in English ports, as given after the sinking of the *Munster* and the *Kerry Head* (which had been plainly marked and flying an Irish flag), was not properly heeded.[78] Boland had complained to Hempel about the sinkings, but the Irish official's grovelling concessions that there may have been some grounds for the sinking of the *City of Limerick,* as she seemed to have had a cargo for Liverpool, would hardly have gratified the British.[79] A small nation ploughing a lonely neutral furrow, could not please all the sides all the time. German mines were still sown in Irish waters. German planes trespassed Irish air space and the Irish government made meek protests. Walshe was 'understanding' – these things happen in wartime.[80] However this Uriah Heap attitude changed abruptly when the Germans dropped bombs on Campile creamery (Co. Wexford) causing causalties.[81] Protests were made in no uncertain terms. The mood was angry. The 'no provoke' mask was dropped. Hempel apologised, but for some reason did not want Warnock to know that he had asked for permission to do so. Warnock was cynical about the 'special treatment' Germany was supposed to be giving to Ireland. Hempel predictably put it all down to British provocation, designed to embroil Ireland in the war against Germany. He reported that the British had not consulted the Irish when they mined the St George's channel to within seven miles of the Irish coast at Dungarvan, but that the Irish would only protest when Irish interests were directly affected; though they did not want their territorial waters used for British shipping traffic.[82] He did report as well that there had been a closing of ranks, consolidating Mr de Valera's position, when it seemed as if the danger were coming from Germany, but maintained that the declaration to respect Irish neutrality had a calming effect and that events were now working in Germany's favour. But Hempel's British 'agent provocateur' excuse no longer explained the open German violations of neutrality, though Walshe in conversation with the German Minister Plenipotentiary 'agreeably' continued to hint at such activities.[83]

On 16 July Hitler had issued his Directive No. 16 for the controversial Operation 'Sea Lion'.[84] In support of this operation, a deception diversion, maybe a secondary attack, in Ireland was conceived. In August (1940) two IRA leaders – Seán Russell and Frank Ryan – left Germany by U-Boat to land in Ireland. Some sort of quisling-type role, harmonised with the proposed landings in Britain, seems to have been envisaged (if that is not too positive a word for these shadowy operations). Hempel had opposed the coming of Russell to Ireland; but the Envoy was nevertheless given a part to play in the operation. A flower-pot was to be placed in the window of the Legation as a signal for Russell that the invasion of Britain was under way.[85] The way the situation was developing it was almost impossible for the German Minister not to become involved, willy-nilly, in some compromising situations.

A message from Berlin (9/9/1940) signed by Kramarz and addressed to Hempel posed requests for military style essential elements of information, if they could be covertly obtained from a friendly source without being compromised. Was there conscription in Ireland? How was mobilisation effected? How many able-bodied men of military age were there? What was the war organisation, equipment and strength of the Irish Army? What was known about dispositions, employment of troops and defences? The report complimented Hempel on his very valuable reports on the effects of the air raids on England and indicated that the greatest detail possible of the effects of the bombings on the civilian population was desirable.[86] Operation 'Eagle', the great German air offensive to achieve air superiority, an essential prerequisite to the launching of the invasion, had started on 15 August.

Hempel sent in his report on the Irish Army on 18 September 1940.[87] By that date the turning point in the Battle of Britain had been reached. After a reverse in the decisive air battle on 17 September, the Führer postponed Operation 'Sea Lion'.[88] 'The German menace to Irish neutrality receded'.[89] The stance of the Irish Defence Forces was a contributory factor.

Hempel's estimate for the total strength of the Irish Army was 659,000. He also mentioned Ireland's successful tradition in waging guerilla warfare against England.[90] The German Minister's report could not be interpreted as holding out prospects of facile victories if invasion were to be attempted, though he did make reference to the shortage of equipment in the Irish Army, Navy and Air Corps. Warnock's reference to the assignment of 'Special Constables' against parachutists when he was giving a resumé to Woermann of the military situation in the North of Ireland, could also be construed as a deterrent. Warnock was conveying the pleasures of the Irish government at German assurances regarding the Canaris injunction against the further insertion of agents and he further allayed German fears concerning bargaining about Northern Ireland to change Ireland's stand on neutrality. These were only press speculations, the Irish representative in Berlin relayed.[91]

Hempel concluded his report to cover himself, by suggesting that a military opinion be consulted, particularly to assess the military potential of the Local Security Force (Group 'A'), which he had distinguished on account of its policing character from the combat Group B, i.e. the Local Defence Force. The Minister himself made no attempt to translate this estimated total figure of his (659,000) into relative combat power units; but he gave enough information to warrant a reconsideration of invasion in conjunction with the proposed invasion of the 'British Isles' – if such an invasion had been really seriously considered in the first place.

Russia remained uppermost in the Führer's predatory plans but, preferably, in his Anglophile mind, with Britain alongside, not against her. A facile victory would have been a great persuader. He underestimated the old British Bulldog, covertly, but significantly, supported by de Valera's 'certain consideration for Britain', in manpower, supplies and intelligence, while aggressively maintaining in essentials sovereignty and self-respect. It was not simplistic. It was not doctrinaire. Within the consideration parameters, it was 'for real'. So was the German threat through Ireland to Britain even though 'Sea Lion' was suspended for the time being. To the extent that long term strategic planning had gone into the *ad hoc* enterprise in the first place, the position of Ireland, in that particular context, had to be reconsidered. It was a tangled criss-crossing.

The fog of war was almost impenetrable. Churchill's will to resist illuminated. Hitler's breach of the Principle of War – Maintenance of the Aim – emerged.

The British muddled through. Between the two, with unique adroitness, de Valera steered his paradoxical policy of considerate neutrality. In the end, relative combat power, in the right place at the right time, decided.

As far as the maintenance of Irish neutrality was concerned, the manifest will to resist of the ill-equipped, half-trained Irish Defence Forces, was a small but significant makeweight in the various relative combat power equations. The Chief of Staff of the Irish Army, General Dan McKenna, radiated reliability, steadfastness, and dour determination.

Hempel was not alone in missing the historical rapport that existed between Derryman McKenna and Cork-born Franklyn, GOC Northern Ireland. Franklyn outmanoeuvred outmoded Churchill and atavistic jingoists to procure elementary armament for McKenna's Emergency Army. McKenna outflanked the unrealistic neutralists who spurned de Valera's warning that neutrality was not an abstract theoretical thing, but a stark matter of reality and survival. Between the two of them, they secured England's southern flank, prevented Ireland being used as a springboard for an attack on Britain and prevented civil war in Ireland.

McKenna's liaisons were kept secret even from the Army. Hempel did not know *all* about them. Neither did Churchill. The two soldiers, McKenna and Franklyn, weighed, on the ground, Éire's 'certain consideration for Britain' in a coincidence of mutual national interests context. Mutual survival was prioritised. That did not eradicate the British threat to Irish security, but choices had to be made. Sectarianism, jingoism and notional abstractions of a non-existent theoretical absolute neutrality, of the type de Valera had warned against, were set aside. These developments were beyond Hempel's black-and-white ambidextrous range. The unstoppable machinery of war ground on, exposing the threat to Éire from both sides in turn.

The German threat was the more unpredictable and erratic. Its knock-on effects of precipitating a preemptive British attack were its most serious consequences. The German High Command and other maverick German players generally avoided directly involving Hempel in unconventional operations. However, there was no escaping some of its side effects and some involvement by him. He was the Envoy extraordinary and Minister plenipotentiary. It was his job to know what was going on. Hempel liked to do his job well.

CHAPTER 7

Invasion Reconsidered, autumn 1940–June 1941

Ireland was important to Luftwaffe aspirations as a potential base for attacks on the north-western ports of England.[1] This factor prompted Hitler to muse that possession of Ireland could have the effect of ending the war and to turn his thoughts towards Hempel.[2] November (1941) came and the Führer had still not launched his invasion armada across the Channel. The fact that his preoccupations were now mainly with Russia did not necessarily mean that he had written off Operation 'Sea Lion', the controversial plan to invade the British Isles. However the inescapable fact of the failure to achieve air superiority in the Battle of Britain did show up the limitations and *ad hoc* nature of the German armada for invasion, assembled in the Channel ports.

Hot pursuit, hard on the heels of Dunkirk, with air cover, fair weather and maybe an airborne landing in support, could possibly have brought off the establishment of a foothold in 'the British Isles'. The Germans, soldiers and civilians, after the fall of France, were possessed of a 'superman' élan, while defeatism[3] was widespread in the British Cabinet and the British Army had been badly defeated in the field at Dunkirk. The momentum of the blitzkrieg had proved to be irresistible. Almost all the equipment of the British Expeditionary Force had been abandoned and the heroic saga of the evacuation of that Force from Dunkirk could not conceal the magnitude of the military defeat.

Hempel, at Ribbentrop's instigation, was later to offer some of this captured equipment to de Valera. This development would seem to mark a change in the concept of handling the 'Ireland Factor', as compared with the methods envisaged with Operation 'Sea Lion'. Anyway, by the time Hitler got around to 'thinking out loud' about a role for Dr Hempel in this respect, the time for physical invasion in 1940 had passed.

Following his *Stufenplan* Hitler had now turned to adopting a military solution in the East:

> After the collapse of the USSR within a few weeks – for that is how Hitler thought of it – Great Britain would be forced into rapid surrender or else come to support the Reich as its junior partner.[4]

The Führer's concepts at this stage were grandiloquent and global. The conceptual content of his soliloque-type remark that Ireland in German hands would spell the end for England can only be surmised. But first of all he decided that enquiries should be made: the German representative in Dublin should find out whether de Valera desired assistance in the form of captured English arms and ammunition which could be transported to him aboard separate ships. The Führer agreed with the assessment of Admiral Raeder, at a conference (31 December 1940) attended by Keitel and Jodl, that the dispatch of an expeditionary force and the occupation of the island of Ireland was impossible in the face of superior enemy naval power,[5] unfavourable geographic conditions and the problems of supply and reinforcement. Hitler's main concern now was to achieve his central war aim, pursued in his policy since 1925, of overrunning Russia. His conviction apparently was that the defeat of Russia would serve him also against Britain: thus he would kill two birds with the one stone.[6] These considerations – unlike those of General Jodl – were not based entirely on calculated strategy: Hitler still hankered to have Britain on his side. As General Halder saw it, the smashing of Russia would shatter Britain. Germany would then, in his opinion, be master of Europe and the Balkans; therefore the destruction of Russia must be made part of the struggle to conquer Britain[7] (in planner's terms, 'The British Isles').

As distinct from Hitler, Ribbentrop regarded Great Britain as Germany's chief enemy.[8] It was mainly at Ribbentrop's insistence that Hempel sought to put pressure on de Valera into accepting military assistance from Germany. Ribbentrop – in spite of an alleged disdain for the Irish[9] – obviously had ideas for fomenting revolution in Ireland, and so getting at Britain 'through the back door', when he recruited Veesenmayer, 'the *coup d'état* specialist', as his 'Special Advisor Ireland'.[10] In a conversation with the Führer

(28/11/1940) the German Foreign Minister mentioned that he was convinced that the Irish would defend themselves to the last against the British and that such an attack would have tremendous repercussions in America.[11] It was at that time that he undertook to instruct the German Minister in Dublin to sound out de Valera as to his intentions, suggesting that Hempel's opening gambit might be to express his concern about the fate of the Legation and, in order to make the necessary preparations, he was to ask de Valera whether he considered an English attack on Ireland probable. Hempel found de Valera difficult to corner in those matters. According to Veesenmayer, the German Envoy was no match for the wily Irish politician.[12] It is not clear whether Hitler's thoughts on Ireland and Hempel envisaged any creative role for the German Minister. Such a role for the German representative in Ireland seemed to have been implied in Ribbentrop's insistent instructions and Veesenmayer's expectations certainly lay in this area: the '*coup d'état* specialist' was to be bitterly disappointed in the Minister Plenipotentiary.[13] Hempel, for his part, was not enamoured with Veesenmayer.

But it is not easy to translate Ribbentrop's concepts, such as they were, into concrete objectives, which presumably were to become Veesenmayer's aims and which, inevitably, had to involve the minister in Ireland:

> was it Dr Veesenmayer who brought Ribbentrop's remarkable wishful thinking about an 'Irish rebellion' into its proper perspective? What exactly did Ribbentrop dream about? Was it about a rebellion of Irish extremists against de Valera, or an all-Irish rising against the English in the event of an invasion of Éire or its harbours by the British, or a rebellion of the 400,000 Irish in the six Ulster counties against the British occupying power.[14]

The obscurity of the Foreign Minister's motivations and concepts did not deter him from harrying directly his diplomatic representative in Dublin to persist with this – in the circumstances and on the surface – tempting offer to de Valera and to persistently pester, almost, the Taoiseach into acceptance.

Prior to this persistence of Ribbentrop's – badgering is not too strong a word – Hempel had managed to reassure and calm the

Irish government somewhat after their near panic arising out of the Held affair.[15] The real weight attaching to those assurances on German intentions to invade Ireland can be measured in some aspects by considering that the plans to transport Seán Russell and Frank Ryan to Ireland (plans which involved Hempel) were in train at that time, and that on 12 August an operation order for a landing in Ireland was issued ('Operation "Grün": Landung Irland'). This order specified landing areas in the Waterford – Wexford area and outlined the extent of the bridgehead – Gorey, Mount Leinster, Thomastown, Clonmel, Dungarvan – in order to advance against the line Dublin, Kildare – the high ground west of 'Mountmeldick' (*sic*), to seize bridgeheads on the north banks of the intervening rivers and canals. If it is granted that this constituted part of a grand deception plan then the extent of deception intended has to be examined against the hard facts of *capabilities*. Trying to divine enemy *intentions* in a military estimate is a futile exercise.

On a tactical level, had the Germans the capability to launch a secondary attack in Ireland to support a main attack on the South of England? Was it meant to be a 'feint' attack? Did deception go as far as simulating a landing? In the latter context there was Hempel's political report that in Ireland the unexpected always happens and also the precedent of the 1916 Rising where, from unlikely beginnings, a revolution took place. A spark was all that was needed. This may have been the possible thinking in the German High Command, whose agent, Goertz, was loose in Ireland at the time, making, by all accounts, significant contacts at official and unofficial levels, and being a piquant social success, loved by the ladies. His presence added a naughty flavour to some parties and it was regarded as a coup by an odd hostess. It was reckoned, in some giddy quarters, to be 'cool'. Therein, lay an added danger to national security consciousness.

On a serious strategic level however there remains the larger question as to whether Operation 'Sea Lion' itself was, from start to finish, a gigantic deception plan to conceal the Führer's preconceived ideas of conquering Russia in pursuit of 'Lebensraum' and a European hegemony, which, when achieved, should automatically bring England to its knees, and on side with their dominant German cousins.

Modifying facts around September 1940 were, on the one hand failure of the Luftwaffe in the 'Battle over England' and on the other, the bad weather conditions prevailing at that time. According to the Halder Diary, the Chief of Staff of the Army was convinced that from 1 July 1940 to 12 October 1940, Hitler had intended to invade the British Isles, if necessary, and if the chances of success appeared to justify the risks. The German soldiers sang '*Wir fahren gegen England*' ('We will march against England') and the planing staffs were working on the invasion of 'the British Isles', which would automatically embroil Hempel. Halder's record that 'it seems incontestable that Hitler did, at least for a period of some weeks, intend to invade the British Isles', has to be taken seriously. In that situation, the British Chief of Staff advised Churchill, encompassment of Ireland was inescapable.

Controversy raged and the matter remains controversial.[16] The existence of the detailed operation order 'Grün' shows that the invasion of Ireland *was* planned. If they could have pulled off the landing, the mechanics of the breakout, given adequate air cover, were feasible. When the dice of war begins to roll, who can precisely predict what would turn up? The axis of the advance and the ground chosen for the bounds were sound from a tactical point of view.[17] The Irish government did have cause for concern, although they were not aware of the full extent of this cause. They insistently voiced this concern and their doubts about German intentions to Hempel, who in turn, acting as the official means of communication between the two governments, tried to reassure them. If subterranean German plans had materialised, Hempel would have, in effect, been lulling the Irish side into a sense of false security. It is unlikely that the German representative was fully aware of all such plans. On the other hand, it is equally unlikely that he would have been totally unaware of them. He probably knew as much as he needed to know. But that assumes a coherence in planning 'Sea Lion' that did not exist. The Germans had no experience of large-scale amphibious operations.

There is enough evidence however to assume that, if the plans for Operation 'Sea Lion', such as we know to have been formulated, had been implemented, the use of force – whether overtly or covertly – would have been directly initiated by the German High Command to take account of the 'Ireland Factor'. That made military sense. By the autumn of 1940 however, with 'Sea Lion' in abeyance, the main theme of German thinking on Ireland would seem to have centred on *persuading* the 'Éire' government to accept German aid in the form of arms to be used against anticipated British aggression. That historic fear was always there. Hempel had no doubt but that a British attack would be resisted by the Irish government, which he pointed out, no longer accepted that Northern Ireland could be used as a bargaining counter to end partition and so persuade them with that bait to depart from their policy of neutrality. There were signs that the British were not going to let up. If anything, while people like Alanbrooke and Eden saw that 'certain consideration' Irish neutrality was in Britain's best interests, the course of the war was inclined to panic some Churchillian 'close quarters' hotheads. There were ominous signs.

Kramarz telegraphed Hempel from Berlin (25/11/1940) that the German Naval Department had picked up and decoded a British message telling the troops that all orders would issue from the 'Irish Commander' and that they were not to fire except on his orders.[18] This illustrated the dilemma of Ireland, in pursuit of preserving a pragmatic neutrality, choosing to face both ways at once. This was the difficulty de Valera had never attempted to conceal:

> Neutrality if you are sincere about it means you will have to fight for your life against one side or the other – whichever attacks you ...
>
> Neutrality is not a cowardly policy if you really mean to defend yourself if attacked. Other nations have not gone crusading until they were attacked.[19]

He always stressed the non-doctrinaire, *ad hoc* nature of his policy of neutrality. It was a purely pragmatic pursuit. ('We do not want to get involved in this war and we merely want to keep our people safe from such consequences as would be involved by being in the war').[20] Therefore Hempel could well have reflected a prevailing mood when he reported (3/10/1940) that the Irish government was giving consideration to the question of reaching an accommodation with the New Order under the Axis power, though he had to include de Valera's reservations as tempering the alleged more positive consideration of Boland and Walshe.[21] Protests to Germany by the Irish government seemed to be more subdued. Hempel got a hearing when he replied to (21/10/1940) representations being made about the bombing of the steamer *Edenvale*. 'incidents like that were to be expected in a War Zone'![22] Walshe's protests about German overflying were calmly made but with a demand for an understanding of his and Warnock's position in lodging protests against German violations of Irish sovereignty from Carrigan Head, Co. Donegal to Carnsore, Co. Wexford (6/10/1940); from Clonakilty to Donegal, where the steamer *Bannthorn* was attacked (11/10/1940) (*aide-mémoire*, 19/10/1940 referred). These aircraft flew in over the coasts of Waterford and Wexford and inland over Tullow and Baltinglass. They were conclusively identified as German.[23] It was with red faces however that the Department of External Affairs and the army withdrew their protests which had alarmist implications regarding the 'French Connection' with the Campile bombings. Hempel ironically reported that the 'puzzle' had been solved: the cause of the excitement and misunderstanding, he explained, had been a 'Stokes Brandt Mortar' shell, which had been left behind in the area by the Irish Army after a training exercise.[24] The initial implication seems to have been that Germans were using captured French ammunition and there is a reference to an inflammatory article to that effect by Stephen King-Hall. It was in fact a *Cartoucherie Française* mortar shell supplied to the Irish Army by the French firm of Edgar Brandt. Hempel's reporting was deadpan; only the British perhaps enjoyed the joke.

The impact of Churchill's anti-Irish utterance (5/11/1940) however was no joke. It demanded circumspection on the part of the Irish government in handling the German threat: it was difficult to be absolutely certain at this stage who would be a future enemy, who maybe a future ally. Consideration of an invasion threat from one side had to be constantly reviewed and reconsidered from the point of view of the possibility of a previous or pre-emptive intervention by the other side. An increasing threat from one side served to heighten the danger of a pre-emptive stroke by the other side. This was the horns of the dilemma of a neutral relying in the last resort on the use of force to defend its neutrality policy. The Irish Chief of Staff, Lt. Gen. Dan McKenna, at a social occasion sharply pulled up an expansive British attaché: 'If you come in we will fight you every step of the way'. At the same time, he was establishing a rapport with his soldier British counterparts on the ground to procure arms for his soldiers. There was no other place they could get them and they 'could not fight with knives and forks'. McKenna, former O/C of the Derry Brigade IRA in the War of Independence, had to concentrate on essentials in procuring arms for his emergency army, if it was to have credibility as a deterrent.

In reconsidering the invasion threat there were many paradoxes. If the Irish government as 1940 went on seemed to become more apprehensive of the British threat than of the German one, that did not mean that the German threat had disappeared. On the contrary, the tendency of the Berlin Political Department to oversimplify and sometimes overestimate the British threat – even to the extent of seeming to wish it or will it – had the effect of increasing the assumptions and expectations of the Germans that they could be called upon to render assistance, at any time.

Hempel, undoubtedly unintentionally, gave the impression that Walshe was 'eating out of his hand'. In making his apologetic protest to Hempel about the sinking of the *Kerry Head* by the Germans, for instance, Walshe managed to wiggle the finger once more at possible British provocation.[25] Warnock's protest too was made 'in a very friendly manner'. His message was that they did not want to make trouble but that the British Press were playing the matter up as an indication that Ireland could not defend itself. Warnock could not be more accommodating, but it would be inept, in the circumstances of relative combat power as between Ireland and Germany, to imply criticism. The fact remained however, that, at this point, Warnock took pains to distance himself from any implied criticism of German actions, specifically repudiating allegations of intimidation motives behind the Campile creamery bombing.[26] A deduction could be made in German eyes that the climate was coming right for intervention. The Irish on the surface were being friendly and understanding. In addition, Hempel had reported a thawing in the attitude of Church circles towards Germany, influenced by the statements of Cardinal McRory who, Hempel constantly stressed, had pro-Axis sympathies.[27] This report of Hempel's referred to 'Kardinal Schitley's Ende Juli Verbot' in support of this trend. Hempel also reported de Valera's position to have been strengthened, remarking that the Taoiseach was well able to handle the IRA: they were up against his (de Valera's) 'half Spanish origins and un-Irish doctrinaire approach'.

Churchill's fulminations added fuel to Ribbentrop's machinations, through Hempel, to supply arms to the Irish. In Ribbentrop's
reckoning, Ireland's difficulty was to be Germany's opportunity.
The only real 'fly in the ointment', as far as 'Wilhelmstrasse' could
discern, was Roosevelt's 'foreign policy exhibitionism',[28] which
branded the Nazi adventure not 'an ordinary war but a revolution',
and that the proper course was not yielding and appeasement but
resistance. The Foreign Minister had instructed Hempel
(6/8/1940) to inform the Irish government of the existence of a
war zone in the waters around Great Britain and that they (the
Germans) would not be responsible for damage to persons or ships
in these waters.[29] The Envoy was to again add that Irish ships would
not be attacked, *if* they followed German instructions as to their
operations. Later Ribbentrop appointed Ambassador Ritter
(9/10/1940), to help him, with particular reference to this area.[30]
He placed him in charge of all FM activities relating to economic
warfare. By a directive of (7/10/1940) Ribbentrop further assigned
to him the handling in the FM of all questions related to foreign
policy. He was immediately subordinate to the Minister of the State
Secretary.

By the time (7/11/1940) Hempel was reporting conversations
with the 'Secretary General' of the Minister of External Affairs (as
he dubbed Walshe) about the remarks made by Churchill in the
House of Commons on Guy Fawkes day of 1940 (5/11/1940),[31]
Roosevelt had been re-elected with a small majority, as anticipated.
When Hempel remarked that it looked as if Britain had now, as a
result of that election, shed her fear of unfavourable backlash in
America to threats to Ireland, Walshe felt, that although Roosevelt
was undoubtedly pro-British, he was still, as the large vote for Wilkie
indicated, strongly dependent on the Irish-American vote.
Hempel's 'radical-nationalist circles' welcomed the wave of anti-
British sentiment in Ireland, following Churchill's hostile rhetoric.
According to the German Minister, Churchill's declamations and
the treatment of the subject in the British Press had caused
'understandable anxiety' in Ireland, which could only work in
Germany's favour.

The German High Command estimated that de Valera's firm
stand against Churchill's verbal onslaughts, inclined the IRA to lend
him support and that, while they (the IRA) were under strict

surveillance, they were less harassed than heretofore. Nevertheless, Hempel reported that the Irish government remained apprehensive of the unlawful organisation and feared that they would obtain substantial quantities of arms and ammunition illegally. The High Command estimate reckoned that the Irish government constantly feared that the IRA-German connection would give the British the pretext they required for invasion and that in those circumstances Ireland would first seek US aid and failing there would turn to Germany for assistance; that the German blockade was beginning to bite, thus alienating the Irish middle classes from Germany; and that the population however was distrustful of all elements with British connections. The estimate's conclusions coincided with Hempel's own opinion, that the abiding consideration of an enormous US backlash would still deter a British invasion.

Hempel expressed the view that the disadvantage for England of attempting to take the ports outweighed any obvious advantage that their possession might bring. They were strongly fortified he said, vulnerable to German air attacks from the French coast and in addition, the cost had to be counted of a war with Ireland and repercussions in the United States. The indications were, that Britain would continue to put on the pressure to extract concessions, but Walshe had told him that de Valera would simply refuse to yield.

Hempel reported de Valera's speech protesting full understanding for England, referring to partition as the stumbling block to friendly relations between their two countries, and vehemently denying that U-Boats would be succoured or advantaged in any way in Irish harbours.[32] 'Und wenn wir für diese sterben müssen, so werden wir für sie sterben' was how Hempel translated de Valera's clinching rallying phrase defying both British and Germans – 'if we must die for this then we will die for it'. This brought applause from all sides of the House, except from the Germanophobe Opposition Deputy, James Dillon. The phrase fascinated Hempel. He never tired of using it. He was no Veesenmayer. 'Hands off' was his advice; at his most adventurous – 'not yet'.

That indeed was fighting talk from the Taoiseach. Hempel telegraphed that he was expecting de Valera to lunch on 14 November 1940 and he looked for guidance from Berlin as how to handle the Irish leader.[33] He enquired in what form he might indicate to de Valera Germany's willingness to render effective assistance to Ireland in the event of a British attack. The German

State Secretary replied to the Dublin Legation that it was in order for Hempel to tell de Valera that determined resistance against any British attempts to violate Irish neutrality would result in 'Ireland being in a front with Germany'.[34] The Ribbentrop-Veesenmayer scenario seemed to be working out and Hempel reacted accordingly.

His activities during this period were preoccupied with Ribbentrop's insistence of pressing German arms on de Valera. The German Foreign Minister was not disposed to take 'no' for an answer. But then, unlike his Envoy, he did not have to deal face-to-face with de Valera. He instructed Hempel to discuss the matter of assistance in the form of arms with other influential persons in Ireland, but preferably with de Valera. He also again directed Hempel's approach: he was to proceed cautiously, not letting on that he was acting on instructions, but to deferentially ask de Valera if it was appropriate for him to enquire from Berlin how Germany viewed the possibility of assistance for Ireland if the British attacked.[35] He prompted Hempel to answer his own question there and then: in that situation the Reich would be ready, willing and able to give Ireland 'vigorous support'. Hempel was then instructed on developing the theme further by giving the impression that he was speaking only for himself. In that view he could informally discuss the 'How' and 'Where' of the operation and by what ships German aid might best be sent. The Foreign Minister in this message also answered a previous query of Hempel's as to what the Legation should do if the Irish government and Foreign Missions left Dublin in the event of a British attack.[36] Whatever happens, Ribbentrop insisted, the radio transmitter and other material were to be kept intact, ready to use, as they would be crucial in the event of German operations being initiated, a contingency always on the cards.

Hempel's reporting contributed to convince Ribbentrop, already previously disposed in this direction, that this course of action of offering arms to Ireland was the best one. Hempel literally reported what he saw. He concluded from a conversation (11/11/1940) with Gerry Boland, the Irish Minister for Justice, that 'in the event of a British attack a request for help addressed to Germany was under active consideration', almost certainly represented the surface situation in uncertain oscillating circumstances.[37] Be that as it may, Dr Hempel was to find the Taoiseach evasive and he reported back to Ribbentrop that a calmer atmosphere seemed to prevail in Dublin and that de Valera was extremely circumspect in avoiding anything that might be construed by Britain as a departure from strict neutrality.[38] The Envoy was given no opportunity for 'any substantial conversation' with de Valera, so he tried to broach the matter at his next meeting with Walshe. Walshe also sidestepped and changed the subject to the anxiety 'many' were expressing, that Germany would sacrifice Ireland to England at the conclusion of the peace. Walshe pointed out that he personally did not agree with that widely held sentiment. Ireland was, in the Irish official's reiterated opinion, important strategically, though he did not rule out England's thirst for revenge for Ireland's neutrality which, according to Hempel was a 'deep sore in her side'. Walshe also instanced to him a British desire to retain control of the Atlantic in order to retain a bridge to Canada and the US to be used in an eventual counter-attack if there were a reverse.

Hempel's report of these conversations indicated that the British thought defeat was inevitable and, for that reason, – and since Roosevelt's re-election – they did not attach as much importance to US reaction as they had previously done. The German Minister acknowledged the strategic importance of Berehaven, Swilly and Foynes, but counselled caution about prevailing rumours as he felt that these could have been circulated by British counter-espionage to induce the Germans to make the first move. He did not seem to be making any progress with de Valera on the arms offer.

Ribbentrop was not deterred. He returned to Hempel to bring the matter up again with de Valera, offering a considerable quantity of arms free of charge, identical with the weapons in use in the Irish Army.[39] Hempel had indicated that the British attack would take the form of a simultaneous thrust from Northern Ireland, together with landings at unfortified ports on the east and south-east coasts of Ireland. This would create the conditions in which the Irish Army would prefer to operate. They would then envisage co-ordination of expected German assistance, anticipated initially as consisting of early effective action by the Luftwaffe. The lessons of the 'Battle of Britain' had not yet sunk in apparently. Hempel thought that the Irish would hold their own at first 'despite a lack of sufficient heavy weapons'.

It was the arms deficiency in the Irish Army that made Ribbentrop's offer via Hempel tempting: it was not to be rejected out of hand. It was true, as the German Minister reported, that the Irish had recently received arms shipments from the US.[40] These however were insignificant and, as the gauche efforts of Frank Aiken confirmed, the pro-British Roosevelt administration was hostile to the delivery of arms to a neutral Ireland.[41] Hempel had also been able to report that it was persistently asserted in IRA circles, that the Germans would attack Northern Ireland in the coming March or April and would then also attack the Irish Free State and support the IRA to overthrow de Valera.[42] It is reasonable to assume that British and American Intelligence would also have been aware of these rumours and would have coupled them with de Valera's alleged ambivalences and utterances. He told a US journalist, Wallace Carroll (20/11/1940) that only an attack could dislodge Ireland from the policy of neutrality and that not even the return of Northern Ireland could change that. There were however other factors in the arms crisis in the army.

In 1938 Lt. Gen. M.J. Costello (later GOC 1st Division) had been sent on an arms purchasing mission but, like Aiken, he too had been rebuffed and stymied by Anglophile Roosevelt.[43] At the time of Ribbentrop's offer the Irish Army was badly in need of arms and equipment, to counter the internal threat (the IRA) and a dual external threat (Germany and Britain). There was a view that the need for arms was so urgent that it did not matter where they came from, so long as they ended up in the hands of the Irish Army.

Gen. McNeill (then on the General Staff – his 2nd Division had not yet been formed) would have been properly pressing, in his official capacity for arms and equipment to bring the army to a state of combat readiness. At another questionable level however, his liaisons with Goertz and Thomsen are likely to have had a bearing on Ribbentrop's insistence. The Anglophobe Foreign Minister concluded that once de Valera's doctrinaire objections to accepting the arms offer had been overcome, the rest would fall into place. If a senior officer like McNeill was anything to go by it looked as if the army was compliant. McNeill's maverick carry-on, whatever its merits or motives, did not represent the tight discipline in General McKenna's new army. Without knowing fully what McNeill was up to, Colonel Bryan strongly disapproved of the company he was keeping.

De Valera, trying to find out as much as he could, did not openly, initially, voice any lofty objections to Hempel. He even drily jested with him to the effect that the German High Command knew its own business best about contingency planning. The Taoiseach's voiced objection was that they would not 'get away' with the gun-running; they would be found out, he contended, and Ireland's neutrality policy would be jeopardised. De Valera, Minister for External Affairs and Taoiseach, saw no chance of having the arms shipped to Ireland unnoticed and for that reason he told the German Minister that Ireland's hazardous situation did not allow the taking of any such risks.[44]

The limits of the risks de Valera was prepared to take were more definitely demonstrated when he refused Hempel permission to bring in extra staff for the Legation in a Luftwaffe plane.[45] The plane was rumoured to have got as far as hovering over Rhinanna: it certainly never landed. Just as de Valera had indicated his willingness to co-operate with Britain to the limit that such co-operation could not be seen to jeopardise the Irish stand,[46] so too was he prepared to listen to the Germans up to a point. That point was well short of the distance he was prepared to go with Britain, even allowing for the fact that the notion of German invincibility was still prevalent. In a reference to the 'Battle of Britain' de Valera's (auto) biographers reflected his view: 'By the end of it emerged what seemed, and still seems, the miracle of the defeat of the Luftwaffe.'[47]

Therefore, it was neither diplomatic nor expeditious to reject out of hand either the previous German offer of an agreement affecting Irish shipping or the present offer to provide arms. The tactic then adopted by the Irish government in each case was to play for time. That tactic however was less easy to adopt when the demand to augment the Legation staff was pressed by Hempel. That would have been clearly visible, defiant, even provocative and dangerously compromising. It obviously had an unacceptable military dimension.

When questions of a military nature had been posited to Hempel previously from his headquarters, he kept himself covered when answering by suggesting that certain aspects of the questions could be handled more comprehensively by a military man.[48] In a conversation between General Warlimont and Ambassador Ritter discussing the extent to which help might be given to Ireland, reference was also made to increasing the legation Staff by an official or officer experienced in military reconnaissance. General

Jodl also wanted the Legation strengthened.[49] Constructions from conversations with 'a high ranking Army Officer "L"' (presumed to be either Major General Hugo McNeill or his cousin, Reserve Officer Colonel Nial McNeill),[50] were also factors in the decision to augment the Legation staff.[51] Hempel had at one point deemed it inadvisable to go further into the enquiries of 'L' (General McNeill), but a concept emerges for a requirement for military type co-operation with the Germans, if the British moved first. That did not accord with de Valera's concept of neutrality with 'a *certain* consideration for Britain'.

Hempel's argument was, that as great latitude was allowed to the Allies in the way as having military and naval attachés at their embassies, a similar consideration should be shown to the Germans. He reported to Weizacker that the British had a naval attaché who probably also had disguised staff; the French had a naval attaché who had been accredited to London before the fall of France; and the Americans had a military and air attaché to allegedly put pressure on de Valera.[52]

Why not grant a like facility to the Germans, he maintained. Like many rules devised during the war, de Valera was well aware that this arrangement favoured the Allies, but he sidestepped Ribbentrop and Hempel in 'Euclidian' fashion. Having explained to Hempel Ireland's daring to remain neutral at all, he insisted that the German officials, proposed to be transferred from America to the Dublin Legation, must use ordinary means of transportation, namely Pan-American passenger line to Lisbon and then to England by British plane. This was impossible: the solution to this problem lay in the absence of any solution.

Ribbentrop fired testy telegraphs at Hempel, expressing annoyance with the Irish. Hempel's advice had been to get in the military advisor under the guise of a replacement for the deceased Legation Secretary Wenzel.[53] Confronted with the Taoiseach's mathematical *reductio ad absurdum* reasoning, he had reluctantly agreed to this impossible proposition of de Valera's. There was nothing more that could be done, unless the Germans wished to force the issue to the point of confrontation. Ribbentrop, with bad grace, gave up the idea of strengthening the Legation staff for the time being. He had to climb down from the position he had taken up on Christmas Day 1940 of instructing Hempel to inform the

'Éireann' authorities that Germany would decide the strength of the Legation staff. On 29 December 1940 he told Hempel not to press further with the matter.[54] De Valera's steel had prevailed over Ribbentrop's bullying.

However, Ribbentrop did not give up so easily on the issue of delivery of arms. He again directed Hempel to discuss with de Valera ways and means of German assistance in the event of a British attack.[55] This time Hempel found de Valera, now back in Ireland after an eye operation in Switzerland, 'entirely non-committal' and more evasive than ever.[56]

A contingent eventual requirement for German assistance remained but Ribbentrop's manipulations were stymied by logistical difficulties and de Valera's adamantine adroitness.[57] Hempel again suggested to Berlin (7/12/1940) that it was advisable to show German interest in the continued existence of an independent Ireland, but again felt that any self-serving German commitment to a united Ireland would be premature.[58]

Nearly three months later (24/2/1941), whether from exasperation or desperation at what seemed to be shilly-shallying on the part of the Irish government, Ribbentrop's instructions to Hempel went much further than Hempel's own proposal.[59] Ireland, the Foreign Minister indicated, could only assert national demands and remain fully independent if England were vanquished. Germany, he continued, subscribed to both those Irish aspirations and then put them both, in the final analysis, 'in the same camp'. It was to no avail: de Valera would not budge. Hempel had made the point that Irish-American activity had given the Taoiseach some immunity from a British attack 'for the time being'.[60] This probably strengthened him to resist the tempting German offer of arms to equip the new national 'Emergency Army', which, increasingly obviously, could not fight without weapons: 'de Valera intervened to make sure that one division at least would be equipped'.[61] That was not enough to restrain the impatient Ribbentrop from prompting Hempel to express 'mild doubts' about the Irish will to resist, when it seemed that they would do nothing practically, outside of theorising, to prepare their defences.[62] The effort made by Ribbentrop to move de Valera through influencing Irish-American opinion 'by spending considerable sums of money' had not worked either.[63] But the captured British weapons were held ready to transport from 13 April 1941. They were of sufficient quantity to make an Irish Divisional Commander's mouth water, particularly as the attitude of Churchill and Roosevelt dampened prospects of getting meaningful supplies from Allied quarters.[64] The cargo prepared for shipment consisted of 46 field guns; 550 machine guns; 10,000 rifles and 1,000 anti-tank grenade throwers – all with necessary and appropriate ammunition.[65]

In German eyes, Roosevelt's resistance to supplying arms to the Irish government could be looked on as a bonus especially when (according to a German report, Telegram 129 12/3/1941) the American League for the Unity and Independence of Ireland, had sent a telegram to de Valera from Chicago stating that it was 'silly, unfair, illogical and unchristian' to request that Ireland would take a course of action that would directly involve it in war 'while its own territorial integrity is being violated and while it is denied the right to secure equipment of the kind needed for its own self-defence'. For Ribbentrop that could read that the scene was set for the use of captured British weapons by the Irish against the British; and most important, it would seem that Irish-American acquiescence (or at least lack of opposition) to such a scheme could be anticipated. The scenario however did not unfold smoothly in that manner for Herr Hempel: de Valera proved to be an insurmountable stumbling block. He had to look both ways.

An analysis of events and utterances up to mid-1941 showed that there was a threat of invasion from both sides. Contact had been established between the British and Irish Secret Service[66] but that did not fully eliminate the British threat. De Valera however was greatly disturbed by the physical manifestations of German violations of neutrality: there was the tangible court evidence of IRA liaisons with the German High Command and there was the insertion of agents who had missions of sabotage and subversion. And that was not all.

The German breaches went beyond undue pressures to augment Legation staffs and persistence with compromising offers of arms assistance; and far beyond Petersen's drunken indiscretions, fracas with an Irish officer and clashes with the police.[67] Hempel had reported that British and American propaganda were turning to good account the dropping of bombs in Drogheda, Terenure, Curragh, Enniskerry, Wexford, the South Circular Road in Dublin and different places on the East coast. The bomb dropped in Wexford had caused considerable damage and casualties and consequently grave disquiet.[68] Hempel relayed an American radio report that the Irish government had threatened to expel him. He complained about an *Irish Times* leading article attributing the Oylegate (Co. Wexford) bombing to the Germans. He repeated that he had made a stiff protest to Walshe, warning them to be careful about such imputations. Walshe took the rebuke quietly, pointing out the adverse effect the bombings were having on Irish public opinion and the capital such actions was providing for British and American propagandists.[69]

Ribbentrop however continued to smoulder at the incomprehensible attitude of the Irish, not alone to the offer of arms but particularly to their obtuseness when it came to a question of reinforcing the Legation staff. All the while, Hermann Goertz from the German High Command was at large, moving it seemed at will, though apparently not entirely unbeknownst to some official circles who apparently had the spy in their sights almost all the time. There were recurring, but measured, protests from the Irish government to Hempel regarding violations of airspace and attacks on Irish shipping.[70] Dillon asked questions in the Dáil about the bombing of Irish ships and the machine-gunning of crews.[71]

All the pressure was not from the German side however. 'The Great White Father', as the German reports refer to Roosevelt, had advised de Valera not to insist on the incorporation of the Six Counties during the war: the message was to wait until the war was over, when US support would be forthcoming to achieve a United Ireland. There was of course a price: Cudahy, Wilkie, Donovan, all leading US political personalities, followed by Prime Minister Menzies of Australia, made a procession to de Valera, with apparently the object of putting pressure on him to modify his stand on neutrality. By May (12/5/1941) Woermann was quoting the Irish Ambassador in Washington as telling the Italian Ambassador in Washington that the 'Great White Father' had sought a declaration – without apparently being fully successful – that England would not attack Ireland. Cordell Hull, however was very definite in his views in which he was supported by the *New Yorker* newspaper, that from a German point of view, nothing could be better than a British invasion of Ireland, under any pretext, or in any form. However, the difference between the British and the German threats was that there were actual German attacks *on what Irish nationalists of all persuasions claimed to be their territory* – as distinct from Allied cajolings and pressures. The first German air raid on Belfast (8/4/1941) killed thirteen people and injured eighty-one. On Easter Tuesday 15 April 1941 an estimated 100 German aircraft again pounded the city. At least 700 lives were lost and 1,511 people injured. De Valera showed the true colour of his sympathies for the democracies and the one nation concept when he dispatched fire brigades from Dublin, Dún Laoire, Drogheda and Dundalk to succour stricken Belfast. The 'niceties' of neutrality did not deter him at a time like that. On 5/6 May two further raids caused extensive incendiary damage. These raids on Belfast shattered the illusion fondly held by the Irish government that the Germans had been respecting the integrity of the 32 Counties in refraining from bombing the Six Counties. On 18 May 1941 Cardinal McRory approached Hempel to have Armagh, his cathedral city, spared from being bombed. Hempel strongly supported (18/5/1941) the Cardinal's request. Armagh was of no military significance, he believed: there was only a division headquarters and a few hundred soldiers there; there were no munitions or aircraft factories or large industry there. The Cardinal, Hempel continued, was a personal friend of his: he was very anti-British and a strong supporter of Irish neutrality and independence as well as having good relations with the Italians.

Hempel's narration of events continued with the regularity of daily bulletins. He reported that several German aircraft pursued by two RAF planes were over Dublin on 29 January 1941 and that Irish anti-aircraft guns fired on them. His succeeding accounts cover what is now known as the 'North Strand Bombing' of Dublin. He reported houses destroyed, 17–20 dead and 150 wounded in that raid (31/5/1941). The Envoy's 'radical nationalist' friends tried to persuade him that the bombing was another example of British provocation. This was carried to ludicrous, counter-productive lengths.[72]

But the evidence produced to the Envoy of German involvement could not be gainsaid. Warnock's protest that 'a light blue coloured plastic material generally cylindrical in shape and bearing the inscription '*hier nicht anheben*', had been found in each bombed area.

It was also reported that the bombs dropped in Malin (Co. Donegal, 5/5/1941) also had German markings (DL 284). Hempel's report to Berlin conceded the position indicated by the evidence and he recommended the keeping of a low profile by the German radio in particular. He pointed out that the efforts to pin blame for the January bombings on the British had had little success.

Kramarz replied to Hempel from Berlin that Liverpool had been the target that night and, while it was improbable that Dublin was mistaken for Liverpool, they did not rule that out. The point of view was expressed that the bombing would not have happened if Dublin had not been blacked out – a complaint that the blackout was favouring the British. Hempel's response was to advise the Foreign Ministry to either accept responsibility as in Campile in 1940 – though he pointed out that reparations would be high – or to use the opportunity to specifically declare intentions. He said that the German successful airborne operation in Crete had reawakened Irish apprehensions. The Irish protest was accompanied by a demand for full compensation and reparation. The incident however did not fully divert the government's mind from anxieties about the British. Walshe, in a further effusion of sychophancy, expressed an opinion to Hempel that the British by bending a guiding beam may have directed the bomber over Dublin.

The British, it was true, had discovered a method of deflecting the beams guiding the German bombs so that they jettisoned their bomb loads over open countryside. This method however, hardly had the precision required to deflect the plane to a specific target like Dublin. The German themselves discountenanced the possibility of the British having acquired German bombs and dropping them. Dr Gogan went further in his fancies: the British, he held, dropped them from reconstructed German planes.

Hempel did admit (2/6/1941) that German aircraft regularly followed routes along the East and South-East coasts. When bombs were dropped again on Arklow (1/6/1941) the British repeated the point of Irish inability to defend themselves. The implication was obvious if the Irish could not defend themselves, the British, to defend their flank, would pre-empt it.

Anglo-Irish relations were further strained by the proposal to introduce conscription in Northern Ireland. The fact remained however that it was German actions which were outraging the government and the people more than Allied pressures. Hempel's account of his summons to de Valera, who expressed the strongest misgivings of German intentions to respect neutrality, leaves no doubt as to the strength of feeling and perplexity caused by the German actions. Walshe, according to the Envoy, took it more coolly; though he somewhat peevishly observed that while Walshe did not appear to be disturbed by British incursions into Irish airspace, he was demanding strict German compliance with the letter of the law. He extenuated that the Irish anti-aircraft fire was ordered only to appease the British and that it was because of this fire that the Germans had dropped their bombs.

A Machiavellian reply from Berlin (29/5/1941) does little to elucidate or explain the bombings. It does reveal however that German planning with regard to Ireland lacked co-ordination of any kind. It notes the failure of Frank Aiken's arms purchasing mission in the US, and comments that Ribbentrop had told Veesenmayer, his *coup d'état* specialist with responsibility for Irish revolution, to put wireless and money at the disposal of the IRA. Plans were hatched for the landing to be made by seaplane in an inland Irish lake. It would seem as if Ribbentrop had given up trying to convince the Irish government through Hempel of the necessity for contingency planning to receive German assistance in the event of a British attack and was going to 'go it alone', through the IRA.

But far greater schemes were afoot which weakened the German threat. On 22 June 1941 Hitler turned his forces against Russia. The British threat remained: 'the weakening of one threat however was balanced by a strengthening of the other'. De Valera never knew for sure whence a blow might come.[73] The reconsideration of the threat of invasion had to be a continuous process, though the more obvious attendant threats from the abortive Operation 'Sea Lion' had receded.

Henceforth, Hempel had to conduct his defensive diplomacy from a less glaring position of strength. Attitudes weather-cocked accordingly, Hempel's overt job became less smooth: his covert role, more hazardous.

CHAPTER 8

From Diplomacy to Spying,
September 1939–November 1941

It was a dilemma, even in peacetime, for the diplomat to know where to draw the line between what might be regarded as legitimate information gathering and what could be construed as spying. That problem was compounded for Dr Hempel as the diplomatic representative of Hitler's Third Reich in neutral Éire in wartime. What particularly complicated the situation was that, in Berlin eyes, it would not have been illogical to conclude that Ireland and Germany had a common enemy in England. 'England's difficulty is Ireland's opportunity' was a traditional Irish slogan for dealing with Britain. Adolf Mahr, formerly of the *Auslandsorganisation* in Dublin, used as a theme in German radio propaganda *'England's Verlegenheit ist Irland's Gelegenheit'* in exhorting Irishmen 'to fight for freedom, to break the yoke of the British Empire'.[1] His exhortation included a wide-ranging, sometimes simplistic and naïve analysis of an approach to the Irish audience, including the Irish-speaking sector. The American factor is also considered. The IRA 'lapped it up as gospel': the majority squirmed.

An IRA Order of the Day (27/5/1941) disingenuously did not blame the Germans for the bombing of Belfast the previous Eastertide but read: 'Already one of the cities has been laid in ruins and thousands of our people killed because, against the will of the Irish people, it has been made a stronghold of British power'.[2] That order called for a new battle to be fought on Irish soil: 'we shall regret, as all people regret, to be compelled to see our land suffer the ravages of war, but we shall know that only final and complete victory can save it from similar ravages, decade after decade, generation after generation'. Although the IRA professed a desire to avoid Civil War, this document accepted, that, in achieving their aim of a *coup d'état* 'in both areas' (i.e. Northern Ireland and Éire), they would be left with 'a weakened people to face the British'. The Minister for Justice, Gerry Boland, in a Dáil reply to Deputy James Dillon said that it was not clear whether the IRA intended a *coup d'état* at home or an attack on the North but that it was the government's intention to take their weapons from them and put them behind bars.[3] Hempel reported the Labour Party's further question on the Military Tribunal and the ensuing exchange between Boland and de Valera and Dillon. De Valera proposed that as there were two parties at war and that as the IRA had declared war on one of the parties it must, therefore, wish to co-operate with the other.

The inherent threat of the IRA to the institutions of the State was even more evident in the fact that the illegal organisation had already established liaison with the *Abwehr* and had prepared a plan (*Artus*) for a German landing in Ireland.[4] Fortunately for the Security of the State and the implementation of the policy of neutrality, this liaison proved to be fitful and inefficient. Lahausen, the head of *Abwehr II* complained that every undertaking proved abortive and that the IRA 'went off and did things on their own without a word to anyone'.[5] Eventually (11/12/1939) relations had deteriorated to the extent that U-Boat commanders repeatedly insisted that they would only undertake to land agents on the Irish coast if they could be assured that the IRA was not informed as to the time and place of the landing.

Notwithstanding this lack of a sense of security and a 'tendency to indiscretion' on the part of the IRA, it seems that Hempel at the outset of the war – to judge from his approaches to Clissmann[6] – was prepared to discreetly make contact with the fringes of this covert 'extreme republican' world.

Clissmann – inadvertently apparently – was 'called up' and had returned to Germany. That left Thomsen, Hempel's second-in-command, to take over the nebulous task, which had been previously allotted to Clissmann. Thomsen could hardly hope to accomplish this mission as expertly and as adroitly as Clissmann presumably could have done: he had neither the background nor the experience. Hempel's attitude to this operation was to turn a 'blind eye' to it '*selbstverständllich ohne merken zu lassen, dass er Wink von uns erhielt*'.[7]

His main concern in that area was to avoid being compromised and to keep up appearances for the Legation. Overtly, he downgraded the IRA.[8] His reservations were based on his estimate of IRA capabilities: their lack of leadership, in his opinion, meant that they lacked the capability for any meaningful action which might have been useful to German purposes at that time. He did not however rule out their potential: the very point he was making was that premature hasty action could damage that potential for future operations.[9] Together with Dr Petersen, he clung to the notion that, in certain circumstances, especially in a situation where England's difficulties might present a national opportunity to end partition, the IRA might have an important role to play. The IRA offer of protection for the Legation in the event of a British invasion does not seem to have offended Hempel's susceptibilities.

Firm evidence of his flirtation in the field of spying and of his reservations and inhibitions in that area is apparent in his relations with Francis Stuart. Stuart for a variety of reasons – domestic, marital, sexual, financial, sense of adventure, escape, his muse, wanting to be near 'the action' etc. – wanted to return to Berlin where he had been a lecturer the previous summer (1939). Intriguingly, whether she wanted to see the back of him for a while or not, his wife Iseult, Maud Gonne's daughter, had arranged, with a little help from Helmut Clissmann, that previous tour. He now enlisted Hempel's aid, telling the Envoy 'in strict confidence' that he belonged to a group of nationalist Irishmen who wished to have a representative in Germany to maintain the previous close links which had been established with the Pfaus Group.[10]

Hempel had been unhappy about the activities of Oscar C. Pfaus of the *Fichtebund*. He complained to Berlin that the action of agencies such as the *Fichtebund*, or the propaganda ministry in making contacts with radical Irish nationalists, should be pursued only with the utmost care.[11] The *Fichtebund* was founded in 1914 in 'memory of the great German philosopher Fichte': it was a propaganda agency using 'culture' as a medium. It called itself the 'union for world veracity', serving 'the cause of peace and understanding' by giving free information direct from the source. It purported to protect human culture and civilisation by disseminating facts about world Bolshevism, its authors and danger.

Pfaus had been in correspondence with a Dr Anna Sloane in New York, through whom he had sought to contact US General Mosely, and with a James Philip Gaffney, also in New York, through whom he hoped to influence Irish-American opinion.[12] He put Gaffney in touch with a Captain Liam D. Walsh of Drimnagh in Dublin. Walsh was General O'Duffy's 'right hand man'. Hempel later reported unfavourably on Walsh, an ex-army officer who had become an agent for the *Fichtebund* and had insinuated himself into employment at the Italian Legation. Walsh had written to Gaffney (22/6/1939) saying that he was very glad to learn that Gaffney was 'doing such good work to help smash the Semitic groups in America' and that he (Walsh) 'would like very much to help in this very necessary work'. When the following year Walsh was uncovered and interned, the Italian representative, Bernardis, erroneously harboured the suspicion that Hempel had planted the *Fichtebund* agent in his Legation whereas, in fact, Hempel had been strongly opposed to *Fichtebund* activities in Ireland.[13] 'Someone', of course, had planted him there.

The Minister Plenipotentiary expressed his opinion to Berlin that the British were only allowing the *Fichtebund* to send their propaganda to subversive elements through the post in order to build up a dossier of breaches of neutrality to be used against the Irish government. He adroitly covered his tracks by requesting that the *Fichtebund* were not to know that he had 'fingered' them. He had already reported the rumours abroad of undercover connections between German intelligence agencies and the IRA.[14] But all his adroitness could not avoid involvement with Walsh. In September 1940 he telegraphed that Walsh's wife was demanding regular payments from the Legation now that Walsh was interned: the *Abwehr* obviously had uses for Walsh, though he would not have been Hempel's choice. Francis Stuart, on the other hand, at the beginning of the war seemed to have the status and discretion that the German Minister felt were desirable in an agent and helped him accordingly.

Stuart, he said, had been selected by his organisation because other efforts to maintain contact had foundered and he vouched for him as the son-in-law of the famous freedom fighter, Maud Gonne MacBride. His point was that if Stuart did not go, some other unsuitable person might go instead. Stuart promised him that he would keep a low profile and Hempel undertook to pay his fare to Germany via the US. The identify of interest between the Envoy and the IRA, in facilitating the return of Stuart to Berlin in wartime, cannot be overlooked in any espionage or subtle subversive context, Hempel's purity-projected image, notwithstanding.

The minister subsequently asked the German Legation in Bern to provide Stuart with money (15/1/1940) and asked their representative Köcher to meet him there personally. Later on however (24/5/1940), after the capture of Held and the arrest of Mrs Stuart, Hempel expressed anxiety about any indiscreet statements Stuart might have made in letters home. He changed his tune. Now he wanted him rebuked for not supporting his wife and family whom he, according to Hempel, had left destitute. Mrs Stuart, Hempel held, did not have enough money to send the children to school.[15] Stuart for his part, though very friendly with Hempel when it suited him, was more inclined to agree with Haller's opinion that the Envoy was 'an old woman'.[16] In their opinion, the German Minister lacked boldness and creativity: there was no daring in him, they thought. Frau Hempel was scathing about their opinion: the 'daring', these 'hurlers-on-the ditch' were demanding, would have undermined his role as minister.

Hempel's proper, professional circumspection surfaced again when he was asked to assist in the return to Ireland of IRA Chief, Seán Russell, then in New York.[17] He convinced the Political Department, which had been receptive to the idea – and had found out that it was technically possible to transport Russell to Ireland by submarine – that the time for such an action had not yet arrived.[18] Veesenmayer was disappointed in Hempel's attitude. ('What a success for Hempel', Frau Hempel exclaimed: 'his way was better'.)

Veesenmayer had concluded that the best course of action to accomplish the mission given to him by Ribbentrop of fomenting rebellion in Ireland, was to let the Irish 'do their own thing': 'give them a chance to prove themselves', as he put it.[19] Though Russell was alleged to lack political acumen,[20] Veesenmayer preferred him to Ryan, whom he regarded as 'too far left'. In the mind of this *coup d'état* specialist both Russell and Ryan had a rapport with de Valera going back to the days whey they were comrades-in-arms together and his assumption, not scotched by Hempel's reportage, was that the IRA and the government differed only as to methods in their separate efforts to achieve the same national objectives, namely a united Ireland. Hempel did not agree totally but failed to specify his position precisely. Frank Ryan's name was not mentioned to him at that stage. As things turned out, when Russell died aboard the submarine (August 1940), Ryan also apparently, was not briefed well enough to take over and carry on. No more than Hempel he had not been fully taken into confidence. The Envoy became more convinced than ever that it was in Germany's best interests to keep Ireland out of the war at this stage and tried to behave circumspectly, diplomatically, accordingly. However, with the best will in the world, from time to time, he had to step sideways to try to find out what the IRA were up to affecting his country.

Woermann reported to Ribbentrop that Hempel had spoken out against sending Russell to Ireland at that time; the Envoy's point, said Woermann, was that, in combat terms, the IRA was not strong enough to produce a successful outcome to operations.[21] There was no lofty principle involved: it was a purely pragmatic assessment. His reaction may have been different, had he formed a different opinion of the IRA's combat-readiness. In any case he would have had little 'stomach' for any type of unconventional combat operations.

He expressed fears that the insertion of Russell would result inevitably in his arrest by the Irish government and that this would reveal the German connection and so further discredit the IRA to the detriment of future employment in Germany's interests. He concluded that only England would then benefit and he drew a flimsy parallel with the landing of Sir Roger Casement from a German U-Boat during World War I. That parallel, paradoxically, could have spurred the Berlin planners. The 1916 Rising despite its military failure had produced a successful revolution from, militarily speaking, the most unpromising beginnings: prisoners could be canonised, the dead would tyranise and do the rest.

So Woermann insisted that the contact with McCarthy, a shadowy figure in the US, be maintained. Perhaps Berlin hoped for a similar '1916' concatenation of events. They forgot that times had changed: Dublin was now in Irish hands.

McCarthy was the mystery man of this period. He was unknown to Irish Army Intelligence.[22] He was the courier between New York and Genoa, the link man between Russell, through the German Consulate in Genoa to the Foreign Ministry in Berlin, the *Abwehr* and finally to Veesenmayer himself (and thence, via the Foreign Ministry, to Hempel). Initially the *Abwehr's* interest was restricted to a demand for sabotage. Ribbentrop was to develop bigger ideas. McCarthy's main object was to get German agreement to 'smuggling' Russell from New York to Europe, with a view to getting German backing for the IRA leader's return to Ireland. Hempel, as was his wont, counselled caution. He got suspicious when he observed that McCarthy and Russell seemed to have the same New York address and perhaps the German Minister in Dublin produced the key to the McCarthy mystery when he queried whether McCarthy and Russell might not in fact be one and the same person: 'McCarthy mit J.R. identisch'.[23] The intriguing query remains unanswered.

In spite of Hempel's misgivings and warnings however, the plans to send Russell and Frank Ryan to Ireland went ahead, culminating in the now well-known drama of Russell dying 'in Frank Ryan's arms' from a perforated ulcer aboard a U-Boat, 100 metres west of Galway in mid-August 1940. This was the time scheduled for the German 'feint' or secondary attack or whatever, on Ireland. In conjunction with 'Sea Lion' and the vain hope of Irish government acquiescence the idea was that would-be fomenters, Russell and Ryan, would 'set the heather blazing'[24] and spark another uprising. However, according to MI5 files released at the Public Records Office in London (April 2000), Russell was allegedly murdered by Ryan because of internal problems and political difficulties within the IRA. There is also a suspicion that Admiral Canaris (smeared by Veesenmayer to me) not wanting to make trouble for his British paymasters, may have had a hand in it. The difficulty with this version of Frank Ryan's part in the affair, is that even though the IRA leaders had drifted apart ideologically, they remained firm friends to the end.

Hempel acknowledged his part in the adventure: the flower-box signal in the main window of his Legation top floor that 'Operation Sea Lion' was under way, giving the green light to Russell to go ahead with his schemes, was a serious involvement, involving a possible link-up with the Operation 'Grün' bridgehead landing in the Wexford area.[25] Wishful thinking rather than hard logistical facts would seem to have predominated the notions. On the other hand, the part played by chance and the impossible in the history of war cannot be discounted. In Ireland, a spark may have been all that was needed to start a rising. That danger, coupled with messianic IRA subversion, remained a serious security threat. The reality of the existence of the agents, particularly Goertz, counselled caution in tendencies to dismiss the danger on logistical grounds.

The German Minister's main concern increased. Whatever happened, he was not going to be compromised: he was going to remain the 'Mr Clean'. The 'flower-pot' story certainly involved him. But while the opening sentence of this incriminating telegram makes the Envoy an accessory to Veesenmayer's aspiration to manipulate Russell and Ryan in an Irish adventure, Hempel had no sooner agreed to the flower-pot arrangement than he qualified it to keep himself covered. He agreed to put the box in the window, but stipulated that it remain there permanently: '*sollten dann möglichst permanent dort bleiben*'.[26] That, in his reckoning, removed any link between it and the Russell/Ryan business. It would have done its job and kept the connection quiet.

The second paragraph of this telegram emphasises once more the minister's desire not to be seen to be openly involved with 'unofficial contacts'. A reliable person, he wrote, wished to be put in touch with Goertz, 'assuming he is still in the country', Hempel hastened to disabuse her; he declined her request saying he had nothing to do with that business. He was concerned with his image. Luckily for Ireland, the German representative was not Veesenmayer. When he advised the German High Command (23/8/1940) to be sure to listen on the 38.25m band the following week-end, he added that receipt of this intelligence through his transmission should not be made known to Goertz. He was disturbed by the spy's activities and wanted to distance himself: there is however ample documentary evidence linking him to the High Command and the agents.

It was a vain hope to imagine that he could wash his hands of Goertz whose status he refused to face up to. The blitzkrieg that brought about the fall of France was an event of enormous political as well as military consequences: old norms had been swept away. Goertz had a place in the German scheme of things – with consequences for Ireland.

For a small neutral country avowed to take on the first invader, some contingency planning was inescapable. The unconventional nature of the challenge had to be taken on board by the military planners. The Janus nature of the Irish neutrality stance insisted that this planning had to be of an *ad hoc* nature: not unnaturally the swaying fortunes of war conditioned the nature of approaches. They did not bargain for a Goertz. Therefore, it is neither ludicrous nor fantastic, in the climate of the times, to acknowledge unorthodox contingency contacts. Hempel reported alleged collusion of two Cabinet ministers and a senator with a notorious IRA man, Hayes.[27] In that twilight area in those momentous times it is not inconceivable that there could occur some blurring and overlapping of the lines normally drawn between customary diplomatic practice and undercover initiatives into which the Envoy was sucked. Procedures were gauche, cumbersome, sometimes farcical, generally overlapping.

Initially, tardy Hempel had to be convinced in writing that Goertz was in fact, officially commissioned.[28] Goertz after all, was more than a mere agent: he was a rival representative, authorised by no less a body than the German High Command. His links with the IRA could compromise Hempel and undermine his official position. Hempel himself envisaged a new radical movement – not the IRA – arising in Ireland, in the framework of a Europe dominated by the Axis powers. In that setting he likened de Valera to Portugal's Salazar.[29]

Like the 'flower-pot' story the melodramatic meeting arranged between Hempel and Goertz at a cocktail party in the Envoy's house in Monkstown has captured the imagination.[30] Goertz was instructed to arrive as a 'guest' and to ask Hempel's maid for the w.c. Maud Gonne MacBride used to say that Hempel was 'frightened out of his wits' at the mere mention of the name of Goertz.[31] Frau Hempel explained that he had to see Goertz to find out what his task was and to get his opinion about the IRA. After the meeting he was satisfied that they both had a similar appreciation of the situation and that Goertz had no aggressive intentions against Ireland. Her husband was not frightened of Goertz, but he found him a burden. Goertz seriously compromised Hempel and his Legation by misreading the IRA's position and the Irish Army's desperation for equipment.

Hempel's telegram of 10 November 1940 stated that due to the lack of heavy weapons and proper defences on the Irish side, the occupation of the ports by the British would be resisted with guerilla warfare and that this could tie down strong British Forces.[32] He later

(6/12/1940) reported that one of the highest-ranking officers in the Irish Army had, on his own initiative, made contact with Thomsen, the Legation Secretary, and appraised him of the Irish Army's expectation of a British attack.[33] Arising from their meetings Hempel reported three possible axes for this attack:

1. Occupation of Lough Swilly which was by far the most important objective. The comment (it is not clear whether it is Hempel's or the Army Officer's) was that, as a glance at the map indicated, defence against such a land attack was pointless.
2. Occupation of Lough Swilly and a further assault by land on the airfields at Rhinanna and Foynes, combined with a seaborne landing at the Mouth of the Shannon.
3. Cork, Wexford, Dublin and eventually Berehaven were also possible objectives.

The army further explained, according to Hempel, that, in the event of a British attack, the Irish Cabinet would probably seek German assistance but first, it was necessary to find out the answers to certain questions as soon as possible: He incorporated the questions in this report:

1. Was Germany prepared in principle to render assistance?: to reply if answer affirmative.
2. Did Germany require Irish airfields? In that case the Irish Army would hold them for as long as possible, though heavy casualties would be unavoidable. Airfields at that point – apart from a few small fields in use by the Irish themselves – had been rendered unusable by sowing obstacles and spiking them with angled railway tracks – and those would have to be cleared if the airfields were required. However if Germany did not need the airfields, they would be only lightly defended. It was not possible to put them out of action for any length of time due to shortage of explosives: Rhinanna – Hempel's report commented on available airfields – was eight times as big as Tempelhof; Fermoy was very poor, and Collinstown and Baldonnel could hardly be held against the British.
3. Could Germany, in the event of an Irish request for help following a British attack, parachute in anti-tank guns (which

1. Eduard Hempel (courtesy German Embassy, Dublin; photograph by Eddy Chandler)

2. Hempel with wife Eva (courtesy Agnes Kramer)

3. A German colony gathering in Dublin, 1938. Left to right: Hempel, Dr Vogelsang, businessman and Dr Adolf Mahr, Director, National Museum, Dublin (courtesy Ingrid Wahr)

4. Hempel at his desk (courtesy Agnes Kramer)

IMPENDING MAJOR CONFLICT IN

RETURNING TO GERMANY

PREPARATIONS FOR A BIG "PUSH"

Troops Hurrying up on Both Sides

FIGHTING IN THE SAAR REGION

Reported Set-back to French Advanced Line

The German Minister, Dr. Eduard Hempel (left), seeing off German nationals who left Dublin last night to return to Germany on "safe conduct" across England. Also in the picture (from left) are Dr. Robert Stumpf and Herr Budina.

FIGHTING on Eastern and Western fronts took on a new note yesterday as the Polish armies halted several German advances staunchly, held on to Warsaw, and drove back Nazi troops coming north from Slovakia.

On the West French soldiers—with hundreds of square miles of enemy territory under their control—made substantial progress, according to last night's official communiqué. Tanks and infantry mopped up German frontal positions, and consolidated gains for the big drive in the Saar River area.

The French advance is situated along the fifty-mile stretch of the River Saar, from Saarbruecken North-West to the Moselle. The German offensive near Sierck, close to the Luxembourg frontier, on Sunday was an attempt to avoid being driven into the Siegfried line. They have made every effort to hold the commanding artillery posts in front of the fortifications.

French newspapers suggest that the Germans' obvious reluctance to occupy the Siegfried line until driven to it by a major offensive indicates mistrust in the solidity of the vaunted "West wall."

OFFICIAL REPORTS

Last night's French war communiqué—issued after an announcement earlier in the day than Sunday night on the whole was calm, and that their troops had been able to make a local advance—was as follows:—

" Despite the resistance of the enemy our attacks have continued to make substantial progress on a front of about twenty kilometres, east of the Saar."

On the other hand, Wilhelmstrasse officials deny any knowledge of Western front fighting beyond minor skirmishes, and attempts by French airmen to bomb the evacuated Saarbruecken aerodrome.

POLISH CAVALRY'S STAND

One of the most gallant actions in Poland is that being fought by Polish cavalry, who still operate in the Corridor region, although the country far in front of them is in German hands. Berlin military authorities state that these Polish troops are expected to surrender soon—and then Germany will give more attention to the West.

The German Official Wireless Station last night claimed that their troops had marched into Lodz, an important industrial centre, seventy miles south-west of Warsaw.

Reports reaching Brussels state that German troops, unable to enter Warsaw from the West, are attempting an attack from the North, and advancing on the Narew River. Polish military leaders point out that this gives Germany a dangerously narrow salient, liable to be cut by the Polish Army in North-East Poland, just below the Lithuanian border.

It was reported from Paris last night that fresh German troops caused the French to lose several hundred yards of German territory yesterday. French observers described the thrust as "without appreciable success" and stopped by a counter-attack.

THRUST AND COUNTER-THRUST

From Reuter's Correspondent.
PARIS, Monday.

The German attack at the north end of the 120-mile front on which the French are pushing into their territory was followed by a night of comparative calm. French observers interpret yesterday's German offensive movement near Sierck, close to the Luxembourg frontier, as an attempt to hold on as long as possible to the advantage posts at the outposts of this line which exclude territory artillery observation posts.

THE SIEGFRIED LINE

The German General Staff, it may be

Maftin, "that he will not engage our divisions in hastily prepared battles."

As a result of the occupation of the Warndt forest covering the approach to Saarbruecken, the French are now threatening Voelklingen, the site of a bundle of railway tracks serving this part of the Saar Basin.

This operation served a double purpose, as, if the forest had remained in German hands, it would have enabled the German thrusters' French communications between Metz and the frontier.

Observers here find cause for considerable satisfaction in the progress of the advance hitherto. Not only have the French left in possession of some hundreds of square miles of German territory, but in what they have taken they have secured themselves in admirable bases for further advances.

The German counter-attacks have failed

Britain to Fight To Bitter End

NO COMPROMISE, SAYS MR. EDEN

BRITAIN'S resolve to fight a very long war to the bitter end to rid the world of Hitlerism, was announced last night by Mr. Anthony Eden (Dominions Secretary), in his broadcast message to the British Empire and the United States of America.

Mr. Eden, in the course of his address declared that, while every inducement was given to Hitler to enter the way of peaceful negotiation, he had chosen instead to embark upon a war of naked aggression.

Floating all the lessons of the past, he said, ignoring or deriding even their own country's experience of British character, the Nazi leaders have preferred once more the path of lawlessness, misery, bloodshed and anarchy.

"Herr Hitler has preferred force. He has made the trouble; he must suffer the decision.

" For us now there will be no turning back. We have no quarrel with the German people, but there can be no lasting peace until Nazism and all it stands for is oppression, cruelty and broken faith is banished from the earth. This is an issue that admits of no compromise.

" We have decided to fight to show that aggression does not pay.

" The people of this country are ready to fight a very long war to the bitter end, if that must be. In aid of the world's Hitlerism and all that Hitlerism employs."

By Herr Hitler's own decision," he added, "our new civilisation must be

BRITISH TROOPS FIGHTING IN FRANCE

From Reuter's Correspondent.
PARIS, Tuesday.

"BRITISH troops are already fighting in large numbers at our side, and their effectiveness will continue to increase," declared M. Roland Dorgelès, French writer of war books, broadcasting here last night.

"The British troops are this time wonderfully prepared," he said.

The French people had already been told that British troops were on the way to support their men in the drive against Germany.

The announcement was made in a statement issued by the French Commissariat of Information on Thursday, part of which read:

"You have been told the military reasons why it was impossible to give you just now precise information regarding British troops in France.

"But it is necessary that you should know that British soldiers are arriving, and that they will be by the side of ours."

The statement also said: "The support that Britain will be able to give us will be infinitely greater than in 1914."

British troops have landed in France, says the Daily Mail, and are in action alongside the French Army. They have taken part in the advances into German territory.

The transport of the B.E.F. has taken several days, and has been carried out successfully without loss of a single life. The despatch of the troops was carried out with the greatest secrecy, so as to reduce to a minimum the danger of attack by submarines or aircraft.

BRITISH VIEW

NO CONFIDENCE IN HITLER'S PROMISES

PEACE ONLY WITH TRUSTWORTHY GOVERNMENT

GOERING'S offering of peace to Britain while his armies and airmen are ravishing Poland received its answer last night.

The Ministry of Information in a bulletin declared that it is considered in official circles that the Nazi Field-Marshal's speech has revealed the bankruptcy of German policy.

Hitler, the Ministry points out, has kept none of his promises to foreign countries, and there is not one country which does not regard the Nazi Government as pursuing a policy which is a menace to the security and independence of all.

It is not surprising that no confidence is felt in any assurance he may give, and Britain is, therefore, justified in requiring that peace should be concluded with a German Government whose word can be trusted.

The German Government, proceeds the bulletin, has also misled the German people—who were promised "peace and honour." They have not got peace, because the German Government have deliberately pursued a policy of violence which has made war inevitable. They have not got honour, because the world recognises the cruelty and treachery of the German Government's charges against Poland.

The "sickening technique," as the Prime Minister called it, has become too familiar. There is not a country in Europe which does not regard the present German Government as pursuing a policy which is a menace to the security and independence of all.

Great Britain is fighting for a return to decency in international relations. Until this is achieved, no country is safe.

Germany may say the same thing. In the West, but the tale of limited German territorial ambitions has been held too often to inspire the slightest confidence. Great Britain does indeed desire another Versailles, but Field Marshal Goering falsely alleges, nor the collapse of Germany, but a just and enduring peace with an honourable German Government.

As regards the economic situation, Field Marshal Goering's remarks can have brought little comfort to his hearers who already, even before the outbreak of war, had been reduced to such meagre war rations.

What is to be said of a Government which frivolously embarks on an unnecessary war in economic conditions the gravity of which even Field Marshal Goering's optimism does not venture to conceal from an audience which is only too well aware of the fact?

ANGLO-IRISH IMPORTS AND EXPORTS

UNDER an open general export licence issued by the British Board of Trade on the 2nd instant, any goods may be exported without any special permit or licence from the United Kingdom to Eire, with the exception of the goods in the following schedule:—

SCHEDULE
Wheat, meal and flour.
Tinned and canned meat, poultry and game.
Meat extracts and essences.
Condensed and dried milk, whole and separated, sweetened and unsweetened.
Fresh plums, greengages and damsons.
Fruit pulp and fruit pectin.
Tinned and bottled fruits.
Vegetables preserved in any way by canning or drying.
Fresh and frozen fish, cured, salted and canned fish.
Silk cocoons, silk raw, waste and noils and silk yarn.

FIFTY GERMANS LEAVE FOR FATHERLAND

SOME fifty members of the German colony in Dublin took advantage of the opportunity afforded them, through an arrangement between the British and Irish Governments, to return last night to the Reich.

They travelled by the mail boat from Dun Laoghaire to Holyhead, on the first stage of their journey, which will bring them in a Dutch ship to Holland, and thence to Germany. The arrangement was evidently hurriedly made; one of the passengers stated that they did not have time to get in touch with a number

6. Hempel giving Nazi salute at the Royal Dublin Horse Show in
   the presence of President Douglas Hyde, Taoiseach Eamon de
   Valera and Tánaiste Seán T. O'Kelly, August 1938

(courtesy Hegarty collection, Film Institute of Ireland)

7. Eamon de Valera at the Royal Dublin Horse Show
(courtesy Hegarty collection, Film Institute of Ireland)

8. Harry Franks, President RDS (1935–38) and President of
Ireland Douglas Hyde (courtesy Hegarty collection, Film Institute of Ireland)

were in very short supply in the Irish Army); Vickers heavy machine guns, anti-tank rifles and French Brandt mortars – generally captured British weapons. This material should be prepared for dispatch, was the army officer's advice, according to the German Minister.

In a second phase, weapon deliveries by sea was the requirement indicated by the army man, who said that Irish ships were not available for this purpose. And, in the third phase, the officer envisaged active German support from a force of 100,000–150,000. Hempel remarked that these conversations took place in the presence of the leader of the disbanded Blueshirts, O'Duffy, who was a friend of the army officer, and that, as he (Hempel) thought O'Duffy to be reckless and impractical, he felt that O'Duffy should not be made privy to any replies to the army officer's queries. It was stated that was also the wish of the 'high ranking officer'. A role for Goertz in such developments was obvious, but not welcome to the minister.

Hempel sent off that part of the telegram at 13.35 hours. Twenty minutes later (13.55), when he was writing the second part, his doubts about the business were increasing.[34] Direct contact with the Legation in such an obvious manner without the knowledge of the Irish government could, the Envoy felt, bring about a difficult situation, particularly when the Irish propensity for indiscretion was taken into account. He recommended that, in future, contact should be effected only through Thomsen ('*nur durch Thomsen Vermittlung gebe*'). In the meantime he would continue to try to influence de Valera, as he had been doing. He distanced himself from Thomsen's contact with the army officer, indicating his own initiatives in sounding out the ground with Walshe and de Valera. His reckoning was that de Valera would treat any undertaking of this nature with caution and reticence and in a purely exploratory manner. The Envoy's concluding reference was to political rather than military aspects of the situation.

His own efforts at this time, coming up to Christmas 1940, were directed to inducting an officer 'experienced in military reconnaissance' – the Irish Army officer had expressed a wish for this, as it would make his liaison task easier and more meaningful. His determined efforts to so augment the Legation staff were, as we have seen, adroitly rebuffed and circumvented by de Valera. The Irish Army Chief of Staff was at lunch at Hempel's (17/12/1940) and recalled being pressurised by the German Minister, with what would appear to have been uncharacteristic aggressiveness,[35] in connection with this bid to augment the Legation staff. The Envoy's report after Christmas (26/11/1941) however, that a British pilot overflying Lough Swilly had been shot down by Irish anti-aircraft fire indicated that the British too were still regarded as potential aggressors.[36] The talk was that the requirement for German assistance was still very much 'on the cards'. The rebuff about augmenting the Legation staff had not quenched the question of rendering aid by supplying arms.

By February 1941 the plot involving the Irish Army connection had thickened to the point of exasperating Hempel. He referred to 'L' – a letter which he had arbitrarily chosen to designate Thomsen's Army contact.[37] He reported that 'L' now wanted to make contact with the IRA because they were supposed to be in touch with the German High Command and they could tell him about the German stance in the event of a British attack. 'L' was apparently getting fed-up waiting for a reply from Thomsen. Hempel conceded 'L's military professionalism but found him to be 'typically Irish, and lacking in balance'. Again he counselled caution in dealing with him, even though Thomsen had a good impression of him. If 'L' invoked the IRA, the position of General O'Duffy, friendly with 'L' but not so friendly with the IRA, would further complicate an already dangerous situation. Indiscretion and the presence of British agents were always possibilities with the IRA, the report went on. Hempel now recommended however that 'L' should be given an answer. His actions could have collapsed the whole neutrality façade.

In a continuation of that telegram from the German Minister, Goertz (K.) enters the scene. In spite of optimism to the contrary in Irish government circles, Hempel felt that a British attack had still to be reckoned with. This obviously was Army Officer 'L's interpretation too, and the reason why, according to Hempel, the officer had made direct contact with Goertz in order to get in touch with the German High Command. Hempel was uneasy and recommended that he should nominate an intermediary who would also be known to Goertz. The German Minister pointed out the risks he ran if he communicated with Goertz and he sought to separate the contact between the High Command agent and 'L', while avoiding revealing the links between Thomsen and 'L'. If Goertz were not suitable, Hempel suggested that he himself communicate with 'L', through an intermediary. It might be better – the Minister Plenipotentiary remarked rather abruptly – if Goertz went home. Without de Valera's acquiescence, the German Minister saw little prospect of any success: however he was doubtful also of the Irish government's chances of success in seeking to buy weapons in the US. Again, Hempel's eternal 'on the other hand' reservations served to sidetrack firm conclusions: the Irish Army, it would seem from his reports, still needed weapons to counter a possible British attack.

Open relations between the Legation and the Irish Army continued – on the surface at any rate – to be cordial and they may be taken as an index to official attitudes and diplomatic relations at this point. A company from the 31st Infantry Battalion with the No. 2 Army Band rendered military honours at the burial in Bantry of five German victims of an aircrash.[38] Thomsen represented Hempel and gave the funeral oration in German. He laid a wreath in Swastika shape on the grave. Many high ranking Irish Army Officers were present. As Thomsen was short of petrol, Hempel reported that the Irish Chief of Staff had put his own car and a high-ranking officer at the Legation Secretary's disposal, to make the journey from Dublin to Bantry. Such deferential solicitude was not so demonstrably evident five months later, after the Führer had committed the *Wehrmacht* to combat in Russia and the German threat of invasion had receded as a consequence. But at this earlier stage – February 1941 – there was nothing definite that could be deduced that should deter Hempel from allowing his Legation Secretary, Thomsen, to remain in clandestine contact with 'L' and the friendly Irish Army, potential allies of the Germans in the event of a British attack on Ireland. 'L' was locquacious, articulate and impressive and the military situation remained fluid. He had to be listened to, at least.

Nevertheless, the German Minister remained apprehensive. He reported that 'L' had hoped to obtain the 'top army job' but the 'Irish government had selected a more solid personality, who enjoyed their full trust'. In this report 'L' is clearly identifiable with General Hugo

McNeill, unlike a previous report which seemed to refer to Reserve Officer Colonel Nial McNeill.[39] Hempel mentioned again that 'L' was acting without the knowledge of the Irish government. 'L', he believed, acknowledged the risks he was taking but maintained that he was acting in the best interests of his country. Hempel was not so sure that 'L' was not just an anti-de Valera adventurer and the links with O'Duffy and the IRA – both of whom wanted a tougher stand against the British – continued to cause the Envoy disquiet. Though he thought it improbable that 'L' was working for England, still he felt it was worth mentioning such a fleeting, disquieting thought. Irish impatience and inclination to indiscretion and exaggeration continued to worry Hempel and he claimed that the British had very good contacts in the Irish Army. He did not reckon that contact with 'L' gave them (the Germans) any guarantee of protection and he now had reservations about involving the Legation in providing answers for 'L's question: it was dangerous, he repeated. The minister recommended that they await the outcome of his own conversations with de Valera before proceeding further with 'L'. After further agonising, he recommended that it would be better to leave the matter of 'sounding out' to himself and, in the same breath, almost as a sigh of relief, he reported (erroneously as it turned out) that Goertz had left Ireland.

It is difficult to reconcile the timings in the three parts of this Telegram No. 154 of 19 February 1941. The first part is timed 17.20 hours; while the second part is timed 11.25 hours. The third part however is timed for that evening, 21.30 hours, and by that time Dr Hempel seemed to have become fully disenchanted with the whole operation of delivering weapons.[40] The pro-British element, he said, was strong in the population and he saw little prospect in keeping such a delivery of weapons secret. The Americans and British, the minister felt, would exploit the situation as evidence of a German plot. Then using a different tone to the distrustful one he used when speaking of 'L', the Envoy stated that he knew that the Irish Army Chief of Staff, General McKenna – whom he looked upon as a dependable national Irishman – took a similar viewpoint. He did not see any opportunity of further discussions with the Irish government: the hard deflating facts of German capability to help could no longer be fudged. Green sunburstery was defused by military estimates of the situation.

However, Hempel undertook to explore the possibility of manipulating a conversation with de Valera to bring up, yet again, the subject of German aid, which he would then qualify and establish any contingency liaison required for the delivery of weapons. The nettle of 'how' precisely that delivery could be effected, was never grasped. He linked this approach with the unofficial queries put forward by 'L' and recommended that further assurances be given of German intent to respect Irish neutrality and Irish national aspirations after the war.

One modifying supposition was that 'L', albeit on his own initiative, might be relaying, at one remove, Irish government tentative thinking on how to grasp this nettle of contingency planning, necessary if, quixotishly, the *first* violator of the neutrality policy were to be opposed. That tune played inexpertly at the wrong speed could become distorted: this could have been the case in 'L's vainglorious interpretations of the government's ultra-cautious approaches to contingency planning. This was a complex matter of extreme delicacy. It was certainly not a matter, at this stage anyway, for any buccaneering element: nor was it a business to be transacted 'over a drink'. In any case 'L' would have been an unlikely choice for such delicate policy. The Director of Intelligence, Colonel Dan Bryan, could not contain his anger when McNeill's maverick carry-on came to his notice.

On the other hand, if the British *had* attacked – and de Valera was never able to rule out that possibility – 'L's theatrical approaches to Hempel and Goertz would have provided an 'on-going' basis for liaison. The conventional chain-of-command is not always the most suitable conduit in unconventional war situations. There is a place for saloon and theatrical threads in the fabric of war.[41] 'L' may have felt that his rank enjoined him to use his initiative without having to seek permission to proceed with his covert probing. There were no indications whatsoever that any such permission would have been forthcoming. Nevertheless, if his activities were suspected, no one apparently shouted 'Stop' either. Like the peace initiative of Rudolf Hess[42] – if it came off, well and good, if not, well that is the lot of contact men: hands are washed of them.

Unlike his counterpart in the South, Major-General 'Mickey-Joe' Costello, 'L' did not stick to his military last. Costello's Intelligence Officer, incidentally, rounded up in Kerry the collaborators of

Goertz who were supposed to help the German agent to escape by sea. According to 'Mickey-Joe', they would have captured Goertz too except that he was under protection of a uniformed member of the Garda Siochána.[43] The Garda in question was allegedly subsequently disciplined and sentenced to five years' imprisonment. Such a spin would index the convolutions and 'the wheels within wheels' of a period in which outcomes were by no means foregone conclusions and hindsight does not reveal all the criss-cross apprehensions, and contradictory appraisals of the time, coupled with the ferocity of 'need to know' sanctions.

Hempel, as far as his telegrams went, did not genuinely seem to have been au fait with these 'wheels within wheels'. If they existed at all they would assuredly have been covert and he may not have needed to know the full extent of McNeill's acquaintance with Goertz.[44] At a higher level he scotched the notion that de Valera would personally liaise with Goertz.[45] Such involvement was inconceivable even to rabid de Valera haters, opponents at both extremes, to his neutrality policy. Machiavellian de Valera may well have been, but undercover conspiratorial nods and winks would have been out of character in the protocol-conscious Taoiseach, punctilious about his 'certain consideration for Britain' being seen to be scrupulously observed externally to the letter as far as the paradox permitted. In view of his sympathies with Central European powers however, it would not have been inconceivable or incredible if such, or more pragmatic adventuresome impulse, were to come from, say, Frank Aiken, who did actually contact Goertz[46] (he later said that Goertz had broken into his house).

Hempel's view was that Goertz and particularly the IRA ('which was in a catastrophic financial situation') were soliciting badly needed money. The Envoy, off his own bat, suggested that a U-Boat deliver £200 sterling to 'a certain island in the West of Ireland'.[47] This was a daring suggestion for the German Minister to make and one which could indeed compromise him. However, he warned against further developments of the contacts between 'L' and Goertz. Goertz, he maintained, could jeopardise a new situation which had arisen since the Envoy's discussion with de Valera. After praising Goertz for his work with the IRA, Hempel thought that the man was too credulous and that the Legation did not want to be mixed up at all in the mechanics of transmitting any money. He knew on good authority, that the IRA was riddled with government and British spies who knew about Goertz. He indicated increasing concern for the safety of Goertz.[48] He maintained that Goertz's contacts with IRA Chief of Staff, Stephen Hayes, compounded the danger. Hayes, now under police protection, had made a confession. He had been working for the Irish government but Hempel warned Petersen not to report the matter.[49] The *Abwehr* acknowledged the Envoy's request about the handling of the money and sought other means of getting £500 to Goertz in Dublin to accomplish his mission. This memo positively identified the 'H' of Hempel's telegrams as Stephen Hayes, the Chief of Staff of the IRA, who had replaced Russell during the latter's trip to the US in 1940.[50]

Hempel relayed the allegations of Hayes's provocation involvement with two Cabinet ministers (Dr J. Ryan and T. Derrig) and an unidentified senator, elaborated on his 'rival', Goertz: he expected him to be apprehended shortly. A copy of the Hayes' confession had been found in a house which the police had raided in pursuit of Goertz. Hempel held that he had it on good authority that the British Secret Service was also involved, so the Legation had perforce to distance itself from Goertz or else the British and Americans – if they could prove a link – would, with great acclamation, demand its expulsion. The case of Hayes, he concluded, emphasised the dangers which could be surmounted only with the greatest circumspection.[51] The implications were that only he, the Minister Plenipotentiary, could surmount the dangers, not Goertz.

He had repeatedly outlined these dangers. In early 1940 Hayes had informed Dr Jim Ryan, the Wexford (also Hayes' County), Minister for Agriculture in the Irish Cabinet, that Russell was going to Germany. Ryan was greatly perturbed at the potential for damage to the Irish State that Russell would possess in Germany and warned, that if Russell returned to Ireland he would be subject only to nominal arrest, whereas otherwise he would take steps to have Russell arrested on the high seas by the British and Americans. Hempel repeated the false rumours of Russell's arrest, murder and burial at sea by the British Secret Service in Gibraltar and recounted Dr Ryan's concern at the problem of quenching Russell's activities without offending Irish-American susceptibilities, as their support was essential to sustain the policy of neutrality. The Envoy thought that it would be a good propaganda move to confirm Hayes' story about Russell's murder and circulate it in the US – if this could be done without exposing the Irish government.[52]

It was in Germany's interests, he maintained, countering a removal proposition, that de Valera remained at the helm. He advised that these IRA-prompted intrigues against de Valera's government could only benefit the British and Americans. He advised that it was in the light of intrigue against themselves, that the Irish government viewed with apprehension Russell's links with Germany. They were not sure whether Russell, seen as a direct threat to them, was alive or dead. They were sure however about Goertz and Held because, Hayes had given Dr Ryan first-hand information on this and while they arrested Held, they allowed Goertz to go free, in order, on the one hand, to discredit the IRA, by associating their organisation with Fifth Column activities and, on the other hand, to keep Goertz under observation, in order to keep tabs on IRA-German liaison activities. The web was tangled. Hempel proffered another 'on the other hand' explanation. In the event of an attack by Britain on Ireland, the Irish government would use Goertz as a liaison officer to effect a secret treaty with Germany.[53] Held, he continued, had told the police of his talks with the Germans and of the plan of German assistance to the IRA for the Northern Ireland operations. On this point the report alleged that Dr Ryan conveyed to Hayes that the Irish government would not get involved so long as the Irish State (i.e. the 26 Counties) itself was not attacked; but that weapons destined for the IRA, badly needed by the Irish government, would be confiscated and further, that the business of Held and Goertz and the link with the IRA had made a bad impression on them regarding German bona fides.

This telegram related that Hayes' information of the 6,000 dollars brought in for the IRA by an Irishwoman living in Spain, was taken as a sign by Dr Ryan that Germany was not taking the illegal organisation all that seriously. Therefore, when they foiled Goertz's attempt to escape by boat, they took care to allow Goertz himself to remain at large.

That version of Hempel's tallies with the 'wheels within wheels' story of Lt. Gen. M.J. Costello that his First Division would have arrested Goertz but for the fact that he was allegedly accompanied by a 'hands off' uniformed Garda Siochána.[53] He refers to Cabinet ministers, Dr Ryan and Derrig, taking Hayes into their confidence regarding the contingent circumstances in which the Irish government was determined to offer 'real resistance' (Hempel used the English words thus in his report). In such circumstances (namely, the imminence of an Allied attack on Ireland), he maintained Goertz would have his uses in reaching a secret understanding between Ireland and Germany. That was indeed the stuff of 'cloak and dagger'.

Then the Envoy seemed to lose some of his cool objectivity. He referred again to the contacts between Hayes, Cabinet ministers Ryan and Goertz and came out bluntly with the opinion that the activities of Goertz were undermining his position, which he claimed, was more important than that of Goertz (*K's Tätigkeit in Irland müsse meine Stellung, die wichtiger sei als die K's, ernstlich gefährden*). To emphasise the dangers the Envoy drew attention to the fact that a brother-in-law of Hayes, named de Lacy, who worked in *The Irish Times*, played a highly suspect part in the Goertz business. Hempel conveyed that portion of the Hayes' confession which had been printed in London.[54] Seán MacBride felt that the British and Irish secret services colluded in it.

The German Minister cautioned that any arrangement involving Goertz could only be unofficial and would have to be conducted with circumspection, because, if it came to the ears of the British government it would furnish them with an instant pretext for the occupation of the ports. He had already warned that, as official German representative, he must keep Goertz at a distance to avoid giving the British an excuse to attain another of their objectives – the expulsion from Éire of the German Legation.[55] Irish goodwill was essential and contacts were important.

He was aware of Thomsen's liaison with an Irish army officer and he met other army officers including, purely formally, General Dan McKenna, the Chief of Staff,[56] to whom he referred in a respectful manner, as did everyone who knew him.[57] Interest in the Irish Army would have been normal practice for the German representative: his predecessors had established that precedent. The advent of Goertz however introduced a new dimension to the Legation's involvement in this area, which could have seriously compromised both Hempel and the Irish Army.

Goertz, after his contacts with Iseult Stuart, Helena Molony, 'V' Held, Jim O'Donovan and subsequently with Miss Maisie O'Mahony (who acted as Chaufeusse/Secretary to him), moved into a house in Dalkey, which had been got for him by a Miss Maura O'Brien. She moved there from Strand Road (Dublin) where she had been living with Mrs Austin Stack. She was picked for this 'fronting' job because she looked innocent. Goertz also stayed from time to time with the Farrell sisters in Dún Laoire (they idolised him) but the house in Dalkey became for a while his headquarters and it had a transmitter installed: Anthony Deery was the signalman. Many people, some allegedly TDs, met Goertz during this period, including one, of whom Goertz said, that he was 'very like a farmer'. Without any further evidence, Dr Ryan's name was mentioned. There is no doubt though that General Hugo McNeill, on his own initiative, visited the German agent on at least a few occasions.[58]

Goertz had the Irish Army in mind from the beginning of his mission and he had an address ready, appealing (over the head of the government) to the Irish Army to co-operate with a German landing when it came. Hayes, according to Hempel, had told the German agent that the Irish Defence Forces were to be strengthened through collaboration between the army and the IRA and had offered the German agent information about the Irish Army. This address, which, coming so soon after the Magazine Fort raid, greatly increased the apprehension of the Irish government, was confiscated when the Special Branch raided Mrs Stack's home at 167 Strand Road. It is not confirmed that the McNeills were aware of the existence of the Goertz address document.

This IRA plan to march on the North worried more people than Hempel – including some IRA members.[59] McNeill, on the other hand, seemed to have shown some sympathy towards this move, as did O'Duffy; and Thomsen, the contact man, evidently did not demur. Hempel's reservations about contacts with McNeill were hitherto confined to what he reckoned to be a personality instability in the army man. The plan to march on the North reinforced that reckoning.

German foreign policy makers, judging by their actions, appeared to have been convinced that as far as Ireland was concerned, sections of the army were at one with the IRA in favouring an aggressive anti-British policy. All that needed to be done, according to that Berlin train of thought, was to repair the relations between the illegal organisations and the supposedly sympathetic government leaders. Hempel reported that Goertz had contacts not alone with 'mavericks' like the McNeills but also with the Head of the Irish Army Intelligence who was also in contact with the Irish government.[60] When 'half the country' apparently was meeting Goertz, it would not have been extraordinary if Irish Army Intelligence had not made it their business to find out what was going on. But Hempel's report was misleading: the Head of Irish Intelligence at the time was not a Major; he was Colonel Dan Bryan and he emphatically had not met Goertz at that stage. He was outraged at the mere suggestion of liaison.[61] However, it might not be unreasonable to assume that surveillance over Goertz was exercised more or less continuously or that contact of some description would have been made with the circles in which the German agent seemed – up to now – to be able to move freely. He was a double threat to the security of the State.

He was now becoming 'too hot to handle' and Hempel accurately predicted his arrest. After that arrest the German Minister hastened to seek advice from Berlin as to how he should proceed to avoid having his association with Goertz compromise his position. The secret transmitter could have compromised him at any time. Although the volume of actual combat intelligence transmitted may have been marginal, there was, if nothing else, the transmission of additional crucial compromising weather reports. The discovery of this Goertz-McNeill-Legation triangle showed the transmitter and the existence of the other agents – in a much more sinister light.[62] Outside of Goertz, however, those other German agents – apart from embarrassing Hempel – constituted more of a consular concern than a threat to his personal position. They had not the capability to compromise him in Berlin and Dublin, in the manner that Goertz, with his Berlin benediction, IRA links and Irish Army liaisons, had.

In less guarded days (February 1940) the Envoy had sounded more knowing about Weber-Drohl (though it had to be dragged out of him) than he had about later arrivals. He expressed disapproval of such ventures in a country overflowing with spies.[63] Weber-Drohl's mission had been to deliver money to the IRA, to invite them to send a representative to Germany, to present plans for landing weapons; to warn them to limit themselves to important military objectives and to avoid wasted efforts. According to an entry in Lahausen's *Abwehr* diary (27/3/1940) Hempel confirmed by a radio transmitted telegram that Weber-Drohl had given the money to the 'Irish Friends'. The German Minister, from his messages, seemed to be 'in the know' at least. Weber-Drohl was sixty years of age and had arthritis. It did not inhibit him from having romantic interludes and, to add to Hempel's consular concerns, indulging in extra-marital procreation.[64] The German agent also wrote 'greener than green' lugubrious ultra-patriotic ballads.[65] Hempel reported (25/10/1941) that Weber-Drohl was free in Dublin but had to be supported by the Legation since 15 October 1941 at the rate of £8 per month. In this report he referred to relevant files destroyed on Tributh, Gartner and Inders.[66] He referred to Weber-Drohl as W.D. and Wr. D., but that use of an obvious initial (he used F.S. for Francis Stuart) did not mean that the Envoy had become less than circumspect in his other approaches.

Stuart, who had arrived in Berlin at the end of January (1940) with a special plea from Hempel for more discretion about the transmission of *Fichtebund* propaganda, confirmed to the *Abwehr* the disjointed nature of IRA operations. This Hempel-helped courier, according to Woermann, did not clearly indicate whether he was sympathetic to Irish nationalist aspirations or not. Stuart did convey that, contrary to instructions, the illegal organisations had used the transmitter received from the US for internal propaganda purposes instead of exclusively for operational communications and so the Irish authorities had little difficulty in locating and seizing the set, though the codes and receiver had remained intact. Jim O'Donovan looked for a replacement. The 'Dr Schmelzer' promised by Weber-Drohl to arrive and rig up a wireless station in Ireland turned out to be Goertz. (Hempel's fond hope at the outset of the war that the Irish government would participate in the erection of a radio station for communication with Berlin had been quickly dissipated.)

From the beginning, communication was a problem. On 29 October 1939, after weeks of intensive, if interrupted, efforts for both the IRA and the Legation, the chief *Abwehr* agent in Ireland, 'V' Held, restored communications. He was pressing for weapons and special items of equipment but the entry in Lahausen's Diary complains that O'Donovan's request did not contain any idea as to how the landing of these weapons was to be effected. Liaison between the *Abwehr* and the IRA was obviously bedevilled by more than technical faults in the transmitter. Different mentalities was the main impediment.

Lack of a sense of the need for security precautions by the IRA in their transmissions was a cause for more than consular concern to the German Minister. Communication from the Legation building during this period was normally by cable. (Code was used for certain messages and the Germans maintained that the British never broke that diplomatic code.) Occasionally the short wave transmitter was used – mainly for the transmission of weather reports.[67] Hempel had transmission and reception problems of his own as have been indicated by his queries for Berlin on the condenser and the wiring and operation of the set, suggesting altered frequencies. In seeking to augment the Legation staff in 1940 it was proposed to send one member who could service the secret transmitter.[68] Operation was an ongoing problem. However, Legation secret communications were a model of efficiency compared with the independent IRA efforts to establish their secret link. Hempel radioed that these efforts at communication between the IRA and the *Abwehr* were attracting the notice of the authorities. He was perturbed as this could draw attention to his own secret set which was being nursed until the time came to use it. The IRA from time to time passed information to the Legation for transmission.[69] Hempel was unimpressed by either the content of the messages or by the IRA approach. They referred to the Irish government as 'the enemy'. Woermann however told Hempel not to worry, that it was unlikely that the Irish authorities would 'get a fix' on a short wave transmitter; it was, he held, an extraterritorial matter, the internal business of the Legation. If a disavowal of the transmitter had to be undertaken he would tell Hempel what to say.[70] That did not stop Hempel from worrying. If the government had British-supplied proof of the existence of the transmitter, a denial by him would result in a serious loss of trust.[71] He sought precedent. What was the position in other countries he queried plaintively.

Hempel's fears were well grounded. The British had located the IRA transmitter in Wicklow and the German Minister reported that they had informed the Irish government that a German Code was being used.[72] The British were alerted to the existence of a transmitter by the unexpected volume of radio traffic. It was thought at first that transmissions were coming from Drogheda. The transmitter in Held's house was useless but there were other transmitters, e.g. Rathmines, Sundrive Road Mills, Clanbrassil Street.

The Envoy's reaction was to lie low and suspend his own secret transmission. In the climate of that time (15/4/1940), with the British waging intensive psychological warfare against Ireland, Hempel got an impression from Walshe that the Irish government 'didn't want to know' about his secret transmitter.[73] For reasons best known to himself – possibly the realistic perception that an ambassador without links to his own government is useless, and adopting 'a first come, first served' defence policy – it took de Valera up until the spring of 1941 to grasp this nettle of doing something about the German secret transmitter. Even then, the demand was only that radio traffic between the Legation and Berlin be cut to a minimum. Hempel resolved, if pressed, to plead that the cutting off of telegraphic facilities before the war had been insupportable, that several unsuccessful attempts had been made with the Irish side to establish communications with Berlin and it was in Irish interests to have such a link. The 'Saga of the Transmitter' went on and Hempel was still using the *Sonderweg* to receive ongoing confidential instructions about how to react to the circumstances following the arrest of Goertz (4/12/1941).[74]

He pointed out that he had warned Goertz about putting his trust in an unreliable person. The Held case vindicated him.[75] There was however no escaping the embroiling *Abwehr* contact with Goertz through his Legation. Messages from Goertz had gone out from Hempel's Legation in official code, for which the minister was responsible.[76] In spite of this, the efforts of the Italian Axis partner in Dublin to make use of the transmitter had been rebuffed by Hempel, and backed up by Berlin,[77] even though they (the Germans) had not been above seeking to use the Rome channel via London before Italy's entry into the war.[78] Telegrams sent via the USA at this stage were designed to camouflage the existence of the Legation transmitter. One of the reasons he could not accommodate the Italians was the constraint to keep its use to a minimum to avoid risk of discovery.[79]

He did not show the same circumspection in reporting Goertz' items of Combat Intelligence. He got into hot water by reporting on the American passenger ship, the *Iroquois*, which was sunk as a result by the German Navy.[80] He reported freely on troop movements and locations, post problems, censorship, the searching of the diplomatic bag, telegraphic delays and on a camouflaged concrete ship which was blocking Belfast harbour to deceive and lure either U-Boats or the Luftwaffe.[81] One of his more specious efforts drew attention to the artistic merit of photographs in the *Irish Independent* by a photographer 'Ph…ew'. There was no photographer's name which could be associated with 'Ph…ew', but there was a very good photograph of an RAF 'Fairey' battle bomber with good air photographs of Norwegian cities. This was at the time of the Invasion of Norway in April 1940,[82] which incidentally Hempel later put about was done to prevent a British attack and *um Finnland zu helfen!*[83]

Weather reports remained a preoccupation with the Envoy, and he took evasive action to ensure their transmission and reception, though German Intelligence placed more reliance on information derived from their machines positioned in the Atlantic.[84] What Hempel does not seem to have been aware of – and this could surely be presented as the greatest violation of neutrality by the Irish side – was that – under British tutelage and British Codes – the Irish Meteorological Office was daily, religiously exporting precious weather reports to London from Collinstown airport. Stephen McWeeney was the diligent, dutiful sender. If there were a danger of the information falling into German hands due to a technical hiccup, the reports were transmitted in a code supplied by the British Commonwealth Office. This was a vital unsung contribution to the British war effort.[85] Extraordinarily, Hempel did not complain: his 'V' men kept him constantly informed about anything else that savoured of re-exporting to Britain. Timber exports for example, he scrutinised with great zeal and made querulous representations to Boland if he sniffed anything at all that could be construed as a breach of neutrality.[86] It was not as if he overlooked sources.

The Curragh internees were tapped for information by Thomsen whom they regarded as an Intelligence Officer.[87] He tried (unsuccessfully) to throw dust in the eyes of the camp staff, allegedly investigating breaches of prisoners' welfare rights. Hempel turned a blind eye to these activities: he and Thomsen collaborated in completing the consequential telegrams to Berlin.[88] Hempel overtly

confined himself to exhorting the internees not to make any
trouble by attempting to escape.[89] Thomsen got on better with the
NCOs than with the officers, who regarded him as 'a strutting Nazi',
with left-wing anti-officer, anti-Junker tendencies.[90] The NCOs
would tell Thomsen things that they would not tell the minister.
They saw him as one of the old school, fuddy-duddy diplomats. The
only thing about him that interested them was the youthfulness of
Frau Hempel: they thought she was his second wife (she was not).

An incident known as the 'food farce' illustrated differences in
mentality and approach between Hempel and Thomsen, his
'Number Two'. The internees asked Thomsen how much money
was available for their food and who paid for it. Thomsen's reply was
to the effect that the Irish government had not yet paid for the
Ardnacrusha Power Station, so they could 'fire away' in ordering
provisions. They went on a shopping spree and ran up a bill for
£3,000 for all sorts of delicacies which was presented to the Irish
authorities.[91] Hempel was furious at this undiplomatic behaviour
and according to the late ex-internee Herr Voigt, he 'blew a gasket'.

Otherwise he gave Thomsen a free hand: the source was too
fruitful to pass up. The internees were well treated, sometimes
allowed out, occasionally permitted to go to Dublin.[92] Sometimes
they visited the Legation. They had a rendezvous in Mrs Bridget
Byrne's café in Liffey Street, which was also a haunt of Weber-Dohl
who, to complicate matters further, also had the finger pointed at
him for being a double agent. For these sex-starved 'POW's' trysts
naturally ensued and love and nature found a way. These liaisons
widened their information-gleaning circles. However, the
significance for information-gathering was not confined to their
romantic contacts. The NCO body in particular were in contact with
Irish workers toing and froing across the Irish Sea, who were able to
provide tit-bits of information, which were passed on to Thomsen
and fed into the intelligence process.[93] The information supplied
covered items ranging from factory locations to accounts of the
effects of Luftwaffe raids. There was a widespread Irish presence in
Britain. A large number of Irish volunteers served in the British
Forces (traditionally Ireland had been a recruiting ground for the
British Army – a facility preserved by the 1922 Treaty but revoked by
Mr de Valera). In addition, there was a very large Irish workforce
(100,000) working in Britain in industry and agriculture. Sir Herbert

Gough in a letter to the London *Times* in August 1944, said that there were 165,000 next-of-kin Irish addresses in the British Forces. Thomsen's egalitarian left-wing leanings made 'chatting up' easy with his NCO contacts.[94] His wife Hilda had the same outlook.

She 'drank like a fish', according to Fleischmann, and similarly called the officers 'big junkers'. She was an architect and worked for Mr Michael Scott, the well-known Dublin architect. Some felt however Thomsen's behaviour was more like Nazi strutting than other attitudes. Thomsen discounted that and gave a plausible reason for joining the 'Reiter SS, the only part of the SS which was acquitted of the charge of being a criminal organisation'. After the war he clashed with the then Irish Ambassador in Bonn, Dr William Warnock, because he felt slighted when he was not invited to an official function at that Embassy. He took the omission as a deliberate snub. Warnock did not deny this. Neither did he acknowledge it. He obviously disapproved. Thomsen's brazen information gathering had undoubtedly contributed to the production of combat intelligence.

Combat intelligence has been defined as being in effect that knowledge of the enemy, weather and geographical features required by a commander in the planning and conduct of tactical operations. These tactical operations at this stage involved air and sea attacks and a possible land invasion of the British Isles (Operation 'Sea-Lion'). Hempel's and Thomsen's contribution therefore was more relevant to a commander's area of interest than to his area of influence. It secured information on surveillance and on some target acquisition, i.e. detection, to permit target analysis. It all added up.

The Envoy also charily reported (15/9/1941) on the human factor, namely the aspiration of Wilheim Masgeik, a steel worker in Haulbowline, to return to Germany.[95] A Captain MacGuinness of the Irish Naval Service, who gave Masgeik to understand that he possessed material relevant to a German invasion, offered to pilot him in a motor boat to the French coast. Careful Hempel did not like the idea: the association with MacGuinness's material on prospects for a German invasion could compromise the Legation. And apart from the consideration that Masgeik would be leaving a wife, two small children and a mother behind him, the Envoy felt that his trustworthiness had to be investigated first of all.

Generally though the bulk of Hempel's reporting could hardly be technically classified as combat intelligence, but classification lines on intelligence work are hard to draw. It is difficult for instance to know how to classify the acerbic thumbnail sketches submitted through or by the Envoy in October 1940[96] (e.g. Murphy (Paris); Kearney (*sic*) (Madrid); MacWhite (Rome); MacCauley (Vatican); Cremin (League of Nations); Dulanty (London); Walshe (Dublin); Boland (Dublin); Lester (Danzig); and Kiernan).[97] This report concluded with the promise of a further instalment from 'Excellence Bewley' though Hempel did not specifically attribute this report to him (Mrs Carter mistakenly credits the German Minister with its composition).[98]

'Excellence Bewley' had had a chequered career before parting company with the Irish government just before the outbreak of the war, when he had been Hempel's opposite number in Berlin. Hempel debunked him.[99] He was supposed to be representing a Swedish Press Agency in Rome, so MacWhite, an ex-French Foreign Legionnaire, who spoke six European languages fluently with a West Cork accent[100] was asked by the Irish government to check up on him. He discovered that there was no such Swedish Agency. The Swedish Ambassador in Rome told him that 'that man's paymaster had a club-foot'. Irish intelligence presumed that 'Club-Foot' was Veesenmayer.[101] If, as Binchy relates, Bewley's paymaster had a club-foot then Bewley must be presumed to have contributed to the convoluted political thinking in Berlin that resulted in actions which made life difficult for Hempel. It is difficult however to logically deduce what picture Bewley painted.

There is little sequential logic or coherence in the intelligence sprawl. Bearing in mind his protested antipathy to de Valera's pro-British stand, he could hardly have contributed to the thinking of the Berlin Political Department, which sought to 'correct' Hempel into thinking that the government and the IRA had the same aims and differed only as to method. Bewley's anti-semiticism has been seen as far back as 1922, when he gleefully showed Binchy, then a student in Munich, a caricature in the *Völkischer Beobachter* portraying de Valera as a Jew. He now had notions that, in the wake of a Nazi victory, he would be Gauleiter of Ireland.[102] However, like the other would-be agents, his wings were now (end of 1941) being clipped by the Irish authorities. He was under surveillance by

MacWhite who hated him. (Bewley had a pronounced Oxford accent; MacWhite, deliberately, never lost his West Cork one.)

The Goertz menace too had lessened. He was now behind bars though he was supposed to have agents and a secret set, *Ulrike*, operating in the North of Ireland. The *Abwehr's* chief agent in Ireland, Jim O'Donovan 'V' Held – was interned in the Curragh. All the other agents had been picked up: in fact the romantic gullible Goertz and the uxorious charlatan Weber-Dohl were the only ones to remain at large for any length of time. Two agents, Walter Simon and Willy Preetz (by chance, a brother-in-law of an Irish army officer) landed by U-Boat in Dingle in June 1940. Their aliases were, Karl Anderson and Paddy Mitchell, respectively.

Their job was to transmit weather reports and reports of convoy movements to Germany. Simon (Anderson) was arrested almost at once. Preetz transmitted to Germany every night for a while from the loft of a small shop in Westland Row before being arrested. In July 1940 'Operation Lobster I' landed an unlikely trio of agents, Gartner, Tributh (South Africans) with an Indian Obed on the South Coast. They were quickly picked up: one of them is alleged to have asked a bus conductor a question in Irish. Schutz (Marschner) was also arrested on landing in Co. Wexford (12/3/1941). They all seemed to have been romantic (in more ways than one apparently – one of them had to be treated for VD the minute he was picked up) – and incredibly naïve. Hempel had dutifully but peevishly reported on them when they landed and were arrested; now that they were interned he was, to his relief, merely their Welfare Officer. However, he still collaborated with Thomsen, processing information milked from them and transmitted it. Still, the German menace could not yet be written off, though the pressures for Ribbentrop's thrusting of arms had eased off.

With regard to Hempel's involvement with the Irish Army there is no evidence to point to the disciplining of General Hugo McNeill or his accomplices in concocting German gun-running schemes. However, General McKenna's insistence on preoccupation with the 'nuts and bolts' of soldiering 'with the equipment they had rather than with the equipment they would like to have', ensured that McNeill would have to stick to his military last to forge a division fit for combat. That left him less time to be bothering the Legation with wild-goose schemes for arms deliveries. Hempel consequently, by the end of 1941, should have had more time to concentrate on the Consular side of his duties. Goertz however, even behind bars continued to cast a shadow over the Envoy. And the Minister Plenipotentiary, whether designedly or not, had sown seeds in his reporting, which encouraged Veesenmayer to attempt to make 'big politics' out of Ireland, in an effort to accomplish the 'Irland Faktor' Mission which had been given to him by Ribbentrop.[103] And double-edged German violations continued. The real danger arose from Allied intervention reaction.

For the most part violations were readily identifiable. They were mainly German. Identification of related IRA subversion, particularly in the cases of inserted agents, was more worrying. Inhibitions about pointing the finger at the Germans were a thing of the past.

PART III
LATE 1941–45, DENOUEMENT

CHAPTER 9

Defensive Diplomacy (mid 1941–mid 1944)

Protests continued to be made to Hempel concerning recurring German violations of Irish neutrality. These violations consisted of the clumsy intrusion of agents, persistent infringements of territorial rights and – 'the unkindest cut of all' – the dropping of bombs on Irish soil. Up to mid 1941 however, the protests made seemed to be muted in some way. Prudent cognisance had to be taken of the general impression shared by Walshe and de Valera, but not by key diplomat, Seán Murphy, of irresistible, invincible German might. Warnock's muted protests to the Germans indicated that what was even more worrying to the Irish authorities was the case for intervention the British would make of it, as proof that the Irish were unable to defend themselves.[1] That was the big worry. In mid 1941 Walshe had seemed to have consistently given Hempel an 'out' by raising the possibility of British provocation: he had put forward that 'beam bent by the British' theory to explain the North Strand bombing.[2] The Irish were resolved not to do or say anything that might give undue offence to the rampant Germans.

De Valera however was no coward: he left Hempel in no doubt but that he considered the bombings an outrage by the Germans and a flagrant breach of neutrality. With particular reference to the bombing of Dublin (31/5/1941) and a bomb dropped near Arklow (1/6/1941), the Irish government formally protested 'in the strongest manner' against the violation of Irish territory by German aircraft 'bringing death and serious injury to persons and property'.[3] Full compensation and reparation were claimed and the German government was asked for 'explicit assurances' that the strictest instructions be given to ensure that no further flights of German aircraft would take place over Irish territory or territorial waters. The German government was also reminded that no satisfactory reply had been received to the protests made to them on the previous January (1941) when 'air bombs bearing German markings' caused loss of life and damage to property in Ireland. It was emphasised that the strain imposed by 'such tragic events' might well become insupportable and the German government were urged 'to comply with the protest'.

Berlin responded, condescendingly, arrogantly. They did not seem to be unduly worried by the protests. The SS *Kyleclare* was attacked by a Junkers 88 aircraft off Brownstown Head, Co. Waterford, in spite of the fact that the ship bore such conspicuous 'Éire' neutralist markings that it was not be possible for Hempel to plead mistaken identity.[4] The fact that the Germans were on the defensive to these protests did not automatically elicit from them immediate acknowledgement and retribution. General von Waldau snidely remarked that the North Strand bombings would not have happened at all if German advice on the blacking out of Dublin had been acted on.[5] It may have been this superior attitude of the Germans that prompted Warnock to add orally to his written protest on that bombing that in spite of 'enemy propaganda' no one believed that the Germans had done the bombing on purpose.[6] Walshe's representations were interpreted by Hempel as 'friendly'. External Affairs used the occasion to put in a word with him to persuade the Germans to desist from bombing Derry, 'as the only industry there was shirt factories'. Hempel responded by reporting back on to the 'occupied area of Ireland', pointing out that 400 nationalists were interned in Crumlin-Road Belfast. The inference was that this was a target to be avoided.[7]

Ribbentrop intervened to outline to Hempel the formal reply he was to make to the Irish protest[8]: it was to be non-committal, but conciliatory, and a press release was to be agreed. Concerning the request to lift the 'blackout', Warnock explained to Woermann that the problem here was that this would give rise to a request from the British for an intensification of the blackout.[9]

Hempel agreed a press release with the Irish government in which the Germans expressed their sincere regret and 'in view of the friendly relations existing between the two countries' were prepared to give compensation 'for the deplorable loss of life and injury to persons and property'.[10] Strictest instructions were to be issued to prevent recurrence. Nevertheless, on 26 July (1941) Hempel had to report that yet another bomb had been dropped: this time in the vicinity of Dundalk by a plane returning from an air raid on Belfast. Fragments of the bomb picked up bore an imprint of the German eagle.

Yet Hempel still persisted with his hints about British and US machinations and provocations. He still insisted that he did not rule out a British attack on Ireland and felt that the danger of such an attack would increase with the entry of the US into the war. He referred in the same breath to the problem of conscription in Northern Ireland and the foundering of Frank Aiken's arms purchasing mission in the US.[11] It is possible then to read some significance into the Envoy's report that de Valera was pleased with the German reply to the Irish protest,[12] especially when the same report refers to Walshe's accommodating attitude[13] and also when the German Minister was given a hearing from both de Valera and Walshe regarding the German point of view on the 'blackout' problem. Then the Envoy reported more specifically on Aiken's return from the US and the failure of the mission, with the exception that the Irish politician *had* got support from Irish-Americans for the neutrality position.

This was followed by a report from Thomsen that nine RAF internees had escaped from the Curragh. (Hempel deferred for guidance a request from the German internee, Oberleutnant Mollenhauer, that representations be made to the Irish government to free a corresponding number of interned Germans.) This tit-for-tat aspiration of the German internees went on throughout this period until after a transfer of RAF internees in November 1943. Hempel reported that only eleven British remained out of the original forty interned and that he was looking for an interview with de Valera to complain about this. He had previously protested to Boland at the transfer of a batch of eleven RAF pilots to Gormanstown, a base convenient to the Border. There was little doubt that the RAF men were treated more leniently than the Luftwaffe crews were.

Hempel refused to recognise the new Irish practice of a 'non-operational' interpretation which favoured the Allies.[14] But he was surprised later to find that the Irish government had been actively negotiating with the British government to arrange the return of German internees. The British Foreign Office was prepared to negotiate accordingly as, in that case, the remainder of the British pilots would be released. Hempel's supposition was that the Swiss practice was based on releasing two Germans for every three British. But he also reported that the British Secret Service were opposed to any such arrangement.[15] He also reported the escape of a German internee and his recapture in Barry, Wales, in the hold of the SS *Lanarone*, which was *en route* to Lisbon.

Of more concern was what he saw (17/4/1941) as high pressure US diplomacy in action in the person of Colonel Donovan visiting de Valera. He had a further related account (11/11/1941) on the American-Irish Defence Association, the activities of Senator Wheeler and the intervention of Colonel Donovan's propaganda staff in Irish affairs. These activities kept him on the defensive. He countered US propaganda in Ireland on 'the Nazi war against the Catholic Church', by issuing Bulletins of his own.[16]

An attack on him by Germanophobe Deputy Dillon however (*'grösster Hasser neuen Deutschland's'*) ensured for Hempel a spreading of the Taoiseach's protective wing. Dillon was a bitter enemy of de Valera's policy of 'neutrality' (*'gleichzeitig scharfer Gegner de Valera's'*). Hempel lodged a formal complaint (29/1/1942) that the Speaker in the Dáil had not intervened to restrain 'an intemperate attack on Germany' by Dillon: an attack, Hempel said, based on the 'so-called confessions' of the IRA Chief of Staff, Stephen Hayes. Dillon and de Valera were foils for one another and Hempel regularly reported their neutrality jousts. Dillon's rhetorical Churchillian affectations were matched by de Valera's flat Bruree polemics. The German Legation was constantly under fire from Dillon, and Hempel was a butt.

He branded Dillon as a German hater and called him a Jew. He recorded Dillon's taunt that de Valera had been quick to protest at the American landing in Northern Ireland but did not protest at all against the German bombing of Belfast. De Valera's retort unintentionally took the IRA line: such a protest should be made, not to Germany, but to those who dragged Northern Ireland into the war against her will.[18] That exasperated outburst at Dillon's posturing did not do justice to de Valera. He openly cast neutrality circumspections aside and sent all available fire brigades to Belfast to succour his Northern brethren. The bombs were not distinguishing prod from papist. To him, they were all Irishmen and and attack on any of them was regarded by him as an attack on Ireland. He responded accordingly.

De Valera himself however was under pressure from all sides from December 1941 onwards: British and American pressures, goads and gibes from James Dillon, in addition to German incursions, alarms and attacks. Hempel heard of additional pressure on him from a chink in the solidarity of his Cabinet, as he, without unanimity, had rebuffed Allied suggestions to enter the war on their side. The Envoy reported two dissenting voices in the Cabinet, but he did not name them, nor name his source.[19] One minister, Seán McEntee, a former leading Belfast republican and veteran of the War of Independence and the republican side in the Civil War, was reported to be strongly, vociferously, pro-British.

All de Valera's apprehension – even for bombings – was not reserved for the Germans: a later (1943) concrete example serves to illustrate such on-going concerns. Ammunition fragments found after an attack on the *Kerlogue* were British. The British admitted their error. The *Kerlogue* was off course – and they offered to pay compensation (Hempel 4/12/1943). This information was released in response to Dillon's persistence in trying to pin it on the Germans.

These on-going concerns with the Allies did not soften Irish attitudes to German violations of neutrality, and if anything, a more peremptory tone had been noticeable in official protests to Berlin (20/10/1941).[20] The Irish government could not understand 'the very long delay' in replying definitely to their protest concerning bombs dropped by German aircraft at several points on Irish territory on 1st, 2nd and 3rd of the previous January. They again reminded the German government that further failure to accept responsibility and to offer speedy reparation, aggravated the bad effects such incidents had on the relations between the two countries. The Irish government impressed 'once more' the necessity for giving the German airmen the strictest instructions to avoid flying over Irish territory and territorial waters. It was not the first time such a protest had been made; but this time the tone was sharper and no reports appear of accommodating remarks from either Warnock or Walshe. In general, Hempel had counselled making concessions to the Irish representations. The bombs must be German and all the Irish government really wanted was a friendly answer.[21] The atmosphere was changing.

Around the autumn of 1941, Hempel's reports had become preoccupied at a diplomatic level with Goertz. They signposted the way to the steps taken that led to the eventual capture of the agent, and raised his presence to a matter of acute inter-governmental concern. Hempel's defensive diplomacy was now immersed, on the one hand, with 'keeping himself covered' in Dublin and, on the other hand, with relaying the party line from Berlin. Clissmann had advised Lahausen on the reply to Woermann's query requesting the *Abwehr's* attitude to the position to be adopted by Hempel on the arrest of Goertz.[22] Hempel was to say, that, naturally, he had heard stories about Goertz but that he had no official information about him. He could state categorically that Goertz had no mission against Ireland otherwise he (Hempel), as official representative, would have known it! He was then advised on an intelligence level to seek a meeting with Goertz to find out how much the agent had disclosed after his arrest. With regard to the other activities of Goertz, such as chartering a military aircraft, Hempel was to say that he could only presume that the agent was simply acting on his own initiative. There is an indication in this directive to a contribution by Clissmann to the incorrigible false assumptions made by the Political Department in Berlin, namely, that 'it was alright' so long as the agents were not acting against Ireland. It was still not fully comprehended in Berlin – acting presumably on Irish source advice – that a cornerstone of de Valera's 'certain consideration for Britain' was his reiterated determination that Ireland would not be used as a base for operations against that country. Hempel had stressed that point time after time. There was an iron resolve in Dublin not to allow Ireland to be used as a base for an attack against England: this was the essence of Irish neutrality.

In seeking to calm the Irish government and avoid compromising himself, Hempel was adamant that Goertz had no authority whatsoever to contact the Irish Army.[23] He protested too much that he knew next to nothing about the activities of Goertz or the agent's mission. His certitude on such a delicate matter, as interference tantamount suborning the Forces of the State, betrayed him. Walshe reacted sharply in his stinging rebuke to him. He was vitriolic about Goertz's contacts with the IRA, 'who constituted a danger to the State'.[24] The agent's outrageous effrontery in attempting to subjoin the army, the cornerstone of the State, touched a raw nerve on the Irish side.

On that point, prickly Walshe kept Hempel on the defensive. When the German Minister expressed his perturbation at de

Valera's 'friendly neutral' reference to the USA in a Cork speech on that country's entry into the war (7/12/1941), Walshe did not reply directly, but rounded on the Envoy that disgraceful incidents like the Goertz affair should never occur again. Eventually however, it was the Irish Minister for Justice, Gerry Boland, who annoyed Hempel most by making capital out of Goertz. Boland's utterances stung Goertz as well, who felt that they had impinged on his honour as an officer. Hempel reported that Goertz had given all his codes and diaries to an Irish Army Officer and that neither he, nor the IRA, ever had any intention of interfering with the integrity and neutrality of Éire, Those were their words: their actions spoke otherwise. Hempel dismissed Boland's accusations of Goertz and the IRA as unfair and ill-informed and made for internal political purposes; he referred to the Minister for Justice as 'insignificant'.[25]

But the Irish government had been very concerned that the presence of Goertz had provided a pretext for unfavourable propaganda against their capability to maintain neutrality (the German agent, it was felt, could have been particularly dangerous in the conscription crisis). After consideration it was resolved, in spite of Hempel's objections, that publicity was a means of countering this propaganda.[26] The reason for this, Hempel had reported, lay in de Valera's continued stress on the threat that existed from *both* the Germans and the Allies. The Envoy in fact had reported the Taoiseach as complaining that the Irish people did not seem to be fully alive to the dangers which were threatening them. They of course, were oblivious of all this '*uisce faoi thalamh*' (water under the ground), and ignorance could be bliss: the 'need to know' rule was enforced.

Anyway the entry of America into the war (coupled with the German attack on Russia) had ostensibly lessened the impact of Germany on Irish affairs.[27] The main danger after 1941 centred on the possibility of injudicious action by the Legation giving the Allies a pretext for intervention. That danger was more real than it appears on the surface. The mere presence of a German representative with his Legation in Dublin was regarded by the Allies as, not just an irritant and an affront, but as a major security risk, not to be endured. The presence of the radio transmitter in the Legation was an obvious target for these doubts and fears. In this area, American impatience was made manifest in less subtle ways than those employed by the more experienced British.

Portents of American pressures were not wanting before the US actually entered the war. On 9 August 1941 Hempel had reported the arrival of a further 400 technicians and workers in Northern Ireland to build a base for 'Lease and Lend', operations.[28] The previous month (26/7/1941) he had reported Deputy Dillon's call for full help, short of sending troops, for the Allied cause because it was a fight for Christianity and Ireland should be on the side of the democracies. He had also reported (1/10/1941) that Irish Senator, Frank McDermott, was campaigning in the USA, 'with a small group of Irish-American renegades for Ireland's entry into the war on the Allied side'.[29] Hempel's inside information seemed to have been so good that he was able to relay de Valera's exact words to describe the American Minister Gray as an *unmöglicher Mann*', an impossible man.[30] According to Hempel, Gray, a relative of Roosevelt's, had full power to acquire bases for US cruisers to counter German U-Boat and Luftwaffe attacks. The German Minister, quoting Cordell Hull's expressed intention not to seek port facilities from Ireland for the present, thought that America's hands were full with the war in the Pacific. Such tensions eased somewhat after de Valera's 'friendly neutral' speech in Cork (14/12/1941) and his assurance that there would be no US attack on Ireland. Gray, however, was reported by Hempel to be a malevolent influence but he was unable to say whether the American representative was pressurising de Valera on his own initiative, or whether he was acting on Washington instructions, to test the Taoiseach. Sumner Wells would give no official guarantee that US troops would not be used against Ireland.[31] The tensions arising from the aggressive attitudes of both belligerents were neverending, in spite of de Valera's expeditious assurances.

Hempel's account (16/12/1941) of sharp words, used to de Valera by Gray and Maffey on a joint call (9/12/1941), confirmed those ongoing Allied pressures for the use of the ports. Hempel held that de Valera's expression of 'a friendly neutral' was made as a concession to these pressures.[32] The day previous to the time referred to in Hempel's report (8/12/1941), Maffey had made his nocturnal delivery to the Taoiseach of Churchill's 'now or never' – 'A Nation Once Again' telegram. It was an offer which de Valera could and did refuse.[33] The shadow of John Redmond, the Irish Party leader, who traded an unfulfilled promise of Home Rule for similar commitments in World

War I, inhibited the ready acceptance of such British suggestions by Irish politicians. Hempel did not refer to the Churchill approach in this report, in which, incidentally, he does refer to his own source of information as being 'personally trustworthy, in general, well-versed in political relationships, but inexperienced, credulous and imprecise'. Who could that have been?

Hempel's inside information did not seem to have provided him with any immunisation to attacks from Walshe, who was increasingly showing him the grumpy side of his character. The deferential days blaming British provocation for every German transgression had gone. This reflected a change in the country's mood. At the outbreak of the war with Russia, Hempel said, there had been a swell of feeling in Germany's favour but that had now changed and no one in Ireland had sympathy for either the Germans or the Japanese, although the entry of America into the war had increased the danger for Ireland. He would not commit himself to predicting an Allied 'Irish adventure'. He concluded that the widespread expectation in the Irish Army was that there would definitely be either a British or American attack, but that there were no significant military indications of this happening immediately. He had reported de Valera's reiterated determination (14/12/1941) to defend Irish neutrality: '. . . *habe (de Valera) festgestellt, dass kein inch des nationalen Territoriums zu Verkauf stünde*'.[34] 'Not an inch' of the national territory was for sale. The landing of American troops in NI nevertheless, caught the Envoy unawares. He reported the news of the landing as 'probably a journalistic sensation'![35]

All this Allied pressure on the Irish government still did not ease the pressure of the Irish government on Hempel. The rankling Goertz imbroglio involving the IRA (Hayes), the Irish Army, General O'Duffy, the Legation, and what was tantamount to hijacking an Irish military aircraft,[36] provided material for Walshe to keep Hempel on the defensive. He never let up. Hempel reported Walshe's doubts about a British–American attack and the Irish official's hopes that America's entry into the war would not have changed German attitudes to Ireland.

Whenever Hempel sought any elucidation, Walshe repeatedly quenched him, going on and on about Goertz's activities, which he kept on 'rubbing' in, had grievously affronted Irish sovereignty. Hempel was never going to be allowed to forget Goertz. He reported that talks were conducted in a generally 'cool atmosphere'. If the Allies had found the Goertz affair a convenient stick with which to beat the Irish government, the latter, in turn, made full use of it to belabour Hempel.

He was scheduled to have a meeting with de Valera in the New Year (1942) and he sought guidance as to how to proceed to try to remedy the deteriorating relationships between the two countries. He recommended that Germany make a fresh declaration of intent to maintain respect for Irish neutrality and – conscious of the increasing Allied pressures for the ports – a statement indicating German willingness to respond to an Irish request for aid in the event of a British or American attack, as well as (with de Valera's concurrence) further talks on the nature of the help. Woermann analysed Hempel's requests, commenting in the process on reports of British rumours of impending German attacks on either Spain, Portugal, Turkey or Ireland. (Woermann did not think it a bad thing to keep the enemy guessing as to German intentions.)[37] He was of the opinion that, as Hempel had already made a declaration to Walshe in December 1940[38] and to de Valera in February 1941,[39] it should not now be necessary to reiterate that position. He could say, that *Germany would continue to respect Irish neutrality so long as Ireland respected it.* He did not approve of the Envoy reopening the question of German aid, though he did agree that Hempel could remind de Valera of Germany's intention to stand by those declarations made in December 1940 and in February 1941. He added that Veesenmayer, who was in Berlin at the time, had been acquainted of the position.

It took Woermann a further telegram (29/12/1941) to tell Hempel to convey to the Irish government that they were over-reacting to the Goertz affair. Woermann gave the same old invalid excuses: Goertz was only operating against England; no one was sent from Germany to operate against Ireland.[40] Hempel replied (9/1/1942) that all efforts on his part to minimise that business had failed. The Irish government had refused to be mollified: a couple of days later however he was able to report some easing of the tension.[41] Notwithstanding that, a Lieutenant-Colonel von Falkenstein of the army planning staff, tangentially telephoned Eisenlohr in the Foreign Ministry to say that, following the sending of American troops to Northern Ireland, the question of delivering weapons to the Government of Éire was considered and that the execution of this concept was deemed by the special staff to be feasible. The army wanted to know whether there were any political snags![42]

The German right hand truly did not know what the left hand was doing. Woermann had already dealt with Hempel's queries in this matter and had ruled out, for the time being, the further pressing of arms on de Valera. If Ireland were attacked, however, he foresaw, 'on the other hand', that the Irish and the Germans would be drawn into a common front and he envisaged preparations – presumably involving Hempel – being made for such a contingency. Kapitän z.s. Bürkner (*OKW Abteilung Ausland*) was informed of this position.[43]

So, apart from the agents – every one of whom was used to reproach Hempel – the scene had been set to keep the German Minister on the defensive. The reality of the Goertz threat to neutrality had been exposed. Furthermore, America was not only in the war but her combat troops were on Northern Ireland soil. In addition, Gray and Maffey had spread the rumour that a German invasion had been planned for March 1942 and on 18 February 1942 Warnock presented another protest giving details of further German violations of Irish air space.[44] Pressure on the German representative was mounting and in those circumstances the presence of the secret transmitter was becoming less and less tolerable to the Allies. Accordingly, the Irish government themselves were constantly on the defensive because they were permitting the existence of that transmitter on their territory.

The changing attitudes towards tolerating the transmitter on the Irish side, in many ways symbolised the changing relationships between Hempel and his Irish counterparts, which were, naturally, conditioned by the changing fortunes of the war. It was a long drawn out story. In April 1941 Walshe intimated to Hempel in a 'careful, understanding, and friendly' fashion that they were aware of the existence of the transmitter.[45] By August (1941) Hempel reported that since the end of June the British House of Commons and Press were making a fuss about the danger of the Legation's transmitter[46] and that de Valera had requested (18/12/1941) the German Minister 'in friendly terms' to restrict the use of the wireless transmitter in the Legation to cases of the utmost urgency and importance.[47] However in the following February (1942) when it was suggested that weather information transmitted by the Legation radio had helped the German battleships *Scharnhorst* and *Gneisenau* to break through the St George's Channel (Operation 'Cerberus'), the issues became more urgent and Hempel's designation of Walshe's representations on the matter as 'friendly' could not disguise the seriousness which de Valera now attributed to the matter.[48]

Walshe confronted the German Minister with texts of recent transmissions which had been supplied by the British. When Hempel pleaded the Hague Convention to support his legal entitlement to use the transmitter, de Valera's adamant instructions once again were to indicate that Ireland would not be used as a base to damage Britain. Hempel quoted in his report from an *Irish Press* leading article to prove that the weather report could not have emanated from Ireland, as the weather in question came from the North-West! That point of view seemed to have had more political motivation than meteorological substance. That 'north-west' weather fiction was maintained. Revealingly, neutrality-wise, weather reports were secretly sent on official line from 'Éire' to Britain every single day of the war; crucially on 6 June 1944, when Eisenhower's decision to go ahead with the D-day landing was decided by a weather report from Blacksod Bay, Co. Mayo.[49]

Hempel's version of British reaction was that they were using Irish neutrality as a scapegoat to salve their loss of prestige in permitting the ships to escape. The set was not confiscated at that time but the Envoy was made fully aware that any further use of the transmitter would lead to its immediate confiscation. Hempel advised giving up using the set for the time being, as it was extremely important to hold on to the set at all costs; he probably had Ribbentrop's charge to him in mind.[50] His counsel was to lie low for the present to preserve the set for future operational use.

Other events kept cropping up in 1942 however which took the focus off the transmitter. Hempel reported that Lieutenant Thornton (Irish Army Air Corps) had been convicted by court martial and sentenced to one and a half years' hard labour.[51] The officer had been charged with the acquisition of an aircraft for the purposes of flying to Brest. Hempel recorded Thornton's relationship with Goertz and the allegation that Thornton was the officer who was supposed to fly the agent back to Germany (in a military aircraft referred to in the alleged contacts between Goertz and General NcNeill).[52] Hempel played down the Goertz connection. Indiscipline, he held, was the reason for Thornton's conviction and punishment; nothing to do with Goertz. He stressed that no evidence was offered at the court martial of the proposed journey to Brest with Goertz. However, accelerating events on the battle front were cutting arguments short.

In earlier days the Irish government had expressed (25/4/1940) appreciation of a U-Boat's friendly handling of the ship *Irish Willow* off the Donegal coast. It was a different story after a German aircraft attacked and sank (2/6/1942) the Irish *City of Bremen* about 130 miles south-west of Mizen Head (the crew was picked up and landed at a Spanish port in (6/6/1942). The Irish government protested most strongly against the attack which, they hammered was a cause of profound resentment to them:

> The sinking of this vessel is not only an attack on Ireland's vital interests, depriving her of sorely needed tonnage and supplies, but it also constitutes a flagrant disregard of Irish neutrality and sovereign rights.[53]

A fortnight later however, Warnock took the sting out of that protest by surmising that the pilot would never have attacked if he had known that the ship was Irish and Hempel reported a rumour in the Irish Army that it was a British pilot who did it. When it was conclusively proved that it was a German attack, Boland quietly pointed out to Hempel that he hoped that it was an accident.[54] The ship (which ironically had been thanked by the Reich in 1939 for rescuing a German crew) was sailing outside convoy and was conspicuously and unmistakably identified as Irish. Thus confronted, Hempel's advice to Berlin was to handle the affair in the friendliest fashion possible and to pay compensation.

In spite of this conciliatory mood, Warnock's watering down and Boland's 'other cheek' quietness, other attitudes on the Irish side towards Germany and Hempel were hardening. Hempel reported a 'rocket' he received from Walshe: the Secretary had phoned the Envoy repeatedly and got no reply. He subsequently sharply rebuked (in French) Hempel who reported: '*Er bitte instandig dies auch nicht wieder zu tun*', it was not to happen again. As always however pressures on Irish neutrality were never from one side only. Hempel reported a flying visit from US representative Bullit to de Valera, though he was unable to explain its political significance: it was totally unexpected.[55]

'Bread and butter' issues also demanded his attention. He reported that, due to shortage of fertiliser, tillage had fallen drastically in 1942 and that there was a tendency to return to cattle raising. This, he explained, had the effect of increasing unemployment and the unemployed were forced to go to England where they were welcomed. In his opinion, a reversion to cattle from tillage, meant increased exports of cattle, bacon and butter, which was to England's advantage: the corollary was Germany's disadvantage. Hempel, on Boland's representation, recommended that Berlin contact the French government, in order to facilitate the import to Ireland of phosphate: imports, which had fallen from approximately 96,000 t. in 1939 to almost 9,000 t. in 1941. In the first six months of 1942 only 598 t. of superphosphate and no rock phosphate was imported. He reported that an attempt to develop phosphate production in County Clare had met with little success.[56] The following year he observed (9/4/1943) that the economic situation was not so bad as to give credence to the rumour that de Valera was showing signs of deviating from his neutrality policy; though he did throw in doubts about the use of a good new airfield, rumoured as being built at Cashel, Co. Tipperary: for whose use, he did not specify. He hinted at British.[57]

At the same time he never took his eye off the political scene. He reported the results of the General Election of 22 April 1943 in which Fianna Fáil lost their absolute majority but still formed the government. The Cosgrave Fine Gael Party (regarded by Hempel as pro-Allied), lost thirteen seats. Hempel attributed the Fine Gael losses to that Party's pro-British leanings, pointing out that the losses were incurred despite a clever well-conducted national government campaign. He cited the *Manchester Guardian,* which was the only British paper to support the Envoy's view, that the results represented support for de Valera's policy of 'strict neutrality'. He advised the German Radio and Press to take the line that de Valera, by his clear energetic and successful policy, had earned the trust of the people. Only for this, Hempel felt that Fianna Fáil losses would have been much higher, especially if all the hardships that the people had to endure were taken into account.[58] Nevertheless, the result was that, as a leader of a minority government, de Valera was in a precarious position and more politically vulnerable than previously. The Taoiseach, however, did not noticeably trim his political sails defensively, but he did have to modify his attitude towards Hempel, by publicly tempering his 'certain' consideration for Britain and being *seen* to be more even-handed. That had many aspects.

Prior to the Italian surrender, 13 September 1943, the Irish government had, with German agreement, chartered an Italian ship – *C Gerolimich* – from the Italian government. The German government, after the Italian surrender, were in no hurry to release the ship as had been arranged, and de Valera had perforce to go 'cap in hand' to Hempel, to solicit his good offices in facilitating its release. He relayed de Valera's explanation that the 1943 harvest had been bad and that if they did not get this ship, he would be left with no option but to ration bread, which would disadvantage him politically, having lost his overall majority in the Dáil in the recent elections. Hempel did not let the opportunity pass and inferred that the difficulties may well have been of the Irish government's own making and may have been caused by a weakening in the Irish resolution to maintain neutrality. He reported de Valera's protestation of their intention to maintain neutrality to the end of the war but alleged that de Valera expressed doubts that small countries could remain neutral in a future war.[59] He had reported Allied pressure to change the Irish neutrality posture to a stance of technical 'non-belligerency', which would be designed, he said, to permit the Allies to use the ports. He had also reported Deputy Dillon citing Portugal as an example for Ireland to follow as, in spite of being neutral, that country was able to assist in countering the U-Boat campaign, by leasing bases in the Azores. Nothing was what it seemed. 'Bread and butter', life and death, not doctrinaire principles were the guiding lines for small nations, struggling desperately to survive by hook or by crook and stay afloat. Dillon's admired Portugal was also sending wolfram throughout the war to make German guns, shells and submarines.

Using the request opening to get in a complaint to de Valera presently about the inadequacies of telegraphic communications, Hempel indicated a willingness to assist. To do otherwise, he explained, would only serve to increase Irish dependence on the Allies. He was instrumental in procuring the ship and the Italian representative later contributed towards having the charter renewed. Wheat was imported accordingly, and thanks, in part anyway, to Hempel's intervention de Valera did not have to ration bread and so run the risk of a defeat in the Dáil and the possible loss of a subsequent general election.

So it was not all defensive diplomacy for the German Minister and indeed, on the grounds of avoiding putting neutrality in jeopardy, his reactions were the opposite of defensive. In his opinion it was the pro-British Irish actions which were doing the jeopardising. On 15 August 1943 he reported that he had good grounds for an official protest at the manner in which the Irish government was releasing Allied pilots.[60] This pragmatic connivance – not to be confused with collusion – on the part of the Irish government was covered up by making a ruling that only those who made forced landings during *operational* flights would be held.[61] Hempel found the distinction between operational and non-operational questionable and he cited numerous instances to illustrate the benevolent attitude shown by the Irish authorities to Allied landings, though he acknowledged that the geographical situation militated against according reciprocal treatment to the Germans. A badly damaged '*Liberator*' landed in Galway (15/1/1943) with six high-ranking officers, including four generals from North Africa (but not Eisenhower, as Hempel had originally speculated). It was transported to Northern Ireland and the officers were facilitated on their way. Hempel was puzzled by Boland's quiver of excuses, especially the Assistant Secretary's assertion that this was normal passenger traffic; that they were only following the example of the Swedes and the Swiss; but, anyway, they would never allow the Foynes line to be used for military purposes. (Normally Hempel had found Boland to be helpful: '*Namentlich Boland erleictert mir meine hiesige Arbeit wesentlich*', 10/4/1943.) British and American mechanics, he complained further, flew in, in civilian attire, to get Allied aircraft back in the air. Although he confessed, that he could not indicate how the Irish government could correspondingly compensate the Germans, on 27 July 1943 he presented a formal note of protest. He had already protested at British violations of airspace, including a protest to Walshe (15/9/1942) at the shooting down of Hauptmann Bernt and his crew by pursuing Spitfires. They made a forced landing in the Tramore area. Nicely-calculating de Valera appeared to be showing openly less forbearance to the Germans. It was difficult for him to keep glowering at them when he was looking for something from them: but he did. The Legation quoted the Taoiseach's reaction to the torpedoing by the Germans of the *Irish Oak* on 19 May 1943. In a Dáil reply de Valera said that 'it was a wanton and inexcusable act. There was no possibility of a mistake, the conditions of visibility were good and the neutral markings on our ships were clear. There was no warning given'.

The Irish approach to the problem of what attitude to adopt to Allied air crews, who were winning the war, was one of realism. De Valera demonstrated that he could bend a little under pressure and this flexibility was simply realistic. In Hempel's eyes, however, it was evidence of bowing to Allied pressures for a milder application of the rules governing internment to their servicemen and, as such, was construed by the German Minister as a breach of neutrality. This was dismissed by the Irish side. In rejecting Hempel's protestations that the Irish government's conduct was scarcely neutral, de Valera pointed out that blow-by-blow parity of treatment was not possible, as returning Germans could bring back significant military information, such as links with the IRA. The Irish did not accept that German pilots in the area could possibly be classified as non-operational, though Hempel and some crews did try on that line, namely that the pilots concerned were on training flights.[62] To him, de Valera's semantics exposed the façade of strict absolute Irish neutrality. But de Valera never said that it was so: he openly acknowledged the vital need to show 'a certain consideration for Britain'. This 'Irish solution' did not mean that it was not real. Serious Britons saw that. The others were irreclaimable.

Hempel maintained a critical approach to Irish actions and attitudes and reported that he had formally warned de Valera that the new Irish practice of interpreting 'operational' and 'non-operational' in favour of the Allies constituted a definite infringement of neutrality. He did not find it that easy to pin de Valera down and his difficulty was apparent when he attempted to analyse a speech (5/10/1943) in which the Taoiseach reasserted, in tones reminiscent of 1940, that if they were attacked by one side they would seek aid from the other. This did not indicate any change in maintaining the policy of neutrality, but at the back of de Valera's *déjà vu* wordings was an awareness of Germany's reduced military capabilities and the Allies' growing strength: *real-politik*. The Taoiseach was really setting his stance for the defensive posture he was to adopt when the anticipated situation came to a crisis point with Gray's presentation of the infamous 'American Note', which de Valera chose to interpret as an ultimatum. A note of defeatism crept into Hempel at this point as he too noted the weight of Allied pressures (without identifying the demands of the American Minister, David Gray). He diagnosed de Valera's main concern as being for the fate of Ireland after the war, if she happened to become embroiled in the conflict against the Allies and if Germany did not emerge a clear-cut victor. The unthinkable could now be expressed by the German representative.

In Hempel's opinion de Valera's expectations of help from Germany had grown less. The fundamental fact was that de Valera never ceased to single-mindedly pursue his anti-partition policy and Germany's possible use towards achieving that aim had diminished drastically. There was also a growing irritation with Germany on the part of the Irish government (in contrast with the forbearance shown when the Germans were winning). They now sharply expressed their annoyance that Francis Stuart had used the German radio to interfere in Irish elections. They had no objections to Germans interesting themselves in Irish affairs, but when the opposition party was attacked on German radio, it could seem as if the government had sought German assistance against Fine Gael.[63] Whatever use might once have been made of the German card to bring about reunification, it was now obviously no longer obtained. And there was no dividends any longer in adopting a compliant position. It seemed that there was not much damage the Germans could do – but they could!

Towards the end of December 1943, literally out of the blue, more 'cowboy' agents (O'Reilly and Kenny) were parachuted into the Kilkee area in Co. Clare, and Hempel was put on the defensive more than he had ever been before. His subsequent telegram to Berlin conveyed a tone of puzzled pain that such events could still occur, apparently without the knowledge of the Foreign Ministry.[64] It gave formidable substance and reinforcement to Gray's pressures on de Valera to remove the diplomatic representatives of the Axis nations.

Hempel reported (22/12/1943) the landing of the two Irishmen (who had been overtaken by the German blitzkreig in 1940 while working in the Channel Islands). One of them, O'Reilly, had been an announcer for some time on German radio. Two transmitters had been brought in and one of the agents told of SS training before being sent to Ireland to carry out espionage against England. They got no chance to operate as they were picked up at once. Not only Hempel, but Veesenmayer also, was outraged at this piece of irresponsibility and further evidence of German disarray. Veesenmayer had actually discarded the proposal to employ John Francis O'Reilly and a companion (Mullally or Kenny) as agents in Ireland. He knew that they were 'chancers' without any training, who would not keep their mouths shut.

It has been intended to insert yet another agent in Ireland and Veesenmayer, in his own handwriting (2/9/1942) intimated that this was in order, but only if a full guarantee were given that Isebart (the agent in question) worked exclusively in Northern Ireland and that the Hamburg *Abwehr* branch reported regularly to the Foreign Ministry Department regarding progress and results, as these were of importance to him with regard to his own special assignment.[65] But from the beginning of 1943 Veesenmayer took steps to discourage the employment of O'Reilly and a companion as agents (Mulally initially; eventually Kenny).[66] He complained bitterly to Canaris when his advice was not taken and the two ill-trained agents landed by parachutes in December 1943 equipped with transmitters for a spying mission. He was not surprised at the reaction of Canaris as he suspected that he was a subverting mole. The spies, O'Reilly and Kenny, landed, not in Northern Ireland, but near Kilkee in Co. Clare and were quickly picked up.

Veesenmayer and Hempel shared the same sense of outrage that such a thing could be done without consultation with the Foreign Ministry Veesenmayer passed on Haller's unflattering memorandum on O'Reilly to the Foreign Ministry. Haller described O'Reilly as a pig-headed opportunist whose father was an RIC man. He graduated from hotel work in London to potato picking in the Channel Islands, factory work in Germany to a chance appointment in the radio service. He wrote scripts for a James Blair ('Pat O'Brien') and made an impression as a broadcaster. Nothing was too bizarre for the broadcasting coterie under Mahr and O'Reilly found himself involved in Irish *coup d'état* pipe dreams. O'Reilly's companion, Mulally, was depicted as an irresponsible, albeit affable, chatterbox. Haller also incidentally referred to an acquaintanceship between O'Reilly and Mulally with Frank Ryan and Francis Stuart in Berlin.[67] Walshe's opinion of the agents harmonised with Haller's. He complained bitterly to Hempel that the American Note crisis was attributable to 'those damned parachutists'.[68]

Walshe paraded Hempel and the Envoy relayed to Berlin de Valera's disturbance at the incident and his stern demand that the Legation transmitter be handed up at once, as it now, without a doubt, constituted a threat to neutrality. The situation had drastically altered. Boland had once confided to Hempel (12/2/1942) that the Irish government's intention to build a special transmitter in the West of Ireland to establish links with the Vatican (purely on Church matters) and with Germany had been opposed by the British, even in peacetime. Its main object – apart from the Vatican link – was to have been the transmission of meteorological information. But those days of cosy academic chatting with Boland about transmitters were now over, as was the luxury that the Irish government had indulged in, of regarding the right to permit – or not to permit – the existence of the transmitter as being symbolically associated with their concept of sovereignty. The need to survive shed pretence. The invasion of Europe was then in the desperate throes of preparation and Churchill was very anxious lest the Axis mission in Dublin could jeopardise that mighty critical undertaking. He was particularly worried that the 'German Ambassador' would send 'a wireless warning of zero even though it was the last he was able to send'.

The British probably knew about the transmitter all along, but said nothing about it. With their code-breaking facility, it provided a ready-made reservoir of information. The imminence of D-day however, when a stray word could jeopardise life-and-death split-second decisions, made confiscation imperative and numbered the transmitter's days.

Hempel again complained that the loss of the transmitter would ensure their total dependence on their enemies for communications. He had also threatened that they would consider reducing the status of the Legation to that of a Trade Representative, as the Irish had done with their office in Berlin, implying that he would be recalled. Walshe remarked obliquely about deciphering problems (presumably British) with messages from the Dublin Legation and the Vatican.[69]

There was also British disquiet (25/1/1944) at the rescue of German shipwrecked sailors by an Irish ship and their landing at an Irish port. The Allies were apprehensive about augmenting a German presence in Ireland as this automatically widened the net of espionage possibilities: the landing in Normandy – Operation 'Overlord' – (6/6/1944) was then less than five months away. Irish attitudes had changed. Walshe was constantly rude and gruff to him, but Hempel put this down to Walshe's poor health. Walshe, he maintained, was the same with other representatives. Walshe did indeed have a reputation for being irritable and vindictive. He blighted some careers and for years one of his staff (Mr McCarthy) only communicated with him by letter. On the other hand he did make a seminal contribution to the creation of the Department of External Affairs.[70]

Hempel also complained of an attack by Irish soldiers on a German internee, Hauptmann Müller. The Germans made a big fuss over this. Müller was admitted to the Curragh Hospital. He had a slight bruise on the side of his face but Thomsen stormed down demanding that Comdt McInerney, the hospital doctor, certify him as having concussion. Müller was a habitual malingerer and exaggerator of his alleged complaints. Hauptmann Mollenhauer, the senior German internee, sent Müller's jacket to Curragh Camp headquarters for cleaning. Müller had been returning late to camp and behaved in an aggressive manner when challenged. But symptomatically, patience with the internees' tantrums had worn thin. The jacket was returned uncleaned.[71]

There was, Hempel continued in this vein, the gravest danger now that Allied pressure would lead to the Irish breaking off diplomatic relations with Germany and this, in effect, would destroy Irish neutrality. Deputy Dillon did not let the opportunity to 'roast' de Valera pass, and Hempel recounted the sharp Dáil repartee between the Taoiseach and the Deputy. Dillon had demanded to know what Hempel had to say about the business of introducing spies to Ireland. Hempel associated Dillon's return in the Dáil (23/2/1944) with 'putting the finger' on the Legation again. Enigmatic de Valera however, was more brusque than ever with

Dillon: he had given all the information on the matter that he proposed to give at that time. Dillon mocked that it was a long way alright to Northumberland Road (the nearby location of the German Legation) and de Valera retorted that it was a longer way still to Dillon's headquarters. Dillon rejoined that wireless messages travel fast, a reference to the German secret transmitter. Hempel reported verbatim.[72]

Less publicly the Taoiseach had prevailed on the German Minister to finally part with his cherished transmitter and to go through the charade of depositing it in a Munster and Leinster Bank safe on 21 December 1943. The set was jointly deposited by Boland, for the Irish side, and Thomsen, for the German side, in a box with a security lock for which only the Germans held the key.[73] That box was then put in a jointly opened steel deed box, which was placed in joint custody in the bank safe. Only four bank directors operating jointly could open the safe. Hempel, keeping himself 'covered' to the last, sought provision for redress in the event of the destruction of the transmitter. It was a ceremony that symbolised facets of the unreal façade involved in the implementation of the policy of qualified neutrality. De Valera told Hempel that he was extremely sorry that this step was necessary and Boland told Thomsen that the Irish government would return the set in the event of an emergency, which Hempel interpreted to mean in the event of an Allied attack on Ireland. The last paragraph of this report from the German Minister is laced with realism. He advised against any attempt to try to replace the set; such action he said would be highly dangerous in the light of an impending allied invasion of Europe.[74] The Envoy seemed to be under no illusions at that stage (7/1/1944) as to which way the tide of the war was flowing.

The transmitter figured prominently in the notorious 'American Note' presented by David Gray to the Taoiseach (21/2/1944) who, fastened on interpreting as an ultimatum the demands – 'as an absolute minimum' – of the American Minister for the removal of Axis representatives in Ireland. The Note referred to the possession of a set by the German Minister and to the radio sets brought in two months previously by the two parachutists.[75] This gave rise to a supposition that the British for whatever reasons had chosen not to inform the Americans about the fate of the transmitter. They were Allies, but as relations between the different commanders in the field index, they were not on friendly terms. The idea that the British indulged in a game of 'one-upmanship' with the Americans appealed to the Department of External Affairs of the period:

> The Americans did not know about the fate of the transmitter and stressed the issue: the British who did, had not chosen not to inform them. And this put the American Minister and his government in a somewhat absurd position. De Valera had the appropriate answer once again, this time countering Anglo-American rather than German pressure.[76]

British Cabinet papers however which were released in 1972, indicated a previous exchange of ideas between Gray and Maffey as to the text of the Note on how to proceed in the matter of forestalling the opportunity for de Valera to spread, on record, this sequestering of the radio sending set from the German Legation. Bad Irish-American relations would suit British post-war Northern Ireland plans. A smaller section of the Foreign Office, conscious of the immense Irish contribution to the Commonwealth and to the war, disapproved of these bully-boy tactics.

At least two Dominion Office officials (Robertson and Wrong) would have preferred an informal approach to exert pressure on Éire and felt that it might have been helpful from the point of view of saving de Valera's face if the Note could have included some evidence against the Axis Legations.[77] De Valera, regardless of the situation, told Kerney (Canada) that Éire would fight invasion from any quarter and – even though the outcome was hopeless – would resist to the last man.[78] There were no cut-and-dried situations in those epochal times. And the counter-productive tactics in dealing with the Irish was to try to threaten or bully them. No one apparently told Gray that.

In a previous report (4/3/1943) on the American's tactlessness, Hempel reported that Gray had sent a letter to the 'American-Irish' Cardinal McRory, criticising de Valera's politics but that the Cardinal had rebuffed him, accusing him of using British-American 'cant'.[79] In the short term Gray lost the American Note encounter. In a general election called in May 1944 de Valera gained seventeen seats and an overall majority again for Fianna Fáil. That fact and the German Minister's reassurance, in response to the Taoiseach's representation, that the German authorities would do their best to save Rome, brought a respite for the pressed Envoy, for whose country 'the sands were running out'. In the longer term, Gray's political purpose to smear de Valera in a post-war anti-partition campaign, which would portray him as having 'frolicked with the German (and Japanese!) representatives' had a damaging effect.[80]

The use of the word 'frolic' was Churchill's. In his victory broadcast (13/5/1945), that great wordsmith was less than felicitous. 'Had it been necessary we would have been forced to come to close quarters with Mr de Valera ... we left the de Valera government to frolic with the Germans and later with the Japanese representatives to their heart's content.'

This charge of 'frolicking' in the sense of 'collaborating' almost, was the essence of the American Note accusation: though it was a full year later when Churchill felt free to fully lend support to Gray's statements. In this period up to mid-1944 neither de Valera nor Hempel had any disposition or reason to be frolicsome about inter-governmental matters. After mid-1944 there was little left – for Hempel certainly – to frolic about. The nearest thing to sportiveness in the relationship, was de Valera's attempt at a thin watery jest about the capability of the German High Command to do its own contingency planning for landing weapons, if required, when the Taoiseach was fobbing off the German Minister's persistent offer of arms assistance.[81] For the greater portion of the war the Minister Plenipotentiary was frequently on the defensive: the atmosphere in inter-governmental relations was not frolicsome; more often than not it was strained. He was frequently explaining German gaffes, transgressions and violations of neutrality, to an increasing exasperated, harassed Irish government.

Initially, he had been a pernickety watchdog, picking out breaches of neutrality by the Irish government, particularly with regard to re-export possibilities. He did later (9/8/1943) report his various démarches, including his protest at the Irish government's release of Allied air crews and the granting of repair facilities to Allied aircraft. He did not protest at the Irish sending location messages in English which was an obvious advantage to the Allies.[82] He himself had violated neutrality by reporting the effects of Luftwaffe bombing on England. As already noted, uninhibited 'export' of that valuable commodity, 'Weather Reports' seemed to have eluded him as protest material: but, being involved in secretly transmitting his own weather reports may have inhibited him. He had his hands full between transmitter sets and arbitrarily inserted agents.[83]

The opening of the 'Second Front' (6/6/1944) did not mean that there was now really nothing left for Herr Hempel to be defensive about. On 27 June 1944 he reported that Goertz was planning an escape from internment. He said that he had tried to dissuade the prisoner from such an attempt as there was a danger in the present situation that such action could still work adversely against Irish neutrality even at this stage of the war.[84] Hempel had taken great pains (unsuccessfully) to avoid publicity about the Goertz affair, from the time of the agent's association with Held to his capture. He had also made the point during Goertz's 'freedom' of the danger of the man falling into British hands. And he had voiced his suspicions of the involvement of the British Secret Service, especially in the matters linking Goertz with the Hayes 'confession'.[85] Even in internment, the turbulence generated by Goertz served to keep the German Minister still on the defensive.

In the matter of self-defence if it were necessary, Hempel was prepared from the outset to use more than diplomatic weapons to defend himself. He had reported that his staff and himself were armed with revolvers. One attendant with a loaded revolver slept in the Legation; windows on the first floor were especially secured; there was continuous protection from the Irish police; he also had a vicious guard dog – a '*bissiger Wachhund*'. He had no intentions of 'turning the other cheek' if it came to protecting his Legation.[86]

He also reported on the Legations of some other countries. The Spanish representative Ontiveras was subject to intimidation because he was pro-German and Hempel attended Mass to give him moral support;[87] the Italian representative had a nervous breakdown which Rome did not know about and Hempel advised that this be taken into account when assessing the Italian's reports.[88] But the Envoy's most intriguing reports refer to the French Legation and the ambivalence of the Irish government towards the situation prevailing there revolving around Vichy, de Gaulle and the North African Committee and involving Laforcade, Albertas ('charakterlos'?) Couvid Drutham and Duhamel.[89] The French Pétainists[90] in Dublin resented Hempel's so-called solicitude as condescending and patronising. They were about to lose diplomatic status while the Germans held on to theirs. They had chips on their shoulders.

Lafocarde's touchy son shot the intruding dog, belonging to the Director of Intelligence, Colonel Dan Bryan. Dan's nightly walks were more mooches, which could be construed as prying. Matters were reaching a climax. Feelings were running high.

The Germans were not alone in feeling the cold winds blow but, unlike the Vichy French, they knew where they stood and they drew comfort from the speeches of Seán McEntee. Seán McEntee referred to the dangers of the increasing spread of communism, following the Soviets' mounting success in battle. Soviet victories brought Marxist implications, impinging on all home fronts – Allied and Axis[91] which caused concern in Catholic circles: *déjà vu.* Bewley could crow 'I told you so', from that point of view. But the remorseless machinery of war was precipitating firm alliances on the winning side and bulldozing fence-sitting. The maintenance of neutrality was becoming increasingly difficult.

Hempel's professed front mission to maintain Irish neutrality could fail. And the German interventionists, particularly Goertz, would, to a large extent, have had only themselves to blame for the Envoy's failures. They had diminished their minister's status, dangerously disturbed the balance of Éire's tightrope 'considerate' neutrality policy given Churchill his 'frolics' and 'close quarters' lines and Gray his pretexts.

In the turbulence of the 'American note affair' the deportment of the Irish Army had a calming effect. It and its Chief of Staff, Lt.-Gen. McKenna, impressed Hempel and he said so. McKenna's main concern at that point was the possibility of some mischievous blurting out of the full extent of Allied-Irish intelligence co-operation, which could be perfidiously misused in the interests of historic hatreds and hostilities. The extent of Hempel's knowledge or suspicion of the extent of this co-operation is not readily quantifiable. The writing was on the wall for the treasonous subversiveness which could be traced through Goertz's career.

CHAPTER 10

Alternative Channels (late 1941–mid 1944)

Routine Spying: Dwindling Efforts

The advent of Goertz (1940) inhibited Hempel's discreet information gathering. Updating details of the Defence Force's organisation, which he had hitherto got away with as routine, now had him looking over his shoulder. His Legation was under the spotlight. The presence of Goertz sharpened the scrutiny.

The very existence of Goertz dominated the attempts by the Allies to persuade the Irish government to come into the war on their side. The exercise of this pressure was the main cause of the high tension that existed in the Irish State in mid-December 1941. Hempel attributed the easing of the tension to some extent to the assurances that he himself had given to the Irish side, in which he had washed his hands of Goertz and his spying. As an index of the easing of the tension he mentioned that the Irish Army generally were allowed Christmas (1941) leave.[1] He found de Valera in good humour when he visited him (31/12/1941).[2]

The reasons for de Valera's good humour on that New Year's Eve are not clear. Hempel reported that a widespread covert smear campaign by rumour was being conducted by the Allies in an effort to undermine him. On the other hand, he surmised that the British may have reluctantly become reconciled to what they saw as the intransigence of de Valera; balancing this against the 'certain consideration' shown, and the possible repercussions from the widespread Irish abroad if they behaved otherwise and seized the ports. The down-to-earth, soldier-to-solider approaches of Lt. Gen. McKenna with his British counterparts on the island radiated, albeit invisibly, a leavening. Where interests coincided, Irish intelligence would pragmatically, without illusion, work hand-in-glove with the British Secret Service. These interests did not always coincide: partition and the ports remained. The 'perfidious Albion', factor would never go away. They did not fully trust one another, but a *modus vivendi* was imperative in the interests of their mutual survival.

Hempel reported a trickle of weapons being delivered from Britain, particularly some badly needed anti-aircraft guns. McKenna was getting a hearing, although Britain's own competing needs were great. He gave Walshe's opinion that the US had its hands full in the Pacific and would not risk upsetting Irish-American opinion by joining with the British in an attack on Ireland. There was, he went on, a drying up of deliveries of goods from the US to Ireland: but he did not see this as seriously endangering Irish neutrality. On the other hand, he did not rule out surprise moves.

For whatever reasons – seen and unseen – Hempel was able to report on an obvious easing of tension coming into 1942. Russia was absorbing the main menace; the ruffled Allies were less restive because Goertz was interned. He was no longer available to subversives as a direct channel of communication to the German High Command. The British had every reason to be satisfied with Irish intelligence co-operation.

The Battle of Britain (September 1940) and the Invasion of Russia (June 1941) had radically modified the German capability to invade the British Isles; so that threat no longer seriously remained. Both British and Irish could breathe a little easier. Hempel reported (4/3/1943) that the German reverse in Russia caused unease in those circles which had looked for a German victory over England and feared the spread of Communism.[3] Very few shared that view. The improving Battle of the Atlantic, preparations for an Allied counter-attack and the capture of Goertz indicated a turning of the tide. Goertz's capture removed a source of temptation and compromise for Cabinet ministers, army officers, and romanticists of all descriptions, as well as a focal point for subversives. The Taoiseach punctiliously only operated through official inter-governmental channels.[4] Hempel's covert associations, leading to other channels of communication, did not alter that overt official position but they did eventually disturb de Valera.

The evidence of the existence of compromising alternative channels of communication outside of the official one, is to be found in the Envoy's own telegram.[5] The suspicion that the *Auslandsorganizaton*[6] had been rendered relatively moribund by the exodus of German nationals at the outbreak of the war[7] is more or less confirmed by him (15/8/1941).[8] He had destroyed confidential documents (with the exception of essential codes and ciphers), dating from the period immediately preceding the outbreak of war. Just before that, selected files had also been burned, although, in his opinion, they contained hardly any compromising material. But he also referred to the *Auslandsorganization* files which had been deposited with him for safe keeping, when the officers of that organisation had returned to Germany. The Envoy indicated that he had only destroyed some of these files, where he deemed that to be advisable, and he requested instructions as to how he should dispose of the balance. This included a register which would be useful, he thought, in the event of a reconstruction of the files being required.[9] Perhaps if the *Auslandsorganization* had been activated to its pre-war capacity it would have been less inhibited than Hempel in handling the offer of an American technician, B.G. Carter, domiciled in London, who had let the Legation know that he was prepared to betray confidential information – but for a sum not less than £25,000. Hempel feared provocation and pointed out to Berlin that the Legation was not to be involved if the matter were pursued.[10] Colonel Bryan from his contacts did not believe that this was covert British pressure on Hempel but admitted that the British did not necessarily tell him everything (nor he, them).

With his own Legation being under such relentless scrutiny it was only natural that Hempel in turn would keep his enemy embassies and legations under observation, to ascertain how they were faring out under the application of the policy of Irish neutrality. He examined the comings and goings in the British diplomatic representation in Dublin which had been opened after the outbreak of the war.[11] At the beginning there had only been a Naval Attaché in the British installation (Greig) but, as the Envoy's report outlined, he was quickly supplemented by a Military Attaché (Price) and an Air Attaché (Haywood), together with appropriate staffs whose true identify was concealed. The Irish government, Hempel added, did not approve of such a large number of attachés and insisted on a declaration by the British of their proper identities. Clumsy censorship of these declarations gave rise to rumours leading to public disquiet as to Allied intentions with regard to the ports. The British representative gave assurances, which were published in the *Daily Mail*.[12] Hempel caustically commented that he had no grounds to doubt these assurances, not least because the

British attachés were of second grade quality and no augmentation of staff had taken place. He reported that Naval Attaché Greig was shortly replaced by Bradley (the name Greig was constantly cropping up). Woodhouse replaced Military Attaché Price after five weeks and Begg replaced Air Attaché Haywood.[13] Mystify and mislead were the aims of the polite diplomatic spying game. They were all 'channels' to their masters and minders.

De Valera's speech in Navan (17/1/1942) left no doubt as to de Valera's position – assurances or no assurances. The Taoiseach reviewed economic and defence pressures, lashed out at Allied propaganda, and issued a strong appeal to join the army. He dismissed smear and recounted his efforts to procure arms. He repeated that they should look danger in the eye and reiterated (in Hempel's words, '*und wenn wir zu sterben hätten, sie auch bereitwillig sterben würden,… es gab keinerlei geheime Geschäfte*' – 'if they had to die, well they were prepared to die … no secret bargains existed'.[14] Hempel's literal factual reporting at this period could lead Berlin to superficially conclude that the Germans and the Irish had a common enemy in the Allies. He intimated – ('delineated' is too strong a word to describe Hempel's reporting) – that a climate conducive to the collection of combat intelligence for the Germans prevailed: the requirement remained, judging from de Valera's fighting talk.

Of the information which Hempel reported it is not possible to accurately assess how much of it was fed to him by provocation. 'N's' reports from British Army sources sound too pat, too good to be true, and often not borne out by subsequent events. Some of the information supplied by the Legation, as distinct from reportage of events, had the appearance of replying to queries which had been professionally broken down into a number of essential elements of information, which collectively would provide the answer sought. If there were a weakness in the reporting it would be in the absence of meaningful sifting by the Envoy. If there were a doubt of provocation about information, Hempel simply said so and transmitted accordingly. However, it was not his job to analyse and translate the information into intelligence; though a more positive contribution to interpretation en route could have been relevant to eventual evaluation. There is an impression of haphazardness and lack of local evaluation as to what degree the information was relevant, reliable, accurate or even plausible. He did not however report everything. He told Frau Hempel of a young German pilot shot down over England being thrown into a furnace alive by an excited mob, but that he did not send that information to Berlin 'as it would only bring revenge and hate'. Was it true? There is no doubt however that what he did report, in a clear breach of neutrality, contributed to combat intelligence, triggering death and destruction.

In a target acquisition operation, Hempel pinpointed in Luton, the Vauxhall Tank Factory, the Percival Aircraft Company, an airfield, a barracks of the Fleet Air Arm School, a Skefto ball-bearing factory and an anti-aircraft location in the vicinity of an electricity plant.[15] This was the type of detailed information returning Irish workers could impart to German internees, who in turn could pass it on to Thomsen. Prior to this he reported that he had learned from a technically inexperienced informant – (without being able to verify the source) – that the British had invented an additive to the column of airplane exhaust which, when focused on, appeared to be a different colour from the German colour which was red. He was unable to say what the British colour was.[16]

He also reported that American troops were equipped with a jeep capable of being quickly converted to an anti-aircraft mounting and on other unorthodox weapon developments in anti-aircraft weapons. In general, these reports gave locations of underground factories; of American and British troop movements (including a comment that the Missouri Regiment in Northern Ireland was composed mostly of Klu-Klux members) and the movement of signal personnel of the 8th (British) Army to India. He relayed a British army engineer's story of sabotage of German bombs dropped in Britain by inserting chewing gum between the fuse and the charge. His report locating a new power station in Larne and an airfield fifteen miles from Derby, contained another anecdote, an unusual 'doggy' story, as well as an orientation on Allied objectives and his own landscape. Thousands of dogs, he said were being trained to spring ashore to explode the minefields.[17] This is not all together that fanciful. The late Dr Walker-Nadell (Glasgow), who landed in Normandy (6/6/44), told me that, on his suggestion, they did precisely that there, but with sheep, saving countless lives. During his lifetime he was concerned lest Animal Rights people got hold of the story to pillory him.

Obviously using the worker-back-from-England link, Thomsen, with Koecher, located aircraft factories in Manchester, Stoke-on-

Trent and Stockford and nine miles from Bermingham (the latter said to be turning out six Sterlings aircraft per week). They stated that American strength in Northern Ireland had reached 36,000 (with 22,000 drowned) and that discipline and training was of a very low standard. There was at present, the report concluded, an increasing number of damaged coastal steamers in Londonderry.

These reports constituted serious hidden breaches of neutrality. Pedestrian though many of them were, they made a more solid contribution to the intelligence process in Berlin than any feedback from the inserted agents. Hempel did enquire with some annoyance from Berlin whether his information was credited in Berlin or not, complaining that it made things difficult for him when he was not aware of other sources of information.[18] At least two of the agents – Goertz and Marschner – compromised Hempel. The return from them in intelligence or spying terms was not commensurate with the risks the Envoy ran on their behalf. Known involvement would have demanded expulsion, certainly by the Allies.

When Marschner escaped from Mountjoy Jail in Dublin (28/2/1942), Hempel and his superiors in Berlin dropped their guard about avoiding involving the Legation. The temporary obsession then seemed to have been to preserve Marschner as an alternative channel of communication in the event of diplomatic relations being broken off. Although Hempel continued to be uneasy about having anything to do with Marschner, he still complied with instructions, relaying even trivial requests from the agent as to how his fiancée, Lilo Henze, was getting on in Hamburg.[19] The telegrams went via the Bern German Legation, signed by the minister there and sent on to Berlin.

While Marschner was at large he was put in touch with McGuinness, an unbalanced petty officer in the Irish Naval Service, who promised to take him to France. Hempel had by this time received further instructions not to give Marschner the £600 or to help him out with a new cover address; but it came too late to avoid involvement. McGuinness was arrested (30/3/1942) and convicted (June 1942) and correspondence found on him, associating him with trying to get military reports to Germany via Petersen, effectively compromised the Legation.[20] In his report on the McGuinness Affair, Hempel referred to McGuinness's gun-running exploits with the 'Irish Jew Briscoe' between 1918 and 1925 and to

McGuinness's unreliability and mercenary outlook. He also enquired regarding the possibility of deciphering Telegram No. 210 of 20 April with Key G. No more than with Marschner, the intelligence dividends from association with McGuinness were negligible. However, with McGuinness now arrested and Marschner recaptured (30/4/1943) (in spite of receiving shelter from the Brugha family, he only succeeded in remaining at large for two months) the Legation could return to its less spectacular system of information-gathering for the intelligence process and take refuge in routine reporting to keep up appearances.

The Oscar Metzke (16/12/1942) case falls outside this category. The Sudeten German, claiming acquaintanceship with Thomsen, approached the Legation with what seemed very pertinent information. He identified in detail the units of a brigade in which he was serving.[21] Hempel suspected provocation but kept himself covered by transmitting the details as delivered. The alleged suicide later in a County Cork Garda Station of this mysterious Sudeten leaves a question mark over his role and Hempel's assessment of him. It is said that his death caused some consternation in Berlin.

Hempel was suspicious of dramatic interventions in intelligence. A Mata-Hari type of agent, Frau Marlow, a Norwegian Jewess married to a Scotsman, who spoke German, Swedish and broken English, was cut down to size by Hempel's cryptic remark that she had bad teeth and – more importantly – had been said by 'W' (presumably Weber-Dohl) to have links with the British Secret Service.[22] (There was a theory that 'W' was a double agent himself.) Marlow was alleged to have infiltrated Hitler's own headquarters. The cast was varied. One rumour had it that the Mata O'Hara (Nora O'Meara) was the illegitimate daughter of General Ian Hamilton. The BBC play *How we licked Hitler* is a stranger-than-fiction sortie into the maze of psychological operations in the Second World War.[23] (According to Veesenmayer they had unquestionably subjoined Admiral Canaris. He promised me the Canaris Diaries to support the charge. He died before that could materalise. There is no tidy indexed documentation to substantiate espionage: only disjointed sprawls.)

Hempel saw British provocation everywhere. He was particularly sensitive to approaches from the Scottish Independence Movement.[24] He seemed to have had a window into the British Secret Service though he generally qualified his sources as being personally reliable, well-versed, but of questionable accuracy and judgement. Hempel had the civil servant's obsession with keeping himself covered. Nevertheless, he passed on verbatim the following British Secret Service report: the Irish Army was very good, in spite of a shortage of armament; and that factor meant that a large force of, say, 100,000 men would be required for a quick occupation of Ireland. In the event of a British/American attack, the Irish defence, in anticipation of German aid, would concentrate in the south under its most capable General Costello. In that event, the report on the army continued, it could be assumed that German-Irish contingency planning would have provided for landing places for the Germans in Southern Ireland.[25] They did not take into account the incompatibilities between Irish and German aspirations and attitudes. The Irish government were playing the preservation of their *ad hoc* neutrality policy by ear; the German 'plans' with regard to Great Britain were ambivalent and lacked consistency. Communication accordingly, was patchy in this grey area, where different mentalities were at work. There were no channels capable of transmitting these endemic imponderables, implications and menaces.

Normal diplomatic channels could not provide full intergovernmental communication in the consequential maze of ephemeral and inconsistent concepts that proliferated. Diplomatic channels are rarely as simple as formal structures and procedures would imply. Nevertheless, it is surprising to come across an 'alternative channel' of communication between Great Britain and the Chief of the Security Police and the SD in Berlin, with a report on Ireland based principally on sources in Church circles.[26] This report indicated that de Valera was pursuing nationalist anti-British policies, instancing the wrecking of British efforts to come to an understanding with the 'Free State' and the continuing ban on the import of British newspapers. The propaganda of the BBC was decried as being ineffective and the report unfavourably compared it with the more 'factual credible' German radio. It held that there was a considerable resurgence of the IRA and that closer cooperation between them and de Valera was expected; that British communist circles were trying (unsuccessfully) to exploit Church–State relations in Germany to influence Irish public opinion; that an American attack on the 'Irish Free State' was expected in early 1943; that the presence of American troops in Northern Ireland shocked the Irish public and indicated how impossible it was for the 'Free State' to pursue a policy of neutrality after this occupation. The conclusion from this report however, was that the anti-British attitude in Ireland (which was aggravated by British economic pressures such as restricting the export of coal) did not automatically mean a positive attitude towards Germany. The Reich, the report maintained, had been rejected because of its attitude to the Catholic Church, e.g. closing schools, convents, etc. While the report depicted the Irish as being undoubtedly anti-British, it nevertheless stated that they remained in sympathy with the US, even though they (i.e. allegedly Church circles in Britain) felt that it was the American intention to make a strong point of the country, and that the Americans would attempt initially to accomplish this by diplomatic approaches and pressures, but would not shrink, if it came to it, from compulsive military considerations. It was a disquieting report.

Bewley was alleged in it to have warned the Germans about de Valera's pro-British schemings, holding that there was no danger of an Allied attack; that the Northern Ireland base sufficed for Allied needs; and that the ports were not essential. He wanted the Germans to openly oppose de Valera. Woermann however, wrote that while they had no illusions about de Valera, they were determined to keep up diplomatic relations with the Irish government as they presently existed.

This report of Woermann's (23/12/1942) is noteworthy in that it indicated mischievous Bewley still obsessed with his vendetta against de Valera irrespective of its detrimental national effect, and also operating as 'an alternative channel'. It also alleged that he made use of some Vatican contacts to communicate with Ireland for intelligence purposes. In that connection it was alleged that a Premonstrant (monk) named Noots visited convents in Europe (including a Belgian convent in Kilnacrott near Ballyjamesduff, Co. Cavan), collecting intelligence linked to the *Tablet* newspaper. Information (including information from Hungary) was then alleged to have been brought by a Swiss lady (a nun?) named Ververs, to Rome for dissemination to Scotland and Ireland. A Monsignor O'Flaherty 'the Vatican Pimpernel' – a Papal diplomat – (though by no means of Nazi inclination; in fact Hempel reported him as being the reporter of German atrocities in Poland) – acted as a courier for Bewley. Hempel got a copy of one of Bewley's letters and queried querulously if Bewley had sent similar letters to anyone else. The Envoy stated that Monsignor O'Flaherty had Northern Ireland connections.[27] This was not accurate. He was a brave Kerryman, who, in spite of having vivid Black-and-Tan memories, risked his life to help British prisoners-of-war escape in Italy. He did the same for the Germans when the tables were turned. Known as the 'Vatican Pimpernel', like his nephew in Ireland, another Hugh O'Flaherty, he put people first and himself second. (Hugh junior was scandalously mistreated for his humanity by pigmy political scribes and pharisees.)

Hempel did not encourage this 'alternative channel' reporting. He queried the efficacy of his own alternative channel – the transmitter – sending weather reports which, in his opinion, were more trouble than they were worth. Canaris agreed with this view. He said that he had nothing to do with Hempel's transmitter and wanted nothing to do with it – he had his own means of getting weather reports. There was no accord between the *Abwehr*, the Navy and the Luftwaffe in this area.[28] Ribbentrop sought unilaterally, unspecifically, (27/2/1942) alternative channels of communication in the event of the Legation's transmitter being put out of action.[29] He wanted communication of some form, even if agents were involved to secure it. He did not care how they were inserted so long as they got the information.

Veesenmayer, on the other hand, supported Hempel's view that the *Abwehr* should have formal Foreign Ministry clearance before inserting agents in Ireland. However, Veesenmayer differed from Hempel, who was professionally and temperamentally averse to such unorthodox adventures. Veesenmayer's objections were not made in principle (at one stage he mooted the interjection of 120 specialists to advise the IRA),[30] but primarily on efficiency and unity of command grounds. Here again he revealed his political limitations and once again, a failure to grasp de Valera's determination for 'consideration for Britain'.

It may not be entirely fair to blame either Veesenmayer for this interpretation, or Hempel for his contribution to it. Though Hempel may be faulted for presenting a less than penetrating positive analysis, the events he reported towards the end of 1942 indicated a state of turbulence in the country, with the people in no mood to demonstrate 'a certain consideration for Britain'. After the hanging of IRA man Williams (3/9/1942), Hempel reported unrest North and South of the Border 'even in strongly pro-British Cork', together with anti-British demonstrations, 'Down with England' and 'Long Live the Republic' slogans. He also reported Irish-American interest in the hanging of Williams, Seán MacBride's great influence with the IRA and the strong criticism of nationalists at the Irish government's reticence in making any representations to the British in the affair. It was held (24/2/1942) that a thin-ice situation in Éire and the frustrations there were aggravated by economic stagnation. Notwithstanding all this, de Valera emerged, convinced he was a man of destiny – the only one capable of shielding Éire's neutrality policy and shepherding his country through the war. Hempel was inclined to agree with that assessment, and sought to distance himself from the inserted agent, especially from O'Reilly and Kenny who were causing so much trouble for everyone.[31]

A telegram of protest to Berlin from him (7/1/1944) concerning them was instrumental in securing a rebuke from Ambassador Ritter, not for the *Abwehr*, but for the SD. They were the ones, the Ambassador's reproach ran, who contravened Veesenmayer's admonitions.[32] Nor did the German Minister encourage Irish agents. His assessment of a retired British Major, K.E. Fitzgerald Lombard, who proffered his services to the Legation, was harsh: 'senile, garrulous, political snob', he called him; yet typically he did not fully eliminate him, and left the matter open by mentioning the retired officer's good connections.[33] (Mrs Carter described him as a homosexual.)

In the case of another would-be agent, Andrews, the German Minister had great reservations which however, were neither specific nor timely enough to deter Veesenmayer (who this time (mid-1943), could be said to be clutching at straws) from pursuing the connection. Andrews appeared to hold out very attractive bait: there were his alleged contacts with General O'Duffy and through him with the IRA in the North – both of whom were said to favour more aggressive action against Britain. O'Duffy proposed raising a Green Division to fight on the Russian front and although Veesenmayer saw no military merit in the idea he felt it could be manipulated for propaganda purposes.[34] To further attract Veesenmayer, was a message (No. 3) that it was possible through O'Duffy to organise 'circles' among Army officers 'many of whom are sympathetic, and antagonistic to the situation in occupied Ireland'. Andrews also sent a message (No. 14) stating that he had a

contact with the supervisor in the Shortt and Harland, Belfast
Aviation Works, a personal friend of O'Duffy's. He added
enigmatically: 'Major-General MacNeill sympathetic'.[35]

There were extenuating circumstances for Veesenmayer's dalliance
with Andrews. His remaining hope of fomenting rebellion in Ireland
after the death of Seán Russell (August 1940) had been Frank Ryan.
He did not like Ryan but he was all he got for this purpose.[36] On 13
January 1943 however, he reported that Ryan had had a stroke, was
hospitalised and would be out of action for months.[37] To spurn
Andrews would have seemed in the circumstances like looking a gift
horse in the mouth. He decided (5/5/1943) to persist with his
Operation 'Mainhau' the code name given by *Abwehr II*, in the spring
of 1940, to the Goertz operation which was intended to involve
Andrews. The Germans were learning nothing about involvement in
Ireland and de Valera's very 'certain consideration for Britain'.

Hempel put that enterprise in perspective when he reported
(6/12/1943) the arrest of Andrews. He indicated that his
information was that Andrews was totally untrustworthy and
unsuitable. But that was too late to deflect confused Veesenmayer. It
was Hempel who had initially put him in touch with Andrews, albeit
with his usual ambidextrous reservations. Another factor
influencing Veesenmayer was Hempel's own growing ambivalence
towards the IRA in Northern Ireland. On the one hand, the Envoy
counselled against doing anything to upset the Irish government
and seemed to report disparagingly that the cache of IRA arms
uncovered by the Northern Ireland police could have had
undesirable consequences if the IRA had used them. On the other
hand, he was not opposed (and indeed was surprisingly
venturesome) to sending three Northern Ireland IRA men, if
necessary by U-Boat, to Germany for training; and to taking steps to
woo the Northern Ireland IRA away from Marxist-Communist
influences. He seemed to be veering towards the chronic mistake
made by the Political Department in Berlin that subversion was
acceptable, provided it was not directed specifically against Éire.
That notion persisted to, time after time, contravene an essential
tenet of de Valera's neutrality policy.[38]

Another extenuating circumstance of Veesenmayer's hanging on
to the Andrew's connection was his growing disenchantment with
the Irish Minister to Spain, Kerney, through whom he had hoped to

establish significant contacts in Ireland which would help him to accomplish his mission.[39] Hempel's reports were factors which helped to heighten Veesenmayer's expectations of making 'big politics' out of Ireland in that manner.[40] Hempel was probably unaware that these particular reports had this effect. It eventually got to a stage where Ribbentrop had to have explanatory notes from his staff to elucidate Hempel's telegrams. By this time (12/12/1942) Ribbentrop was trying to replace Thomsen who was said to be sick.[41] Whether it was on account of the sickness or whether he wanted a first hand pre-invasion account of the situation in Ireland from a returned Thomsen is not clear. The ill-planned insertion of scouting O'Reilly and Kenny occurred a couple of weeks afterwards.

Hempel's involvement in the Veesenmayer/Kerney Affair [42]

Veesenmayer accepted Hempel's assessment that he was more important than the agent Goertz.[43] The *coup d'état* specialist was also aware that Ribbentrop had his own reasons for protecting Hempel: although he supported aiding the IRA, he did not want him to be openly involved.[44] Then Veesenmayer was informed by Woermann that Helmut Clissmann, who was to be Veesenmayer's precursor and emissary to Leopold Kerney, the Irish Minister in Spain, had deduced, from a Hempel telegram, that 'L', was the Irish Minister for Agriculture, Ryan. That indeed looked like the makings of 'big politics'.[45] It is not clear how Clissmann arrived at this alleged conclusion. It was not exactly what Hempel had said. Maybe Clissmann concluded that the man behind Hempel's 'L' was the real 'L'. Hempel's arbitrary use of capitals could confuse. He had previously used 'L' to designate the two MacNeills.

Woermann thought that Hempel's telegrams (the three parts of Nos 367, 319 and 289 from Dublin) had a bearing on the Spanish excursion planned by Veesenmayer, so he sent him copies of them, having first shown them to Clissmann, before the latter departed on his authorised 'Madrid Mission' to Kerney. Veesenmayer in a Memorandum to Woermann (24/11/1941) had already indicated the conclusions he had drawn from Hempel's telegrams. As a result, he said, the communications which Clissmann had brought back from Spain arising out of his contacts with Kerney, merited far-reaching consideration. He took it that Hempel's telegrams had thrown a new positive light on that development, forgetting that Hempel was never positive about anything.

Veesenmayer quoted Hempel's telegram (No. 367, P. 3) that the IRA had elite potential and were a rallying point for the spirit of Irish nationalism.[46] This view, Veesenmayer said, coincided with Kerney's opinion, as allegedly expressed to Clissmann, and with the last radio message from Goertz. To Veesenmayer, the message was that the IRA were an organisation of extraordinary importance. He took from Hempel that the differences between IRA and government policies were more cosmetic and semantic than fundamental. Kerney, Clissmann alleged, had minimised the Hayes affair by surmising that the latter might have had a role as 'go between' for some of de Valera's colleagues. Veesenmayer's summary extolled the IRA's fighting record: he felt that now de Valera was more in tune with the IRA and the changing times, and since 1926 had many successes against England. The fact that Hayes's attackers came from Northern Ireland, where the British Secret Service had a wide influence, made them suspect: they were either paid agents, provocateurs or infiltrators. However, he did not think that the time had yet come for a British attack, and if it did, contrary to Kerney's alleged opinion, he did not believe that the Irish Army was capable of prolonged resistance. He saw the deterrent to Britain lying mainly on Irish-American reaction, as Roosevelt had also to take this factor into account.

Veesenmayer had no difficulty in 'writing off' Goertz: he had outlived his usefulness. In this matter Hempel could be satisfied that his damning reporting had the desired effect. Goertz's arrest devalued him further. Berlin branded the agent's aberrations as being due to a nervous breakdown, resulting from his long period of isolation in Ireland.[47] The High Command were convinced that Goertz was under close observation from both the Irish and British Secret Service: he had become a liability. Hempel had recommended the agent's repatriation though he did not say exactly how this was to be effected.

An important deduction which Veesenmayer managed to draw from Hempel's reports – over and above what the Envoy intended – was the implication that it was possible for de Valera to assign an undercover role to Dr Ryan to foster liaison with what Veesenmayer deemed to be a more tractable wing of the IRA, namely that wing led by Hayes. If that supposition were correct, Veesenmayer thought, that in view of Minister Kerney's unexpected openness, it merited special attention. He gathered from Clissmann's meetings with Kerney, that in an emergency, Kerney would be empowered to make representations for aid to Germany. Kerney, he said, was a careful and reserved Irish nationalist and a close friend of de Valera's: the implication therefore was that this was a serious business, to be conducted at a high level.

Veesenmayer gave priority to the healing of the rift between de Valera and the IRA and he had Frank Ryan in mind as the agent to effect this rapprochement. He could see no good reason why de Valera and the IRA should be fighting each other when they could combine to everyone's advantage against the common enemy – England. It is doubtful if Hempel would be in accord with all Veesenmayer's attitudes which the memorandum indicated had been influenced by his telegrams. The German Minister, who deduced his mission as being the preservation of Irish neutrality, could hardly have approved of Veesenmayer's resolve to strengthen the manipulation – no matter how prudently – of the '*Irland Faktor*' against the England 'bastion', as Veesenmayer described it. The *coup d'état* specialist intended to further discuss 'ways and means' of fomenting the 'revolution', with Frank Ryan as his chief instrument for that purpose. Part of Veesenmayer's problem in making a complete estimate of the situation on fomenting this 'rebellion' stemmed from his difficulty in harmonising his interpretation of Hempel's telegrams with what he understood Clissmann had said that Kerney said.

Eventually Sonnleithner, according to a report from his Special Train (*Sonderzug*) in Westphalia, sent Veesenmayer himself to meet Kerney and informed the Führer of that position.[48] This did little more than confirm earlier accounts of previous meetings. Kerney, according to Veesenmayer, did convey that Ireland's only hope of eventual reunification lay in a decisive German victory. He was not alone in wishful thinking. The wounds of the Black-and-Tans and British strong-arm actions in Ireland were still raw and a thirst for retribution remained. Mrs Kiernan (Delia Murphy), wife of the Irish Ambassador to the Vatican, made no secret of similar sentiments, while at the same time, paradoxically, assisting British prisoners-of-war to escape German clutches in Nazi-occupied Italy. Cardinal

McRory was also pro-Axis to the extent that he was anti-British. Veesenmayer hoped to link such sentiments to a lucky roll of the dice in war where anything can happen. But the fortunes of war were not favouring Nazi Germany just then.[49]

But nothing concrete transpired: the 'big politics' undertaking came to nothing. Veesenmayer was not impressed by Kerney and considered him to be vacillating. He complained that the Irish emissary 'hummed and hawed' too much, that he was very nervous, very unsure of himself and very reticent. He somewhat cattily ascribed all that and the lack of progress of the talks, to Kerney not being, as he put it, 'a career diplomat'.[50] The Irish minister, in Veesenmayer's opinion, was ambitious to be 'in on a great act, probably to impress de Valera', but lacked the nerve to go ahead with it and see it through. On the other hand Hempel *was* a career diplomat but that fact did not spare him from Veesenmayer's lash. Veesenmayer did not consider that Irish attitudes might modify and change as prospects of a decisive German victory receded following mortal reverses on the Russian front. He looked for local scapegoats to explain the failure of his *coup d'état* mission from Ribbentrop.

With regard to Hempel's part in the affair, Veesenmayer was more exasperated than bitter. He was annoyed with himself for having allowed Hempel's reports 'to lead him up the garden path'. That was never Hempel's intention: his style of reporting could lead to misinterpretation, especially if predispositions towards the IRA already existed. He exasperated Veesenmayer.

Hempel, he felt, was 'a nice fellow' but 'weak and harmless': always soft, always anxious to please, careful, non-committal, who just reported and reported and reported, without doing anything, with neither an opinion or recommendation of his own to offer. In his opinion, Hempel was a good observer who saw all sides, but was indecisive, concluding his reports with 'on the one hand' but 'again on the other hand'. The best the would-be fomenter of revolution could bring himself to say in Hempel's favour was that the Envoy was 'a good reporter'. He felt that the Minister Plenipotentiary was no match for a 'world class' wily politician like de Valera and that the Envoy did not represent Germany's proper interests forcibly enough, but continually took counsel of his magnified fears. In Veesenmayer's book, Hempel, on account of his trepidations rather than his principles, constituted a weak link in a possible wartime chain wherein, 'antennal' daring, vision and 'guts' to take weighed risks were essentials. He found Hempel wanting in those martial requirements.

However, at the beginning of 1944 Veesenmayer and Hempel had been able to make common cause in furiously protesting at the Security Services' interjection of the agents O'Reilly and Kenny. In this they were supported by Canaris and the Foreign Ministry, as represented by Weizacker.[51] But the unison between Hempel, Veesenmayer, Canaris and the Foreign Ministry in this instance was merely a semblance of any cohesion or co-ordination. It was not real. Ribbentrop was becoming increasingly alienated and despised by the other Nazi leaders and Veesenmayer was convinced that Canaris was actively working to the detriment of Nazi Germany. He had long been uneasy about the 'peculiar people' with whom Canaris surrounded himself, and he was increasingly of the opinion, in his own words, that the *Abwehr* chief was 'the fly in the ointment', continually 'snookering, foiling and fouling-up' matters relating to any Irish intervention. The extraordinary clumsy amateurish attempts to insert agents and the nature of British intelligence 'tip-offs' to the Irish government could lend credence to this accusation: but Veesenmayer did not identify anything precisely in this area.

There was a point of view – rumoured to be harboured at official levels – that Kerney's talks with Clissmann and Veesenmayer, however well intentioned, could, if they had become known to Allied intelligence, have constituted the gravest threat of the war to Irish neutrality. When this opinion was voiced by the late Professor Desmond Williams, Kerney sued him: he was supported in his testimony by Clissmann. Veesenmayer's own signed reports however authenticated his discussions with Kerney and underline their seriousness. The case was settled out of court with Professor Williams unjustly paying damages.[52] Veesenmayer, for his part, felt that both Kerney and Hempel, in their respective areas, struck chameleon attitudes and played with words which misled him into having expectations, which thankfully for Ireland, failed to materialise. It was a close run thing. The compulsions of the Second Front would have given short shrift to any such a reckless endangering adventure.

CHAPTER 11

Towards Defeat, summer 1944–45

Hempel's reports

The success of the hazardous, incredibly daring, Normandy Invasion (June 1944) made clear that the 'unconditional surrender' of the German Forces was now an attainable Allied objective.[1] Spurred by the imminence of a defeat, the full SS State closed ranks. The attempt on Hitler's life (20/7/1944) accelerated that impetus, as the unresponsive Allies did not take seriously the existence of real resistance to Hitler. If they had done so, and capitalised on it, there was a possibility that a further nine months of intensified carnage could have been avoided. Roosevelt's fixed ideas on the 'unconditional surrender' concept, ensured that 'a German was a German' and that was that: 'the only good German was a dead one'.

The old *Beamtenstadt*, of which Hempel's family had been pillars, had merged comparatively easily with the *Volksgenossenstadt*, where the survival of the State had become the overriding factor. The virtues of loyalty and obedience, which Hempel and his generation had cherished, and which had hitherto done little to halt the progression of a Nazi 'take-over', now under pressure of war, served to ease the transition to an SS State.[2] Hempel continued to function in Dublin as the German representative of this State. '*Befehl ist Befehl*' – 'an order is an order' still pervaded to muzzle and spancel ordinary German citizens.

Frau Hempel continued to crucially support her husband in his duties and retained her genuine honourable German patriotism, which however (as happened with many others of her class) had been subsumed by the propaganda pervasiveness of the master myth-maker, Goebbels, and woven into the Nazi philosophy. This is not to say that she was a Nazi and she denied that they had been used by Goebbels, and their innate virtues of order and obedience abused. Her husband was very much influenced by her: it was her steadfastness and wifely support which sustained him in the dark days ahead. She was a fine example of all that is best in German women, but very few Germans of that indoctrinated generation were immune from Siegfried illusions.

Some Germans, even after the reverse in Normandy, still retained notions of a *deus ex machina* intervention to turn the tide. Over a week after D-day (13/6/1944), a 'flying-bomb' (a guided missile), VI attack on Britain started. Paris was liberated on 25 August 1944, but on 8 September 1944 the first German rocket bomb, V2, fell on England. The V2s were more unpredictable and nerve-wrecking than the V1s. It is doubtful if the target acquisition data which Hempel previously supplied would have been a factor in the targeting of these 'buzz bombs' and rockets. They were inherently inaccurate: fall of shot was random and haphazard. It was not possible to precisely target them; they had a devastating effect on strained-to-breaking-point civilian morale.[3]

The situation should have allowed Hempel more opportunity to concentrate on his designated consular rather than the unspoken, covert side of his mission. However, the antics of Goertz, even in prison, once more served to distract him.

Goertz no longer received the special treatment he was supposed to have got when he was interned initially in Arbour Hill, where it was alleged the prisoner occasionally got strawberries and cream from General MacNeill's wife, who lived next door in army married quarters. He was transferred to Athlone. To Hempel he had become the nuisance personally, which he had been politically and militarily.

He had heard confidentially that Goertz was planning to escape from internment to Northern Ireland, but his friends had strongly advised against such an escapade. He stressed how this move, even at this late stage of the war, could still jeopardise Irish neutrality.[4] Following this, von Grote advised the Reichsführer (7/7/1944) that Hempel should in no way be involved in anything connected with the projected escape of Goertz.[5] But the 'buck was not to be passed' so easily. A reply from the Reichsführer's office to von Grote (18/7/1944) indicated that Hempel would have to make up his own mind, as they were not in a position to judge all the aspects or possibilities of the case. Only Hempel, they pointed out, as the man in the spot, was in a proper position to make these judgements. That did not suit the Envoy at all, who preferred to give 'I am directed' replies where decision making was concerned. (Frau Hempel would not concede this indecisiveness at all but the facts and the language speak for themselves.)

Goertz, through intermediaries, kept pressing the German Minister for £400 to assist his escape and Hempel was not able to make up his mind. He referred the matter once more to headquarters. He sent a telegram on the dangerous political complications and consequences of dragging the Legation into the affair. Goertz, he said, was labouring under a misconception and the prospects of effecting a successful escape were so slim as to be almost non-existent. Von Grote once more lent him bureaucratic support (11/9/1944) in his efforts to avoid having the Legation become involved in this escape bid. Hempel was not disposed to follow the logic of his own reasoning in the matter; but Berlin was even less disposed to take his decisions for him. On 18 September 1944 the *Reichsführer Reichssicherheitshauptamt, Militärisches Amt* (who undoubtedly, considering the remorseless progress of the war from a German point of view, must have had more important matters to deal with) wrote back that it was a matter for Hempel himself. The Minister Plenipotentiary would simply have to make up his own mind as to how to proceed. This was tantamount to a rebuff: but Hempel's apprehension, while it may have been indicative of the so-called Civil Service incapability of making a decision, has to be viewed against the increasing irrationality and arbitrariness with which the affairs of the SS State were now run.[6] It was embarrassing for the ultra-correct Envoy, ever concerned with punctiliously keeping up appearances, to find that communications addressed to him concerning Goertz still carried headings for the infiltration operation, '*Unternehmen Mainau*'. He had always been afraid that something like this could happen. Apart from proprieties, this was a sterile unrealistic proposition based on spurious premises.[7] Hempel would have been even more apprehensive had he known that the messages smuggled out of the Athlone Internment camp for Goertz fell first into the hands of Irish intelligence, who promptly passed their contents on to bland British intelligence, which could just as readily bite the hand that fed it.

Irish Army intelligence had broken the Goertz code and intercepted the agents' outgoing messages. Van Loon, Goertz's cell-mate, however, later insisted that they had got through, citing a secretly coded advertisement in *The Irish Times* to prove it. There are rarely Euclidean QED solutions to intelligence problems. The breaking of German codes remains a subject of debate. Andrews had used the code given to Goertz and the Germans themselves had difficulty deciphering it. With '*Ultra*' however, the British broke most codes.

Ireland's secret weapon in this field was Dr Richard Hayes of the

National Library. He is said to have helped the British break a troublesome code during the 1944 Ardennes Offensive, though Constantine Fitzgibbon, then on the Allied intelligence staff, testily refuted this. The fact remains that, after the war, MI5 invited 'Hayes to have a week at London's expense'. He had the time of his life. Hayes also decoded codes in salvaged cannisters, which had been jettisoned from a German submarine and washed up on the Cork coast. They were picked up post-haste by Ed Lalor (SAS) for the Allies in Normandy. There was never any acclaim. Such acclaim, in any case, would have embarrassed doctrinaire neutralists who made a religion of 'neutrality'. It may be true, however, that the Irish never broke all Hempel's own codes and his communication, by whatever means, was ongoing. The British apparently did not, and the British and Irish intelligence services worked hand-in-glove, but one never knows. The Irish side did fox Goertz into handing over his coded messages to their 'plant', Sergeant Power.[8] Hempel was cuter.

If the following sensational claim is correct, Hempel was still in contact with his masters and was prepared apparently, when the occasion demanded, to operate in areas extending beyond the conventional consular ones. Towards the end of the summer (1944) a cousin of Hempel's friend, Dr Gogan, returned from England, where he had been working in an aircraft factory.[9] His name was Russell, a one-time RFC pilot and former Officer Commanding of the Irish Army Air Corps. He told Gogan of preparations in England for an airborne landing in Holland. Gogan immediately rushed Russell out to Hempel's where, he said, the Envoy interviewed the cross-channel worker at great length and reported accordingly. How Hempel reported is not clear. Frau Hempel was adamant that he was getting messages through, via Switzerland right up to the end. Nothing was transparent.[10] Gogan did not say how it was reported, but he was convinced that the information supplied was responsible for the repulse by the Germans of the Allied attempt at an airborne landing at Arnhem: Operation 'Market Garden' (17/9/1944). The Second SS Panzer Corps were in position in the Arnhem area, not limping and badly mauled as Montgomery had anticipated, but poised in a high state of combat readiness.[11] The rest is history if you want to believe the consequences. There is no doubt about the happening. Dr Gogan was an honourable man. Likewise Frau Hempel remembered it.

Dr Gogan had fought in the 1916 Rising and was implacably

anti-British, persisting in spite of the evidence, that the British had engineered the North Strand bombing. Still the sequences of facts from Russell to Hempel to Arnhem are incontrovertible and Dr Gogan's integrity is unimpeachable. Readers should draw their own conclusions as to whether his claim is 'tenuous' or not.

Hempel's Efforts to Protect German Interests

There were of course other German interests of a consular nature to be protected at home and looking after the interests of the other internees as well as Goertz formed a major portion of this concern. The German Minister had been specifically instructed by the High Command to look after the internees.[12] In addition to the agents landed both by sea and by parachute, a most important contact man, Warner B. Unland, who had been kept under surveillance for some time by the Irish authorities before being picked up, was also interned.[13] His wife remained free to worry Hempel. She complained to him that the complaints Marschner (Schutz) had made to him during his escape from Mountjoy were ill-founded. These presumably affected her husband. Schutz and Goertz were to be the most troublesome internees. Their actions could have compromised Hempel politically. However, Goertz's letters smuggled out of internment by a (wrongly) supposedly suborned army Sergeant Power, for Germany via Hempel, were bagged *en route* by army intelligence. Goertz was set up and notified of his promotion. This moved him greatly. Hempel was being used by both sides, each intent on misleading the other.[14]

While Gunter Schutz, alias Marschner, was at large Hempel was instructed to help him to get on with the espionage job for six months, to give him plenty of money and to procure identification papers. Fortunately for the Envoy's concern to avoid being compromised, Schutz had neither the stature nor the luck to warrant this type of assistance. He was picked up, so Hempel, to his relief, was spared involvement. He just did not want to get involved in any shape or form.

He did assist the internees as instructed but he kept his distance. He did not write to them or visit them; but he did send books, tobacco and soap and arranged for the Red Cross parcels to be delivered. Persistently pestered by Goertz, he used Red Cross agencies to continually console the erratic agent with the good news that his wife and family were safe in Hamburg, and that his home had escaped being damaged by the bombing. This expressed concern made Goertz feel, in the latter part of 1944, that he could enlist the German Minister's aid in escaping. He obviously did not know Hempel. The thought of the complications and the inevitable consequential compromise horrified the Envoy. Frau Hempel pointed out that the escape of Goertz at that point, apart at all from being unwise fundamentally, would have been unsafe for the agent himself. In any case Hempel had no intention of putting himself out unduly to try to solve all the internees' problems, including their financial ones. He was determined not to get too mixed up with them if he could avoid it. He accepted however that there were some unavoidable contacts in wartime.

He regarded Mrs Unland as one such. She was a lively character who kept him 'on his toes' looking for expenses for herself and her husband. These incidental, inescapable financial problems of the internees took up a good portion of his time.[15] His financial accounts, in spite of the other pressures of the war on the East and West Fronts, and in the air, were carefully checked at headquarters and minor errors were adjusted.[16]

That did not shut out the war. The time was approaching for the last German counter-offensive to try to reach Antwerp from the snow-filled Ardennes through the Meuse river in Belgium (The Battle of the Bulge: December 1944). Hempel did not regard that last throw of the dice as a reason for not keeping his accounts straight. Bruchmanns did the bookkeeping. Every penny was accounted for and, whatever he felt about them, he was conscientious in looking after the needs of the internees.   He successfully passed on their request that their monthly cigarette money be increased from three to four pounds per internee.[17]

The mundane and the melodramatic walked hand-in-hand in considering a plea from the amazing Weber-Dohl for his release on medical grounds, and for a visit by his son from London.[18] Hempel was increasingly conscious of the compromising threat posed by the agents since 1940. He was not sorry to see them all interned out of harm's way: and that included Weber-Drohl. He had himself to think about. In the latter half of 1944 there was nothing they could do outside, as far as he was concerned, but cause trouble. In his eyes they had been inept, inefficient and unfortunate; a nuisance and a menace.

At the end of 1944 his recorded telegrams ceased abruptly. It seems unlikely that the compulsive reporter should suddenly cease reporting. In the Foreign and Commonwealth Office, all German documents relating to Ireland terminated in 1944, so in 1945 there are no more captured telegrams to 'reveal' Hempel's mind on matters affecting the denouement of diplomatic relations between the two countries.[19] From his wife, we know that he continuously, meticulously pursued the externals of his office, sending messages through Switzerland, right up to the end. No record of the Gogan-Russell Arnhem message was located but such top secret messages are not filed or indexed. Frau Hempel was adamant that it was sent but did not say how. Obviously convention and protocol were set aside, when needs must.

He was normally very conscious – maybe excessively so – of the importance of protocol and like most diplomats he had come to revere protocol as an end in itself: a game of conventions and rules to be played out relentlessly, regardless. In this rigid adherence to the protocol of externals Hempel was matched on occasion by de Valera; de Valera though was more Machiavellian. The most controversial illustration of this was de Valera's call on Hempel to express sympathy on the death of Hitler.[20]

Hitler's Death: Winding Up of Legation

The Battle of the Bulge illustrated once more that the German Army was expert in tactics but weak on strategy. The plan for the battle was said to have 'originated with Hitler'.[21] The set-back sent Hitler scurrying back to Berlin in mid-January 1945 and almost immediately he opted for the troglodyte existence in the bunker until the time came for him to carry out, for the record, his rehearsed suicide.[22] In contrast to these elaborately stage-managed exits of Hitler and Goebbels, which were not without manifest physical courage, Ribbentrop, Hempel's minister, went into hiding in Hamburg, in the apartment of his mistress. The deserted Wilhelmstrasse, 'the old smart diplomatic quarter', was 'now Germany's boulevard of broken dreams'.[23] Hempel was crushed and humiliated, though Frau Hempel insisted that the humiliation arose from Hitler committing suicide instead of dying fighting.

Hitler died on 30 April 1945 and, when his death was announced, de Valera accompanied by Joseph P. Walshe, the Secretary to the Department of External Affairs, paid a formal call of condolence on the German Minister (3/5/1945). This action brought an outcry of outrage from the Allied press. The Irish public in general however, smarting from the contemptuous dismissal of their country's enormous contribution to the war effort in all fields, while maintaining its sovereignty and self-respect, many took a vicarious pleasure in the reaction provided. A letter to *The Times* of London referred to de Valera as 'a totalitarian termite incapable of departing in any circumstances from the conventions of diplomacy – a Casiabianca of the protocol'.[24] But the Taoiseach justified his actions: his point of view was that so long as Éire retained diplomatic relations with Germany 'to have failed to call upon the German representative would have been an act of unpardonable discourtesy to the German nation and to Dr Hempel himself'. He did not intend to add to Hempel's humiliation in the hour of defeat (ironically that was just what he did). He wrote: 'during the whole of the war, Dr Hempel's conduct was irreproachable. He was always friendly and invariably correct in marked contrast with Gray.' The Taoiseach and Minister for External Affairs gave other reasons for his actions such as that it was 'important that it should never be inferred that these formal acts imply the passing of any judgements, good or bad'.[25] De Valera felt that he had acted correctly and wisely. The superfluous letter he wrote in addition was offered for sale in London later. A younger generation of Hempel's unaware of the personal call, thought that letter was what all the furore had been about and could not understand all that fuss 'about a letter'.

The grandiloquent gesture fell flat. The 'condolers' found Hempel in a distressed and inconsolable state. He kept wringing his hands and crying repetitively: 'It's all so humiliating; it's all so humiliating'. It is not clear whether he was referring to Germany having lost the war or to the implications of the visit. The visitors were disappointed in him. They had expected a more stoic heroic composure: but his repeated use of the word 'humiliating' upset them. They tried to excuse the unhappy choice of word by allowing for the fact that Hempel was a foreigner, but had to remind themselves that the Envoy's English was very good. The dramatisation of the visit seemed to have been lost on the German Minister. The deflated deputation were disappointed in him.[26] It fell flatter than flat.

Frau Hempel had a different impression of the events: she was present. She never saw her husband 'wringing his hands' but she explained that eczema on the back of his hands did cause itching and scratching. Her version – and she was there – was that they very quickly spoke of matters other than the death of Hitler, such as the fate of their family in Germany. Hitler's death was no surprise to her husband, she said 'he had seen it coming'. They realised instinctively that de Valera's visit would bring trouble. She stressed that the Taoiseach visited Hempel's home rather than the Legation.[27] Some saw this move as more de Valera Machiavallianism.

A week later Hempel visited de Valera to hand over his Legation: the war was over and German passion was spent.[28] According to one source, some members of the German colony (not the Hempels) relieved the Legation of portable items like typewriters and duplicators before the close down. Frau Hempel's version is that they were simply recovering stuff left in for stocktaking and that anyway, it was better than what eventually happened to them. On 10 May 1945, the key of the Legation was handed over to David Gray as the representative of the American Occupation Force in Germany – 'plenipotentiary of the new "new authority" in Germany'.[29] Hempel's post-war efforts to set up in business, according to Frau Hempel, were frustrated by British influences.[30]

Hempel and the Death of Goertz

Goertz still turned out to be a nemesis who, from the moment of his arrival in May 1940, had cast a shadow over Hempel. Even in death he tormented him. Hempel was pilloried by the friends of Goertz for not attending his funeral.

Judge Wyse Power advised him not to attend. The Hempels had intended to go but the advice was that it would be impolitic to do so and Hempel, being the man he was, 'the fixed person for a fixed job', one of 'the technicians of diplomacy', conformed, naturally.[31]

The coffin was wrapped in the swastika (should have been under the 'schwarz-weiss-rot', the German colours, Frau Hempel sniffed). The faithful Farrell sisters wore Goertz's decorations throughout the funeral. They were paying homage to the incurably romantic *Abwehr* man who, unlike the hapless Hempels, was not subject to the restraints of diplomatic bureaucracy. However, differences aside, on the night of the famous 'where's the w.c.' password, a certain rapport generated between the *Wilhelmatrasse* diplomat and the High Command Spy. That feeling may have prompted Boland to seek Hempel's aid in the ensuing Goertz debacle.

Goertz was pathologically, probably with good reason, apprehensive of falling into British or Russian hands. When the Department of Justice granted him asylum and released him from internment, he stayed on in Ireland, taking a low-paid job as Secretary of the Save the German Children Fund. After the war, however, de Valera yielded to Allied insistence that the spies in Ireland be repatriated to undergo investigation. They were reinterned preparatory to deportation. Goertz's worst fears were realised. He panicked and enlisted Hempel's aid for a reprieve. Hempel did intervene with both de Valera and Boland and assurances were given accordingly to Goertz that he had nothing to fear in returning. Goertz refused to be pacified when Boland and Hempel visited him in Mountjoy. He was later released on parole.

He looked for advice from an ex-internee, Luftwaffe navigator, George Fleischmann, who had managed to stay on in Ireland when other internees were being repatriated. He was making a name for himself as a film maker. (Dan Breen, the TD, violently anti-British from his War of Independence days, helped him. He offered Fleischmann a hide-out in Kilkenny and Tipperary when he was evading repatriation. As it turned out Fleischmann was able to use other influences to stay.)[32] Goertz asked the ex-navigator's opinion as to what he thought was 'going on', as he had been invited to dinner with the Hempels in Dún Laoghaire; Boland was also to be a guest. Fleischmann told him that, whatever it was, it could not be bad: the best thing was to accept Hempel's invitation to dinner, see how things turned out and afterwards they would meet in the Royal Marine Hotel to discuss the outcome.

It was four o'clock in the morning when a very agitated Goertz emerged from Hempel's house to meet up with Fleischmann again. Fleischmann could not calm him. The proposition put to him by Boland, with Hempel's equivocal backing, was to consider an offer from the Americans to work for them.

Goertz did not recognise Cold War realignments, and the prospect of working for his former enemies appalled him: he would never change sides. Fleischmann advised him pragmatically. The Americans would look after his wife and son in Hamburg: he should 'play along' for a while and then, if he found it too distasteful, take evasive action. Goertz was not convinced, but agreed to think it over. They walked through the night tossing and turning the problem. Boland, according to what Fleischmann said that Goertz said, had given the agent, in Hempel's hearing, until the following Saturday to make up his mind, whether to accept the American offer or not, telling him not to worry about his parole, which was due to expire that same Saturday. That would be taken care of.

In Frau Hempel's reasoning it was not really an offer as such: there were more 'ifs' and 'buts' and 'mights' in it than 'wills and shalls'. Addled Goertz went to the West for the rest of the week to calm his nerves and clear his mind. He was invited to lunch at Hempel's on his return after his arranged visit to the Aliens' office. He did not turn up for the lunch. He killed himself instead.

When Goertz duly went along to the Aliens' office for an extension of his parole, a Special Branch man met him and told him that a Dakota plane was waiting to fly him back to Germany. In Fleischmann's opinion, the hyper-sensitive Goertz felt that he had been betrayed, tricked and trapped, and badly let down by Hempel and Boland. The Clongownian 'chaps' approach of Boland did not seem to have established the necessary rapport with Goertz. And the starchy pedantic Hempel was not the best choice to play the role of 'ein guter Kamerad'. Fleischmann felt that he had gone a good part of the way to repair those deficiencies – not far enough obviously.

An inexcusable bureaucratic slip-up between the Department of External Affairs and the Department of Justice stopped the Hempel-witnessed undertaking given by Boland to Goertz. Colonel Bryan felt that they (Army intelligence) would have handled it better. They would have asked Goertz if there was anything else against him outside of his pre-war period in custody in England, after he had been apprehended for spying there. If the answer was negative they would have appealed to his sense of duty and patriotism – that the mission he would be going on would not so much be working for the Americans but serving his country against the Russians, in the only way possible in the circumstances. Dr Boland, who had done so much for Hempel and Irish-German relations, did not spare himself preparing what he hoped would be a palatable proposition for Dr Goertz. He was very upset at his suicide.[33]

The story of Goertz's suicide is well known. A military funeral was sought: the nearest he got to it was being buried in Fleischmann's old Luftwaffe Greatcoat. The Misses Farrell in Dún Laoghaire, with whom 'the Doctor' used to stay, unaware of any suggestion of bureaucratic bungling, bitterly blamed Hempel for his death.[34] Following his revered protocol, he had sounded out the Irish government to see if approval would be forthcoming for his attendance at the funeral. That reply was negative: the judge's warning copper-fastened it for the diplomat.[35] His non-attendance at the funeral did not enhance his reputation in Ireland, a country where funerals are special, and a feeling persisted, unfairly, in 'Goertz circles' that Hempel had been less than magnanimous or helpful in his treatment of the well-loved and romantic agent. Yet again, the Envoy was misunderstood on the one hand, and exposed on the other. That, in essence, was the story of his life as Hitler's Envoy Extraordinary and Minister Plenipotentiary in a paradoxically neutral Éire (26 Counties), which had a land-linked controversial neighbour, Northern Ireland (6 Counties) at war.

Epilogue

'What you saw was what you got', was one cryptic verdict on the protocolled diplomat. That does not tell us much about the middle-aged, allegedly dry-as-dust, cold-fish civil servant, who wooed and won a beautiful German maiden half his age, had five children by her, and lived happily ever after with her. We know his CV but we do not know the secret of that success.

We know that he was born in Saxony in 1887, fought as a cavalry officer with a Saxonian regiment in the 1914–18 war, became a professional civil servant attached to the German Foreign Office in (1919): that Dublin conveyed diplomatically in 1937 they did not want a Nazi as the German representative in Dublin and got Hempel instead.

He loved the order, the correctness, the rules of diplomacy. The form was all. The Irish government intended its declaration of neutrality to be a declaration of sovereignty. That demanded a liturgy and a religious reverence for protocol appearances. Appearances and externals were of prime importance. Against that background, Hempel's success as a diplomat in Ireland had to be measured. He satisfied de Valera: and the British. To his credit he did not satisfy Ribbentrop and Veesenmayer.

There is a German saying that there are two ways in this world to judge a man: the kind of woman he marries and the way 'he dies'.[1] Hempel scored highly on both counts. Frau Hempel disarmingly told me that they 'romped' (her word) on the bed the day before he died at the age of 85. They were devoted to each other throughout.

She was a magnificent woman in everything except perhaps in a blind spot of 'pop star' infatuation for Hitler, which she shared with the majority of German women of the period. They saw Hitler as the saviour of Germany. He had solved the unemployment problem, built roads (autobahn) and tamed an inflation which was destroying the family and society. He had given back self-respect to the Fatherland.

The conventional territory for German women in male-dominated Germany, '*Kinder, Küche, Kirche*' (children, kitchen, church), did not encourage female questioning beyond observing, 'if the Führer only knew'[2] as a response when things went wrong. It enhanced femininity at the expense of feminism. Frau Hempel thrived on it.

During her time in the Legation, she caused many a staid bureaucratic heart, even in their later years, to beat a little faster, such was her striking beauty. She was an endless topic of second-wife erotic speculation among the cut-off German internees in the Curragh: this she was not. Hempel was both a father figure and a little boy figure for her. He would have been lost without her.

His own pursuits and hobbies were intellectual and he remained somewhat remote even from his family. He was always ultra-correct: even at home he was always 'the boss' and demanded to be treated with respect. The girls stood to attention to him. Frau Hempel summed up – that he was 'fair but strict'. The Hempels were aware of their importance and the habits of the diplomat dominated the household.

The children saw very little of their parents. They had their meals at the other end of a very large house and only saw them when they queued up to say good morning and good night. Occasionally in a bout of togetherness, the children would be summoned to have their midday meal with them but they were not supposed to speak unless spoken to and they were too scared to indulge in any chatter. The parents conversed in French so that they could speak freely. There was a lack of communication.

He was a modest man in his own way though he is alleged to have been quick 'to get up on his high horse'. He was quite impractical in ordinary matters and 'couldn't drive a nail'.[3] He punctiliously attired for each and every occasion: if he were going to the beach he donned beach wear with not a button out of place and so on. He would dress ceremoniously to attend to the bees and then have to be rescued by his wife when the bees turned angry and buzzed him. Frau Hempel liked bees and initially did not need protection until one day they turned on her too.

She kept the house going in every way and provided for the family from the proceeds of her confectionery business. Dr Hempel, through no fault of his own, except maybe a lack of adaptability and flexibility, was unable to turn his hand to making a living, now that he was out of office. Still he liked to pace about as master of the house and she indulged him. Once when the drains were blocked he called 'a conference' with the other occupants of the house, the O'Flanagans. After lengthy convoluted deliberations, leading nowhere, they eventually solved the problem themselves, simply and directly. But Hempel revelled in the conferring for its own sake, even though it tangented from the problem-solving in question.

Other relations were of a more sombre nature. Thomsen's exhibitionist railing against the Nazis after the war infuriated Eva Hempel because of its hypocrisy: her later, changed comment was that 'Thomsen had been the biggest Nazi of the lot'. Thomsen refuted this:

> After the attacks against the *Auswärtiges Amt* to employ former leading Nazis everybody who wanted to return to the Foreign Services had to be agreed upon by a special Bundestag Committee composed of members of all parties. Only after having received a green light by the committee did the Foreign Office recall one for service.[4]

Thomsen was recalled with ambassador rank to serve in Iceland and Africa. Frau Hempel explained that no one who held her husband's rank under Hitler received that rank back. The de-Nazification process apparently washed whiter than white or else somebody was still 'looking after their own'. The Cold War took the heat out of the de-Nazification process. Russia was now the visible enemy.

Hempel went back to his pre-war job – looking after Foreign Office furniture and accommodation. Ironically he did not do as well on recall as Thomsen, but then he was older. Warnock termed Hempel's post 'some sort of Board of Works job'. He recalled mischievously that not even the stolid ex-Envoy was immune from Cupid's trip-wires. On one such trip to Switzerland he met 'an old flame' – the wife of the Austrian Ambassador.[5] Of course nothing improper occurred: he had a wife who remained eternally young and beautiful, though according to Warnock, the old flames did apparently briefly flicker. The fate of other contemporaries of Hempel on the losing side was not so felicitous.

The Irish government did not help those who had 'bucked' them. For his family's sake (the Bewleys were an established highly respected Dublin Quaker family), they made an exception of

Charles Bewley: but they were quite vindictive with Francis Stuart. He was not helped when he was getting rough treatment from the French, and his passport was not renewed. Thomsen was dealt with differently: he was simply not invited to anything. On one occasion he turned up fuming at a function in Bonn during Warnock's ambassadorship there, demanding explanations for not being invited. He did not get any.

By contrast, the good offices of Sir John Maffey were invoked to facilitate the return of Hempel to Germany in 1949. Maffey, at de Valera's request, was also instrumental in saving Bewley – who had been regarded by Hempel as such a mischievous anachronism and an annoyance – from being shot after he had been captured by the Americans in their advance up through Italy. The wording of Maffey's petition would not have pleased the wayward de Valera-phobe, who never lost an opportunity to detract from de Valera for his alleged pro-Britishness. Bewley, the self-styled 'true republican', according to Maffey, 'came from a very loyal British family; he was well connected, with a brother in the Treasury, etc. and his execution would cause a great deal of embarrassment'.[6] The post-war paths of Hempel and Bewley did not cross. There was no love lost between them.

Hempel had only two years left to serve after his return to Germany (1949) and subsequent recall to the Foreign Ministry. He retired on pension in 1952 and lived privately at his home in Freiburg until his death (12/11/1972). He was the only surviving member of his family. His younger brother, who had accompanied Eduard on the extended tour of the Far East in 1913, had been killed in the Battle of the Somme in 1918. He spurned publicity.

He had had some unhappy experiences with the Irish press generally[7] and when P.P. O'Reilly interviewed him on his retirement, the Radio Éireann reporter found the ex-Envoy still hemmed in by diplomatic protocol. He was old and he did not feel free to make the same caustic comments on Irish weaknesses that he had made in his telegrams.[8]

However, this obsession with protocol was what made Hempel a crucial link in keeping up neutrality appearances. He invariably said the right thing and put a good face on things. Conversely, this trait, luckily for Ireland, did not enhance the German representative's usefulness to Veesenmayer, the *coup d'état* specialist who had the mission from Ribbenbtrop of fomenting rebellion in Ireland. He needed a more devious envoy, a swash-buckling 'Siegfried', for his purposes. Hempel was no intriguer. He had given a lifetime of service to the Foreign Office and was a dedicated career diplomat who believed in its form.

His death was reported in the *Irish Independent* (13/11/1972). His career was outlined: when he arrived in Dublin (1937), he discovered that he was the only non-party man in the German Legation. The report held that Hempel was so unaware of what was happening around in the Legation that it was widely believed that the real head of the Legation was the wartime First Secretary, Herr Thomsen, a member of the SS. Hempel, the report alleged, was kept completely in the dark regarding widespread intrigues by Nazi spies in Ireland and German dealings with the IRA. Thomsen condemned the *Independent* story as nonsense.[9] It underestimated Hempel. The British knew better and esteemed him professionally: 'It was his (Cranborne's) belief that the German Minister (Hempel) had on the whole behaved well'. According to Frau Hempel, her husband knew what people were saying about Thomsen, but did not believe it. Thomsen, in the Envoy's opinion, was just young and ambitious. Hempel was in control, or so he thought. Dan Bryan felt that they had 'perhaps been too hard on Thomsen'.[10]

There is no evidence that British satisfaction with Hempel implied a satisfaction with the way he may have responded to provocation baits. Provocation was part of ongoing psychological warfare (now psychological operations). Hempel was apprehensive of this and generally tried 'to keep himself covered'. This 'Beamter' syndrome in turn contributed to a lack of certitude: his inconclusive reporting, seeing all sides – 'on the one hand but on the other hand' – infuriated and finally frustrated Veesenmayer.

If the British knew – and there was not much that they did not know – they would have approved of the manner in which the German Minister happened to 'drag his feet' in matters which would have served to promote the adventuresomeness of Veesenmayer, involving the IRA. It is a sombre question as to how the dutiful Envoy would have reacted, had he been aware that his master Ribbentrop was the author and formulator of Veesenmayer's mission to foment rebellion in Ireland, but he was well aware that both of these were of a different opinion to himself. Intriguingly, he was not altogether in the dark either. It seemed to have been mere fortuitousness and expediency – 'backing it each way' – that induced Ribbentrop to keep Hempel out of *direct* involvement with the IRA. If Hempel had encouraged the Irish adventure, the resultant shattering of the policy of neutrality would have been disastrous, not only for the Allies and the Germans alike, but principally, for Ireland.

Hempel was right in his analysis that the majority of the Irish people had put their trust in de Valera to pursue a policy of neutrality and in his conclusion that de Valera was the man of destiny to see that policy through its difficult, tortuous course. He plotted his own course accordingly. He served Ireland well. Ireland was lucky to have had him. He was lucky to have been in Ireland. All his family fell in love with Ireland. Sadly however, the ruinous happenings in the concentration camps, which came to light at the end of the war, devastated and alienated the younger members. Their strict upbringing had given them very high standards. Belsen and Auschwitz were shattering shocks to them. However, they showed great resilience and got on with life in their chosen environments. So did many of the forceful characters who were caught up in the war.

Helmut Clissmann became a successful businessman. He founded the now thriving German Society.[11] Fleischmann made a name for himself in the film world.[12] He was born in Austria in 1921 and qualified at the Film Academy in Berlin. He worked as a cameraman at UFA Studios and the 1936 Olympics. After his internment he remained in Ireland and founded Hibernia Films. He produced news reels, filmed activities of the Defence Forces, ESB, Aer Lingus and various government departments such as agriculture, health and foreign affairs. Between 1947 and 1989 he made up to seventy films including one on Yeats. It was quite an achievement for a Luftwaffe reconaissance photographer who crash-landed and was interned for 'the duration'. In 1951 he filmed *Return to Glennascaul* and later was second unit director on John Huston's *Moby Dick*. He returned to Germany in 1959 to work for Rank from depressed 'tigerless' Ireland, but returned in the sixties to work on the first ever TV broadcast in the Republic. He continued to make commercial films.

Monsignor Hugh O'Flaherty, 'the Vatican Pimpernel', is perhaps the most noteworthy character to flit across the pages. There is a glimpse of him allegedly slipping a Kilnacroth message to Bewley. He put his life on the line, succouring, in turn, German and British prisoners of war. He took great risks. Intriguingly, the contrary Bewley was a close friend of his: they discussed liturgy.[13] He was the uncle of Judge Hugh O'Flaherty.

Francis Stuart, the novelist, was another contemporary talent who blossomed in spite of official discouragement. He became a member of Aosdána, an affiliation of artists established by the Arts Council in 1983, by which time he and his German wife, Madelaine, had well shaken the dust of wantonly incinerated Dresden from their feet.

The craggy Northern Irish Protestant born in Australia (1902) of Irish parents was not a stylish writer to begin with but by dint of persistent chiseling he eventually made an outstanding contribution to literature, notably with his autobiographical novel *Black List: Section H* (1971).

He was brought up in Ireland and educated in England. He received a Royal Irish Academy award for his privately published first collection of poetry in 1924. He turned to novel writing in the 1930s, without however any best-selling 'impact'. He published eight further unremarkable novels between 1933 and 1940 and he had two forgettable plays produced by the Abbey Theatre.

In 1940 Hempel helped him – then an IRA agent – to take up a post as lecturer at the University of Berlin, where he remained for the duration of World War II. Between 1942 and 1944 he made a series of radio broadcasts[14] to Ireland which greatly embarrassed the Irish government. They were instrumental in his post-war detention by the French until 1946. They were a lugubrious mish-mash, invoking 'the most dangerous of all tyrannies – the tyranny of the dead'.[15] He contributed to IRA irresponsibility and was a threat to the security of the State. Hempel's pedestrianism acted, on the one hand, as a cover for this threat, and on the other hand, as a deterrent to it. As Veesenmayer would complain, what you thought you saw, was sometimes what you did not get.

Hempel's appearance of correctness was an essential component in keeping up the façade of Irish neutrality, which paradoxically, permitted 'a certain consideration for Britain'. The Irish solution to a British survival problem allowed supplies, manpower, intelligence, weather, to be given to Britain. Hindsight acknowledges that Irish style neutrality was not only the best solution for both Britain and Ireland, but the only rational solution to the wartime problem.

It was indeed 'a close run thing', confirming de Valera's expressed belief that it could not be repeated in future global wars. In such circumstances, Ireland would perforce show 'a certain consideration' for Europe. Survival is increasingly predicated on interdependency.

As the war progressed it became increasingly plain to de Valera that his brand of ambivalent neutrality would not work in future and could only be contemplated from a position of barrier physical features, e.g. like nearest-to-neutral Switzerland, or with some other compelling deterrent. One way or another, it could only be contrived from a position of armed strength.

From the outset de Valera had stressed that Irish neutrality in World War II was a matter of expediency, not doctrine. He made it clear to Hempel that his 'certain consideration for Britain' anomaly would be accorded to Germany, in similar circumstances. Pavlovian Hempel did not question Dev's 'similar circumstances', bearing out Veesenmayer's contention that he was no match for Éire's Taoiseach and Minister for External Affairs, Eamon de Valera. Hempel may not have pleased Veesenmayer (which gratified Frau Hempel), or the fragmented Nazis and their IRA collaborators, but he suited de Valera who, mistakenly, marked his appreciation by his visit to him on Hitler's death.

Hempel had an impossible mission but, from his point of view, he accomplished it by helping to keep Éire neutral. A subversionary streak in a mission has a chameleon quality which allows myopia. He did his best to act properly according to his lights, and within his remit.

Herr Hempel was a Minister First Class, appointed by the uniquely evil Adolf Hitler and accredited by the King of England to represent Hitler's lawless Nazi regime in neutral Éire, which had reduced the King to a rubber stamp in External Affairs and to whom England was the 'ancient enemy'.

Hempel articulated his mission in neutrality terms. However, that mission could only be accomplished within de Valera's terms of 'certain consideration for Britain'. On the one hand, then, Hempel's voiced mission could be said to have been actually accomplished. De Valera acknowledged the part the German envoy played in what essentially had to contain elements of charade to be presentable: 'he was invariably correct'. On the other hand ...

Notes

NOTES to Chapter 1

1. Conversation with the late Lt. Gen. P.A. Mulcahy.
2. *Irish Times* 19/5/1976 (The 'Fifty years of Fianna Fáil' by Professor John A. Murphy).
3. Ibid.
4. Earl of Longford and T.P. O'Neill, *Éamon de Valera* (Dublin 1970), p.258.
5. J.I. McCracken, *Representative Government in Ireland* (Dublin 1958), p.197; pp.257–8.
6. C.H. Bewley, *Memoirs of a Wild Goose* op. cit. elaborates on German obsequiousness to the British Foreign Office.
7. Radio Éireann, 1977 Thomas Davis Lecture by Professor Kevin Nowlan UCD, referring to German attitudes towards minorities.
8. PAAA 6531 Abschrift zu III E. 1352 Anlage I.
9. PAAA Abt. III Handelsbeziehungen Irlande zu Deutschland Band I (13/8/1932).
10. PAAA Abt. III Vol. 1 (9/11/1932).
11. *Irish Independent* (Letters) (30/12/1932).
12. PAAA R2/10013 folio 1 (6/1/1932).
13. PAAA R2 9914 folios 1–98 (4/1/1935).
14. F & CO 453 951–4 (28/2/1936).
15. F & CO 455 921–92 (31/1/1934) also PAAA Ha Pol Clodius, Serial No. 2167 H.
16. G2/15 S 9439 State Papers' Office (21/1/1937).
17. Enno Stephan, *Spies in Ireland* (1963), p.30.
18. The German historian Andreas Hillgruber discovered the existence of Hitler's *Stufenplan: – Kontinuität und Diskontinuität in der deutschen Aussenpolitik von Bismarck bis Hitler* (Düsseldorf 3rd Edn 1971).
    – *Problems des zweiten Weltkriege*
    – *Hitler's Strategie, Politik und Kriegsführung 1940–41*, Frankfurt a.m. 1945.
    – *Deutschlands Rolle in der Vorgeschichte der beiden Weltkriege*, Göttingen 1967.
19. Klaus Hildebrand, *The Foreign Policy of the Third Reich* (1973), p.vii.
20. Ibid., p.19 and p.23.
21. Letter from Frau Hempel (5/6/1977). C. Carter, *The Shamrock and the Swastika* (Palo Alto 1977), p.28.
22. *Hitler: Deutschland und die Mächte* by Horst Dickel, p.507. Also PAAA Abt. III Handelsbeziehungen Ed. 2 Bericht Schleemann B 531 23/5/1934.
23. *Journal of Commonwealth Political Studies* Vol. VIII (1970), pp.206–28. See also

Deirdre McMahon's thesis on Malcolm McDonald (UCD) and her later book, *Republicans and Imperialists – Anglo-Irish Relations in the 1930s* (Yale University Press 1984).

24. *Journal of Commonwealth Political Studies* Vol. VIII (1970) (Mr de Valera's Dominion: Irish Relations with Britain and the Commonwealth 1932–8, p.206); *The Commonwealth Experience* by P.N.S. Mansergh (London 1969), p.239.

25. Longford and O'Neill op. cit. p.267. Also *Dáil Eireann Debates XXI, 1455* (16/11/1927) on neutrality and *Irish Neutrality and the War Years* by Ryle Dwyer, p.5.

26. PAAA Abt. III Politik Ireland. Militärangelegenheiten (IV) (28/4/1927).

27. Longford and O'Neill op. cit., p.286.

28. Ibid., p.279.

29. *Journal of Commonwealth Political Studies* Vol. VIII (1970), p.208.

30. Ibid.

31. See Note 23.

32. PRO Premier 1/273, p.257–61.

33. *Journal of Commonwealth Political Studies* Vol. VIII (1970), p.224 also PRO CAB 27, 524, 34th meeting (9/6/1937).

34. Robert Briscoe, a Fianna Fáil TD, later to become Lord Mayor of Dublin, was a Jew.

35. *London Times* (16/1/1937).

36. *New York Times* (19/5/1937) – speech to a large audience of priests in the Archbishopric of Chicago.

37. Inaugural sermon in the Basilica of St Therese.

38. R. Smylie, Editor of *The Irish Times,* never seemed to tire reminding his readers of his POW experiences in Germany in World War I.

39. Article 44: Repealed by Referendum 1972. (4th and 5th Amendments).

40. F & CO E 037299 (22/7/1934).

41. F & CO E 037297–9 (30/7/1936).

42. F & CO E 037300–303 (1/8/1936).

43. F & CO E 037304–305 (22/2/1937).

44. F & CO E 037307–309 (18/3/1937).

45. F & CO E 037310–314 (31/5/1937).

46. State Papers G2/14 S. 9834 (21/5/1937).

47. See Note 12, Chapter 2.

NOTES to Chapter 2

1. PRO D.O. 35/654/70/5 (21/8/1937).

2. Based on interviews with, and letters from, Frau Eva Hempel, Eduard Hempel's widow (Eduard was the elder brother).

3. Shown as 'Frau' Ahlmann on F & CO record card. Many of the German internees in Curagh (Herr Voigt, Scarlettstown) thought that she was Hempel's second wife – she was so young looking and the age gap seemed so great.

4. First-born. Born in Oslo.
5. Later dubbed by Hempel 'the government paper'.
6. *Irish Independent* (8/7/1937). As an indication of social patterns of the day the leading article dealt with the difficulties in getting domestic servants.
7. *The Irish Times* (8/7/1937). The proprietary interest of *The Irish Times* in matters German, stemming from the editor's (Smyllie) POW experiences in Germany has already been referred to (See Note 38, Chapter 1) and constitutes a shadowy strand in the Intelligence skein referred to later with reference to Larry de Lacy of *The Irish Times*, a brother-in-law of Stephen Hayes, the IRA Chief of Staff.
8. Present were Mr Séan Murphy, Asst Secretary to the Dept of External Affairs and Dr Rynne of the same Dept; Dr Koester, Counsellor of the German Legation and Frau Koester; Herr F.E. Müller, Chancellor of the Legation; Herr R. Wenzel, Consular Secretary, Frau Wenzel and Fräulein Wenzel. Fräulein Bier and six of the German Legation Staff, Dr Stumpf representing the German colony, Capt. Robert McGurk, Harbour Master Dún Laoire and Alderman Byrne, Lord Mayor of Dublin. *(The Irish Times)* (8.7.1937). Alderman Alfie Byrne was a well-known Dublin public figure of the period. His name was later put forward as a candidate for the first presidency but he subsequently withdrew. The German Legation reported accordingly; as they saw a possibility of 'Graf Eduard Taffe' – a Czech of Irish descent – also being a runner.
9. *The Irish Times* (13/7/1937) had a photograph of the children. The other two Hempel children, Berthold and Agnes, were both born in Dublin, where Berthold died in 1948.
10. The Hempel family finally settled for a house in Gortleitragh, Sloperton, Dún Laoire.
11. Interview with Frau Clissmann (August 1976).
12. Letter from the Foreign Ministry in Bonn (13/9/77) gives the following details:
    (a) Dr Georg von Dehn-Schmidt
         Born 9/2/1876 in Guhrau, Bez. Breslau died 14/7/1937.
         1923–30 Consul General in Dublin (since 1929 also Chargé d'Affaires in Dublin.
         1930–34 Minister First Class in Dublin.
         1934 transferred as Minister First Class to Bucharest.
    (b) Wilhelm von Kuhlmann
         Born 20/1/1879 in Königsberg/Brussels.
         Died 16/1/1937 in Wiesbaden.
         1934–37 Minister First Class in Dublin: during a protracted illness from 1936–37 he was represented by Dr Schroetter.
    (c) Dr Erich Schroetter
         Born 8/4/1875 in Osterode/Harz.
         Died on 14/7/1946.
         Unattached Legation Councillor charged with the temporary representation of the Legation in Dublin 1936–37. (Described as

'Vortragender Legatioinsrat Z.D. 1936 mit der zeitweiigen Vertretung der Gesandtschaf in Dublin beauftragt' – rather than as Geschäftsträger, Chargé d'Affaires).

(d) Dr Eduard Hempel
Born 6/6/1887 in Pirna/Sachsen.
Died 12/11/1972 in Wildtal, Freiburg/Breisgau 1937–45 Minister First Class in Dublin.

13. *The Irish Times* (22/7/1937) *Nichevo* i.e. Smyllie, the editor.

14. Airey Neave, *Nuremberg* (1978), p.348.

15. Letter from Frau Hempel (5/6/1977).

16. PAAA Abt. III Politik 9 Ed. 1 re turning down Nuremberg Party Rally invitation in 1934.

17. *The Irish Times* (22/7/1937). Interview and stories from Prof. Binchy.

18. Gordon Craig, *The Diplomats* (Princeton 1953), p.140.

19. *The Irish Times* (18/1/1936).

20. PAAA Abt. III Band 3 Telegram No. 21 29/10/1934.

21. *The Worker* (11/1/1936) Vol. III No. 44. The left-wing paper also lambasted Lombard Murphy Belton, Alec McCabe, Aileen O'Brien (*Independent*).

22. Seán McEntee, a Belfast veteran of the War of Independence and the Civil War, a Minister in de Valera's Government, said to have, uncharacteristically, pro-British leanings. Alfie was Alderman Alfie Byrne, Lord Mayor of Dublin, who would not normally have been associated with extreme republican sentiment. (See Note 8) (CYMS: the Catholic Young Men's Society).

23. *The Irish Workers' Voice* (15/2/1936) Vol. VII No. 18.

24. See Note 12 (c).

25. PAAA Abt. III Handelsbeziehungen – Bd. IV for the role of the *Auslandsorganisation* in Dublin. See also *Chef Auslandsorganisation* Bd. II Irland. Further references in Gordon A. Craig op. cit. and P. Seabury, *Wilhelmstrasse.*

26. Hitler's Order of Jan. 1937 (DGFP).

27. Gordon A. Craig op. cit. p.478 (The *Allgemeine Zeitung* cited in Hitler's Speeches I 1068).

28. Ibid. i.e. Gordon A. Craig op. cit. p.435.

29. BA Koblenz RS DAM 9322 (7/2/1937). (See also PAAA *Chef Auslandsorganisation* (22/11/1935) and (16/1/1936).

30. Ibid.

31. Ibid. (v. 3067) and 10/2/1937 'unseren Lektoren, Herr Clissmann, gegen die Intrigen Stellen zu schützen'.

32. F & CO 6320/E471481–2. The documents include the letter from Ruberty of the office of AO dated 6 July 1937 which shed light on the reasons for the removal of Herr Schroetter German Minister in 1937.

33. *Irish Independent* report under caption 'Hitler's Envoy Dies' (13/11/1972).

34. See Notes 26, 27, 44.

35. Also conversation with a contemporary diplomat of Hempel, Dr William Warnock in Bern 1975.

36. A card in the F & CO (without serial no. or reference) gives us the following information on Thomsen:

'Geb. 11/7/1885 Berlin evangelisch (this date appears to be incorrect and should read 1905 perhaps – he was a much younger man than Hempel).

SS-Untersturmführer

Beschliessung? A Dipl. Ing. Hiltrud Werner

Von Eggeling. Berlin 8/10/1936 Tochter Renate

Sybille Th. Geb. 21/7/1938

Universität Bonn 1926/27

Universität Kiel 1927/28

Universität Cambridge 1928/29

Landwirtschaftliche Hochschule Bonn 1929/30

Universität Bonn 1930/33

Diplom Landwirt 1938

1933/36

Geschäftsführer D. Wirtschaftsausschusses D.

Deutschen Gesellschaft F. Völkerbandsfragen

Mitarbeit an einer Forschungsaufgabe d. Rockefeller-Stiftung

Attache 1. Auswärtigen Amt 15/2/1934

Attache 1. Referat Protokoll 16/1/1935

Diplomatisch-Konsular Prüfung 24/6/1936

Attache in Oslo 9/10/1936

Legatioinsserkretär 4/7/1938

Versetzung in Dublin 25/10/1938

Erster Legationssekretär Dublin 20/11/1938

Gesandtschaftsrat Dublin 12/6/1942

(A similar card of 'rough-work' exists for Hempel).

37. Letters from Henning Thomsen to Jos. T. Carroll author of *Ireland in the War Years 1939–45* (Newton Abbot 1975). I would like to thank Mr Carroll for letting me have photostats of these letters and allowing me to use them.

38. There are two cards of the kind already referred to (see Note 36) for Hempel in the F & CO. The first card gives his party number as 6087607 with 1 July 1938 as the accompanying date. The second card gives the number DVP 28–33 with no date. This second card lists Hempel as being a member of the Association of Higher Saxon Civil Servants until he left the Saxon State Service in 1926; a member of the Anthropological Society 1919–25 (but inactive after 1921) and that his languages were English, French and Norwegian.

39. He pointed out (letter 25/11/1972) that: 'As such distinguished men as Prince Bernard of the Netherlands and many friends of the 'Prince (*sic*) of Edinburgh' had belonged to the Reiter (Mounted) SS, at the Nuremberg Trials, the Reiter SS was the only part of the SS acquitted of the charge to be a criminal organisation'. Membership obviously did not tell against Thomsen when he was re-employed after the war by the Foreign Ministry, who had a directive not to employ former leading Nazis. His age gave him the edge over Hempel in re-employment.

40. Letter from Thomsen, ten days before his death, to Jos. Carroll (21/12/1972).

41. Hildebrand op. cit. Ch. 3. p.49; p.51; p.52. See also SGFP DI Doc. 19 (The Hossbach Memorandum) 5/11/1937.

42. McMahon op. cit. Hildebrand op. cit. Chapter 2. See Chapter 1, Note 24.

43. Gordon A. Craig op. cit. Introduction. Also *Diplomats and Diplomacy in the Early Weimar Republic* (Holborn).

44. Gordon A. Craig op. cit. p.418.

45. *The Times* (London 16/4/1936) reported that an announcement of the reorganisation 'appeared by mistake in a single edition of a German newspaper':
'The new system is really a reversion to that favoured by Bismarck which lasted until 1918. Its purpose is to use greater cohesion and unity in the conduct of German foreign policy.
The principal change consists in the disappearance of the Eastern European and British Departments of the Foreign Office. They were united into a single Political Department at the head of which was Dr Dieckhoff.
The Political Department was subdivided into four departments on a geographical basis: Far East, Near East (including Northern European States and part of the Balkans); the rest of Europe, exclusive of Great Britain; and Great Britain and overseas countries. Dr Dieckhoff was responsible directly to Herrn von Bülow, the Permanent Under-Secretary of State, and as head of this highly important department will obviously play an important part in the shaping of German Foreign Policy. Besides the Political Department there are, under the new system, departments for Personnel (Freiherr von Grünau); Law (Dr Gaus), Economics (Dr Ritter); Culture (Dr Stieve) and Press (Dr Aschmann). Many changes in the diplomatic service were pending as there were vacancies in London, Madrid, Oslo, Copenhagen, Bucharest and Athens.'

46. Gordon Craig op. cit. p.428.

47. Seabury op. cit. pp.166–7. See also *A Study of German Diplomats under the Nazi Regime* (University of California Press) p.168.

48. Stephan op. cit. p.25 (see Chapters 4 and 8).

49. Seabury op. cit. pp.41–67, 87–8.

50. Gordon Craig op. cit. pp.428, 468.

51. F.H. Boland (born 1940) was Assistant Secretary at the Irish Department of External Affairs 1938–46; Secretary 1946–50; Ambassador to Britain 1950–56 and Irish representative at the United Nations 1956–64. In 1960 he was elected President of the 15th Assembly of the UN. Ryle Dwyer, *Irish Neutrality and the USA, 1939–47* (Dublin 1977) p.231.

52. Interview 7/10/1975.

53. See Charles Bewley's autobiography *Memoirs of a Wild Goose* (op. cit.). He was not replaced simply because 'he was pro-fascist', as Stephan op. cit. p.51 implies, but for his wayward recalcitrance and unprofessional conduct.

54. Bewley's name is mentioned at the conclusion of a waspish report on the personalities of External Affairs forwarded apparently by Hempel on

11/10/1940. This report was not compiled by Hempel as Carter op. cit., p.54 implies but by 'a prominent Irishman' (probably Bewley), who did it on request. (F & CO 825/280051–7). The vignettes cover Walshe, Graf O'Kelly, O'Briain, Murphy, 'Kearney' (spelled incorrectly), MacWhite, MaCauley, Cremins, Dulanty, Brennan, Hearne, Boland, Lester and Kiernan. As a supplement to the report an elaboration of the former Irish representative in Berlin, 'Excellence Bewley', was submitted to the Department of External Affairs. It had been intended to publish it as a newspaper article but the extension of the war caused the authors to desist from this. There is no date on the report itself but it is undoubtedly Bewley's in a period just at the beginning of the war. In an interview (May 1979) with Prof. Binchy he jested that if Bewley had become Gauleiter of Ireland he would probably have got Binchy off the hook for the critical and caustic article he wrote about Hitler back in 1933.

55. Patrick Keatinge, *The Formulation of Irish Foreign Policy* (Dublin 1974), p.55.
56. Ibid. pp.110–11.
57. In 1927 when the Minister for Industry and Commerce (Mr P. McGilligan) doubled for the Minister for External Affairs, Walshe acquired a great deal of experience and became McGilligan's right hand man. BA Koblenz R4311/1446 (21/May/1931).
58. Conversations with Dr Warnock and Prof. Binchy.
59. Interview with Dr Warnock, Ambassador to Switzerland August 1975. See also F & CO 825/280051/2 (11/10/1940), but probably compiled earlier.
60. Conversations with Colonel Dan Bryan, former Director of Intelligence.
61. DGFP DI. Telegram No. 28 AI (A166) p.50 17/11/1937. Re Walshe see also F & CO 825/280051–057. (October 1940).

NOTES to Chapter 3

1. Bewley op. cit. pp.158–9.
2. Hildebrand op. cit. p.52. See also *Historische Zeitschrift 218 (1974)* p.74 ('mit England'; 'ohne England'; notfalls gegen England') Chapters 1 and 2 also refer.
3. *DGFP D I* p.XV. (*DGFP D I Doc 108* p.190 26/1/1938). See also Heinemann, *Hitler's First Foreign Minister Constantin Von Neureth, Diplomat and Statesman* (Berkeley 1979).
4. Hildebrand op. cit. p.6.
5. Keatinge op. cit. p.5.
6. Dickel op. cit. p.566, Note 5.
7. *DGFP D I* Telegram No. 28 (17/11/1937).
8. Hempel's report (23/7/1937) was accompanied by an *Irish Press* photograph (22/7/1937).
9. F & CO E 471545–7 Telegram A. 177 30/11/1937.
10. *Innere Politik: Parlaments und Parteiwesen* Pol II 134 A. 105 (3/8/1937 and 13/11/1937): A. 177 (30/11/1937).
11. Ibid. 3035/38.

12. PAAA *Politische Beziehungen zwischen England und Irland* E 037315–8 (17/7/1937).
13. A. 183. 386429, 20/11/1937.
14. PAAA *Innere Politik Parlaments und Parteiwesen Telegram* A. 105 (3/8/1937).
15. IRA. See J. Bowyer Bell, *The Secret Army: The IRA since 1916* (1970); *The IRA* by Tim Pat Coogan; Stephan op. cit.
16. PAAA *Innere Politik und Parteiwesen* Pol II 134 (13/11/1937).
17. PAAA *Innere Politick Parlaments und Parteiwesen.* Pol II 134 Irland 5 (6/12/1937).
18. Ibid. B. 1290 9/11/1937.
19. Ibid. B. 1306 13/12/1937.
20. PAAA A. 183 (386 428–447) (20/12/1937).
21. A 198 (20/12/1937) 386448–386450.
22. A 208 29/12/1937).
23. Longford and O'Neill, op. cit. pp.293, 295.
24. Ibid. p.360.
25. F & CO E 037318–037323 (30312/37).
26. Ibid. See also Longford and O'Neill op. cit. p.295–300 for special position of Roman Catholic Church in the Constitution.
27. F & CO E.037318–037323 (30/12/1937).
28. Interview with former government Minister Frank Aiken (27/2/1976).
29. PAAA Pol II 1430/38 House of Commons 4/5/1938 Longford and O'Neill op. cit. pp.259–300.
30. 'On the Eve of War' by Kevin B. Nowlan, p.4 (from *Ireland in the War Years and after 1939–51* edited by Kevin B. Nowlan and T. Desmond Williams).
31. F & CO E. 037381–037323 (30/12/1937).
32. F & CO E 037324-5 (15/1/1938).
33. F & CO E 037338–037341 (5/4/1938) see also PAAA Po 3 Engl/Irland E 037324–037325 (Woermann) 15/1/1938 E 037326 (19/1/2938); E 037327 (28/1/1938) E 037328–037329 (26/1/1938).
34. PAAA D 304 (Reinhardt Liverpool) 14/2/1938.
35. PAAA Pol II 144/38 A. 26 (15/1/1938).
36. PAAA Pol II 160/38 (16/1/1938).
37. Ibid. 386452–386454. See also Pol II 11938 E 426792–426793 (14/1/1938).
38. PAAA Pol II A. 726 (386482) 11/2/1938.
39. PAAA A104 (18/3/1938) E 037333–037336.
40. PAAA A 152 (15/5/1938) E 037342–3.
41. Ibid. (E037343) and PAAA A167 (17/5/1938) 387530–387544.
42. PAAA A103 (18/3/1938) E 037333–037336.
43. PAAA Pol II 1241 Po 3 Engl/Irland No. 5 (26/4/1938) (E 426831).
44. PAAA Ha-Pol Clodius E 471395–E471399 (5/5/1938).
45. PAAA A 167 (17/5/1938) 387530–544.
46. Ibid. (387540).
47. PAAA Ha-Pol Wiehl A 166 (21/5/1938).
48. PAAA Po 3 Engl/Irland A 246 (14/7/1938).
49. PAAA Po 3 Engl/Irland A 415 (17/10/1938) 387550–387555.

50. F & CO A 417 (18/10/1938) E037316–037351.
51. F & CO A 404 14/11/1938 E 037352–4.
52. PAAA (abschrift zu 2 VI 3244) (3/11/1938).
53. PAAA *Irland 36 Judenfragen* A 523 7/12/1938.
54. Interview with Moore Lewy, son of the late Professor Lewy (13/2/1979), conversations with Professor Binchy.
55. See Note 54.
56. *DGFP D. VII* p.XVII.
57. *DGFP C IV Doc. 285* (8/1/1939).
58. Coogan op. cit. Chapter 5 (ultimatum: pp.127–8).
59. F & CO E 037366–9 (15/2/1939).
60. F & CO E 037355–9 (16/12/1939).
61. F & CO E 037360–5. (17/2/1939).
62. William Shirer, *The Rise and Fall of the Third Reich* (1960), pp.469–75 (including Hitler's reply).
63. PAAA Po 3 Engl/Irland No. 753 (28/4/39) 387596–8. *Irish Independent* (28/4/1939).
64. PAAA Pol II Nr. 968 27/5/1939 387604–619.
65. Conversation with Veesenmayer; notes from Woermann (July 1977).
66. PAAA Po II Wu 968 (27/5/1939).
67. It is interesting to speculate if these different 'voices' within the Cabinet represented a machiavellian hedging of bets to be placed to maximise any benefits which might derive from either an Allied or a German victory.
68. Interview with Dr Frederick Boland (Sept. 1975) who said that Frank Aiken was sympathetic to the 'Central European Powers'.
69. PAAA Pol II (2001139 No. 1067 6/6/1939.
70. See *A Personal reminiscence of the Volunteers* by Lt. Col. M. Feehan (retd) *An Cosantoir* February 1978.
71. F & CO Pol II No. 1308 1/7/1939 (E 037384–387).
72. F & CO 91/100053 (*The Sunday Times* 6/8/1979 p.8).
73. *DGFP D VII* p.X.
74. *DGFP D VII* Doc. 303 (Telegram No. 47) 26/8/1939.
75. *DGFP D VII* Doc. 428 (29/8/1939) p. 422 also 91/100057–56.
76. Longford and O'Neill op. cit. p.473.
77. *DDFP VII* Doc. 494 p.471 (Telegram No. 52 31/8/1939).
78. Hempel later discussed this translation: 'doctrinaire' he maintained was intended to convey that de Valera approached problems in a theoretical way. Longford and O'Neill op. cit. p.346.
79. K. Nowlan and T.D. Williams, (eds) *Ireland in the War Years and After* (Dublin 1969) p.14.
80. Ibid. p.5. Also Dáil Éireann Parliamentary Debates 1 xxiv, 719).
81. F & CO 037360–5 (17/2/1939) *dass die Aufrechterhaltung irischer Neutralität im Kriegsfall kaum möglich sei* pp.3/4. ('maintaining Irish neutrality in the case of war is scarcely possible').
82. Ibid., p.4.
83. *DGFP DVII* Doc 484 Telegram No. 52 (31/8/1939).

NOTES to Chapter 4

1. Interview with Herr Clissmann (November 1976).
2. Gordon Craig op. cit. p.428 *et seqq.*
3. Geyr von Schweppenburg, *Erinnerungen eines Militärataches London 1933–37* (Stuttgart 1949) p.15.
4. Gordon Craig op. cit. (Introduction).
5. Ibid. See also p.480 *et seq.* for the 'rigid bureaucratic ethic' and 'Germany's aims versus Hitler's methods'.
6. *DGFP DI* Doc. 33 (22/11/1937) p.68.
7. *DGFP DI* Doc. 40 (25/11/1937) p.77.
8. Stephan op. cit. pp.34, 35.
9. HMSO White Paper 1921.
10. I AAA *Abt III Politik Irland Militärangelegenheiten* (28/4/1927). Hempel continued the practice. In his reports on the army he referred to his sources of information '*Vertrauensleute*' – indicating a covert source, A. 37 (18/1/1938). He did not try to hide it. See also E. 037368–9.
11. Ibid. (March 1924–April 1936).
12. The departure on courses to the US of Maj. Gen H. McNeill Assistant Chief of Staff, Colonel M.J. Costello, Captain P. Berry, Artillery Lieutenant Charley Trodden and Infantry Officer S. Collins-Powell.
13. PAAA *Abt. III Agenten – und Spionagewesen Irland* 1928. (There is no other evidence to support allegations against Egestorff. He was married to a Catholic Irishwoman and made a film 'Turf instead of Coal'. He was having difficulty getting back into either Britain or Ireland after the war).
14. Coogan op. cit. p.94.
15. PAAA Akt III Band 3 February 1926–5/7/35.
16. Von Schweppenburg op. cit. pp. 15, 25, 46, 47, 109.
17. PRO Prem 1.273 x/k 5595 PRO CAB 53.35 x/k 5595 (12/1/1938). See also PRO CAB 27, 527. 1.5.c. (32) 13.
18. Stephan op. cit. p.20. See also Chapter 3. This same paper had a cartoon in 1922 depicting de Valera as a Jew – something Bewley maliciously pointed out to Binchy who was a student in Munich at the time (conversation with Prof. Binchy). Binchy opined that de Valera was 'too big to be a Jew' but Bewley apparently was loath to relinquish his relish for a pejorative concept of de Valera.
19. F & CO E 471515–7 (24/6/1936).
20. Coogan op. cit. Chapter 5.
21. Stephan op. cit. p.26.
22. Ibid. Chapter 2. To Enno Stephan must go the credit for unearthing these stories of Spies in Ireland. No one else could have done it. He was introduced to key IRA figures of the period in pubs by the 'Pope' O'Mahony. Stephan's personality and integrity did the rest. Mrs Carter (*Shamrock and Swastika*) embroidered on this: but the spade work was Stephan's.
23. For *Abwehr* organisation see Stephan, op. cit. p.26. It was divided into an administrative headquarters and three divisions. See also *Lahausen's Diary on Ireland.*

24. Captain L. Walsh has left some papers to the National Library (incl. Microfilm 6539). They are very scrappy and incoherent, attempting occasionally to attribute a messianic mission to O'Duffy (who had led the Irish Brigade in the Spanish Civil War). Liam Gogan indicated (8/12/1976) that he frequently met O'Duffy at Hempel's.
25. Stephan op. cit. p.22.
26. Ibid. p.38.
27. Ibid. p.47.
28. Interview with Jim O'Donovan (11/9/1975).
29. 'Militär Geographische Angaben über Irland' by Comdt. Colm Cox *An Cosantoir*, March 1975.
30. Stephan op. cit. pp.35, 36.
31. Letter from Schroetter to Berlin (7/2/1937).
32. See Bowyer Bell op. cit. for IRA split.
33. Stephan op. cit. p.36.
34. Carter op. cit. p.95.
35. PAAA *Chef Auslandsorganisation* 22/11/1935 and 16/1/1936.
36. Interview with Dr Moore Lewy (14/3/1979).
37. Interview with Col. Dan Bryan, Director of Intelligence (November 1976).
38. *German Military Intelligence* by Paul Leverkuehn, p.33.
39. Interview with Helmut Clissmann (16/2/1976).
40. *The Worker* 11/1/1936, Vol. VII No. 44.
41. Conversation with Douglas Gageby a contemporary in TCD of Clissmann's and son-in-law of Seán Lester, who has written an excellent biography, *The Last Secretary General, Seán Lester and the League of Nations* (Dublin 1999).
42. BA Koblenz R51 DAM 932 No. 4047 24/1/1936.
43. *Irish Worker's Voice* Vol. VII No. 60 2/5/1936.
44. Interview with Seán MacBride, September 1978.
45. Carter op. cit. p.197.
46. Interview with Herr Veesenmayer, July 1977; see also Brissard op. cit.
47. Carroll op. cit. p.36.
48. Bewley op. cit.
49. Ibid.
50. *DGFP D VIII* Doc. 605 p.768 10/2/1940. (Reply refers to Hempel's telegrams previously sent 91/100148–48; 91/100156).
51. See Note 71, Chapter 3.
52. There were coded messages in Jim O'Donovan's papers in the National library, which Mr van Loon indicated were translatable.

NOTES to Chapter 5

1. Bewley, op. cit.
2. Longford and O'Neill, op. cit. p.290.
3. Hitler's Directive 'Case White' (3/4/1939) for the attack on Poland, Shirer op. cit. Chapter 17 and 18 p.14.
4. François Fonvieille-Alquier, *The French and the Phoney War 1939–40*, p.14.

5. Envinnerungen eines Militär-Attaches Freiherr Geyr von Schweppenburg, London 1933–37, p.112.
6. *Irish Press* Photo (2/9/1939).
7. Ibid. 4/9/1939 (See Chapter 3).
8. State Papers G2 Sch D (22/8/1939).
9. Ibid. Sch E.
10. State Papers S. 11387 (24/8/1939).
11. Ibid. 1/9/1939.
12. State Papers G2/86 S. 11417 (22/9/1939) Longford and O'Neill, op. cit. p.350.
13. Carroll op. cit. p.16 and confidential intelligence source. Ten years previously in a book written in German and published in Germany, Rynne had accurately predicted Ireland's stand on neutrality. *Die Völkerrechtliche Stellung Irland's'* (Duncker & Hümblot).
14. Carroll op. cit. p.13.
15. Bewley op. cit. Part II Chapter 1, p.1.
16. F & CO 91/100054 (8/8/1939). See also 91/100094 (9/11/1939).
17. F & CO 100064 (25/9/1939); 91/100084 (16/10/1939; 91/100087 (20/10/1939); 91/100093 (2/10/1939); 91/100094 (9/11/1939); 91/100066 (16/11/1939). See also Telegram No. 183 (30/12/1937) p.34 and Telegram 15 (10/10/1938) Par.
18. Longford and O'Neill op. cit. p.360. F & CO 91/1000167 (5/3/1940), for a comparison with Hempel's first recommendation see Note 16.
19. PAAA *Innere Politik Parlaments und Parteiwesen* A 143 (23/2/1939) (See Part I).
20. *DGFP VII* Doc. 484. 471 (31/8/1939). See also Doc. 428. F & CO 91/100057–8 (29/8/1939).
21. F & CO 91/100062 (1/9/1939).
22. F & CO 91/100067 (27/9/1939).
23. F & CO 91/100068/69/70 (29/9/1939).
24. Dickel op. cit. p.192.
25. F & CO 91/100071 (3/10/1939).
26. F & CO 91/100077 (7/10/1939) 91/100080/81 (9/10/1939).
27. F & CO 91/100082 (11/10/1939); 91/100083 (14/10/1939).
28. F & CO 91/100086/7 (20/10/1939).
29. F & CO 91/100085 (18/10/1939) (Woermann on instruction to naval forces) F & CO 91/1000114 (4/12/1939). (Boland's reassurance re re-exports).
30. F & CO 91/100068 (29/9/1939).
31. *DGFP D VIII* Doc. 216 p.241 (8/10/1939).
32. *DGFP D VIII* Doc. 335 p.405 (14/11/1939).
33. *DGFP D VIII* Doc. 401 p.466 (30/11/1939).
34. *DGFP D VIII* Doc. 335 p.405 (14/11/1939).
35. F & CO 91/100120 (13/12/1939).
36. See Note 34.
37. F & CO 91/100109 (21/11/1939); 91/100122/3 (17/12/1939). See also F & CO 100122/3 (17/12/1939).
38. *DGFP D. IX* Doc. No. 18 (28/3/1940) (memorandum by the Director of the Political Department).

39. Stephan op. cit. pp.104–6.
40. *DGFP D IX* Doc. No. 18 (28/3/1940). (See also Documents 562 (24/1/1940) and 605 (10/2/1940).
41. *DGFP D VIII* Doc. 216 (8/10/1939).
42. 'On the other hand' reportage played on his mind. Interview with Veesenmayer July 1977.
43. F & CO 371/22985 (3/10/1939).
44. B. Martin, *Friedensinitiativen und Machtpolitik im zweiten Weltkrieg 1939–42* (Dusseldorf 1974), p.204. See also C/1545/267/62 Halifax Memorandum English Bishops 4/XXXII/17 and London *Times* (8/2/1940).
45. F & CO 91/100088 (24/10/1940).
46. *DGFP D VIII* Doc. 559 p.691 (Note).
47. *DGFP D VIII* p.690 Doc. 559 (22/1/1940).
48. F & CO 91/100170 (8/5/1940); *Irish Press* (1/3/1940); (2/3/1940); (4/3/1940). See also Carroll op. cit. pp.16 and 17.
49. *DGFP D VIII;* Telegram No. 40 (22/1/1940) p.690. There is some confusion as to whether the name is 'Gregg' or 'Craig'. The Board of Editors is convinced that Craig is the name intended (footnote 1, p.690). Hempel felt that he was more interested in trade treaties than in peace initiatives, 91/100170 (8/3/1940). As a matter of coincidence the name of the British naval attaché appointed incognito initially (1939), according to Hempel, was Graig 91/100887–8 (12/1/1942).
50. John Duke of Bedford, *A Silver-Plated Spoon*, p.157.
51. F & CO 91/100160 (21/2/1940).
52. F & CO 91/100155–56 (10/2/1940) (*DGFP D VIII* Doc. 605). See Chapter 4 – News Agency reports in *Irish Press* (1/3/1940) for German 'forming up' for battle.
53. *Irish Press* (4/3/1940) (Agency report).
54. Martin op. cit. pp.64, 202, 315. PAAA Telegram No. 709 (3/10/1939); No. 40 (23/1/1940) No. 410 (21/7/1940).
55. Martin has done a remarkable amount of revealing research in this area. Forty-five pages of Cabinet papers covering the period 4/5 October 1939 will not be released until 2015. See Carroll op. cit. pp.16 and 17. For Duke of Windsor reference (*kritische Ausserungen des Herzogs von Windsor über die englische Politik*). See Martin op. cit. p.202.
56. *DGFP D VIII* p.694 Telegram No. 40 (22/1/1940), F & CO 91/100143 (23/1/1940).
57. F & CO 91/100069/70 (30/9/1939). See also Note 22.
58. F & CO 91/100100/1 (10/11/1939).
59. F & CO 91/100107 (16/11/1939).
60. F & CO 91/100114 (4/12/1939).
61. F & CO 91/100112 (30/11/1939); 91/100125 (18/12/1939) *DGFP C VIII* Doc. No. 401 p.406 (30/11/1939).
62. F & CO 91/100132 (23/12/1939).
63. *DGFP D VIII* Doc. No. 216 p.241 (8/10/1939).
64. *DGFP D IX* Doc. 310 p.422 (20/5/1940).

65. Interview with F.H. Boland (20/9/1975).
66. Interview with Francis Stuart (29/10/1975).
67. Interview with Mrs Petersen (17/2/1976). See also Carter op. cit. pp.33, 34, 164. Enno Stephan told me (July 1977) that Petersen died in tragic circumstances around the beginning of the 1970s in Bonn where he had been living with his niece. He had returned to journalism after the war.
68. F & CO 91/100139 (11/1/1940); 91/100187 (8/5/1940).
69. F & CO E. 307486/7 (6/1/1940).
70. *An Cosantóir* series History of Irish Naval Service. (See also *An Cosantóir* June 1977. December 1977; Carter op. cit. Chapter 6 'Violations of Irish Neutrality').
71. F & CO 91/100196 (10/5/1940).
72. F & CO 91/100193 (13/5/1940).
73. F & CO 91/101121 (15/12/1939). *Irish Press* (1/12/1939); (2/12/1939); (5/12/1939); (6/12/1939).
74. *DGFP D VIII* Doc. 216 p.241 (8/10/1939).
75. F & CO 91/100129 (23/12/1939).
76. Karin Wolf, *Sir Roger Casement und die deutsch-irischchen Beziehungen* p.114.
77. E. de Valera, *Ireland's Stand: A Selection of the Speeches of E. de Valera during the War 1939–45* (Dublin 1946), p.18.
78. Carter op. cit. p.28.
79. Hildebrand op. cit. p.96. Chapter 5 'The Idea of a "Partition of the World" (1939–40)'.
80. *DGFP D I*, p.VXI.

NOTES to Chapter 6

1.   Longford and O'Neill op. cit. p.350.
2.   Andre Bresaul, *The Biography of Admiral Canaris*, p.190.
3.   Longford and O'Neill, op. cit. p.364.
4.   F & CO 91/100195/6/7 (13/5/1940); (16/5/1940).
5.   *DGFP D IX* Doc. 291, p.401 (21/5/1940), F & CO 91/100200 (16/5/1940).
6.   F & CO 91/100190 (10/5/1940).
7.   Longford and O'Neill op. cit. p.361 'De Valera did not see him ...'.
8.   F & CO 91/100200 (16/5/1940) Telegram No. 239 (14/5/1940).
9.   *DGFP DIX* Doc. 291 p.401 (21/5/1940).
10. Ibid.
11. Ibid.
12. Conversations with the late Dr Warnock, see also F & CO 91/100301 (19/7/1940) re Woermann on Warnock's anti-British attitude.
13. See Note 7.
14. *DGFP DIX* Doc. 310 p.422 (23/5/1940). This telegram is continued in F & CO 91/100211/2 (25/5/1940). Here Hempel also refers to the open sympathy for the IRA manifest among certain elements of the Volunteer Force (a territorial component of the Defence Forces now called out on Permanent Service).

15. *DGFP DIX* Doc. 314 p.431 (24/5/1940) (See Chapter 8).
16. Telegram 181 91/4/1940): 'Not found', per *DGFP D IX* p.431. See also Stephan op. cit. p.306 (Index) and Carter op. cit. p.21 (Index).
17. According to confidential sources, Hamilton was friendly with Joe Andrews (Chapter 10) and both of them 'shopped' Goertz (Chapter 8) to Gray, the American minister. Hamilton was more of an 'adventurer' than an 'agent'.
18. The *Goebbels Diaries* translated and edited by Louis P. Lochner, Foreword (out of print). See also Trevor-Roper's *The Goebbels Diaries* (1978).
19. *DGFP DIX* Doc. 314 p.431 (24/5/1940), footnote expressing opinion of Board of Editors. See also F & CO 91/100188 (Telegram No. 224) 6/5/1940 and Stephan op. cit. Chapter 6 ('Atlas the Strong') Chapter 8.
20. Wife of Francis Stuart, lecturer in Berlin University. (Chapter 8) F & CO 91/100215 (25/5/1940).
21. Conversation with Michael Keane of the National Library (12/6/1978) who recalls talking to the Hempel family in Laragh during an outing.
22. Telegram No. 282 (29/5/1940), see also Doc. No. 208 Militär-Archiv Frieburg.
23. *DGF DIX* Doc. 314 p.431 (24/5/1940).
24. *DGFP DIX* Doc. 361 p.476, see also F & CO 91/100218 (1/6/1940). See Chapter 5 for reference to 'Iroquois'.
25. *DGFP D VIII* Doc. 358 p.405 (14/11/1939), see also Telegram No. 123 (8/11/1939) and F & CO 91/100097 and F & CO 91/100103.
26. *DGFP DIX* Doc. 362 p.491 (1/6/1940).
27. Stephan op. cit. p.108–113, p.122. Carter op. cit. p.149.
28. Longford and O'Neill op. cit. p.366.
29. Lt. Col. Dudley Clarke, *Seven Assignments* (1948), p.184; Carroll op. cit. pp.43–5, 62. One of the contact makers returned later as a Military Attaché, according to Col. Dan Bryan.
30. Carroll op. cit. p.42.
31. Ibid. p.44, 49.
32. PRO Premier 4/53/2 (30/6/1940).
33. Ibid.
34. PRO 4/53/2 (24/6/1940).
35. Ibid. (18/6/1940).
36. F & CO 91/100279 (6/7/1940).
37. Carter op. cit. p.56.
38. W.E. Ironside, *The Ironside Diaries* (1962), p.238 (27/3/1940).
39. F & CO 91/100157 (13/2/1940) ('Black-and-Tan' was one of the branches of the British Terrorist Forces in the Anglo-Irish war 1919–21; so called from the motley colour of their dress).
40. F & CO 91/100273 (6/7/1940).
41. F & CO 91/100277 (6/7/1940).
42. Carroll op. cit. p.64. *DGFP DX* Doc. 79 p.89. Telegram No. 347 (1/7/1940).
43. Confidential source.
44. F & CO 91/100230–1 Telegram No. 293 (4/6/1940). F & CO 91/100233–5 Telegram No. 302 (7/6/1940). F & CO 91/100236 Telegram No. 303

(8/6/1940). Background documents to the Political Department's further thinking, e.g. Pol II 1372 g. have not yet been found.

45.   *DGFP DIX* Doc. 437 p.573 (15/6/1940). This is in reply to Telegram No. 293 91/100230–1, (4/6/1940); No. 302 91/100233–5 (7/6/1940); and No. 303 91/100236 (8/6/1940).

46.   F & CO 91/100244–6 (17/6/1940). *DGFP DIX* Doc. 473 p.601 (17/6/1940).

47.   Carroll op. cit. p.63.

48.   Interview given by Hitler to Karl von Wiegand *New York Journal* (14/6/1940). DGFP DIX p.602: a footnote refers to an entry in this connection in the *War of the Operation Division: German Naval Staff* (3/6/1940).

49.   *DGFP DIX* Doc. 506 p.637 (21/6/1940). F & C 91/100247–51 Telegram 320 (17/6/1940); Telegram 324 (19/6/1940).

50.   Ibid.

51.   Longford and O'Neill op. cit. pp.365–8, for de Valera's part. Hempel's report (Note 46 refers) dealt with Craigavon's part.

52.   F & CO 91/100247/8 (21/6/1940).

53.   *DGFP DIX* Doc. No. 506 p.638 (21/6/1940).

54.   F & CO 91/100310 (30/7/1940).

55.   *DGFP DIX* p.639. Footnote 5. Telegram No. 196 (26/6/1940).

56.   *DGFP DIX* Doc. 437 p.573 (15/6/1940) See Note 42.

57.   F & CO F3/0420 Telegram 340 (26/6/1940); *DGFP DXI* Doc. No. 35 (27/6/1940).

58.   F & CO 91/100271 Telegram 349 (3/7/1940); *DGFP DX* Doc. No. 35 (27/6/1940).

59.   *DGFP DX* Doc. 79, 89 Telegram No. 347 (1/7/1940) F & CO 91/100265–70 Telegram No. 345 (30/6/1940).

60.   Ibid.

61.   Carroll op. cit. p.60 and 135 – interview with F.H. Boland (20/9/1940) F & CO 91/100256 Telegram No. 533 (24/6/1940).

62.   F & CO 91/100282 (8/7/1940); 91/100285 – refers to (15/6/1940).

63.   F & CO 91/100280 (8/7/1940) (See Chapter 3).

64.   See Carroll, op. cit. Chapter 3: 'Britain plays the Unity Card'. For Hempel's report on pressure from the British and particularly the US Press for the return of the ports and for Ireland to side with Britain see F & CO 91/100309–10 No. 434 (30/7/1940).

65.   F & CO 91/100265–70 Telegram 345 (30/6/1940).

66.   *DGFP DX* Doc. 100 (3/7/1940).

67.   *DGFP DX* Doc. 149 (11/7/1940). See also 91/100118 (8/12/1939) and Telegram No. 183 (20/12/1937).

68.   *DGFP DX* Doc. 210 Telegram No. 410 p.262 (21/7/1940). See Chapter 8 for further account of agents).

69.   *DGFP DX* Doc. 199 p.259 (19/7/1940).

70.   *DGFP DX* Doc. 266 p.379 Telegram 437 (31/7/1940) See also F & CO 91/100300–10 for Hempel's version of developments in the Irish political situation. *Irish Neutrality and the USA 1939–41* by T. Ryle Dwyer, p.84.

71.   W.L. Langer and S.E. Gleason, *The Challenge of Isolation 1937–40* (New York

1952) pp.484, 485, 522, 718. See also F & CO 91/100211–12 (25/5/1940); Letter of the president to Gray, (15/8/1940) Roosevelt papers Box 72; Ryle Dwyer op. cit.

72. *DGFP DX* Doc. 266 p.379 (31/7/1940); F & CO 91/100309–13 (31/7/1940). See also Doc. 292.

73. Ibid. 'This was what the Entente attempted to do with Czechoslovakia etc. against us after the World War, with the well-known unfortunate consequences'.

74. Admiral Ritter was Ambassador on Special Assignments in the Foreign Office 1939–45. *DGFP DIX* Doc. 367. p.496 (1/6/1940). Also *DGFP DIX* Doc. 396 (6/6/1940) from High Command of Navy to Foreign Ministry.

75. *DGFP DX* Doc. 292 p.290 (6/8/1940). See also Document 3507 Telegram 267 (16/8/1940) F & CO 2186/472342–43. For Intensification of Sea Warfare see also *DGFP DVIII* Doc. Nos 352, 361, 367. And Führer's Conference on Naval Affairs *Brassey's Naval Annual 1948*, pp.57, 71, 77.

76. Telegram 508 (F & CO 91/100346–49) (25/8/1940). See also 91/100370–2 (2/9/1940) and 9960/ 696288 (1/11/1940).

77. Longford and O'Neill op. cit. p.372.

78. F & CO 91/100319–21 (5/8/1940). See Chapter 5.

79. F & CO 91/100308 (27/4/1940).

80. F & CO Telegram 402 (19/7/1940); Telegram 555 (11/9/1940).

81. Carter op. cit. p.88–9. See also F & CO 91/100316 (3/8/1940) 100280 (8/7/1941) and 100307 (26/7/1940).

82. F & CO 91/100308 (26/7/1940).

83. PAAA Pol M 10926 Telegram 444 (4/8/1940) bombing of *Kerry Head.*

84. In *Das Unternehmen See-Löwe* by Karl Klee Munster Verlag Göttingen (particular reference to pp.140–2 Vol. 1). Ronald Wheatley, *Operation 'Sea Lion'* (1958) p.4; Footnote 3; Shirer op. cit. *Churchill's Memoirs* Vol. II, p.19 (July 1940).

85. Telegram No. 473 (15/8/1940).

86. Telegram No. 300 (9/9/1940).

87. F & CO 91/100383–4 (18/9/1940). See also Telegram No. 566 (15/9/1940).

88. Shirer op. cit. p.781.

89. Longford and O'Neill op. cit. p.373.

90. F & CO 91/100383–4 (18/9/1940). Dr Hempel refers to his report A. 120 (16/2/1940) and gives 8,000 as the figure for the Regular Army nucleus of the Defence Forces with 4,000 Reservists and 17,000 Volunteers. As a result of the 'Call to Arms' (June 1940) he added 180,000. He did not put a figure on the Local Security Forces (Group A police duties, Group B combat duties) but he arrived at a total estimated figure for the army of 659,000 (*Gesamtbestand Armee wird z. Zt. auf etwas 659,000 Mann geschätzt).*

91. F & CO 91/100305 (24/7/1940).

NOTES to Chapter 7

1. *Kriegstagebuch des OKW* (Wehrmachtführungstab) by P.E. Schramm I, p.191 (27/11/1941).

2.   Dickel op. cit. p.574. *'Die Bemerkung Hitlers am 27/11/, das Irland in deutschen Händen das Ende Englands bedeutet, nimmt Irland-Pläne auf, vom AA und dem OKW seit der Churchill-Rede am 5.11 diskutiert werden'.*

3.   The full story of how widespread or otherwise this defeatism was has still to be written when Cabinet papers are released this century as scheduled. See also Gregory Blaxland, *Destination Dúnkirk* (London 1973) for the extent of the military defeat.

4.   Hildebrand op. cit. p.105.

5.   *Brassey's Naval Annual 1948* pp.156–9. *War Diary of the Wehrmacht ops. Staff* (December 1940–March 24 1941). See Chapter 1 for reference to *Stufenplan*.

6.   Hildebrand op. cit. p.105.

7.   Ibid. pp.109–10.

8.   Hildebrand op. cit. pp.115–16.

9.   Coogan op. cit. p.217. Stephan op. cit. p.163. Kurt Haller's opinion: 'Ribbentrop ... had in general an exceedingly low opinion of the Irish. Incapable of hiding his disdain for them').

10.   Stephan op. cit. p.104.

11.   *DGFP DXI* Doc. 416 p.427 (28/11/1940).

12.   Interview with Dr Veesenmayer, Darmstadt July 1977.

13.   Ibid.

14.   Stephan op. cit. p.106.

15.   F & CO 91/100298 (16/7/1940).

16.   '"Gruen": German Military Plans and Ireland 1940' by Professor Charles Burdeck (California State University, San Jose); *An Cosantóir* March 1974. For the British Chief of Staff's advice to Churchill see Mary C. Bromage, *Ireland* (University of Notre Dame Press), p.145.

17.   *'Wir fahren gegen Irland?'* by Comdt. Colm Cox *An Cosantóir* May 1974.

18.   F & CO 91/100275 (5/7/1940) (Hempel); F & C 307561 (25/11/1940) (Kramarz to Hempel). See also 91/100275 (5/7/1940).

19.   Carroll op. cit. p.168. See also F & CO 91/101260 (17/11/1943) *'Neutralität sei keine Feiglings Politik, sondern eine schwer durchfuhrede Politik'.*

20.   Longford and O'Neill op. cit. p.349.

21.   F & CO Telegram 627 (2 Fortsetzung) (3/10/1940).

22.   F & CO Telegram 669 (24/10/1940), Telegram 682 (29/10/1940), Telegram 685 (30.10.1940).

23.   F & CO 91/100419 (26/10/1940).

24.   F & CO 91/100397 (27/9/1940); 91/100401 (1/10/1940).

25.   F & CO 100316–7 (3/8/1940).

26.   F & CO 91/1100401 (1/10/1940).

27.   F & CO 30954 (Irland 1920–43) cites a telegram (5/11/1940) relating where the Italian representative, who it said knew the Cardinal well, told Hempel of the Cardinal's pro-Axis leanings. Hempel was later to point out that the Cardinal was an exception amongst the clergy in this regard.

28.   *DGFO DXI* Doc. December 1991, p.259 (19/12464-67) (21/7/1940).

29.   *DGFP DX* Doc. 292 (see also 291) p.420 (51/34332–33 and 51/34333–35 (6/8/1940).

30. Ritter 1780/406615 (9/10/1939).

31. *DGFP DXI* Doc. 300 p.493. 91/100424–25 (7/11/1940). See also Note 65, Chapter 6.

32. F & CO 91/100426–28 (8/11/1940). For German High Command Estimate 9177/409 (24/12/1940) (Militärarchiv Freiburg).

33. F & CO 91/100429 (10/11/1940). In HMSO DGFP references 'the breakfast' became 'a luncheon'.

34. *DGFP DXI* Doc. 330 p.570 91/100432–33 (13/11/1940).

35. *DGFP DXI* Doc. 407 p.718 91/100443–44 (26/11/1940).

36. F & CO 91/100438–9 (23/11/1940) (See Chapter 8).

37. F & CO 91/100434–5 (11/11/1940).

38. *DGFP DXI* Doc. 419 91/100447–60; 91/100451–52 (4/12/1940) 91/100453–54 (29/11/1940).

39. *DGFP DXI* Doc. 455 p.793 91/100456–7 (5/12/1940).

40. See Note 59 (Ibid.).

41. Carroll op. cit. pp.101–7.

42. See Note 59.

43. Lt. Gen. Costello ('Mickey Joe' as he was popularly known) in a radio interview with P.P. O'Reilly (24/6/1978) indicated how Roosevelt's pro-British attitude jeopardised his mission.

44. *DGFP DVII* Doc. 523 p.882 91/100475–7 (17/12/1940) (See Chapter 8 for Thomsen/Goertz links).

45. *DGFP DXII* Doc. 576 p.973 91/100502–4 (29/12/1940).

46. Longford and O'Neill op. cit. p.379.

47. Ibid. p.373.

48. F & CO 91/100383–4 (18/9/1940). See also F & CO 307545–6 (28/29/11/1940). *'Das OKW scheint dabei in erster Linie an einen aktiven Offizier zu denken, der allerdings GETARNT ALS BEAMTER...'* He was looking for an active officer, *disguised as a civil servant.*

49. *DGFP DXI* Doc. 333 p.572 (1005/307564–65) (14/11/1940).

50. The reference in F & CO 100465 (No. 790) (6/12/1940) points to Col. Nial McNeill, a Reserve Officer, Director of Ordnance Survey, a cousin of Gen. Hugo McNeill. Nial became Intelligence Officer of the 2nd Div. before becoming O/C 4th Inf. Brigade... *'insebesondere angebahnte Fühlungsnahme Thomsens mit hiesiger Armee genügen konte um so mehr als dieser in Eigenschaft als Reserveofffizier über verhältnismässig gute Vorbedingungen verfügt'.* Telegrams Nos 774 and 787 (5/12/1940) also refer. See further F & CO 91/100629–32 4/12/1941; 91/100647–52 (19/2/1941) and Chapter 8.

51. F & CO 912/100629–32 4/3/1941. *DGFP DXII* Doc. 79 p.152 91/10055–6 (24/2/1941) (See also, re Irish Army, Telegram 841 of 20312/40).

52. F & CO 91/100464–65 ((6/12/1940).

53. Ibid.

54. F & CO Collection entitled Ireland. Ambassador Ritter (Bundle 4) Serial No. 5 (307436–570) containing items from (14/11/1940– 18/8/1941).

55. *DGFP DXII* Doc. 79 p.152 91/100655–6 (24/2/1941).

56. *DGFP DXII* Doc. 150 p.270 191/100666–67 (11/3/1941).

57. *DGFP DXII* Doc. 164 p.290 1005/307445 (13/3/1940).
58. *SGFP DXI* Doc. 466 p.804 10/100462–63 (7/12/1940).
59. *DGFP DXII* Doc. 79 p.152 91/100655–56 (24/2/1941).
60. *DGFP DXI* Doc. 485 p.832 91/100469–70 (10/12/1940).
61. Longford and O'Neill op. cit. p.372.
62. *DGFP DXII* Doc. 79 p.152 91/100655–56 (24/12/1941).
63. *DGFP DXI* Doc. 710 p.1198 19/100610–11 (26/1/1941) and Doc. 721 p.1230 91/100014–16 (28/1/1941).
64. F & CO Collection entitled 'Ireland – Ambassador Ritter' (Bundle 4) Serial No 1065 (367436–307570) Item 10 (13/3/1941).
65. Ibid. (Serial No. 307445).
66. Confidential Intelligence Source.
67. Hempel's Telegram No. 847 (Ambassador Ritter's Collection – Bundle 4) (23/12/1940).
68. F & CO 91/100544–5 (5/1/1941) (and generally F & CO 91/11 100511–100945, first half of 1941.)
69. F & CO 91/11 100511–100945 Telegram 56 of (16/11/1941) and Telegram 59 (17/1/1941).
70. F & CO 91/11 100511–100945 – Telegram No. 104 (3/2/1941).
71. F & CO 91/100661 (Telegram 175 (26/2/1941).
72. Interview with Dr Gogan (8/12/1976).
73. Longford and O'Neill op. cit. p.392.

NOTES to Chapter 8

1. *PAAA (24/80) Rundfunk propaganda nach Irland* (18/5/41). Memorandum (247496–247510).
2. IRA Order of the Day, 'Conscription and After' (27/5/1941) from Jim O'Donovan's papers in the National Library Ms 21155. See also Order Special, 33/9/117 'To each member', in same papers.
3. Stephan op. cit. pp.69/70. The IRA constituted an ongoing problem. See F & CO 91/100902 (29/2/1942). See also Chapter 6, the 'Artus' plan.
4. *DGFP DVIII* Doc. 605, p.760 (10/12/1940). See also The *Irish Times* (3/6/1958) 'They spied in England'. Based on E. von Lahausen, *German Secret Service War Diary of General von Lahausen* (London 1958). Chapter dealing with Ireland reprinted. P. Leverknehn, *German Military Intelligence,* p.11, p.33.
5. Lahausen Diary.
6. Interview with Herr Clissmann 1976.
7. F & Co 91/100467 (9/12/1940). (See also D11 523 p.882, F & CO 91/100475–77 (17/12/1940).
8. Longford and O'Neill op. cit. p.358. *DGFP D VIII* Doc. 355 (p.405) (14/11/1939) F & CO 91/100103.
9. *DGFP DVIII* Doc. 358 p.405 (14/11/1939) See also Stephan op. cit. p.2.
10. F & CO 91/100126 (20/12/1939) (See Chapter 4).
11. *DGFP DIX* Doc. 465 p.545 (16/12/1939).

12. Letters from Pfaus and Liam D. Walsh kindly lent to me by Enno Stephan.
13. Carroll op. cit. p.135–6. Carter op. cit. p.252, Note 5. Hempel's reports 91/100272 (4/7/1940); 91/100369 (2/9/1940); 91/100387 (18/9/1940); 91/100388 (23/9/1940). Liam Walsh's Papers on Eoin O'Duffy National Library Micro film 6539 (not revealing on this period: an unrefined eulogy and hero-worship of O'Duffy).
14. F & CO 91/100097 (Telegram No. 123) (9/11/1939).
15. *DGFP DIX* Doc. 314 p.431 (24/5/1940) and Telegram No. 272 (25/5/1940): Mrs Stuart's financial straits Telegram 614 (30/9/1940) (See also F & CO 91/100142 (15/1/1940) and 91/100147 (25/1/1940).
16. Interview with Francis Stuart (29/10/1975). See also *Journal of Irish Literature* edited by Robert Hogan (this edition by J.H. Nattersdad) January 1976. Stuart, an Antrim Protestant, was converted to Catholicism and Republicanism by the MacBride family. His real interest was in writing.
17. *DGFP DVIII* Doc. 562 p.693 (24/1/1940).
18. *DGFP DVIII* Doc. 605 p.760 (10/2/1940).
19. Interview with Veesenmayer (July 1977). See Chapters 6,7,11.
20. Kees van Hoek, 'Secret Agents in Ireland' *Sunday Chronicle* (May 1954).
21. F & CO 100155–6 (10/2/1940).
22. Confidential source.
23. F & CO 91/100149 (27/1/1940). The late Professor F.X. Martin O.S.A. was working on a life of Seán Russell.
24. Line from rebel song of the 1798 Rising which took place mainly in Co. Wexford. For MI5 claim that Ryan murdered Russell see *Irish Times* (April 2000).
25. F & CO 100334 (15/6/1940).
26. Ibid. See also F & CO 91/101440 (20/10/1941) from Washington (25/10/1941).
27. F & CO 91/100793–4 (20/10/1941). Hayes was a senior IRA figure later involved in an sensational kidnapping episode.
28. F & CO 91/100343 (25/8/1940). 'Erbitte im Interesse Vermeidung etwaiger Provokation ob... (portion missing) angeblicher Dr H.K. Legitimiert. See also *DGFP DIX* Doc. 314 (P.431) (24/5/1940) Doc. 361 (P.490) (1/6/1940).
29. F & CO 91/100408 (8/10/1940).
30. 'Where is the w.c. please' by Donal O'Donovan (son of 'V' Held, Jim O'Donovan) *Irish Times* (1978) reviewing *The Shamrock and the Swastika* by Mrs Carter.
31. Separate interviews with Miss Farrell (26/2/1976) and with Miss Maura O'Brien (25/4/1977), harbourers of Goertz. They were besotted with him.
32. F & CO 91/100431 (10/11/1940).
33. F & CO 91/100458–60 (6/12/1940). Thomsen in a letter to Mr Joseph Carroll later (21/12/1972) wrote: 'Dr Hempel has frequently used single letters in his reports for safety reasons. They were picked at random. I do not think that he and Hugo McNeill were at so intimate terms to discuss personalities of the Irish Army. It was with the knowledge of the Irish government that certain personalities kept contact with members of the

German Legation. That is done everywhere and to mutual advantage. There are things one does not say officially. I do not think Hugo McNeill was one of them'. He would say that!

34. F & CO 91/100461 (Fortsetzung) (6/12/1940).
35. Carroll op. cit. p.76–7. (See also Chapter 7).
36. F & CO 91/100608 (22/1/1940).
37. F & CO 91/100629–30 (4/2/1941).
38. F & CO 91/100636–37 (8/2/1941).
39. F & CO 91/100647–52 (19/2/1941) See also F & CO E. 307550–51 (6/12/1940). (Nial McNeill) & E. 307553 (5/12/1940) (Hugo McNeill).
40. F & CO 91/100652 (19/2/1941).
41. When bringing Brig. Gen. Dorman O'Gowan from Cavan to the Military College to give a lecture, he told me that what sustained him mentally during the North African Campaign was resorting to the device of regarding the whole business as a play, a piece of theatre.
42. Veesenmayer told me that, in his opinion, Hitler was aware of the gamble Hess took in flying to Britain and acquiesced in the adventure.
43. Radio Éireann broadcast on the Emergency with Lt. Gen. M.J. Costello (p.p.O'Reilly) (1978). Gen. Costello's remark was regarded as vainglorious by some and prompts the observation that there are many unsung heroes like Captain Nick Leonard of the Irish Army and Sergeant Mickey Gill of the Garda Siochána to whom the State owes a debt for their key roles in preserving security during the Emergency.
44. F & CO P1/100021–32 (4/2/1941).
45. F & CO 91/100674 (27/3/1941) (also confidential source).
46. Confidential intelligence source.
47. F & CO 91/100674 (27/3/1941).
48. F & CO 91/302003 (15/9/1941).
49. F & CO 91/302006 (27/9/1941).
50. Paaa Nr. 1690/41 g.kdos Abw. II/2 (302008) (29/9/1941).
51. See Note 29; also F & CO 91/101441 (25/10/1941) F & CO 91/101423–4 (2/11/1941); 91/101427–29 (8/11/1941).
52. F & CO 91/101428 (29/10/1941). See also footnote 4 to *ADAP EI* Doc. 25 (16/12/1941).
53. See Note 45. Gen. Costello's implications seem to have been that Goertz would not have 'got away with it' in his divisional area. GHQ is thought to have instructed him to arrest Goertz irrespective of who was with him: the Garda in question is alleged to have got five years' imprisonment.
54. Seán MacBride has also indicated that de Lacy played a suspicious part in the imbroglio spinning around the Hayes 'Confessions', which involved the British and Irish Secret Service, the IRA, and through Goertz and McNeill, the German Legation. Hempel also reported measures taken by the Irish government against *The Irish Times,* whose editorial sympathies lay openly with the Allies. Interview with Seán MacBride (1977).
55. 91/101440–1 (25/10/1941).
56. Carroll op. cit. p.76.

57. F & Co 91/100647 (19/2/1941) (e.g.).
58. Interview with Miss Maura O'Brien. See also Stephan op. cit. Chapter 7 (25/4/1977).
59. Interview with Miss Maura O'Brien: 'When Helena Molony heard of IRA plan to march on North she felt that it "would have led to carnage and tried to steer Goertz away from the IRA to meet other people"'.
60. *ADAP EI* (191/100857–59 (21.12.1941).
61. Ibid. Footnote 6 identifies the Major as 'Bryan'. When I drew Col. Bryan's attention to this he was outraged and indicated his intention to seek to have this offending footnote retracted.
62. Stephan op. cit.; Carter op. cit. Part III; Carroll op. cit. Chapter 4.
63. Stephan op. cit. Chapter 6 'Atlas the Strong'; F & CO 91/100172 (21.3.1940); 91/100188 (6/5/1940). Weber-Drohl gave new code words as follows: 91/100185 (29/4/1940). 'Mackarel' for Ireland; 'Bulldog' for England; 'Bullfrog' for Portugal. Enno Stephan informed me that a new contact address for their couriers and agents had been found by the IRA in England but that an attempt to establish a courier route via Portugal fell through and that it took many months to establish a secret link via Spain.
64. The story is that Weber-Drohl cohabited with a soldier's daughter in Arbour Hill married quarters. The Department of Defence became involved when the girl's mother claimed children's allowance for Drohl's baby.
65. These ballads, e.g. 'God Save Ireland' can be read in Jim O'Donovan's papers in the National Library, MS 21155.
66. F & CO 91/302024 (25/10/1941).
67. F & CO 91/100066 (25/9/1939); 91/100069 (28/9/1939); 91/100073 (30/9/1939); 91/100175 (4/10/1939). Thomsen in a letter to Jos. Carroll (25/11/1972) stated that it was not correct to assert that the Irish government requested the German Legation not to send cipher telegrams. He wrote that until the US entered the war the German Legation sent their messages via Washington, and later (with the permission of the British government!) via Switzerland. These telegrams however, he said, only arrived after a long delay when they lost their news value. He maintained that the transmitter was not used (except in one exceptional case which he did not specify) when the way via Switzerland was opened.
68. F & CO 307544 (7/12/1940).
69. Carter op. cit. p.27 refers to a 'confidential government source' for information in this context. Mrs Carter had conversations – among others – with Col. Dan Bryan and Dr Hayes (National Library) who was the 'only real code expert in the country'.
70. F & CO 91/100138 (15/1/1940).
71. F & CO 91/100145 (24/1/1940).
72. F & CO 91/100179 (9/4/1941).
73. F & CO 91/10012 (15/4/1940). See also 91/100162 (6/4/1940; (British Cabinet papers quoted by J. Carroll) Hempel's Telegrams (191/100686–7) (4/4/1941); (9/5/1941); *DGFP DXI* Doc. 407 (26/11/1940).
74. F & CO 91/100841 (4/12/1941) (See Chapter 9).

75. F & CO 91/100915 (8/12/1941)

76. F & CO *Abwehr* 961/301979 (2/7/1941).

77. F & CO 091/100546 (5/1/1941); 91/100687–8 (11/4/1941).

78. F & CO 91/100152 (9/2/1940).

79. F & CO 91/100137 (10/1/1940) 'Tarnung Senders durch gelegentlich Telegramme über USA'.

80. See Chapter 5, Note 25.

81. F & CO 91/100091–2 (25/10/1939).

82. F & CO 91/100180 (13/4/1940).

83. F & CO 91/100193 (13/5/1940).

84. Two of these weather buoys were recovered from the sea and a well-known officer in Clancy Barracks, 'Webley' Doyle, dismantled them.

85. Confidential sources. The full story of our export of 'Weather Reports' to Britain is an interesting example of how crucial de Valera's 'certain consideration for Britain' was. They tipped the scales in deciding the timing of the Second Front (June 1944).

86. F & CO 91/100100 (10/11/1939); 91/100106–7 (16/11/1939) (17/11/1939).

87. Interview with Herr Voigt, Scarlettstown, Newsbridge former internee (NCO) (18/12/1976).

88. Letter from the late Herr Thomsen to Mr Joe Carroll (25/4/1972) (kindly lent to me for use by Mr J. Carroll): 'During the many years we worked together there has never been any difference of opinion between Dr Hempel and me. We have every day for four to five hours discussed what we had heard and drafted together the reports to the Auswärtiges Amt'.

89. Interview with Fleischmann former internee (officer) (26/2/1976).

90. Ibid.

91. The total number of 'belligerent internees' listed alphabetically in the Irish Army 'Archives' is in the region of 270.

92. *The Games of the Foxes* by Ladislos Farago, referred to by Ryle Dwyer in *Irish Neutrality and the US* p.198.

93. Mr Anthony Weyner, PO 35 Box 1228; Carroll op. cit. p.182.

94. Interview with Fleischmann; Carter op. cit. p.29; Carroll letter (25/11/72).

95. F & CO 91/100778 (15/9/1941).

96. F & CO 91/280051–57 (11/10/1940).

97. Dr Kiernan, the report said, during his period as Director General of Radio Eireann, allowed every group except Republicans, freedom of expression and in the Spanish Civil War broadcast victory for the 'forces of democracy' over the 'rebellious generals'; he was someone who could not be suspected of being either friendly to the Germans or hostile to the Jews, nevertheless the King of England would not accredit him and de Valera did not dare to have the Irish President sign for him.

98. Prof. Binchy is certain that these are the work of Bewley. Mrs Carter erroneously attributes these vignettes to Hempel (op. cit. pp.48–9). Prof. Binchy also points out various remarks in the report that fixed the time of composition in the first months of the war rather than October 1940. From

the 'inside' comments made, he felt that Hempel could not have written it. This is stressed to illustrate a Bewley approach to exerting influence even in Hempel's own domain.

99. F & CO 91/101086 (23/12/1942).

100. Conversation with Prof. Binchy who knew Bewley intimately. Binchy would gladly have exchanged jobs when he got the Berlin vacancy and Bewley got the Vatican post. Bewley had a brother in the British Treasury and a brother-in-law of Bewley's mother, Sir Arthur Pim of Oxford University, looked after his wayward Irish relation in his will. Bewley was greatly influenced by the controversial Jesuit, Father Martindale.

101. Conversation with Col. Dan Bryan, Director of Irish Army Intelligence. There was no positive identification as to who 'Club Foot' really was: most likely Veesenmayer, though Goebbels too had a corresponding disability.

102. Interview with Prof. Binchy. F & CO 91/101086–7 (23/12/1942). See also 91/111 100946–101324 (1/4/1942) – (31/12/1943) (with particular reference to F & CO Item 4 'Bewley discussing future of Éire in case of a German victory).

103. Stephan op. cit. p.247, citing Kurt Haller.

NOTES to Chapter 9

1. F & CO 91/100 319.21 (5/8/1940).

2. Longford and O'Neill op. cit. p.391 states: 'Churchill has later suggested, in his history of the war, that the Dublin bombing might have been caused by the deflection of the beams on which the Germans were flying, but the explanation was not known at the time'. (See F & CO 91/1000750 (13/6/1941). It would seem as if Boland and Walshe did not tell de Valera everything they suspected. They did have, it would seem, their suspicions about the beam at the time. More accurate information (short of the full story) is available nowadays about the beam technicalities.

3. F & CO 91/100731 (3/6/1941) (aide-mémoire delivered by Warnock).

4. F & CO 91/100744 (7/6/1941).

5. F & CO 91/100734 (4/6/1941).

6. F & CO 91/100741 (9/6/1941)

7. F & CO 91/100737 (31/5/1941).

8. F & CO 91/100 738.9.40 (8/6/1941).

9. F & CO 91/100741 (9/6/1941).

10. F & CO 91100735 (13/6/1941).

11. F & CO 91/10077408–9 (9/6/1941).

12. F & CO 91/100750 (13/6/1941).

13. See Note 2 above.

14. F & CO 91/100751 (20/6/1941).

15. F & CO 91/100753 (23/6/1941), 11/100897 (23/1/1942), 91/10097 (23/1/1942) and 91/100953 (28/3/1942). See also 91/101253 (13/11/1943) and 91/101266–8 (22/11/1943) for RAF transfers.

16. F & CO 91/100830 (11/11/1941). See also 91/101130–3 (18/4/1943) for

US propaganda in Iceland and Hempel's counter-measures.

17. F & CO 91/100754 (17/7/1941).
18. F & CO 91/100902–3 (29/1/1942); 91/101255/7 (10/1/1943) – 91/101258–60 (17/11/1943); 101212/5 (20/11/1943); 91/101279 (4/12/1943) *(Kerlogue)*.
19. F & CO 91/100882 (8/1/1942).
20. F & CO 91/100807 (30/10/1941).
21. F & CO 91/100782 (24/9/1941).
22. F & CO 91/101418/9 (4/12/1941).
23. F & CO 91/100853 (16/13/1941).
24. F & CO 91/100857–9 (10/12/1941); 100857–62 (7/12/1941).
25. F & CO 91/100855–6 (16/12/1941). Telegram 357 (30/12/1942); 91/100187 (14/9/1943); 91/10188–91 (19/7/1943).
26. Longford and O'Neill op. cit. pp.384–7.
27. Ibid. p.384.
28. F & CO 91/100770 (9/8/1941).
29. F & CO 91/100785 (1/10/1941).
30. F & CO 91/100827 (4/11/1941).
31. F & CO 100827–9 (10/11/1941); 91/100892–5; includes reference to Telegram 379 which characterises Gray; (10/1/1942). *Sunday Express* (9/1/1942). See also Note 19 and 91/100916 F (12/2/1942).
32. *ADAP EI* Dec. 24 p.38–9 F & CO 91/100855–6 (16/12/1941).
33. Longford and O'Neill op. cit. pp.390–1.
34. F & CO 91/100860–1 (15/12/1941); 91/100889–91 (13/1/1942); 91/100899 (26/1/1942); 91/100900–1 (28/1/1942).
35. F & CO 100899 (26/1/1941).
36. *ADAP EI* Dec. 25 pp.40–1 (16/12/1941) re military aircraft. See also F & CO 91/100883/5 (6/1/1942). Hempel's account of Thomsen declining an invitation to contact Goertz and 91/100866 (8/1/1942).
37. *ADAP EI* Dec. pp.100–2 (27/11/1941).
38. *ADAP D XII* Dec. 523 (Dec. 1940).
39. *ADAP DXII* Dec No. 79, Dec. No. 150 (February 1941).
40. *ADAP EI* Dec G9. p.128 (29/12/1941).
41. F & CO 91/101353–6 (6/1/1942).
42. *ADAP EI* Dec. 221, p.396 (9/2/1942).
43. Ibid., Note 1. See also 91/100 907–8 (undated) F & CO 91/100 910 (12/3/1947).
44. F & CO 100921 (18/2/1942).
45. F & CO 91/100 686–7 (11/4/1941)
46. F & CO 91/100 764 (10/8/1941).
47. F & CO 1005/307436–307570. (Ambassador Ritter Bundle 4). Item No. 7 (18/8/1941).
48. *ADAP EI* Dec. 250 pp.491–3 (19/2/1942).
49. Irish Intelligence also adopted this defensive line, namely that 'north-west' weather in the Channel ruled out Ireland as source. W. Stagg, in his book on meteorological factors affecting D-Day (1944) decisions, shows that a report

from Blacksod Bay prompted Eisenhower (contrary to American staff officer conclusions) to go ahead with the landing on Normandy (per confidential source). Weather reports from Ireland *were* more than relevant: they were critical.

50. *SGFP D XI* Dec. 407, p.718 (26/11/1940).
51. F & CO 100935 (13/3/1942).
52. Telegram No. 420 (21/11/1941) (See Chapter 8).
53. F & CO 91/100 985 (17/6/1942); 91/10S987 (30/1/1942); 91/100988 (13/6/1942); 91/100988 (19/6/1942); 91/100993 (17/6/12942). For the *Irish Willow*'s encounter with the U-Boat, see 91/100965 (25/4/1942).
54. F & Co 91/101068 (27/10/1942).
55. F & CO 91/280080 (18/8/1942).
56. Militärchiv Frieberg Nr. 106–F (25/8/1942).
57. Militärarchiv Friebureg Nr. 200 (9/4/1943).
58. PAAA Akten Büro St. S. Irland Band 111, Telegram No. 281 (28/6/1943).
59. F & CO 91/101224–7 (9/10/1963); 91/101251/2 (9/11/1943).
60. F & CO 362677–9 (15/8/1943); see also 91/101098 (14/2/1943); 91/101103 (18/2/1943); 91/101212 (29/9/1943).
61. Longford and O'Neill op. cit. p.401.
62. Ibid. p.422–3; 91/101293/5 (13/12/1943). 91/101297–9 (14/12/1943). See also 91/101024 (15/9/1942); 91/101129 (10/4/1943) (Hempel's praise for Boland) 91/101155 (22/5/1943); 91/101156–9 (27/5/1943).
63. Ibid. p.403. 91/101160 (1/6/1943). See also F & CO 91/101300 (13/12/1943); 91/101298 (14/12/1943).
64. F & CO 362683–4 (22/12/1943). O'Reilly's father was nicknamed Casement. He was one of the RIC men who arrested Casement when he was put ashore in Kerry from a German submarine in 1916. Later when his son escaped from Mountjoy Prison, he handed him up, collected the reward and invested it in a pub for John Francis to make provision for his release.
65. F & CO 302088 (21/8/1942).
66. F & CO 302118–20 (13/1/1943); 302121–3 (29/1/1943); 302123 (28/1/1943); 302149–50 (25/1/1944); 32158 (14/1/1944).
67. F & CO 302157–60 (14/1/1944).
68. Carroll op. cit. p.142; F & CO 302167 (8/2/1944).
69. Ibid. See also 91/100918 (12/2/1942); 91/101274 (2/12/1943) 91/101310/11 (17/12/1943), 91/101312–5 (18/12/1943). For Churchill's fears see Carroll op. cit. p.140–1 and Churchill 5 'Closing the Ring'.
70. Dr Michael Rynne pays tribute to his stature and his contribution to influencing the implementation of the neutrality policy. He felt at that time that Walshe's biography was overdue. Since then Professor Dermot Keogh has paid fulsome tribute to him, misplaced in my opinion: few of his contemporaries would have argeed with this general assessment.
71. Military Archives, German internees.
72. F & CO 301273–4.
73. F & CO 302175 (25/4/1944). See Note 25 (also F & CO GB/64).
74. F & CO 302161/2 (4/1/1944).

75. F & CO 1423/362691 (19/3/1944). Re American note see also Carroll op. cit. Chapter 9 and Ryle Dwyer op. cit. Chapter 10.
76. Interview with F.H. Boland (7/10/1975). Longford and O'Neill op. cit. p.398. Nowland and Williams op. cit. p.39. Nowland and Williams op. cit. p.39. Another point of view (F.H. Boland) was that the British were not averse to using the Americans as a stick to beat the Irish.
77. PRO P3/113/5. Telegram 614, p.128. (26/2/1944).
78. PRO P3/133/5. Telegram 611, p.123.
79. F & CO 91/101116–7 (4/3/1943).
80. Ryle Dwyer op. cit. pp.216–17.
81. *DGTP DXII* Dec 150 p.270 (11/3/1941). F & CO 91/100666–7 (11/3/1941).
82. F & CO 1423 362–6–75 – 362691 (August 1943 – October 1944).
83. Interview with F.H. Boland (7/10/1975).
84. See Note 25; F & CO GB/64.
85. Telegram No. 267 (27/6/1944), which also refers to Telegram 90 (11/11/1943).
86. F & CO 91/100686–7 (11/4/1941): 91/100764 (10/3/1941): 91/101363–5 (8/12/1941): 91/101374–6 (21/12/1941): 91/101356–66 (27/12/1941).
87. F & CO 91/100774, par. 3 (15/8/1941).
88. F & CO 91/101120 (12/3/1943).
89. F & CO 91/101016 (9/9/1942); 91/101122–3 (21/3/1943).
90. F & CO 91/101206–7 (21/9/1943): 101231/2 (14/10/1943) 101248–9 (8/11/1943) and 101282–3 (6/12/1943). Confidential source whose French wife supported Pétain.
91. F & CO 101067 (5/6/1943); 101169/70 (24/6/1943).

NOTES to Chapter 10

1. F & CO 91/100886 (8/1/1942).
2. F & CO 91/100892–5 (6/1/1942).
3. F & CO 91/1001116/7 (4/3/1943).
4. Longford and O'Neill op. cit. p.494.
5. See Chapters 4 and 8.
6. See Chapter 2, pp.28–9; Chapter 4, p.96.
7. Carroll op. cit. p.36.
8. This report was made just a year after the 'Flower Pot' signal plan.
9. F & CXO 91/100774 (par. 102) (15/9/1941).
10. F & CO 302033 (11/2/1941).
11. See Chapter 5.
12. *Daily Mail* (7/1/1942), P.4.
13. F & CO 100887–8 (12/1/1942).
14. F & CO 91/100889–91 (18/1/1942).
15. F & CO 91/302046 10/2/1942).
16. F & CO 91/302045 (10/2/1942). (Telegram 90). See also Carter op. cit. p.40. She seems to have linked Telegrams 90 and 92 and identified the electrical plant at Luton as the place where the British worked on an additive to change

the column of airplane exhaust. This is not all that evident from Hempel's reports: unless perhaps Mrs Carter is interpolating other information with the last sentence of this report 'Zwischen Gasanstalt und dem links der Straße London–Luton gelegen Elektrizstätswork Flak'.

17. F & CO 91/101107/8 (18/2/1942. See also 91/100961 (13/4/1942); 91/100975 (19/5/1943); 91/101088 (4/1/1943); 91/101093 (9/1/1943); 91/101094 (14/1/1943); 91/101119 (3/3/1942). See also Note 23 re BBC play on psychological operations in World War II.

18. F & CO 91/101002 (1/7/1942).

19. F & CO 91/100922/3 (28/2/1947). F & CO 301148–50 (7/3/1942). Stephan op. cit. pp.200–4: p.209. Carter op. cit. pp.201–10. Coogan op. cit., pp.223–4. See also Chapter 8, p.234.

20. F & CO 91/302069–70 (3/6/1942).

21. F & CO 91/302105–8 (10/12/1942); also confidential source.

22. Telegram No. (30/4/1942). For theory that Weber-Dohl was used by Allies or a double agent see Ryle Dwyer op. cit. p.198.

23. James P. O'Donnell, *The Berlin Bunker* (1979), Chapter 7. Incidentally, the attempt to emulate Casement's Irish Brigade (WWI) was also infiltrated by British agents. (As an example Enno Stephan drew my attention to an article in *Der Spiegel* (25/3/1968) (p.82) by Thomas Cushing, who was a member of the Brigade (Stephan op. cit. p.240), and became an employee of the British Ministry of Defence.

24. F & CO 91/101197–9 (13/8/1943) 91/101218 (1/10/1943).

25. F & CO 91/100857 (31/3/1942).

26. PAAA 280072–79 (19/8/1942). Denomination of Church circles not stated; presumably RC.

27. F & CO 91/101086–7 (23/12/1942); 91/101070 (16/11/1942); 91/101080 (2/12/1942) (Kilnacroth); 104 91/101015 (8/9/1942) (Hempel on Bewley).

28. F & CO 100929 (27/2/1942). See Chapter 9 for further information on Veesenmayer's opinion of Canaris.

29. F & CO 91/100930 (27/2/1942).

30. F & CO 91/101335–38 (23/1/1943). See also Nowlan and Williams op. cit. p.18. The 120 dwindled to 12 and the eventual attempt ended up with 3 (including Clissmann). See also Stephan op. cit. Chapter 17 and Carter op. cit. Chapter 16.

31. F & CO 101013–4 (3/9/1942); 91/101022–3 (8/9/1942).

32. F & CO 302149–50 (25/1/1944).

33. F & Co 302101–2 (22/12/1942). There does not seem to be any documentary evidence for Mrs Carter's (op. cit. p.44) defamatory description of him as a homosexual.

34. F & CO 302134–5 (5/4/1943).

35. F & CO 91/101330–33 (5/5/1943).

36. Interview with Dr Veesenmayer, July 1977.

37. F & CO 91/101335–38 (23/1/1943).

38. F & CO 302142 (6/12/1943); 91/101013/4 (3/9/1942); 91/101017 (4/9/1942); 91/101090 (5/1/1943); 91/101023/3 (8/9/1942); 91/101026

(10/9/1942); 91/101072/3 (21/11/1942); 91/101124 (21/3/1943); 91/101096 (9/2/1943); 91/101124 (21/3/1943).

39.   F & CO 91/101336 (par. 5) (23/1/1943).
40.   See Chapter 8 (end).
41.   F & CO 91/101291–2 (12/112/1943).
42.   See Appendices XIX to XXIV.
43.   F & CO 91/101431 (3/11/1941). See Chapter 8.
44.   See also F & CO 91/101450 (21/6/1941) and 91/101457–9 (undated).
45.   See Chapter 8 (end); Stephan op. cit. pp.242–7.
46.   F & CO 91/101410–17 (24/11/1941).
47.   F & CO 101363 (27/12/1941); 302030–1 (1/12/1941).
48.   F & CO 91/101041–2 (5/10/1942).
49.   F & CO Deutsche Botschaft im Vatican 626221–626229. The selected items from this field of miscellaneous papers include reports of pro-German utterances by Irish Catholic clergy and representatives abroad during the earlier part of the war. An allegation is made that Cardinal McRory was pro-Axis and anti-British, attaching more weight to one word of the Führer's than to all the protests of the British (626227 (5/11/1942); cf. with Hempel's telegram of (2/11/1941); 626227–9, for the period end of November 1941, gives an interesting 'run down' on Ambassador Kiernan and his wife (see Chapter 5) – referring to Kiernan as one of de Valera's 'Old Guard' and quoting Mrs Kiernan in such a way as to indicate an identity of views with the ones Kerney is alleged to have expressed.
50.   Kerney was appointed personally by de Valera when the Fianna Fáil government first came into power (1931). He had been a thorn in the side of the first Free State government. They had to get rid of him.
51.   F & Co 302145 (14/1/1944); 302157–60 (14/11/1944); 302147 (20/1/1944); 302149–50 (25/1/1944); dates do not run in sequence with serial nos.
52.   *The Leader* (31/1/1953) see also Stephan op. cit. p.247; and Carter op. cit. p.119 re rebuke Kerney is alleged to have received from de Valera.

NOTES to Chapter 11

1.   B.H. Liddell Hart, *History of the Second World War* (1970), Chapter 3 ('The Liberation of France') and p.477 re 'unconditional surrender'.
2.   Hildebrand. op. cit. pp.196, 107, 109, 110, 116. Re *Beamtenstaat* and *Volksgenossenstaat* see also John Lukacs, *The Last European War* (London 1976) p.324 and W. Bolerson, *The Limits of Hitler's Power* (Chicago, 1968) p.438. Re virtues of obedience and allegiance, see Kenneth Macksey, *Kesserling: The Making of the Luftwaffe* (1978) pp.103–4; p.161 ('The Struggle for Bureaucratic Self-preservation').
3.   Liddell Hart op. cit. pp.576, 706. Allied victory – and the successful steerage of the neutrality policy were in fact 'close-run things enough'.
4.   Telegram No. 267 (27/6/1974). See also Telegram No. 90 (11/11/1943).
5.   PAAA: RSHA Mil Amt, Abt *Abwehr* 1 (6/7/1944).

6. Film records (BBC TV) of the trials of the participants in the July plot to assassinate Hitler illustrate the hysterical gangsterism that gripped the Third Reich. A minor slip was enough to bring denunciation and 'removal'. In any case, Hempel was out of his consular depth in this non-governmental area and simply did not want to be mixed up in it.

7. F & CO 301396 (10/8/1944).

8. Confidential intelligence source. It is certain that Stephan (op. cit. p.273) was incorrect when he said that Goertz found 'a bribable Irishman' in Sergeant Power, 'who was in constant financial difficulties'. Power, in fact, brought the message to the Irish authorities. The British incidentally, perhaps as a legacy from their Empire, had one of the most effective intelligence systems in the world. By contrast – though they were completely effective against German infiltration attempts – Irish intelligence was relatively small fry, but they did their jobs with dispatch and no incompatible fanfare.

9. Interview with Dr L.S. Gogan (8/12/1976): He was unreserved in his affection for both of the Hempels (Dr Gogan may have been one source of the 'responsible radical nationalist opinion', to which Hempel constantly refers in his telegrams). Thomsen he regarded as the Nazi overseer here. He had a poor opinion of IRA capabilities. He avoided questions as to whether Dr Ryan was 'L' and answered it by saying that one day Dan Breen said that the LDF and the LSF were being run by British and Free State officers and that next day they were under army control. Dan Breen's activities in the period remain questionable. Dr Gogan refused to accord heroworship to Frank Ryan, though he liked him.

10. See Chapter 8, Note 85 where reference to photograph of Fairey Aircraft is cloaked by a reference to a photographer 'Ph-ew'.

11. Montgomery op. cit. pp.274–6.

12. F & CO 301257 (9/7/1942).

13. Carter op. cit. p.208. Mrs Carter's chapter on 'The Internment Camp' at Athlone is indicative of what is probably the most useful and original research in her work. She seemed to have established a rapport with retired army officers similar to the rapport Stephan managed to inspire in his dealings with retired IRA men. These retired army men were very forthcoming to Mrs Carter, as the notes in her book indicate. She also acknowledges (p.12) the invaluable 'inside' information she got from Dr Hayes ('H.G.'), the code expert. ('There is no one to do this job since he died (1976)', according to Col. Bryan.) Prof. Murphy of UCC has remarked on the advantage an outsider has in conducting this type of investigative research. It is to be hoped that the documents referred to in the personal possession of the retired officers in question, will in time, make their way into military archives.

14. Stephan op. cit. p.273, who states, referring to Goertz's letter: 'As the angry old ladies, Mary and Bridie Farrell recall, these letters were delivered in Dublin to a Miss Cantwell who saw to their onward delivery – not however to Northern Ireland as van Loon and the Farrell sisters agreed – but to the German Embassy in Dublin. Goertz's coded messages were transmitted from there to Germany by the embassy transmitter.' There remains a gap in the

different accounts as to what actually happened. Confidential sources closer to the action hold that Goertz's messages (whatever about a leaking of them to the British) never got beyond an army officer's flat in Leeson Street (Dublin), after the involvement with Sergeant Power was heavily acted out. Much earlier Joe Walshe had been highly indignant when Hempel had asked him to convey news of Goertz's promotion to the agent. Walshe took that request as adding insult to injury and the message was not passed on at that time. Later on however, whether because they relented or were bereft of other ideas, those playing this game of encoded 'tig' with Goertz incorporated the news of his promotion in one message which overwhelmed the emotional *Abwehr* agent.

15. Carter op. cit. pp.211, 212.
16. F & CO 301400 (17/11/1944).
17. Telegram No. 257 (16/6/1944). (See also Telegram No. 90 (11/1/1943.)
18. F & CO 91/101151 (15/5/1943). (See also 301331–2 (15/5/1943).
19. Hempel was the most diligent document burner of all the diplomats. But that also applied to selected pre-1945 documents as well and does not account for the gap in the captured documents. The Russians may still have some of the salvaged ones.
20. Carroll op. cit. p.176.
21. O'Donnell op. cit. p.17, Footnote 1.
22. Ibid. Chapter 8.
23. Ibid. pp.57, 111.
24. On the same day (3/5/1945) that Gen. Eisenhower proclaimed that Hitler did not die 'a hero's death', *The Times* gave $4\frac{1}{2}$ lines to de Valera's expression of condolences to the German Minister. Subsequent correspondence was more in sorrow than in anger. Exceptionally too, Commander McDermott insisted that the Taoiseach did the proper thing. That brought the following letter (17/5/1945): 'Will Mr de Valera be grateful to Commander McDermott for exhibiting him as a totalitarian termite incapable of departing in any circumstances from the conventions of diplomacy – a Casiabianca of the Protocol?'

Dr Michael Rynne recalls that the bulk of ordinary Irish people felt that de Valera had done the decent thing in visiting Hempel (see Note 27); the atrocity stories of Belsen and the other camps were not known at that time. However, the visit did not serve to console distraught, humiliated Hempel. (Confidential source.)

25. Longford and O'Neill op. cit. pp.411–12.
26. Confidential source. Allowances should be made for Hempel's stress in the circumstances.
27. Letter from Mr Joe Carroll (13/3/1977), saying that Frau Hempel had written to him about his book *Ireland in the War Years,* pointing out that de Valera called on Hempel after Hitler's death at the residence in Monkstown and not at the Legation. The war was not yet over. Normally and formerly, it could be said, that the logical place to tender formal condolences was the Legation. Professor Williams traced devious de Valera thinking in choosing to

call on Hempel's home rather than to the Legation. Dr Rynne on the other hand, felt that Hempel's home was the proper place to go, as the Legation in Northumberland Road was a grubby little location. Dr Rynne incidentally feels that Carroll (op. cit. pp.160–1) misjudged the mood of the Irish people at the time: there was a wider understanding at home and among Irish-Americans for de Valera's actions, than Carroll conveyed. De Valera, Dr Rynne held, did not need the famous reply to Churchill's speech to make any redress for his tendering of condolences.

28. Stephan op. cit. p.288; Wolf op. cit. p.163.
29. Interview with F.H. Boland. See also Carroll op. cit. p.177.
30. Interview with Frau Hempel (22/8/1975).
31. Seabury op. cit. pp.vii, ix.
32. Interview with George Fleischmann (19/2/1976), who told me the story of Goertz's 'last supper' with Hempel and Boland. See also F & CO 91/101185–6 (13/7/1943) and 91/101199–6 (7/8/1943).
33. Confidential source.
34. Interview with the Misses Farrell (20/2/1976).
35. Stephan op. cit. p.212.

NOTES to Epilogue

1. O'Donnell op. cit. p.212.
2. Ibid. pp.101–12.
3. Interview (1976) with Dr Harry and Mrs Ita O'Flanagan, who had rented a flat from the Hempels. Goertz, according to Van Loon, was similarly clumsy with his hands; though one would not think so from the cross he fashioned for his grave in Glencree.
4. Letter from Thomsen to Mr J.T. Carroll (25/11/1973) – for the use of which I thank Mr Carroll.
5. Interview with Dr W. Warnock (19/11/1976).
6. Conversations with Prof. Binchy.
7. E.g John Murdock's interview with Dr Hempel, *Sunday Press* (Nov./Dec. 1963) which greatly offended and embarrassed both the Hempels and Enne Stephan.
8. F & CO 91/101051/4 (11) (22/10/1943). There are frequent examples of this attitude of Hempels.
9. Conversations: Frau Hempel, W. Warnock, Joe Carroll.
10. PRO P3/133/5 P. (21/2/1944). Colonel Bryan was widely acknowledged – by Liddell Hart, among others – to have been a very effective Director of Intelligence. He was not disposed to show a similar leniency towards the alleged 'going-ons' of the MacNeills – though he personally was not aware that they were in contact with the Legation and Goertz at that time. For further information on MacNeill see *The Leader* 31/1/1953 and 28/3/1953. Viscount Cranbourne was Secretary of State for Dominions 1943–45, *Who's Who British Members of Parliament, Vol. III 1919–45* (Sussex: Harvester).
11. Goethe Institut, 37 Merrion Square, Dublin 2.

12.   Emma Keogh, Librarian, Film Institute of Ireland. Linda O'Nolan, Film Base News Sept./Oct. 1989.
13.   J.P. Duggan, 'Undiplomatic Diplomat', *Studies*, Vol. 90, No. 358 (Summer 2001).
14.   Copies of these broadcasts are available in the German archives. See also David O'Donoghue, *Hitler's Irish Voices* (Belfast 1998), p.236. The Arts Council, Pat Moore.
15.   J.C. Beckett, *The Making of Modern Ireland* (1969), p.441.

Sources

1. Archival

National Library, Dublin

Entries in R.J. Hayes Manuscript Sources for the History of Irish Civilization, 1965.

(1) Germany, Relations with:
Mss. 13,073–92: Papers of Roger Casement, with some of his cousin Gertrude Bannister aft. Mrs Parry: about 4,000 documents, 1969–1916: Many letters to Casement, written incl. J.M. Plunkett, H.W. Nevinson, Douglas Hyde, John Devoy; letters by him; papers on his family; documents on his national activities, his journeys to the United States and Germany, his investigations in the Congo and Putumayo, his trial, 1916; some literary papers (Background to Veesenmayer's reference to 1916: '*1916 war kein Beispiel*').

(2) Germany, Relations with:
Ms. 13,100: Letters addressed to friends in Ireland by J. Doran, a prisoner of war in Germany, 1916–1917, referring to Casement's brigade and to Fr Crotty, chaplain to the prisoners (Veesenmayer's 1916 references).
Germany: Relations with:
Germany, Auswärtiges Amt. Büro des Staats-sekretäres. Irland. Telegrams between the German Legation in Dublin and the German Foreign Office, mainly regarding the neutrality of Ireland (from a film copy in the Public Record Office, London).
n.4682 p.4670.

(3) Germany: Relations with:
Germany: Auswärtiges Amt: Büro des Staatssekretäres. Irland. Telegrams between the German Legation in Dublin and the German Foreign Office, mainly regarding the neutrality of Ireland. Jan. 1942–Dec. 1943; Dec. 1942–May, 1941. (From a film copy in the Public Record Office, London).
n.4683 p.4671.

(4) Germany: Relations with:
Germany: Auswärtiges Amt: Telegrams between the German Legation in Dublin and the German Foreign Office. Agenten in Irland, 1942–4. Office of Ambassador Ritter, 1940–41, 1943–4. Handakten Clodius, mostly on commercial relations, 1940. (From a film copy in the Public Record Office, London). n.4684 p.4672

(See also National Archives, Particular reference to Frank McDermotts' letters on Hempel 999/84/5 (20-4-71 and 99/?? 6 (30-4-72) (previously Four Courts). Also files S9439 and S9984 previously State Papers Office

Politisches Archiv des Auswartigen Amtes, Bonn

(1) General
PAAA, England Nr. 80 (Irland), Bd 11–16.
PAAA Politische Beziehungen zwischen Irland und Deutschland, Bd 1 und 2.
PAAA Abt 111 Pol 1–13 (Irland) (1/9/21-3/4/36)
PAAA Büro St. S., Deutsch-Englische Beziehungen (19/6/40)-31/12/40).
PAAA Ha-Pol Clodius (Irland), Bd 2 und 3
PAAA Akten Botschafter Ritter (1940–1944)
PAAA U.St. S., Irland (Veesenmayer)
PAAA Abt 111 Handelsbeziehungen Irlands zu Deutschland (dl; Bd IV)
PAAA Pol Abt 11 Politische Beziehungen zwischen, England und Irland Bd 1, 11.
PAAA Bürostatsekretar Irland, B1 1,2,3.
(i.e.   1 (8.39-12.40) 91/100052-510
            2 (1.41-3.42) 91/100512-945
            3 (4.42-12.43) 91/100947-1324.
PAAA Rundfunkpoliksche Abteilung 1939-45 Bd 7;8; 27-42.
PAAA Ha-Pol 1936 off 1,11a, 11b; 111; Paket 12; Fach 183–186 Paket 9.15.

(2) Kent Catalogue Vol. II
Ireland file references: pp.10; 11; 28; 29. 163–8; 266; 879.

(3) Kent Catalogue Vol. III
Lists all important files of period 1936–45 except those of Missions and Consulates (Vol IV). Ireland file references: pp. 5; 20; 32; 41; 44; 53; 57; 62; 171; 198; 208; 329; 336; 346; 382; 427; 471.

(4) Kent Catalogue Vol. IV
Lists the files of the major European missions and consulates and some non-European. A note indicates that deficiencies, especially of records in the non-European area, is due to the loss and destruction of entire sets of files during and after World War II. From the Hempel point of view this collection is

disappointing and a further reminder of his compulsive burning of files. It brings to mind that Hempel actually wrote to the German Foreign Ministry, even though he was then out of office, to seek to suppress Enno Stephan's *Spies in Ireland.* Hempel feared that it would damage German–Irish relations. The AA in turn get down the line to Stephan's employers to seek to muzzle him. Stephan stood firm on his democratic rights and refused to be muzzled. Aid came to Stephan from an unexpected quarter: the *Bundesnachrichtendienst* (Intelligence) opposed Hempel and said that, on the contrary, publication of such a work could only improve relations by shedding historical light. Jupp Hoven was another to indicate virulent dissent at the publication and indicated to Stephan, as an example to be followed apparently, that Goertz took the honourable way out rather than betray his comrades by revelation. (Conversation with Enno Stephan July 1977). One surmise to explain that situation is that some (Germans) wanted to know more than Hempel deemed it politic to reveal. Hempel's actions indicated a suspicion that there was something to hide. Ireland file references: p. 41 (Bern); 315, 328 (Madrid); 386 (Oslo); 392, 434 (Paris); 563/4 (Rome); 713 (Vatican); 720 (Sophia); 760 (Warsaw); 678 amd 558 Political relations between Ireland and Italy 1938–39. Hoven (a fellow student of Clissmann's in TCD) was most unco-operative with me (author) in Germany.

Bundesarchiv Koblenz

Sammlung Brammer (101/12); *Sammlung Traub* (110/11)
Sammlung Oberheitmann; Korrespondenz H. Clissmann's, Deutsche Akademie, R57, DAM 932; R2 9914 (folio 1–98); R2/10013 fol. 1; R2 10218 fol 1; R2/24603 (*Internationale Vertrage*); R.4311/4311/1445e Irland; *Akten der Reichskanzlei sowie des Finanz-und Wirtschaftressorts; Aktenbande aus der Adjutantur des Führers.* SS Akten (Irland); Auslandsnachrichten dienst (Irland) Resort Schellenberg (Irland); *Slg Schlumack,* 291–296a N15/–26 NS22/485. Koblenz disappointing in Hempel area.

Militäranchiv Freiburg

Operation '*Herbstreise*' (incorporating Operation '*Grun*') (N.B.)
Operations 'Seelöwe (Seelöwe); 'Haifisch' and 'Harpune'.
Various political, economic and naval files referring to Ireland (e.g. RW5/v: RWG/V and Wi/1).

Foreign and Commonwealth Office, London

(1) Serial 1612N 386396 – 386508.
Political relations between Britain and Ireland. Vol 1 (May 1936–April 1938).

Selected items.–
(i)   (24 November 1936). Éireann Minister in Berlin asks that in publications the name 'Irish Free State' should not appear under the general heading of 'England' but should be given separate space as in the case of other British Dominions.
(ii)   (12 December 1936). Report on law abolishing post of Governor General in Dublin.
(iii)   (19 November 1937). Secretary of State for External Affairs discusses with German Minister favourable political position of Germany caused by Italy joining the Comintern Pact.
(iv)   (20 December 1937). Lengthy report on significance of new Irish Constitution and position of Eire within the British Commonwealth.
(v)   (18 January 1938). Report on British–Irish Conference in London.

(2) Serial 16128. 387528–387624.

Selected items:
(i)   (17 May 1938). Report from German Legation in Dublin on Anglo-Irish relations as a result of Agreement of 25 April 1938.
(ii)   (17 October 1938). Report on Ireland during and after Sudeten crisis.
(iii)   German Legation reports on Irish armament questions.

(3) Serial No. 3730 M

Supplementary to Serials 1612N, 1618H and 3158H (German Foreign Ministry: Pol 11 Po 3: England–Ireland). 24 items selected: 51 items unfilmed.
Selected items:
(i)   (30 July 1936) EO37217 Ber. A 42 Koester Dublin to AA. Statements by Irish politicians indicating that Ireland would be neutral in the event of a European conflict.
(ii)   (1 August 1936) E 037300–303. Ber. A43 Koester Dublin to AA. Irish refusal to participate in the Coronation celebrations.
(iii)   (25 February 1937) Schroetter Dublin to AA. Ireland and the Oath of Allegiance.
(iv)   (18 May 1937). Schroetter Dublin to AA Radio speech by de Valera on Anglo-Irish Relations.
(v)   (21 May 1937). Schroetter Dublin to AA. De Valera's declaration re Ireland's non-participation in the Imperial Conference.
(vi)   (17 July 1937) EO37315–7. Ber. A98g. Schroetter to AA. Political feeling in N. Ireland.
(vii)   (30 December 1937) EO37318–323 Hempel-Dublin to AA. Proclamation of new Éire constitution.

(viii)   (15 January 1938) EO37324–5 Ber A 192 g. Woermann (London) to AA. Reaction in N. Ireland to Éire constitution.

(ix)   (18 January 1938) EO37236. Telegram 19 Woermann to AA. Progress of the Anglo-Irish talks; N. Ireland and Irish unity.

(x)   (19 January 1938) EO37327 Tel 21 Woermann to AA. The Anglo-Irish talks.

(xi)   (26 January 1938) EO37328–9 Ber A 455 Woermann to AA N. Ireland and the Anglo-Irish talks.

(xii)   (23 February 1938) EO37330–2 Ber A. 871 J. Woermann to AA N. Ireland elections.

(xiii)   18 March 1938) EO37333–336 Ber. A 104 Hempel Dublin to AA. The situation reached in the Anglo-Irish conversations.

(xiv)   (5 May 1938) EO37338–341 Berlin BI365 G. Beilfeld (London) to AA.. N. Irish opinion and the Anglo-Irish Agreement.

(xv)   (13 May 1938) EO37342–345. Ber. A 152 Hempel to AA. Defence Questions discussed in Irish Senate.

(xvi)   (18 October 1938) EO373346–351 Ber. A.417 to AA. De Valera on N. Ireland.

(xvii)   (20 November 1938) EO37352–354 Ser. A. 484. Hempel to AA. De Valera on Anglo-Irish relations.

(xviii)   (16 February 1939) EO37355–9 Ber. A 120 G. Hempel AA. The suppositions on which Irish defence expenditure for 1939 would rest.

(xix)   (17 February 1939) EO37360–5 Ber. A 127 g. Hempel to AA. De Valera's speech on Ireland's attitude in the event of war.

(xx)   (15 February 1939) EO37366–9 Ber. A 103 g Hempel to AA. Conversation with de Valera on the subject of the IRA and outrages in N. Ireland.

(xxi)   (23 February 1939) EO37370–5 Ber. A143 g. Thomsen Dublin to AA. De Valera on Irish Neutrality.

(xxii)   (28 January 1939) EO37376–80 Hempel to AA. Renewed IRA activities.

(xxiii)   (1 July 1931) EO37381–7. Ber. 1308 Hempel to AA. Dáil debate on Neutrality.

(xxiv)   29 July 1939) EO37388–91 Ber. Hempel to AA. British measures against IRA.

(4) *Collection entitled Éire Vol 1. Serial 91/1:100051–100510* (there are gaps in this sequence: some, but not all, of these missing telegrams are available in PAAA, Bonn).
Numerous Telegrams between the German Legation in Dublin and the German Foreign Office from August 1939 to December 1940, mainly regarding the neutrality of Éire.

(5) *Collection entitled Éire Vol. II. Serial No. 91/11: 100511–100945: 1 January 1941–31 March 1942.*
Selected items.
Telegrams between the German Legation in Dublin and the German Foreign Office dealing with:

(i)	Dropping of bombs on Dublin and other towns in Éire.
(ii)	Question of resistance if neutrality violated.
(iii)	Influence of Irish in USA.
(iv)	Fear of invasion of Ports in Éire by Great Britain.
(v)	Wendel Wilkie's visit to Dublin and report of speech by him in the National Press club. Telegram from German Ambassador, Washington. No. 450 of 18 February 1941.
(vi)	Offer of German assistance to Éire in case of attack by Britain – Ribbentrop to German Ambassador Dublin; No. 97 dated 24 February 1941 and reply to letter in Telegram No. 218 dated 11 March 1941.
(vii)	A secret wireless station used by German Legation, Dublin.
(viii)	Activities of German agents in Éire.
(ix)	Appeal of pro-German section of town of Derry in Ulster that that town should not be bombed.
(x)	Appeal by Archbishop of Armagh that that town should not be bombed.

(6) *Collection entitled Éire Vol. III: Serial No. 91/III: 100946–101324: 1 April 1942–31 December 1943.*
Selected items:

(i)	German Legations connection with spies in Ireland.
(ii)	Protests of Irish Government against attacks on Irish ships.
(iii)	Reports on military movements and numbers of troops in Ulster and England.
(iv)	Former Irish Minister in Berlin, Bewley, discussing the future of Éire in case of a German victory.
(v)	Reporting particulars of British preparations for invasion of the Continent.

(7) *Collection entitled Ireland (Veesenmayer) Serial No. 91/IV: 101325–101470 May 1941–5 May 1943.*
Selected items.

(i)	Plan 'Mainau' of Mr Andrews for action with Germany in connection with Irish fascist organisations 'Blue Shirts'.
(ii)	Reports of SS Oberfuhrer Veesenmayer regarding activities of his

group of 120 men in the matter of Ireland.

(iii)   Report of dropping Hauptmann Dr Hermann Goertz by parachute over Ireland on 5/6 May 1940 to carry out action with the IRA to assist German War Plans.

(References to 'Von Herr Clissmann der Abwehrabteilung 11 ubergebene Telegramme (Dublin): No. 289 (22/9/41); 342 (20/10/41); 367 (29/10/41); 371 (2/11/41); 387 (6/11/41); 443 (3/12/41); 442 (5/12/41); 443 (8/12/41).

(8) *Collection entitled: Ireland Serial No. 1423: 362675–362691. August 1942–October 1944.*
Selected items:

(i)   (9 August 1943): Telegram from German Minister at Dublin surveying series of alleged breaches of neutrality by the Irish Government. Hempel refers to the release of air crews, the granting of aircraft repair facilities, and reports on his various demarcates.

(ii)   (5 October 1943): Telegram from German Minister at Dublin reporting on discussion with de Valera, during which he presumed that if Éire were the victim of aggression from one side, she would receive all possible assistance from the other.

(iii)   (25 January 1944): Telegram from German Minister at Dublin reporting ever increasing Allied pressure on Éireann Government for severance of diplomatic relations with Germany. Hempel states that he is observing political trends very minutely in order to prevent any breach in relations.

(9) *Collection entitled: Intelligence (Abwehr): Ireland. Serial No. 961: 301977–302176.*
These documents are concerned with the activity of German secret agents in Ireland and with the help rendered by the German Legation in Dublin. Several names and addresses are contained in the correspondence. Agent reports that General O'Duffy prepared to send a 'Green Division' to Russia.

(10) *Serial No 957: 301141–301404*
Certain documents concerning the activities of German agents in Éire and help extended to those agents by German Legation in Dublin. Several names are given ('including names of Eireann sympathisers').

(11) *Collection entitled: Ireland (Ambassador Ritter Bundle 4): Serial No. 1005: 307436–307570.*
(i)   (14 November 1940). General Warlimont informs Ambassador

Ritter that in event of British attack on Éire the only assistance Germany could offer would be (1) Concentration of U-Boats around ports occupied by British, (2) Extension of air raids to ports occupied by British. The use of airborne troops is ruled out owing to supply line difficulties.

(ii)   (18 December 1940). German desire to send two military officers to be attached to German Legation in Dublin as civilians.

(iii)   (6 December 1940). High-ranking officer in Éireann army asks what help Germany could give in event of British attack; asks for deliveries of British weapons captured by Germans.

(iv)   (21 December 1940). Éireann authorities request Germans not to strengthen staff at Legation at Dublin.

(v)   (25 December 1940). Ribbentrop instructs German Minister in Dublin to inform Éireann authorities that Germany will decide the strength of Legation staff.

(vi)   (29 December 1940). Ribbentrop instructs German Minister in Dublin not to press further in the matter of increasing staff of Legation.

(vii)   (18 August 1941). De Valera requests German Minister in friendly terms to restrict use of wireless transmitter in Legation to cases of utmost urgency and importance.

(viii) (22 February 1941). Short report of conversation between Wendell Wilkie and de Valera on Éire's neutrality.

(ix)   (24 February 1941). Ribbentrop instructs German Minister in Dublin to assure de Valera of Germany's readiness to aid Éire in event of British attack.

(12) *Miscellaneous: Loesch collection: Serial 825: GB59: 6329: 3015 3096: 3199.*

Public Records Office, London

War Cabinet, Foreign Office and Dominions Office papers (transferred to Public Records Office, Kew).

Imperial War Museum London

Co. Ref. No.	Title	Date
AL 1933	Canaris/La Hausen fragments	(5/3/37)
MI 14/68	Deception measures	(7/8/41–28/10/41)
MI 14/81	Deception measures	"
MI 14/86	Deception measures	"

MI 14/87	Deception measures	"
1678 (2)	La Hausen's Diary	(12/5/37–12/4/41)
		(14/4/41–3/8/43)

The War Journal of Fritz Halder.
AL 1770 Hitler's ideas of a British (19/3/43) Legion against Bolshevism;
John Amery.
MI 14/402 *Fall 'Grün'* (12/8/40–20/9/40).
Betr.   *Ausbildung der Pioniere*
             Ausbildung der Artillerie
Organisatorische u. techniche Vorbereitungen
Art der Durchführung
Anordrungen für die Verwendung der Artillerie
Aufgaben und Verrwendung der Pioniere
Anordnung für die Geheimhattung
Erganzungen zur Bezugverfügung
See Transportsmeldung
Vorlaüfige Stärkemeldung
(These are listed to indicate detail of planning (deception measures).
AL 1491. Letter of Hempel German Ambassador (17/12/40) to Ireland
offering arms and German help against England.
AL 1048/2. Plans for Invasion of British Isles. (The Führer's thoughts as
relayed by his adjutant (AL2828) and General Jodi's summary of the
situation with reference to the Invasion of the United Kingdom.
(M14/14/112) do not refer to Ireland.)

2. Manuscripts

Bewley Memoirs from Dr Bewley (since published by Lilliput Press)
Goertz Letters etc. Enno Stephan
J. O'Donovan (including letters from Goertz and Weber Drohl)
Miss Maura O'Brien, Enno Stephan, Prof. Williams
National Library Ms 21155 Acc 3199
Liam Walsh's (incl. Eoin O'Duffy) National Library P6539
(Miss O'Brien kindly accepted my suggestion that the Goertz letters and
other papers be given to the National Library and Mr O'Looney arranged
for their collection.)

3. Personal interviews

Prof. D.A. Binchy
Dr Geoffrey Bewley
F.H. Boland

Miss Mona Brase
Col. Dan Bryan
Jos. T. Carroll
Helmut and Mrs Clissmann
Horst Dickel
Misses Farrell
George Fleischmann
Douglas Gageby
Dr L.S. Gogan
Frau Eva Hempel
Mrs Caitriona Hertz
Jan van Loon
Seán MacBride
Seamus Mallin
Miss Sheila Murphy
Miss Maura O'Brien
Patrick O'Connell Buckley
James L. O'Donovan
Dr Harry and Mrs O'Flanagan
Anthony Powell
P.P. O'Reilly
Michael Scott
Enno Stephan
Francis Stuart
Arthur Voigt
Dr W. Warnock
R.R.A. Wheatley
Dr Edmund Veesenmayer
Prof. Desmond Williams

4. Letters/Conversations

Dr H. Becker
Lt. Col. D. Beglin
Dr David Bewley
R.D. and Thea Boyd
Mrs Carolle Carter
Fr S.J. Clyne (for Archbishop O Fiaich)
Tim Pat Coogan
Con Cremin
Máire Cruise O'Brien
Col. E. de Buitléir
James Dillon
Dr Reinhard R. Doerries

Ruth Dudley Edwards
Bartholomew Egan OFM
Dr R. Fechter
Robert Fisk
Col. James Fitzgerald Lombard
Dr Giessler
Mrs Hayes
Dr Andy Hempel
Ms Agnes Hempel
Prof. Dr Klaus Hildebrand
Ken Hiscock
Harold Hoven
Dr Maria Keipert
Hilary F. Lawton S.J.
Col. F.E. Lee
Herr Loos
Mrs Jacqueline McGilligan
Sean Mallin
Una Mallin
Anthony Maraco
Dr Bernd Martin
Ron Mellor
Lothar A. Merta
Seán McEntee
Mrs Caitriona Miles (for Professor Delargy)
Capt. Jack Millar
Peadar O'Donnell
Mrs Kay Petersen
Dr Pretsch
Dr Felician Prill
Philip Prill
Philip Reed
Dr Michael Rynne
Oberst i.g. Sauvant
Franz Selinger
W.K. Smurthwaite
Dr Franz von Sonnleithner
Kurt Ticher
M Toomey
Rudolf Veesenmayer
Dr Ernst Woermann.

5. Newspapers; periodicals; articles; published documents

Newspapers

Irish Independent, Irish Press, Irish Times, The Worker, The Irish Worker's Voice, Daily Express, Daily Mail, Daily Telegraph, Sunday Chronicle, Manchester Guardian, The Times, New York Journal, New York Times, Allgemeine Zeitung, Volkischer Beobachter, Sunday Independent.

Periodicals

Archivalische Zeitschrift (1968), *Der Archiver* (1972) (n.b. *Zur Lage des Archivwesens in der Republik Irland by P. Kahlenberg*, pp. 175–182), *An Cosantoir, The Bell, Journal of Commonwealth Political Studies, Historische Zeitschrift Journal of Modern History, Nation und Staat; The Leader, Der Speigel, Statesman and Nation, Studies.*

Articles

Anon., 'MacNeill', *The Leader*, 28 March 1953.

Anon, 'Ireland in the Vortex', *The Round Table*, No. 121, December 1940.

Binchy, D.A., 'Adolf Hitler' *Studies*, March 1933.

Binchy, D.A., 'Paul von Hindenburg', *Studies*, June 1937.

Brennan, Robert, 'Wartime Mission in Washington', *Irish Press*, June–July 1958.

Brodrick, Charles, 'Gruen: German Military Plans and Ireland, 1940', *An Cosantoir*, March 1974.

Cox, Colm 'Wir fahren gegen Irland', *An Cosantoir*, May 1974, March 1975.

Dickel, H., *Irland als Faktor der deutsehen Aussenpolitik von 1933–1945: Eine propadeutische Skizze – Hitler, Deutschland und die Mächte Bonner Schriften zur Politik und Zeitgeschichte*

Dwyer, T. Ryle, 'The Irish diplomats used as U.S. spies', *Sunday Independent*, 24 June 1984.

Goertz, Hermann, 'Mission to Ireland', *Irish Times*, 25 August–10 September, 1947.

Harkness, David, 'Mr de Valera's Dominion: Irish Relations with Britain and the Commonwealth, 1932–39', *Journal of Commonwealth Political Studies*, Vol. VIII, 1970.

Murdoch, J., 'Interviews with Dr Hempel', *Sunday Press*, November–December 1963. (These articles contained many inaccuracies and caused much distress: they were refuted.)

O'Reilly, John, 'I was a spy in Ireland', *Sunday Dispatch*, July/August 1952.

Rugby, Lord (Sir John Maffey), 'Lord Rugby remembers', *Irish Times*, 3 June 1962.

Stuart, Francis, 'Frank Ryan in Germany', *The Bell*, November 1950.
Van Hoek, Kees, 'Secret Agents in Ireland', *Sunday Chronicle*, June 1954.
Williams, T. Desmond, 'Study in Neutrality', *The Leader*, January–April 1953.
Williams, T. Desmond, 'Neutrality', *Irish Press*, June–July 1953.

Published Documents

Akten zur deutschen auswärtigen Politik (ADAP) Series É Band 1 Gottingen
(1969). *Documents of German Foreign Policy* DI–XIII (DCFP) HMSO
(1949–64).
Dáil Debates 1939–1945 Dublin – *International Military Tribunal Nuremberg*
(1949) Vols – 142 Nuremberg.
Seanad Debates 1939–1945 Dublin.

Micro Film

P. 4670
P. 4672
P. 4671
P. 4672 (See National Library of Ireland)

Maps

Militärgeographisch Angaben über Irland Süd – und Ostkuste (von Mizen Head
bis Malin Head).
Text-und Bildheft mit Kartenanlagen Abgessclossen am 31 Mai 1941.
Generalstab des Heeres
Abteilung für Kriegskarten und Vermessungswesen
(IV Mil. Geo Berlin 1941 15 October 1941.
(Military College Library, Curragh).

6. Bibliography

(All books are published in London unless otherwise indicated)

Anderson, M.S. *The Ascendancy of Europe 1815–1914* (1972).
Beckett J.C., *The Making of Modern Ireland* (1969).
Bedford, John Duke of, *A Silver Plated Spoon* (Cassell Report Survey
    1959).
Bell, J. Bowyer, *The Secret Army: The IRA since 1916* (1970).
Bewley, C.H., *Memoirs of a Wild Goose* (Dublin 1989).
Blaxland, G., *Destination Dunkirk* (1973).

Block, Jonathan and Patrick Fitzgerald, *British Intelligence and Covert Action* (1983).

Bolerson W., *The Limits of Hitler's Power* (Chicago 1968).

Bowman, John, *De Valera and the Ulster Question* (Oxford 1983).

Brassey, *Brassey's Naval Annual* (1948).

Brissard, A., *The Biography of Admiral Canaris* (1973).

Brissard, A., *The Nazi Secret Service* (1974).

Bullock, A., *Hitler: A Study in Tyranny* (1968).

Butcher, H., *Three Years with Eisenhower: Personal Diary 1942–1945* (1950).

Carroll, Joseph T., *Ireland in the War Years 1939–45* (Newton Abbot 1975).

Carter, C., *The Shamrock and the Swastika*, (Palo Alto 1977).

Chamberlain, N., *The Struggle for Peace* (1939).

Chatfield, A E. M., *The Navy and Defence: the autobiography of Admiral of the Fleet Lord Chatfield*, Vol. 2, 'It Might Happen Again' (1942, 1947).

Churchill, W. S., *The Second World War*, Vols 1–6 (1960).

Cienciella, A.M., *Poland and the Western Powers, 1938–39* (1968).

Clarke, D., *Seven Assignments* (1948).

Colvin, I., *Canaris, Chief of Intelligence* (1973).

Coogan, T.P., *The IRA* (1970).

Cooper, Matthew, *The German Army 1933–1945* (1978).

Craig Gordon, A., *The Diplomats 1919–39* (Princeton 1953).

Demeter, Karl, *The German Officer Corps in Society and State, 1850–1945* (1962).

de Valera, E., *Peace and War: Speeches on International Affairs* (Dublin 1944).

Ireland's Stand: A Selection of the Speeches of E. de Valera during the War 1939–45 (Dublin 1946).

Donitz, K. Deutsche, *Strategie zur See im Zweiten Weltkreig* (Frankfurt a.m. 1972).

Duff Cooper, *Operation Heartbreak* (1950).

Duggan John P., *Neutral Ireland and the Third Reich* (Dublin 1985).

A History of the Irish Army (Dublin 1989).

Memoirs of a Wild Goose (i.e. Bewley's Memoirs' co-edited; joint published; foreword) (Dublin 1989).

Dulles, A., *Germany's Underground* (New York 1947).

Dulles, A., *The Craft of Intelligence* (1964).

Dulles, A., *The Secret Surrender* (1967).

Dulles, A., *Great True Spy Stories* (1969).

Dwyer, T. Ryle, *Irish Neutrality and the USA, 1939–47* (Dublin 1977).

Edwards, Ruth Dudley, *An Atlas of Irish History* (1973).

Eisenhower, D., *Crusade in Europe* (1948).

Farago, L., *German Psychological Warfare* (New York 1942).

War of Wits: The Anatomy of Espionage and Intelligence (1956).

The Game of the Foxes (1971).

Fisk, Robert, *In Time of War* (1983).

Fleming, P., *Invasion 1940* (1959).

Fonvielle Alquier, F., *The French and the Phoney War, 1939–40* (1973).

Gageby D., *The Last Secretary General, Seán Lester and the League of Nations* (Dublin 1999).

Gallagher, Joseph Peter, *The Scarlet Pimpernel of the Vatican* (1967).

Garlinski, J., *Intercept: Secrets of the Enigma War* (1979).

von Gersdorff, U., *Geschichte und Militargeschichte* (Frankfurt a.m. 1974).

Halder, F., *Kriegstagebuch Bd III* (Stuttgart 1964).

Harkness, D.W., *The Restless Dominion* (1969).

Heinemann, John, *Hitler's First Foreign Minister, Constantin von Neurath, Diplomat and Statesman* (Berkeley 1979).

Hildebrand, K., *The Foreign Policy of the Third Reich* (1973).

Hillgruber, A., *Kontinuität und Discontinuität in der Deutschen Aussempolitik von Bismarc bis Hitler* (Düsseldorf 1971).

Hillgruber, A., *Hitler's Strategic, Politik und Kreigsfuhrung 1940–41*, (Frankfurt a.m. 1945).

Deutschland's Rolle in der Vorgeschichte der beiden Weltkreige (Göttingen 1967).

Hitler, A., *Mein Kampf* (1939).

Hogan, V.P., 'The Neutrality of Ireland in World War II' (unpublished doctoral thesis for University of Notre Dame, 1948).

Hull, Cordell, *The Memoirs of Cordell Hull*, 2 vols (1948).

Huntington, Samuel P., *The Soldier and the State* (Cambridge, Mass. 1972).

Ironside, W.E., *The Ironside Diaries* (1962).

Kahn, O., *Hitler's Spies: German Military Intelligence in World War II* (1978).

Kavanagh, Comdt. P.D., *Irish Defence Forces Handbook* (Dublin 1974).

Keatinge, P., *The Formulation of Irish Foreign Policy* (Dublin 1974). *A Place among the Nations*, Dublin (1978).

Kehal, K., *Kreisen Manager im Dritten Reich* (Düsseldorf 1973).

Klee, K., *Das Unternehmen 'Seelöwe'* (Göttingen 1958).

Dokumente zum Unternehmen 'Seelowe' (Göttingen 1959).

Kordt, K., *Nicht aus den Akten* (Stuttgart 1950).

von Lahausen, E., *Secret War Diary of General von Lahausen* (1958).

Langer, W.L., and S. E. Gleeson, *The Challenge of Isolation, 1937–40* (New York 1952).

Leverkuehn, P., *Der Geheime Nachrichtendienst der deutschen Wehrmacht in Kreige* (Frankfurt a.m. 1957).

Liddell Hart, B.H., *History of the Second World War* (1970).

Longford, Earl of, and T.P. O'Neill, *Eamon de Valera* (Dublin 1970).

Lukacs, J., *The Last European War* (1971).

Macksey, K., *Kesserling: The Making of the Luftwaffe* (1978).

McCracken, J.I., *Representative Government in Ireland* (1958).

McMahon D., 'Malcolm McDonald – Anglo Irish Relations 1935–36' (MA Thesis UCD 1995). *Republicans and Imperialists – Anglo-Irish Relations in the 1930's* (Yale 1984).

Mansergh, P.N.S., *The Commonwealth Experience* (1969).

Mansergh, P.N.S., *Survey of British Commonwealth Affairs*, vol 2.

Mansergh, P.N.S., *Problems of Wartime Co-operation and Post-War Change, 1939–52* (1958).

Martin, B., *Friedensinitiativen und Machtpolitik in zweiten Weltkreig 1939–42* (Düsseldorf 1974).

Montgomery, B.I., *Memoirs* (1958).

Namier, Sir L., *Diplomatic Prelude 1936–1940* (1948).

Neave, A., *Nuremberg* (1978).

Nowlan K, and T.D. Williams, eds, *Ireland in the War Years and After* (Dublin 1969).

O'Donnell, J.P., *The Berlin Bunker* (1979).

O'Donoghue David, *Hitler's Irish Voices* (Belfast 1998).

O'Halpin, Eunan, *Defending Ireland: The Irish State and Its Enemies since 1922* (Oxford 1999).

Petersen, G.W., *The Limits of Hitler's Power* (Chicago 1968).

von Ribbentrop, J., *Memoirs* (1954).

Schellenberg, W., *The Schellenberg Memoirs* (1956).

Schramm, P. E., *Kriegstagebuch des OKW (Wehrmachtführungstab)* (Frankfurt a.m. 1961).

von Schweppenburg, G., *Errinerungen eines Militärattaches* (Stuttgart 1949).

Seabury, P., *Wilhelmstrasse* (Berkeley 1954).

Shebab, H.M., 'Irish Defence Policy 1922–50' (M. Litt. Thesis for UCD 1975).

Shirer, W.I., *The Rise and Fall of the Third Reich* (1960).

Smith, R.H., *OSS: The Secret History of America's First Central Intelligence Agency* (Berkeley 1972).

Stagg, J.N., *Forecast for Overlord: June 6 1944* (1971).

Stephan, Enno, *Spies in Ireland* (1963).

Stephan, Werner, *Joseph Goebbels – Däemon einer Diktatur* (Stuttgart 1949).

Stuart, Francis, *The Victor and the Vanquished* (1954).

Sturm, Hubert, *Hakenkreuz und Kleebatt: Irland, die Allierten und das Dritte Reich 1933–45* (Frankfurt a.m. 1984).

Taylor, A.J.P., *The Origins of the Second World War* (1961).

Trevor-Roper Hugh, *The Goebbels Diaries* (1978).

Hitler's War Directions 1939–45 (1964).

Wagner, G., *Lagevorträge des Oberbefehlshabers der Kriegsmarine vor Hitler 1939–45* (Munich 1972).

Warlimont, W., *Inside Hitler's Headquarters* (1964).

Welles, S., *The Time for Decision* (1944).

von Weizacker, E., *Memoirs* (1951).

West, Nigel, *MI5: British Security Operations (1909–1945)* (Toronto 1981).

West, Rebecca, *A Train of Powder* (1955).

Wheatley, R., *Operation 'Sealion'* (1958).

Wheeler-Bennett, J.W., *The Nemesis of Power* (1954).

Wilmot, Chester, *The Struggle for Europe* (New York 1952).

Wolf Karin, *Sir Roger Casement und die deutsch-irishen Beziehungen* (Berlin 1972).

Young, A.P., *The 'X' Documents: the Secret History of Foreign Office contacts with the German Resistance 1937–39* (1974).

Appendix 1
Hempel's Curriculum Vitae

Hempel, Eduard
Born 6.6.1887
Prot.
Parents; Karl Konstantin H., Government Privy Councillor
(*Amptshauptmann*, Saxon) Olga Elwine (née Ponfick)
m 24.5.1928, Eva nee Ahlemann
(Father: George A., pruss-officer)
Children: Andreas, Constantin; Liv; Bernt, Agnes.

Grammar School in Bautzen, Fridericanum Grammar School in Davos –
1906 *Abitur* in Wertheim/Baden; 1906 to 1910. University education in
Munich, Heidelberg, Berlin and Leipzig: Law – 15.6.1910 1st State
Examination, 28.6.1910 Dr. Jur; 1.10.1910 to 30.9.1911 one year voluntary
service; from 1.2.1912. Justice and Administrative service in Kingdom of
Saxony – 14.2.1920 2nd State Examination; 2.8.1914 to 7.1.1919 Military
Service: 15.10.194 Reserve Lieutenant, from 1.5.1917 on the staff of the
Military Administrator in Rumania; 1.12.1920 Higher Civil Servant
(*Regierungsassessor*) – 1928 to 4.7.1933. <u>DVP (Deutsche Volkpartei)</u> (self
dissolution), 1.7.1938 <u>NSDAP</u> (National Socialist).

29.3.1921	Transfer to Saxon Legation in Berlin. Assistant – Legations Secretary.
14.6.1924	Legation Secretary 1st class, Counsellor.
7.1926	Diplomatic consular examination.
31.5.1928	Oslo Legation
23.12.1929	1st Counsellor of the Legation
29.10.1932	Special duties (Personnel, Administrative, Buildings) 11.3.1933 Counsellor
22.6.1937 to 8.5.1945	Minister in Dublin Remained in Dublin.
31.1.1950	Chancellor's office, Foreign Affairs (from 15.3.1951 Foreign Office relief envoy), Dept 1 (Personnel and Administration) Real Estate and buildings at home and abroad.
18.12.1951	Retirement.
12.11.1972	Death in Wildtal near Freiburg im Breisgau.

Sources: Auswärtiges Amt., Berlin. J.P. Duggan, 'Herr Hempel at   the

German Legation in Dublin 1937-1945', MLitt thesis, Trinity College
Dublin, 1980. Ibid., *Neutral Ireland and the Third Reich* (Dublin, 1985).
The Hempel family. Earl of Longford and T. P. O'Neill, Eamon de Valera
(Dublin, 1970).

Appendix 2

Hitler's letter to George VI appointing Hempel, 22 June 1937
(translation)

Adolf Hitler
German Reichskanzler
To
His Majesty
King of Great Britain, Ireland and the British Lands[1] beyond the Seas,
Defender of the Faith, Emperor of the India
Your Majesty!

Arising from the demise of Envoy von Kuhlmann, German Minister in Dublin, I have decided to replace him with Dr. Eduard Hempel.

His proven qualities lead me to expect that he will worthily represent Your Majesty in fostering good relations between the two peoples.

Dr. Hempel would be honoured if, as recommended, Your Majesty would accept him as Envoy Extraordinary and Minister Plenipotentiary.

I beg to request that he be accepted with goodwill in anything he undertakes in good faith in my name or in the service of the German Government.

I avail of the occasion to assure Your Majesty of my highest esteem and genuine friendship as well as my best wishes for the well-being of Your Majesty and the future prosperity of the Irish Free State.

Berlin, 22 June 1937.

(Sg) Adolf Hitler

(Sg) Freiherr von Neurath.

---

1. 'Dominions' not specified. German demand for the return of colonies was vociferous at the time.

Adolf Hitler
Deutsche Reichskanzler
an
Seine Majestät
den König von Gross Britannien, Irland und
der Überseeischen Britischen Lande, Verteidiger
des Glaubens, Kaiser von Indien

Euere Majestät!

Von den Wunsche geleitet, den durch das Ableben des Gesandten von Kuhlmann erledigten Posten des Deutschen Gesandten in Dublin wieder zu besetzen, habe ich beschlossen, diesen Posten dem Vortragenden Legationsrat

Dr. Eduard Hempel

zu übertragen.

Seine bewährten Eigenschaften berechtigen mich zu der Erwartung, dass es ihm gelingen werde, sich Euerer Majestät Wohlwollen zu erwerben und die Beziehungen guten Einvernehmens zwischen beiden Volkorn zu festigen und zu vertifen.

Herr Dr. Hempel wird die Ehre haben, Euerer Majestät dieses Schrieben zu überreichen, dass ihn in der Eigenschaft eines ausserordentlichen Gesandten und bevollmächtigten Ministers des deutschen Reichs beglaubigen soll.

Ich bitte, ihn mit Wohlwollen aufzunehmen und ihm in allen was er in meinem Namen oder in Auftrage der deutschen Reichsregierung vorautragen berfufen sein wird, vollen lauben zu acceptieren.

Ich benutze auch diesen Anlass, um Euerer Majestät die Versicherung meiner vollkommensten Hochachtung und aufrichtigen Freundschafl zum Ausdruck zu bringen und damit zugleich meinen besten Wünsche für das Wohlergehen Euerer Majestät und für das Blühen und Gedeihen des Irischen Freistaats zu verbinden.

Berlin, den 22 Juni 1937.

(Sg) ADOLF HITLER.

(Sg) FREIHERR VON NEURATH

Appendix 3
Sean Russell's letter to Dr Luther, 21 October 1936

Sean Russell,   Seville Hotel, New York, N.Y.
   Quartermaster General
   of the I.R.A.   October 21, 1936.

His Excellency Dr. Hans Luther,
German Ambassador to the U.S.
Washington, D.C.

Your Excellency:

The Government of the Republic desires me to call to your attention a news item reporting refusal by the Irish "Free State' government of landing rights in our country for your international air service. As special Envoy to the United States and Quartermaster General of the Irish Republican Army, I am asked to express to you on behalf of ~~the~~ my government the sincere regret of our people that the German nation, in return for past friendships to us, should be refused a right apparently conceded without question to England, the traditional enemy of the Irish race.

The "Free Sate" government depends for its very existence on the British parliament, whose puppet it is and the action taken must be viewed rather as the carrying out of the directions of the master than the expression of the free will of the people from whom it pretends to derive its authority.

The government of the Republic and the people of Ireland are, and will continue to be, mindful of the debt they owe to the German people and their government for assistance calculated to rid our country of that foreign rule that now uses the so-called "Free State" as its domestic agent. That this is true is attested by the fact that our Chief of Staff, many senior officers and our best men are in jail and that those who would prepare the army and the people of the republic for a successful termination to our countries centuries of struggle to be free have earned the undying enmity and the ceaseless persecution of that which, while it pretends to having kept the faith with Pearse and Casement, is so belied by its every act that nobody is in doubt that the future will but mirror its past.

It was not for such an end that we enlisted your aid in the past. It was because we sought then to end such rule that we might be free from treason at home and tyranny from abroad. We ask that you believe this as we would have you believe, too, that Republican Ireland is disposed to, and shall be glad of the opportunity when she may make return to her friends in Germany

for valued assistance in the early days of the present phase of our fight. – With
esteem for you and your people, I beg to remain, on behalf of the
Government and people of the Republic,

Gratefully and sincerely yours,

Sean Russell, Special Envoy of

Ireland to the USA.

Appendix 4
Chiefs of Staff outline Britain's position (extract)

The purposes for which we require to use the ports ourselves.

12. The purposes for which the Admiralty require to use the ports are set out in paragraphs (3) to (10) above. As regards the requirements of the Royal Air Force, Berehaven is envisaged in Trade Protection plans as a base for reconnaissance squadrons. The requirements of trade protection could, however, be met, though with some added difficulty, without the use of ports in Ireland. Air patrols for anti-submarine and trade protection work could be maintained from such places as the Scilly Isles or Milford Haven.

Military measures necessary to ensure the use of the ports.

13. In the foregoing paragraphs, we have explained the importance of the ports to the conduct of the war. We now turn to consideration of the military measures which would be necessary to ensure their security in the conditions hypothecated in Question (2).

14. Our peace-time garrisons at the ports would clearly require reinforcement. We do not anticipate that this operation would present serious difficulty, but it would have to be carried out promptly before the peace-time garrisons were overwhelmed. Regular troops would thus have to be employed at first, although they could be relieved by Territorial Army troops later. The operation has never been examined in detail, but, merely to prevent the ports being captured by Ireland, one Infantry Brigade Group per port should be sufficient, but in order to enable the ports to be used safely by the Navy, the hinterland of each port would have to be occupied, and as a rough estimate a division with A.A. defences would be required for each. This estimate is based on the present state of the Irish army and air force, with a hostile population behind them, but no firm figure could be given without detailed local reconnaissance.

15. Whether or not the importance of the ports as summarised in paragraphs (3) to (10) above would justify the very considerable military effort as assessed in paragraph (14) above, cannot be determined in advance of the event. The decision would have to be taken by the Cabinet of the day in the light of the then existing circumstances.

Question (3).—If the Ports had previously been handed over to Ireland, and if on the outbreak of war Ireland were to deny us their use, would the importance of the ports be so great as to warrant military operations to regain the possession and use of them?

16. This question envisages either a neutral or hostile Ireland. The importance of the ports as summarised above is, of course, a constant factor; but the military operations that would be necessary to regain possession of them, in the conditions hypothecated in this question, would be considerably more formidable than the reinforcement of our existing garrisons, involving as it would combined operations, comparable to the Gallipoli landing, in the face of opposition.

17. Without detailed study, it is impossible to estimate the precise size of the expeditionary force that would be necessary, but we are advised that, as a rough estimate, at least three divisions would be immediately required to capture the ports, even in their present unmodernised condition. The more highly the ports were armed, the harder, of course, would be the operation.

18. As in the case of Question (2), the decision as to whether or not the importance of the ports would justify the military effort necessary to capture them would have to be taken by the Cabinet of the day in the light of the then existing circumstances.

19. It will be seen from our examination of Questions (2) and (3), that the retention or capture of the ports, in the face of a hostile attitude on the part of Ireland, would at best involve a most formidable military commitment, and might, even so, be impossible.

20. But a hostile attitude on the part of Ireland has even more serious implications than the possible denial to us of the use of the ports. As stated in paragraph (11), we require the control of the ports in order that we may deny their use to the enemy. The use by the enemy, not only of these ports, but of the entire Irish territory as a base for operations against this country would clearly envisage a most serious position. In such circumstances, the retention or capture of these ports would not be sufficient, and it might be necessary to contemplate complete occupation of Ireland to prevent its being used as a base for hostile action, either by submarines or aircraft, against this country or Northern Ireland or our sea-borne trade, or for land operations against Northern Ireland. It is very clear therefore that, in order to avoid so intolerable a situation arising, no effort should be spared to ensure that friendly relations with Ireland are maintained.

21. Although, therefore, we endorsed the views of the Deputy Chiefs of Staff as expressed in C.I.D. Paper No. 416–C to the effect that we should insist on a complete assurance from Ireland " of the availability of these ports for use by our forces and for the adequacy of their defences, in the interests of the safety of the territory and communications of the Irish Free State no less than of the United Kingdom . . . . before any technical discussions are instituted to cover the actual process of handing over; " we consider that it would be preferable to waive insistence on a formal undertaking which might be politically impracticable for Mr. de Valera to give, and which would not necessarily have any value in the event, if by so doing we could secure a satisfactory agreement with Ireland.

(Signed)   CHATFIELD.
                C. L. NEWALL.
                GORT.

2 *Whitehall Gardens, S.W.* 1,
    January 12, 1938.

Appendix 5

Hempel's War Zone warning to de Valera, 17 August 1940

DEUTSCHE GESANDTSCLAFT,
DUBLIN

August 17th, 1940

Excellency,

Under instructions received from the Government of the German Reich, I have the honour to notify the Irish Government of the following:

In consequence of the development which the war has taken during the last weeks, England has now become the centre of warlike operations at sea and in the air. In the waters around England, therefore, warlike actions have to be reckoned with which exclude safe passage of merchant ships through these waters. In consequence, the whole sea area around England has become a theatre of warlike operations. Every ship which passes through these waters exposes itself to destruction not only by mines but also by the active weapons of war. The German Government therefore warns anew and very urgently against the passing through the endangerd areas. It must be suggested to the Irish Government to take also on its own initiative steps which it deems to be adequate in order to prevent Irish citizens and Irish ships from entering into the endangered areas. The waters within the following geographical points have to be regarded as endangered:

From the French Atlantic Coast at

	47°	30′	N 2°	40′ W to
point	45°		N 5°	W to
point	45°		N20°	W to
point	58°		N20°	W to
point	62°		N 3°	E to

hence southwards to the Belgian Coast and further on following the Belgian and French Coasts to the first-mentioned point.

His Excellency Eamon de Valera, T.D.,
    Minister for External Affairs,
        Government Buildings,
            Dublin.

The German Government assumes no responsibility for damages which might be suffered within those areas by ships or persons.

This warning will be notified at the same time to all other Governments of neutral States participating in sea trade.

In spite of the fact that the waters round England are endangered through warlike measures, the German Government nevertheless wishes to facilitate to Ireland the supply of vitally essential goods. It therefore is prepared to have special regard for Irish ships. The German Armed Forces will not attack ships under the Irish Flag which are specially marked and announced by the Government of Ireland, provided that such ships and their loads will be announced by wire previously in due time, will conform to the orders given by the German Armed Forces and will carry only such goods which will remain in Ireland according to a guarantee to be given by the Irish Government. The fixing of the modalities should be the subject of a special agreement which I am authorised to enter into negotiations about immediately.

Accept, Excellency, the renewed assurance of my highest consideration.

                    E. Hempel.

Appendix 6

German record showing Clissmann's involvement with Kerney, Irish Minister to Spain. Professor Desmond Williams exposed this liaison in *The Leader* (c. 1947). He was sued. He lost. This documentation was unavailable then.

Record of conversation between the Irish Minister to Spain, Mr. L.H. Kerney and H. Clissmann, 8 and 11 November 1941 in Madrid (translated extract).

Mr. Kerney, who three days ago returned from several months holiday in Ireland, welcomed the undersigned very warmly. He spoke openly and frankly and I was convinced that if the occasion arose he would welcome further meetings.

1. <u>Political Situation in Ireland</u>. He described the political situation in Ireland as very satisfactory and said that de Valera enjoyed majority support, which convinced him that his policy of Neutrality, which had been successful up to this point could maintain the degree of independence which had been achieved with difficulty. De Valera had also won over nationalist Ireland.

Hostile demands from the more Anglophile Cosgrave opposition carried no weight. As a result of the secure supply situation, which could be decisive, the country, in spite of the significant shortage of raw materials and fuel, could sustain itself economically, even in a prolonged war. With a small merchant fleet of 12 ships they had made a very gratifying beginning.

The Irish Army Command clearly considered that a well-trained Army of about 200,000 was adequate to offer serious resistance to any aggression in spite of a serious shortage of heavy weapons, particularly anti-tank and anti-aircraft artillery.

We should consider whether it would be possible for Germany to agree to the secret purchase of special weapons to have them delivered from Germany to Ireland via Spain in available Irish ships. The undersigned, as requested, appraised K. of how to contact him in Berlin by telegraph.

2. From the wide-ranging foreign policy review of K's, it can be taken that the main concern of the Irish government was the occupation of Ireland in this war, essentially, by Great Britain and the United States. According to K, Great Britain recognised that an invasion would cost more than it was worth and, that the U.S. probably deduced from Minister Frank Aiken that such a step would lead to strong resistance and large-scale sabotage from influential Irish-America which could even lead to civil war. However the setting up of American air and sea bases in Northern Ireland and the development of German-American relations was a source of great threat to the Island.

K repeatedly stressed the unassailable determination to defend Ireland against any aggression. American and English aggression alike would be opposed without sentimentality.

The Irish government enjoys full freedom of action and was not tied by any secret agreements. On the contrary, de Valera's unwavering object was to secure the reunification of the six partitioned counties with the South as soon as possible, to break the connection with England and establish a truly independent State.

This process of gradually breaking links was reflected in the appointment by de Valera of Charges d'Affaires to the Irish diplomatic missions in neutral countries like Portugal and the Vatican in order to avoid in this way accreditation of Irish Ministers by the British King. The German estimate of the Irish situation was that the Irish government would regard an Anglo-American victory as copperfasting partition, while a German victory, which weakened Great Britain, alone could guarantee the freedom and unity of Ireland. It follows that Germany must regard de Valera as a potential ally.

K. described the IRA as a still significant factor in Ireland especially in the North.......'99% of the Nationalists in the North eagerly looked forward to liberation by Germany. The IRA contained worthwhile political potential which de Valera sees as a threat and deals with accordingly, as it (the IRA) might refuse to acknowledge his political leadership'.

Various small incidents such as the Held Affair and the landing of German agents with transmitters in Ireland in 1940, plus the possibility that Sean Russell was still in Germany, gave the Irish government special concern about German intentions in Ireland. There are many rumours circulating about Sean Russell, making the Irish and German government and Frank Ryan responsible for his death. He and his government, as well as Irish-Americans in the U.S. and the IRA, believe that Russell died in August 1940 from natural causes in the presence of Ryan. So long however, as there was no confirmation, his (K's) government was compelled to consider the possibility of Russell being concealed in Germany. Such a supposition must naturally do damage to Irish-German relations. Before the arrival of the undersigned in Madrid, K. had already, through his wife, made contact with Frank Ryan and a friend of Frank Ryan's in the U.S. in order to confirm Russell's death. He accepted that during the war the German government could make no official statement. He urged that confirmation through Ryan could be used by him to reassure de Valera. He could not see that such a confirmation would damage Germany in the slightest since Sean Russell's political views were well known and in wartime every state would avail of every opportunity to gain information. Indeed he was convinced that such a statement easing tension would be in the interests of German-Irish relations.

His government made an important distinction between Russell and Ryan whom he admired and spoke very highly of. Ryan would put national interests before those of an organisation. Russell, on the contrary, would act differently. Russell allegedly destroyed by his IRA bombing campaign in England de Valera's plan for settling the Ulster question. So long however that Ryan could not play an open role of which the Irish government would be aware, its members would fear that he would become Russell's successor in Germany. K. himself hoped that he would one day see Frank Ryan as a 'go-between' with de Valera.

H. Clissmann

Appendix 7

Sonnleithner (from Führer level) confirms liaison involving
Veesenmayer, Ribbentrop's *coup d'état* specialist for Ireland

Special train, Westfalia, 5 Oct 1942.
No. 1229, 510.
1) Telko
2) G. transmission for Minister Hewel Werwolf
Notice for the Führer
Secret
SS. Oberführer Veesenmayer sent by me to Madrid had two detailed
discussions with the Irish Minister, Kerney. As I had given V. a covert
mission for the purpose neither a German nor a Spaniard in Madrid
knew of his real mission. The most important results of these
discussions with Kerney were:

1. Kerney is convinced that de Valera will oppose to the utmost any
    invasion no matter which side it comes from. De Valera
    repeatedly made clear to him that he would also oppose an
    American invasion.
2. Kerney takes it for granted that in the event of an English or
    American invasion, de Valera would immediately apply to
    Germany for assistance.
3. Kerney thinks that in the event of an English-American invasion
    the rift between de Valera and the IRA would be automatically set
    aside. De Valera himself came from the IRA where he had a
    leading position and, in the event of war, he would not be untrue
    to his basic beliefs.
4. In spite of de Valera's determination to maintain neutrality, in
    Kerney's opinion, this would not be pushed to the limit, but, in
    the event of reasonable prospect of success, he would declare war
    in order to liberate Northern Ireland.
5. Kerney holds that it is decisive, in concert with progress of
    German aid being made available, that the German government
    should simultaneously declare that it has no interests in Ireland
    and that German troops would remain on Irish soil only for as
    long as the common war against the Allies demanded it. Further-
    more, Irish trust would be significantly strengthened through the
    recognition of a free, united, and independent Ireland.

6. The Irish Defence Minister, Frank Aiken, who was in America last Autumn, succeeded in winning over the Irish in the USA, whose influence is not to be underestimated, to follow de Valera's political line.
7. Kerney acknowledged the accommodating attitude in the matter of compensation for Irish ships sank by us. He said however that Ireland would consider it more important to replace them by other ships.

Poste Pole, 5 October 1942

Sonnleithner

Appendix 8

Hempel's covert flower-pot signal to harmonise IRA rising with Operation 'Sea Lion'

Dublin 15 August 1940

Top Secret

(Ref Telegram of 13, No. 261 and of 7,No 246).

1) In the event of future operations flower pots can be placed in the main window of the Mezzanine and should, as far as possible, remain there permanently.

2) In the course of a brief conversation a trustworthy person enquired whether R, if he were still in the country, were to be informed. I refused to admit that I had anything to do with the matter.

Hempel.

Appendix 9
Hempel's covert involvement as information collector/transmitter

Dublin 23 August 1940

Top Secret

Please advise the High Command immediately to listen this Saturday and Sunday to the Gustl-Hour on the 38.25 metre band. Receipt of this information from me is on no account to be communicated to G. (Dr. H.K.).

Hempel.

Appendix 10
American note threat

INWARD TELEGRAM
(Sent by teleprinter)

CYPHER (TYPEX)   COPY NO..2...

FROM: EIRE (REP.)

TO: D.O.

D. 21st Feb.,1944.   5.33 p.m.
R. 21st   "   "   5.35 p.m.
____

IMMEDIATE

No.24 MOST SECRET & PERSONAL.

Following for Machtig. Begins.

American Minister handed in the Note this afternoon. Mr. de Valera said that as a Sovereign neutral state they could not accede to the request. It was his belief that German Minister had on the whole behaved well. Eire Government were satisfied that their control was strict enough to eliminate danger of espionage. So long as he was head of the Government the reply would be in the negative.

2.   Asked as to whether he would give formal reply here to the American Legation or through his representative in Washington, Mr. de Valera said that he would consider this point.

3.   I suggest that our note be handed in without delay. Ends.

Appendix 11

Woermann's note on Bewley's shadowy activities involving Curia

Berlin 23 December 1942

In the last few days Bewley, the former Irish Minister in Berlin, who now lives in Rome, has twice sought me out. He identifies with the IRA and is very hostile to de Valera.

This is a record of the conversations:

1. In Bewley's opinion, we have a wrong impression of de Valera. Actually he is a friend of England. His concerns are to keep Ireland in the British Commonwealth. Bewley's assertions are designed to bring us into open confrontation with de Valera.

    I replied that while we had no illusions about de Valera we consider it important to maintain present good relations with the Irish government.

2. Bewley is convinced that an English or American incursion in Ireland or a demand for a reoccupation of the Treaty ports is not anticipated. The experience from the war confirmed that in the new strategic situation the occupation of Ireland or the Irish ports was not necessary as the North of Ireland provided sufficient suitable services. The same applies to the situation in the Air.

3. In Ireland at present large amounts of money are being earned through business with England. All those profiting from the war are hostile to Germany.

    Friends of Germany, outside of the IRA in particular, strange as it may sound, are to be found among the clergy, as these do not profit from the war.

    Bewley's direct contact with Ireland is, according to his own statements, very slight. Nevertheless he has managed through some clergy involved in the Curia, to get, in some cases, information in and out of the country.

Woermann.

Appendix 12

Commander-in-Chief of Navy's report to Führer's on supporting Ireland against Britain, 30 December 1940

High Command, Navy

REPORT OF THE C.-IN-C., NAVY, TO THE FUEHRER ON DECEMBER 3, 1940, AT 1630

Also present: Chief of Staff, O.K.W.
General Jodl.
Commander von Puttkamer.

1. Ireland.—The C.-in-C., Navy, puts forth the views contained in Appendix I, after summarising his general point of view as follows:

APPENDIX

The Question of Supporting Ireland against Britain

I. The first condition necessary for transfer of troops is naval supremacy along the routes to be used. This naval supremacy could never be attained by us in view of the vastly superior British Home Fleet, not even for the duration of one transport operation.

The ratio between the British and German Fleets is as follows:

Battleships	..	.. at least 2 to 1.
Cruisers	..	.. at least 20 to 3.
Destroyers	..	.. about 70 to 6 or 8 at the most.

The possibility of surprise is ruled out, due to the necessity of starting from the French coast.

II. The geographical position is extremely unfavourable, since the coast of Wales and Cornwall extends like a wedge toward our line of approach; the distance from enemy bases to Ireland is less than that from the ports of embarkation in north-western France. In contrast to the Norway operation, it would not be possible to establish, by means of a surprise attack, a supply line which could be defended. Such a supply line is of decisive importance for the success of the operation.

III. The island has no defended bases or anchorages at all. Although the Irish might willingly open their ports to us, they would also be open to the enemy pursuing us. There would be no time for planned harbour and coastal fortifications, and undisturbed disembarkation of the expeditionary force is unlikely. It would not be possible to send supplies in view of the superior sea power of the enemy and the limited area through which the approach would have to be made.

IV. To a defending force, cut off and left to its own devices, the topography of the country does not afford as much protection against modern weapons as the Narvik region for example. Without supplies and reinforcements, an expeditionary force would soon feel the increasing pressure of a British expeditionary force brought over under the protection of British naval power; sooner or later our own troops would face a situation similar to Namsos or Dunkirk.

V. Support by the Air force would depend on the weather. Ireland, the westernmost island of any size in the northern Atlantic, is known to have a heavy rainfall and consequently low clouds and very frequent damp and foggy weather. Air support would have to come primarily from the mainland, since the airfield accommodation in Ireland would not meet our requirements; it would scarcely be possible to expand them because we could not supply equipment. Every attempt at transporting troops by Ju52's would be in great danger from British fighters, which are again increasing in numbers.

VI. It is concluded therefore that it would not be possible to follow up an Irish request for help by sending an expeditionary force and occupying the island, in view of the enemy's superior naval force, the unfavourable geographical conditions and the impossibility of forwarding supplies. Troops landed in Ireland without supplies of foodstuffs, weapons, and ammunition would sooner or later be wiped out by an enemy whose supply routes are difficult to attack.

VII. It will be possible in the winter months to bring occasional blockade-runners with weapons and ammunition into Irish harbours and bays, as long as there is still no state of war between Britain and Ireland, and as long as the Irish co-operate.

*   *   *   *   *   *

Notwithstanding these and other threats against her, Britain proceeded to strike hard at the weakest points of the Axis. On December 9 the first Western Desert offensive began, and with outstanding success the British Army, assisted by the Navy and air force, drove the Italians back out of Libya.

In spite of the situation in the Mediterranean, however, Hitler issued his first clear directive for the invasion of Russia on December 18.

Appendix 13

Woermann's memorandum, 10 February 1940

No. 605

91/100155-56

Memorandum by the Director of the Political Department

St.S. No. 136 g. Rs.   BERLIN, February 10, 1940.

With reference to telegram No. 7 [1] from Genoa and telegrams Nos. 50 [2] and 52 [3] from Dublin re Ireland.

1. The Irish Republican Army (IRA) is a secret militant society which fights for the union of Northern Ireland with the Irish Republic and the complete separation of Ireland from the British Empire. This is also the ultimate objective of the present Irish Government. The difference between the Government and the IRA lies mainly in the method. The Government hopes to attain its objective by legal political means while the IRA tries to achieve success by terrorist means. Most of the members of the present Irish Government formerly belonged also to the IRA.

By reason of its militant attitude toward England the IRA is a natural ally of Germany.

2. The Intelligence Department [*Abwehr*] already has strictly secret connections with the IRA, a part of which utilized a channel which is now closed as the result of the war. The Intelligence Department knows of McCarthy's presence in Italy and attaches the greatest value to resuming the connection at once. It has asked the Foreign Ministry today to inform the Consulate General at Genoa that it will immediately dispatch there two of its representatives for the purpose of establishing contact with McCarthy. The Intelligence Department has been asked to establish contact only after the Consulate General at Genoa gives the cue for it. The interest of the Intelligence Department is confined to the promotion of acts of sabotage.

3. It is technically possible to take John Russell (Irish name: Sean Russell) to Ireland aboard a German submarine.

4. In his telegram No. 50 of January 27, which is herewith enclosed,[4] Minister Hempel, upon inquiry, expressed himself against dispatching John Russell to Ireland at the present moment. He is of the opinion that the IRA in Ireland does not have enough striking power to bring about success. He fears that John Russell's arrival and Germany's part therein will become known, that this will lead to a further discrediting of the IRA, and that England will profit therefrom in the end. Thus an incident would be created that would be parallel to the landing of Sir Roger Casement by a German submarine in the World War.

5. In the opinion of the Political Department such an action may very well be considered. However, the proper time for it would not arrive until Great Britain is in considerable difficulties all along the line. The operation would then have to be carried out, if possible suddenly, in connection with other operations within the British Empire or at its periphery. For the present, Minister Hempel's objections are shared. If it learned of Russell's arrival, the Irish Government would in all probability have him arrested and, if German complicity became known, as could be expected, it would have to take the necessary steps with reference to us. Irish neutrality would thereby be jeopardized.

6. It is therefore proposed that the contact with McCarthy be maintained so that the plan can be pursued further at the proper moment. Since the Intelligence Department already has connections with McCarthy, it is suggested that for the time being such connections not be established through another channel as well.

Submitted herewith to the Foreign Minister.

WOERMANN

---

[1] Document No. 562.

[2] Not printed (91/100148–49).

[3] Not printed (91/100150).

*See footnote 2

Appendix 14

Ritter's memorandum, 'Should Ireland be Excluded or Included in a Blockade of England?'

SHOULD IRELAND BE EXCLUDED OR INCLUDED IN A BLOCKADE OF ENGLAND?

I. Effect on England.

1. If Ireland remains outside the blockade, that is, if the line of blockade is drawn between Ireland and England, England would be cut off from one of its food bases. Ireland has until now supplied about 5 percent of England's food requirements, mainly meat and some dairy products.

Raw materials would not be lost to England because Ireland has until now supplied practically nothing. England would be unable, or relieved of the necessity, to supply Ireland with coal (hitherto an exchange of meat for coal).

2. If Ireland is included in the blockade, that is, if ships moving between Ireland and England are not attacked as part of the blockade measures, England would be able to continue obtaining the mentioned food supplies from Ireland for some time. The shipments, however, would probably be greatly curtailed before long because

Ireland would be compelled, after being cut off from its overseas source of livestock feed, to conserve its own diminished production primarily for home consumption. Ireland would in that case supply only as much food to England as she must in order to get an absolutely necessary supply of coal from England.

II. Effect on Ireland.

Ireland, if need be, would be able to feed herself for a long time by readapting some of her food habits. Ireland possesses almost no industrial raw materials and, particularly, no coal.

1. If Ireland remains outside the blockade, that is, if the line of blockade is drawn between Ireland and England, Ireland would be able to obtain livestock feed and raw materials from overseas, as in the past, provided she is able to find the required shipping space. Her food supply would therefore not be impaired. She would, however, be cut off from her source of coal. Obtaining a substitute supply from the United States would not be easy considering the lack of shipping space of her own. Being cut off from her English coal base is therefore likely to affect Ireland seriously.

2. Inclusion of Ireland in the blockade would cut her off from her overseas livestock feed base. Her food base would thus be contracted, but the country would not starve.

Being cut off from overseas raw material sources would in that case affect Ireland not very severely because the country is not highly industrialized. It would on the other hand be able to some extent to continue obtaining its coal supply from England.

Thus the outcome for Ireland is in either case that she can subsist in a pinch. If excluded from the blockade, her food situation would be more favorable, but she would lack coal. If included in the blockade, Ireland would still be able to get her coal, but in the matter of her food supply she would have to undergo certain adjustments and restrictions.

III. Considerations I and II view only the *economic* consequences in each case. From the *political* standpoint it must not be overlooked that inclusion of Ireland in the blockade would be a violation of Ireland's neutrality. Such a violation might give rise to the idea in Ireland that in an emergency Ireland was to some extent still linked to England for better or worse. This would also have repercussions in the United States in view of the strong Irish element there.

IV. The economic and political considerations lead to the conclusion that excluding Ireland from the blockade would be preferable.

The possibilities and effects from the standpoint of naval operations are a matter that can be judged only by the Navy.[*]

RITTER

[*] See document No. 296.

Appendix 15
That *Aide Memoire* on Neutrality of 12 September 1939

Dr Rynne's letter (19/5/77) refers. He remembers the Deak and Jessup book which contained the Irish declaration of neutrality well; (he checked the galley proofs). The book, he said, has a 'dark-greyish, cream-coloured' paper cover, was about $2\frac{1}{2}''$ thick and he paid £13 (air mail) to order it for External Affairs from N.Y. He could put his hand on it in the Legal Library, he said (but unfortunately Library has been shifted since his day). The Library of Congress have investigated, but have failed to locate. The Dept. of Foreign Affairs has been extremely helpful and turned all their Deak and Jessups inside out: but unfortunately there was no sign of Dr Rynne's 'dark-greyish, cream-coloured paperback' containing the 12th September 1939 *Aide Memoire* on Neutrality – a copy of which had been handed to Herr Hempel. Its disappearance is hardly likely to have been a 'mini-Watergate' as Dr Rynne jocosely remarked (though Maffey and Joe Walshe had been very strongly opposed to its publication).

I have written (as suggested by Foreign Affairs) to Mr Aidan Mulloy in U.N. N.Y. – (seeing it was published in New York) – to try to track down this elusive *Aide Memoire* in the hopes of having a 'mini-scoop' for thesis: incidentally, Dr. Rynne does not feel that Carroll (op. cit. p. 15/16) has got his summary of the contents of the *Aide Memoire* quite right.

A 'mini-Watergate' the elusiveness of this *Aide Memoire* may not be: but from the opacity of this thesis a mini-mystery it certainly is, as if somehow the wills of Maffey and Joe Walshe for its suppression had finally prevailed. There may be a simple but still elusive explanation. It was an important document: though the British snubbed it, the German reception was conditional and Walshe frowned on it, for de Valera it was a protocol cornerstone.

Dr Rynne's letter on the disappearance of his book

SYDENHAM HOUSE,
SYDENHAM ROAD,
DUNDRUM, DUBLIN. 14.
10th September, 197⸱

Dear Lieut.Colonel Luggan,

Thanks for your note of 29th August covering photocopies from the Library of Congress (which I return in case you haven't duplicates).

Certainly, the plot keeps on thickening re "Neutrality Laws & Regulations of the World". Should we accept that the book never existed unless in an alleged 1938 edition before war and neutrality became vital issues ?

If one felt sufficiently frustrated to contact the Librarian, Reading Room, British Museum, the gamble might pay off. These people, if cautious, are comparatively honest ; they once allowed me to take notes from a British-Government-banned book called "An Unwanted Defence of Roger Casement" by G.B. Shaw in a private room. You would need a friend with a current Reader's Ticket.

Otherwise the law booksellers of Chancery Lane could help viz. Sweet& Maxwell, Butterworth or Stevens. One of these might even divulge the name of a well-known secondhand law bookshop in London which (like Foyle's) has practically everything in the law line. Unfortunately, I have forgotten this information.

Excuse type and delay in replying - I am still struggling with the postal backlog.

Yours sincerely,

Michael Rynne.

Appendix 16

Veesenmayer's proposal for the Ireland operation, 24 August 1941

BERLIN, August 24, 1941.

Attention Counsellor of Legation Weber, Foreign Secretariat "Westfalen".

In accordance with the Foreign Minister's directive of August 17[1] I herewith transmit attached a proposal for the Ireland operation which I have prepared with the request that it be submitted to the Foreign Minister as promptly as possible.

VEESENMAYER

[Enclosure]
PROPOSAL FOR THE IRELAND OPERATION[2]

BERLIN, August 24, 1941.

The latest possible date for this operation appears to be the time from September 15 to 25, 1941. Prerequisites are dark, clear nights before the autumn gales begin.

A thoroughgoing personal discussion on July 11 in Lorient with Lieutenant Colonel von Harlinghausen, bearer of the Knight's Insignia of the Iron Cross with Oak Leaves, brought out that he is willing to transport by airplane the three men who are to go on this mission. He does not anticipate particular difficulties for this operation; he has prepared a well-adapted Heinkel 59 (especially seaworthy and noiseless) and assigned an experienced aircraft pilot who has repeatedly carried out undertakings of this sort with success. The over-all responsibility is in his own hands.

The landing will take place only if the landing place can be definitely identified and no particular risks are present. The descent will be made by gliding in from a great height and the debarkation by rubber boat. Each of the three men will receive an English folding bicycle to take along so as to have greater mobility on land.

After careful examination and by common agreement Brandon Bay was chosen as the landing place; it is a bay of Dingle Peninsula which is favoured for the following reasons:

---

[1] Not found.

[2] A note by Ribbentrop at the top of this document indicates that it was put into the special portfolio where the Foreign Minister kept documents which he intended to show Hitler (Führerwappe).

[3] A special formation for commando warefare.

1. Favourable air approach from Brest, where the start is to take place.

2. Sheltered location and hence good prospects of safe debarkation.

3. The men who are to be landed will have available to them numerous safe hiding places on Dingle Peninsula which, as a result of the short distances, can all be reached within an hour's march.

4. There is a possibility of quickly crossing over to the Valencia Peninsula [island] with the help of friendly fishermen.

5. Lough Gill, an inland lake near the landing place, offers especially favourable facilities for hiding the luggage to be taken along (radio equipment and money). The Dingle Peninsula is furthermore much favoured by tourists, which will make our men less conspicuous.

Participants in the enterprise are the Irishman Frank Ryan and two men who, up to this time, were members of the training regiment Brandenburg,[3] Sergeant Clissmann and Private First Class Reiger.

Frank Ryan participated in the enterprise with Sean Russell and after the latter's death on the U-boat he returned here as directed.[4] He is one of the leading Irish nationalists, has been for many years a member of the leaders' council of the Irish Republican Army, and a particpant in numerous fights against England. In 1929 the Secret Service carried out an unsuccessful assassination attempt against him, and he has often been in jail since. He has extensive connections with the Irish republican circles up to de Valera's closest entourage and to de Valera himself, as well as to the Irish regular army, the nationalist Irishmen in Northern Ireland, and especially to leading Irishmen in America.[5]

Clissmann lived for over 5 years in Ireland (1933–34 and 1936–39), married the daughter of a well-known Irish nationalist, and has been on close terms of friendship with Frank Ryan ever since 1930. He has undergone military training, has already participated in an operation against England, speaks perfect English with an Irish

[4]   Nothing more on this matter has been found in German Foreign Ministry files. For earlier contacts of German agencies with Sean Russell Chief of Staff of the Irish Republican Army (IRA), a secret militant nationalist organization see vol. VIII of this series, documents No. 562 and 605. According to a published account by a former German Abwehr official Sean Russell died of natural causes on board a German submarine which was to take him to Ireland. See Paul Leverkuehn, *German Military Intelligence* (London, 1954), pp. 104–105.

[5]   Further accounts of Ryan's activities are found in Veesenmayer's memorandum to Woermann of Nov. 24 (91/101400–17) and Clissmann's memorandum to Woermann of Dec. 5 (91/101391–97). these documents discuss the policies and personalities of the Irish Republican Army and that organization's relations with the Irish Government and with Germany.

accent, and has extensive connections in Ireland.

Rieger, who also had military training, speaks English perfectly and is a specially trained radio operator.

The operation was initiated and prepared in cooperation with the High Command of the Wehrmacht, Department II of the Abwehr, and by joint agreement is submitted for approval.

The military objectives assigned to Clissmann, according to a letter of August 23 from the High Command of the Wehrmacht to the Foreign Ministry (enclosure I[6]), are as follows:

(1) Establishing liaison with the Irish Republican Army and activating the sabotage operations of the Irish Republican Army, on the English island, and at the same time bringing the Irish Republican Army the sum of money which it is expecting.

(2) Establishing radio communications by means of a radio set [*Afu Gerät*] which is to be taken along.

(3) Transmitting military information, including weather reports, since at de Valera's demand radio traffic of the Legation with the Foreign Ministry had to be cut down to the very minimum.[7]

(4) Preparation of underground resistance in the event of Ireland's occupation by the English or Americans.

Supplementing item (3) a telegram of August 22 from Operational Staff to the Foreign Ministry is also attached (enclosure II).[8] References in the files of the Foreign Ministry appear in radiogram No. 207 from Dublin, No. 2800 from Washington.[9]

In addition to the foreoing military tasks there are the following political tasks for Frank Rynn and Clissmann:

(1) To establish a generally effective liaison with the Irish Republican Army.

(2) To transmit an urgently needed financial subsidy to the Irish Republican Army, for which purpose the Foreign Minister has made available 40,000 pounds sterling.

(3) If expedient, to attempt bringing about an understanding between the Irish Republican Army and de Valera, which the latter

---

[6] Not printed (F17/053).

[7] Hempel had reported such requests by the Irish Government in telegrams Nos. 318 of April. 11 (91/100686–88) and 383 of May 9 (91/100703).

[8] This telegram expressed the interest of the Luftwaffe in obtaining weather reports from Ireland (F17/054).

[9] In this telegram of Aug. 12 (91/100772–73) which was transmitted via Washington Hempel reported de Valera's urgent request that radio transmissions from the Legation be limited to exceptional cases. In view of de Valera's statements Hempel strongly recommended that the Embassy transmitter cease broadcasting weather reports.

has so far tried in vain. That is the very task for which Frank Ryan has the most promising qualifications. Politically this could promote the strengthening of the all-Irish policy of neutrality and, if necessary, of the Irish national will to resist. From the point of view of propaganda Frank Ryan has a particularly marked influence with the Irish in America which, if skilfully mobilized, can be politically useful.

(4) The possibility of influencing through Clissmann the attitude and policies of the Irish nationalist activitists.

(5) To furnish the Reich with a clear picture of Ireland's domestic and external situation through objective reporting.

(6) To observe carefully English and American efforts in southern and northern Ireland.

(7) In the event of Ireland's occupation by England or America, to organize the resistance, thereby to tie down enemy forces to the greatest possible extent.

To carry out this operation later than the middle of September 1941 is, aside from the weather, not advisable for the following reasons:

(1) With the progress of the war in the east, Ireland is becoming more and more a focal point of English-American interests. That involves intensified surveillance and accordingly slimmer chances of success for the proposed operation.

(2) After the landing has been accomplished, at least 4 to 8 weeks are required for the start of operations.

(3) It appears inadvisable to restrain Frank Ryan any longer because being a confirmed activist, his powers of resistance and willingness for action are beginning to slacken after a forced stay in Germany of over a year's duration; and in the event of too long an absence from Ireland the effectiveness of his influence is bound to suffer there, too.[10]

VEESENMAYER

---

[10]   Marginal notes:

In Ribbentrop's handwriting: "September, 1–2 months."

In Sonnleithner's handwriting: "Octobcr, or November, or December."

"U.St.S Woermann arrange whatever is necessary. Submit again after 5 days. R[Intelen], Sept. 6."

Through a minute of Sept. 6 (91/101448) Woermann informed Clissmann that Ribbentrop, after consultation with Hitler, had decided to postpone the project. In the absence of Veesenmayer the Foreign Ministry would consult with the Wehrmacht if the project could be undertaken at the end of October, in November, or December.

Appendix 17

Veesenmayer's observations, 24 November 1941 (translated extracts)

De Valera, himself a former member of the IRA, obviously recognised very early on that physical force alone could not solve the trouble with England. Consequently the IRA came to regard him as the enemy of Ireland's fight for freedom and this gave them grounds for directing part of their armed struggle against de Valera, his supporters and his methods.

The Irish Minister for Agriculture, Ryan seems to me to be depicted as a simple, not particularly politically active man, who nevertheless has a close relationship with de Valera. It is therefore quite possible that de Valera has chosen him to cultivate a well-camouflaged relationship with the splinter wing of the IRA. It is also possible that these activities brought him in contact with Hayes, as they both came from Wexford. The telegrams and his knowledge of the presence of Kruse give grounds for regarding the relationship as credible. If this supposition is true it deserves special attention bearing in mind the unexpected frankness of Minister Kerney in his encounter with Clissmann. It can therefore be more or less taken as contingency planning by de Valera, in the event of an outbreak of hostilities with England, to seriously consider the question of a call for German assistance. The exchanges between Clissmann and Kerney, as well as Kerney's expressed wish to intensify contacts on both sides, lead to the conclusion that he is empowered, in an emergency to make contact with the German government.

Under the present circumstances, I consider it a priority, other things being equal, to strive for a reconciliation between de Valera and the IRA, which should at least be valid for the duration of the war. I have already indicated the same considerations in bringing Frank Ryan to Ireland: he is the most suitable person to accomplish the delicate mission. From Kerney's conversations with Clissmann, I am once more convinced that Frank Ryan would be taken very seriously by de Valera. Moreover it can be assumed that the leadership of the IRA really long for an Envoy from Germany. Such circumstances would give Frank Ryan a chance, by skilful operation, to contribute seriously towards disrupting the plans of the British Secret Service. Nowadays there is no compelling reason for de Valera and the IRA to fight each other. On the contrary they could ideally complement each other by appropriate division of labour in the struggle against the common enemy, England.

Belgrade, 24 November 1941.

Veesenmayer.

Index